Deaths Reported by the
Long Islander
1878-1890

David Roberts

Heritage Books, Inc

Published 1998 by

HERITAGE BOOKS, INC.
1540E Pointer Ridge Place
Bowie, Maryland 20716
1-800-398-7709
www.heritagebooks.com

ISBN 0-7884-0950-6

A Complete Catalog Listing Hundreds of Titles
On History, Genealogy, and Americana
Available Free Upon Request

Table of Contents

page #

Preface------------------------------------iv

Entries------------------------------------1

Counties Listing
Long Island Gazetteer---------------267
NY State Gazetteer------------------282
United States Gazetteer------------285

Index-------------------------------------291

DEATHS REPORTED BY THE LONG ISLANDER
1878-1890

INTRODUCTION AND PURPOSE

Newspapers are an important source of genealogical data, but finding the data in the papers
can be difficult without some type of index.
This present volume will offer the researcher
an alphabetical listing of death notices abstracted from the Long Islander for the years
1878 through 1890; a separate index of other
persons mentioned in these death notices; and
a gazetteer of geographical places mentioned
in the notices. It is hoped that this work
will assist in Long Island and related genealogical research.

DEVELOPMENT OF THE PROJECT

This listing has evolved over the past decade,
following the discovery in an 1879 paper of a
list of persons who died during the year 1878.
Additional year-end summaries were found into
the early 1930's. Could these lists be
indexed?

After some time, it was discovered that much
more material was to be found in the text of
the newspaper itself. The starting date of
this index has remained 1878, but the scope is
now much wider than the year-end summaries of
local deaths. With purchase of microfilm from
the Huntington Historical Society and the
introduction of home computers, the project
became a reality.

ABSTRACTION POLICIES

All deaths listed in the "Died" column have
been included, as have all obituary notices.
Many more deaths, however, are to be found in
the news columns from various communities on
Long Island. These deaths have been included
and form a major part of the listings in this
work.

Often, the "Village Notes" column had reports of the deaths of former Huntington area residents and occasionally of current residents, who were not listed in the "Died" column. Most of the deaths mentioned in the community columns from eastern Queens County, now Nassau County, or other parts of Suffolk County were not listed in the "Died" column. Items picked up from local papers in Suffolk and Queens Counties or from Brooklyn and New York City papers generally were not listed in the "Died" column. Deaths of national figures were often subjects of editorials or short articles. These also were generally not listed in the "Died" column, but all have been included in this listing.

Accounts of contested wills, fires, railroad and steamboat accidents, murder trials, large bequests to community institutions, explosions, drownings, natural disasters and the like all provided the names of deceased persons not mentioned in the "Died" column.

All persons who could be reasonably identified were included in the list of deceased persons. Not included were vague accounts in community news columns which could not be identified, such as "so-and-so attended his aunt's funeral" If there was no way to identify the aunt, she was not included.

Often a column would state that "so-and-so was not expected to live." Unless it was reported later that the person had died, this person was not included in the listing.

During the early 1880's and again around 1890, the paper carried a brief column of national news. Often these columns contained news of murders, executions and suicides from various parts of the United States. Unless there was some Long Island, Brooklyn, Westchester County or near-by coastal Connecticut connection, these items were not included in the listings.

POLICY ON NAMES

A reasonable effort was made to identify a person by his full name. Full identification was not always possible, however.

For example, "Mr. Brush" and "Mrs. Brush" were the only identifications that could be found for the deaths of a former Hicksville couple from a Florida yellow fever epidemic in 1888. For cases of this type, and there were many, he is listed as "BRUSH, Mr." and she "BRUSH, Mrs." and the names appear at the start of the listings for deceased persons named Brush.

Sometimes, assumptions must be made. For example, Rev. E. Gutweiler of the Reformed Church in Hicksville, lost his mother in 1888, his sister in 1889 and his father in 1890. His sister was listed by her full name, but the parents were listed only as the mother and then the father of Rev. Gutweiler. The assumptions were that the Reverend's mother was "Mrs. Gutweiler" and his father was "Mr. Gutweiler." There is always a danger of a mistake in this type of assumption, but when reasonable, it was made.

A six-month old child of John Collins died and the funeral was held in Commack in 1885. In cases of this type, with no child's name given, the dead baby was alphabetized as "COLLINS, child," or in the case of Henry and Matilda Beebe's 17 day old baby who died in 1880 as "BEEBE, infant." Deaths of this type would appear in the listings at the beginning of the surname in question.

Mrs. S. C. Clark died at Hempstead in 1886. Was her name Sarah Catherine or was she married to Samuel C. Clark ? Since it is impossible to tell, she is listed as "CLARK, Mrs. S. C."

Mrs. Samuel Carman died at St. James in 1888. Since we know her husband's name, but not her given name, she is listed as "CARMAN, Mrs. Samuel" and alphabetized as Samuel in the listing of persons named Carman.

Where a woman's given name is known, she is indexed under her given name, and her husband is listed in the abstraction portion of the text. Most of the married women and widows fall into this category.

Sometimes cross-references are necessary because the same person was given two names by the newspaper. For example, Thaddeus Gritman was shot by his friend in a bizarre accident in 1886. In the account of the friend's manslaughter trial in 1887, the victim is called Thaddeus Griffin. Which was Thaddeus's correct surname? Since this is not known, both surnames are listed.

No effort has been made to standardize surnames. August Kerps of Hicksville lost a daughter in 1886 and in 1890 August Kerbs lost a son. August Kerps and August Kerbs are probably the same individual, but we can not assume that to be the case. The researcher must check alternate spellings, especially for non-English surnames, since names have not been given a standard spelling.

POLICY ON DATES

Generally, the "Died" column gives the date of death. Often the date is given in the community columns, but frequently the date is listed as "Monday of last week" or "on Wednesday" or some similar citation. For this situation, the date was figured using the Perpetual Calendar from a recent edition of the World Almanac. There is always a possibility that a date could be a week off if the interpretation of "on Wednesday" was incorrect.

Sometimes, the dates given are too vague to be identified. A person died "last week" or

"recently." In these cases, the date of the
paper is included as a time reference for the
death.

AFRICAN AMERICANS

Persons noted in the newspaper as "colored" or
"black" or "mulatto" or some other term used
to denote African Americans are marked with a
"*" for easy identification. At times, a person was clearly related to an African American
or listed as being the member of an A. M. E.
or other black church, yet not listed in the
paper as "colored." In these cases, a [*?] is
placed after the name to indicate the person
probably was an African American. Other African Americans may be listed with no "*,"
simply because nothing was suggested in the
newspaper as to race, even though the newspaper generally made a point of identifying an
individual as being "colored." Most people
listed with no "* " are probably white, but
there may be exceptions to this generaliz-
ation.

NATIVE AMERICANS

A few persons noted as "Indian" in the listing
were so identified in the newspaper. Most
often, the individual was connected with the
Shinnecock or other Native American group in
eastern Suffolk County. Other individuals, of
mixed Native American-African American heritage, may have been called "colored" by the
newspaper and would then be marked with a "*."

CONDITION OF MICROFILM

The newspapers for the years 1878 to 1890 were
read on microfilm. Generally, the microfilm
quality was good, but in some cases there were
problems: the entry was too dark or it was too
faded to be read clearly; the entry was cut
off in the microfilming process; or the actual
newspaper was torn or folded. In such cases, a

reasonable effort was made to figure out the
citation, but often the entire citation was
omitted from the listing because it was
unreadable.

In a few cases, only part of the name was
readable. These persons are listed with a [ ]
around the unreadable portion of the name.

The small type used, especially in the "Died"
column, might have caused mistakes in reading
dates of death or ages.

On a few occasions, especially in the early
1880's, the center pages of the paper were not
microfilmed. The filmer photographed only the
front and back pages, missing pages 2 and 3
which contained most of the news. In such
cases, the deaths of those people recorded on
those unfilmed pages could not be abstracted.
Fortunately, these cases were relatively few
in number.

ADDED MATERIAL

If material was added to the citation by the
abstracter, the added material has been enclosed with [ ]. For example, the death of General Mc Clellan was noted in an 1885 paper.
The Long Islander called him only "General Mc
Clellan" but he is included in the listing as
"MC CLELLAN, General [George B.]," and as that
paper only reported the date of his death, the
place of his death is listed as [Orange, N.J.]
and a short three line biography is included,
also in [ ]. Standard references were used for
added material on important people.

QUOTED MATERIAL

If phrases were quoted directly from the newspaper, they are enclosed in quote marks, such
as in the account of the execution of murderer
William Kemmler in the electric chair in 1890

as the "first electricide in history" or the
1890 death of Mary "Aunt Polly" Ackerly "after
a long life of usefulness."

SAMPLE ENTRIES

> ABBOTT, Daniel - 86 years; d. 28 March
> 1890 at Syosset

This example tells us Daniel Abbott was 86
years old when he died on 28 March 1890 at
Syosset, but we know little about him, his
relatives or the cause of his death. Many
citations only tell us this much, with some
not even giving this much data.

> ABRAMS, Benjamin - 56 years; drowned 2
> June 1882 at Fire Island Inlet

In this example, we know the cause of Benjamin
Abrams's death, but not much more than we knew
in Daniel Abbott's case.

> ARMSTRONG, John J. - d. 18 October 1886
> at Jamaica; native of Mineola; lawyer;
> Queens County District Attorney 1859;
> Queens County Judge 1865-1885

We know facts about John J. Armstrong's career
as a lawyer, D. A. and judge. We know he was a
native of Mineola and that he died in Jamaica,
but do not know his age or the cause of his
death or anything about his family.

> ACKERLY Catherine A. - 74 y 2 m 19 d;
> d. at Crab Meadow; funeral 7 February
> 1887; wife of William Ackerly

We know Catherine A. Ackerly's exact age, the
place of her death, but not the date, the date
of her funeral and the fact that she was the
wife of William Ackerly. However, we know
nothing about the cause of her death or any
other relative except the name of her husband.

BAYLES   James M. - 74 years ; d. 29 March
    1889 at Port Jefferson; b. 18 January
    1815; ship builder by trade;   founded
    J. M. Bayles & Son 1861; son of Elisha
    Bayles; husband of Desire Ann Hawkins;
    father of James E. Bayles, Samuel H.
    Bayles, G. Frank Bayles; Mrs. A. Curtis
    Almy, Hamilton T. Bayles, S. Taber
    Bayles and Havens S. Bayles.

Here we know James M. Bayles's birth and death
date, the place of his death, his occupation
and something of his career, his father by
name, his wife by maiden name and the list of
his children, including a married daughter.
Even so, we do not know his birthplace nor the
cause of his death nor the given name of his
daughter, Mrs. Almy. All the names listed in
the citation, except for James M. Bayles himself, appear in the "Index of Persons Mentioned."

Citations vary and much vital genealogical and
biographical has been extracted, but some
citations tell us much more than others.
Because of the wide variance in what could be
found in a citation, a standardized "field"
format was not used in presenting the data.

ERRORS

Every effort was made to keep errors to a
minimum, but in a work of this size, there are
bound to be mistakes.

Some errors were made by the typesetters when
the paper was being printed. In a few cases,
persons were listed as having died on a date
later in the month than the paper's date. In
other cases, letters were transposed. Mistakes
were silently corrected if it was an obvious
error, such as transposed letters. Otherwise,
the error was noted and sometimes a possible
solution was be noted with a [?].

Factual errors were impossible to correct and
were left as stated in the newspaper. Some-

times, a person was reported to have died and
in the subsequent issue a correction was
printed announcing that the newspaper was in
error and the person in question was still
alive. In these cases, the person's name was
removed from the listing. In other cases, a
correction as to the details of the death,
funeral, family relationships and other
factual data might show up in a paper a week
or two after the initial reporting. In such
cases, the listing data has been corrected to
reflect the paper's own corrections.

More serious errors may have been made reading
the tiny type often used in notices in the
"Died" column and numerals such as 3 and 8
could have been confused. Likewise, poor
quality of microfilm may have caused errors.
Dates may be off by one week in some cases,
due to misinterpretation of phrases such as
"last Wednesday." Transcription errors could
have been made by the abstracter. The manuscript has been proofed and it is hoped that
errors are at a minimum. Please contact the
abstracter if you find an error that can be
corrected.

ALL SECONDARY GENEALOGICAL RESOURCES NEED TO
BE CHECKED AGAINST AN ORIGINAL SOURCE. THIS
WORK IS NO EXCEPTION.

SPECIAL THANKS

The abstracter wishes to thank Janice Hummel
of the Lexington Park Branch, St. Mary's
County Memorial Library, Lexington Park, Maryland, and Bleecker Harrison of the St. Mary's
County Historical Society, Leonardtown, Maryland, for use of microfilm readers. Without
their cooperation, this work could not have
been accomplished.

James H. Ogden, III, historian at Chickamauga
and Chattanooga National Military Park, Fort
Oglethorpe, Georgia, a former student and

long-time friend of the compiler, and Harvey
L. Lineback of Hollywood, Maryland, genealogist and long-time friend of the compiler,
both made valuable suggestions that were
incorporated into this work. Mr. Lineback also
assisted in the early stages of proofing the
manuscript.

Harry Macy, Jr. and Henry B. Hoff, both of the
New York Genealogical and Biographical Society
made valuable suggestions. Mr. Macy, Mr. Hoff
and David Kerkhof of the Suffolk County Historical Society, Riverhead, N. Y., helped lo-
cate many places for the gazetteer.

The greatest thanks, however, is given to
Lynea E. Bowdish of Hollywood, Maryland, wife
and friend of the compiler. Without her sup-
port and encouragement, this work would not
have been completed.

August 1996

David Roberts
24435 Lakeland Drive
Hollywood, Maryland 20636-9614

(301) 373-5251

----- Billy [Italian] - d. 27 January 1885 at
    Shelter Island; killed by falling tree
-----Frank [Italian] - d. 22 October 1888 at
    Shore Swamp, Oyster Bay; killed in cave in
    while working on railroad; interment at
    Brookville
[ ]IGGS, Mrs. William - 70 yrs 1 mo; funeral
    10 March 1889 at Northport; interment at
    Comac
[ ]PER, Mrs. Benjamin - 65 years; funeral
    3 July 1889 at Northport
ABBOT, Daniel - 86 years; d. 28 March 1890 at
    Syosset
ABBOTT, Eddie - 3 years; drowned 13 July 1887
    at Patchogue
ABBOTT, Nathaniel B. - drowned "seven weeks
    ago" [31 January 1891 paper]; drowned
    December 1890 [28 March 1891 paper]; fell
    from sloop "St. Clair" into East River, New
    York City, off Blackwell's Island found
    floating near a pier "last week" [28 March
    1891]; funeral 25 March 1891 at Port
    Jefferson; resident of Port Jefferson
ABRAMS, Benjamin - 56 years; drowned 2 June
    1882 at Fire Island Inlet
ABRAMS, Hiram - d. "two weeks ago" at Free-
    port; Civil War Veteran; 19 October 1889
    paper
ABRAMS, Jarvis - 45 years; disappeared "six
    weeks ago"; suicide, found hanging in tree
    at Valley Stream; 17 November 1888 paper
ACKERLY, child - ca. 6 years; d. 28 July 1885;
    Northport item; son of William Ackerly
ACKERLY, Augusta [male] - d. 14 October 1890
    at Patchogue; son of Elvena Ackerly
ACKERLY, Catherine A. - 74 y 2 m 19 d; d. at
    Crab Meadow; funeral 7 February 1887; wife
    of William Ackerly
ACKERLY, Gilbert - 74 y 11 m 11 d; d. 14 Feb-
    ruary 1887 at Dix Hills
ACKERLY, Henry S. - 79 y 4 m 8 d; d. 25 Sept-
    ember 1889 at Northport; piano manufacturer
ACKERLY, Isaac - 85 years; d. 13 May 1887 at
    Southold
ACKERLY, Jacob - 84 years; d. 4 November 1879
    at Centreport

ACKERLY, Mary - 90 yrs 1 d; d. 5 March 1890 at
    Centreport; "Aunt Polly"; "after a long life
    of usefulness"
ACKERLY, Neil - 6 y 2 m 10 d; d. 22 December
    1886 at Northport; son of N. S. and Mary M.
    Ackerly
ACKERLY, Mrs. Orville B. - death recorded;
    21 November 1879 paper
ACKERLY, Phebe - 82 years; d. 13 January 1890
    at Northport; Dix Hills native; widow of
    Henry Ackerly; mother of James Ackerly
ACKERLY, Philetus - 44 y 11 m 1 d; d. 6 Dec-
    ember 1888 at Northport; brother of William
    Ackerly
ACKERLY, Richard R. - 70 y 4 m 25 d; d. 5 Feb-
    ruary 1884 at Northport
ACKERLY, William - interment 19 November 1888;
    Northport item; brother of Philetus Ackerly
ACKLEY, Harry E. - funeral 1 December 1889 at
    Hempstead
ADAMS, Alfred * - 15 years; drowned 30 July
    1887 in Lake Agawam, Southampton
ADAMS, Benjamin Franklin - 52 y 1 m 13 d;
    d. 6 June 1890 at Cold Spring Harbor
ADAMS, Mrs. Benjamin Franklin - resident of
    Cold Spring; interment at New York City;
    15 May 1885 paper
ADAMS, Charles - d. 31 December 1888 at
    Smithtown
ADAMS, Grosvenor S. - ca. 69 years; d. at
    Greenport; 4 May 1883 paper; President
    of First National Bank of Greenport
ADAMS, John Q. - 35 years; d. 17 February 1880
    at Huntington
ADAMS, Joseph - 77 years; d. 16 December 1885
    at Cold Spring
ADAMS, Luke - 84 years; d. 19 July 1880 at
    Smithtown
ADAMS, Mary Ann H. - 46 years; d. 10 October
    1880 at Huntington; daughter of James Adams
ADAMS, Sarah - funeral 16 March 1890 at Orient
ADLER, Rebecca - drowned 14 July 1883 at
    Rockaway Beach
AGNEW, Samuel - 66 yrs 5 mos; d. 11 September
    1881 at Cold Spring

AITKEN, Mrs. Irving - 2 July 1880 paper;
   resident of Sea Cliff; "Seawanhaka" fire on
   East River
AITKIN, Walter - 71 years; d. 21 February 1885
   at Hudson, N. Y.; brother of Thomas Aitkin
AKERS, George - d. 17 November 1884 at
   Flushing; fell from roof of skating rink
ALBERTSON, Elizabeth C. - d. 28 September 1889
   at Ridgewood; interment at Westbury; widow
   of Hicks Albertson; mother-in-law of Cornell
   Mott
ALDRICH, John - 71 years; d. 7 December 1878
   at Aquebogue; found dead in bed
ALEXANDER, Fred C. - 6 months; d. 17 July 1885
   at Miller's Place
ALEXANDER, Henry * - 19 years; d. 30 June 1890
   at Uniondale; native of Jamaica, West
   Indies; working picking cherries 27 June
   1890 in a tree at Island Trees; hit by
   stones thrown by boy; fell out of tree,
   broke neck and fractured spinal column;
   taken to Uniondale poorhouse where he died.
   Queens County Grand Jury discharged the boy,
   Joseph Saleighman, 8 September 1890 because
   "evidence not sufficient to indict" in death
   of Henry Alexander.
ALEXANDER, William - 41 Years; d. 12 May 1878
   at Huntington; served in Co. E., 127 NY
   Vols., Civil War
ALFRIEND, Edward Francis - 7 months;
   d. 6 August 1888 at Cold Spring Harbor; son
   of Edward M. and Nellie Alfriend
ALLEN, child - 3 years; d. 14 August 1879 at
   West Jamaica; child of George Allen; fell
   into boiling water
ALLEN, Gideon - d. 29 July 1883 "suddenly
   while sitting on the stoop of Hultz's
   Hotel"; resident of Port Washington;
   brother-in-law of Thomas McKee
ALLEN, Gilbert - suicide 19 July 1885 at
   Bellmore
ALLEN, Mary - d. 23 July 1890 at Brooklyn;
   swallowed false teeth while unconscious
ALLEN, Tustram B. - ca. 22 years; d. 10 Octo-
   ber 1884 at Half Hollow Hills; hunting
   accident; son of Tustram Allen

ALSOP, John - 75 y 1 m 16 d; d. 16 January
1888 at Huntington; native of New York City;
husband of Margaret Rapelye

ALSOP, Mrs. William - d. 25 February 1889 at
New York City; summer resident of East Neck

ALSOP, William M. - d. 2 April 1883 at New
York City; resident of East Neck

ALTAFF, Hattie - 15 y 10m 11 d; d. 10 June
1878 at Greenlawn

ALTRITT, Charles J. - 50 years; suicide 21 May
1884 at Fresh Pond, Queens County

ALVA, Alexander - 27 years; death recorded
4 September 1885 paper; resident of Bath,
Maine; brother of Mrs. Rowell of Huntington

AMIDON, Francis H. - 74 years; d. 22 July 1886
at Cold Spring Harbor; resident of New York
City

ANABLE, Henry S. - 73 years; d. 16 September
1887 at Flushing; resident of Long Island
City

ANDERSON, August - 37 years; d. Lloyd's Neck;
11 June 1887 paper

ANDERSON, Azariah - 72 years; d. 8 February
1888 at Riverhead

ANDERSON, Edward - 89 years; suicide 28 October 1887 at St. Johnland; cut throat and
drowned himself in Sunk Meadow Creek

ANDERSON, Ellen * - 1 mo 15 days; d. 1 July
1888 at Huntington; daughter of Maria
Anderson

ANDERSON, George - drowned 5 September 1886 at
Flushing; resident of New York City

ANDERSON, Johann - 24 years; drowned 26 August
1885; washed overboard from ship during
storm on voyage from New York to Nassau

ANDERSON, Reuben - d. 9 July 1885; Babylon
item; interment at Cypress Hills

ANDREW, "Major" - d. 11 January 1879 at
Washington, D. C.; formerly of Huntington;
father of Redrick Andrew

ANGERVINE, Lewis W. -77 years; d. 5 March 1884
at Hempstead; former Queens County Treasurer

APPLEBEY, Mattie B. - 39 years; d. 22 June
1878 at New York City; stomach cancer; wife
of Lucian O. Applebey

APPLEBY, Mary A. - 80 years; d. 29 February
1888 at Huntington

4

APPLY, Kate - drowned 16 August 1884 at Sea
Cliff
ARCHER, Edward H. - 2 days; d. 24 July 1887 at
Cold Spring
ARCHER, Oliver W. - 2 mos 17 days; d. 13 July
1890 at Cold Spring Harbor; son of Thomas B.
and Esther Archer
ARCHER, Rebecca J. - 70 y 9 m 11 d; d. 30 Nov-
ember 1884 at Greenlawn; wife of Floyd D.
Archer; mother of Mrs. George Howarth
ARCHER, Thomas E. - 1 yr 7 mos; d. 17 August
1879 at Cold Spring; son of Thomas and
Esther Archer
ARME, Walter - ca. 28 years; drowned about
1 May 1882 at New York City
ARMSTRONG, infant - d. 14 August 1887 at Pine
Hollow; child of William Armstrong
ARMSTRONG, George W. - 6 mos 14 days;
d.1 August 1878 at Huntington
ARMSTRONG, John J. - d. 18 October 1886 at
Jamaica; native of Mineola; lawyer; Queens
County District Attorney 1859; Queens County
Judge 1865-1885
ARMSTRONG, Louise - funeral 23 February 1888
at Oyster Bay
ARMSTRONG, Samuel T. - 78 years; d. 12 January
1878 at Saybrook, Connecticut; blind
inventor of machines for making rubber goods
ARNET, Amanda - 26 years; d. 16 May 1878 at
Oyster Bay; wife of Nelson Arnet
ARNOLD, Richard - d. 8 April 1886 at New York
City; owner of Arnold, Constable & Company;
had country residence at West Islip
ARTHUR, Mr. - d. 13 November 1890 at South
Hampton, Connecticut; brother of D. A.
Arthur of Northport
ARTHUR, Chester A. - d. 18 November 1886 [at
New York City]; President of the United
States [1881-1885]
ARTHUR, Emmet - 36 years; d. 15 November 1882
at New York City; interment at Smithtown
ARTHUR, Franklin O. - 68 years; d. 7 June 1879
at Smithtown Branch; dentist
ARTHUR, Jeremiah N. - 73 years; d. 25 Septem-
ber 1883 at St. Johnland

5

ARTHUR, Mary - 47 y 1 m 3 d; d. 26 June 1881
at Crab Meadow; wife of Isaac B. Arthur

ARTHUR, Mattie G. - 20 y 3 m 18 d; d. 12 May
1880 at Crab Meadow; wife of Scudder Arthur

ARTHUR, Robert S. - 7 mos 12 days; d. 23 October 1882 at Northport; son of Daniel A. and
Nettie M. Arthur

ASH, Mrs. - d. 28 May 1885 at Hicksville

ASH, James - "late of the village of Hicksville"; notice to creditors; 11 August 1888
paper

ASHPURVIS, Annie - 6 years; d. 6 October 1886
at New York City; burned by exploding lamp;
sung "Nearer, My God to Thee" before dying

ASTOR, John Jacob - d. 22 February 1890 [at
New York City]; "The deceased was worth
probably $200,000,000."

ATCHINSON, Alexander- 65 years; drowned
24 June 1879 at Lloyd's Neck; formerly of
Lloyd's Neck; resident of Brooklyn; funeral
at East New York

ATTWATER, Mrs. E. M. - 57 years; d. 15 April
1879 at Jacksonville, Florida

ATWATER, Mary A. - 84 yrs 6 mos; d. 25 December 1885 at New York City

ATWATER, Samuel Hobart - 38 years; 19 February 1884 at Brooklyn; former resident of
Huntington

AUBREY, Julius - murdered 19 July 1885 by
Joseph Cerovsky; judicial examination held
by Judge McKenna at Newtown

AUER, Frederick - 8 years; d. 25 January 1887
at Hicksville; scarlet fever; son of George
Auer

AUER, George - 53 years; d. 3 January 1890 at
Hicksville; foreman of Hicksville-Westbury
section of Long Island Railroad

AUGUSTA - Dowager Empress of Germany; 79 yrs.;
d. 7 January 1890 at Berlin, Germany

AVERY, infant - 1 mos 6 days; d. 28 March 1885
at East Northport; son of Charles and Mary
J. Avery

AVERY, Solomon - 69 y 9m 22 d; d. 17 November
1880 at East Northport

6

BABCOCK, David S. - 63 years; d. 24 August
1885 at Stonington, Connecticut; hit by
railroad train; President of Stonington
Steamboat Company; resident of Brooklyn
BACH, Catharine - 73 yrs 3 mos; d. 1 March
1886 at Hicksville
BADEAU, William S. - found dead in the road
30 April 1888 at Smithtown Landing
BADGLEY, Stephen L. - 50 years; d. 12 March
1888 at Brentwood; schoolteacher
BAKER Mrs. - death recorded 1 June 1883
paper; wife of editor of Stamford Herald
BAKER Mrs. - d. 11 October 1890 at Orange, New
Jersey; mother of Rev. E. Folsom Baker;
Cold Spring item
BAKER, Ashley C. - 89 years; d. 10 March 1884
at Flushing; father of Charles R. Baker;
veteran of the War of 1812
BAKER, Ella - 20 y 8 m 15 d; d. 24 February
1886 at Oyster Bay Cove; daughter of Edward
and Sarah A. Baker
BAKER, Emma - d. 15 November 1884 at Winfield;
found dead on the floor; wife of William
Baker
BAKER, Isaac H. - 26 y 2 m 20 d; suicide
14 March 1881 at Elwood; son of Uriah Baker
BAKER, James I. - d. 13 May 1886 at New York
City; President of Suffolk County Medical
Society
BAKER, John - 15 y 6 m 8 d; d. 13 August 1886
at Melville; son of John Baker
BAKER, Mary - 72 years; d. 24 January 1885 at
Brooklyn
BAKER, Mary C. - 35 years; d. 24 December 1879
at Elwood; daughter of Uriah and Mary Baker
BAKER, Richard - d. 9 December 1889 at Oyster
Bay Cove; "old resident"
BAKER, Theodore - 12 yrs 7 days; d. 7 August
1886 at Melville; son of John Baker
BAKER, Uriah - 81 y 3 m 22 d; d. 5 March 1886
at Brooklyn; interment at East Northport
BAKER, William - 85 y 8 m 15 d; d. 15 September-
ber 1884 at Comac
BALDWIN, Abigail - 70 y 8 m 15 d; d. 20 Dec-
ember 1878 at Cold Spring
BALDWIN, Abram H. - 41 y 10 m 5 d; d. 29 Nov-
ember 1886 at East Neck

7

BALDWIN, Alexander R. - 81 yrs 11 mos;
d. 1 March 1882 at Dix Hills

BALDWIN, Ashmer - 87 yrs 4 mos; d. 30 January
1884 at Wading River; former resident of
Cold Spring

BALDWIN, Charles H. - 40 years; d. 19 August
1885 at Brooklyn son of John A. Baldwin;
b. 10 June 1845 in Sullivan County, N. Y.;
furniture dealer in Williamsburgh; former
resident of Huntington 1857-1864

BALDWIN, Edward E. - d. 18 July 1890; funeral
at Northport

BALDWIN, Ella - 13 years; funeral 25 September
1883 at Woodbury

BALDWIN, Frederick A. - 48 years; d. 10 December 1881 at Morris Plains, N. J.; interment
at Cold Spring

BALDWIN, Hannah - 48 y 4 m 6 d; d. 29 April
1881 at Woodbury; wife of Robert Baldwin

BALDWIN, Mary - 85 years; d. 25 August 1890 at
Hempstead; "old and respected resident";
survived by five children

BALDWIN, Mary - 90 years; d. "recently"
8 November 1890 paper; widow of Michael
Baldwin; sister of H. A. Burtis;
Hempstead item

BALDWIN, Mary Isabella - 20 yrs 6 mos;
d. 12 December 1879 at Woodbury; daughter of
Robert and Hannah Baldwin

BALDWIN, Mary P. - 82 y 11 m 6 d; d. 16 November 1882 at Dix Hills

BALDWIN, Rebecca Ann - 68 years; d. 16 October
1886 at Brooklyn; interment at Huntington;
wife of John A. Baldwin; former resident of
Huntington

BALDWIN, Robert V. - 58 yrs 5 mos; d. 11 November 1888 at Woodbury

BALDWIN, Sadie - ca. 9 years; d. 5 October
1886 at Mount Sinai; daughter of William
Baldwin

BALDWIN, Unity - 55 years; d. 13 August 1883
at Huntington; wife of William Baldwin

BALLAGH, Jane - 70 yrs 7 mos; d. 13 August
1883 at Vernon Valley; widow of Robert
Ballagh

BALLAGH, Jane C. - 43 y 2 m 15 d; d. 22 September 1884 at Vernon Valley; interment at Brooklyn

BALLAGH, William - 81 years; d. 27 July 1880 at Huntington

BALLTON, Baver * - 9 y 4 m 23 d; d. 20 May 1878 at Old Fields

BALLTON, Benjamin P. * - 4 mos 15 days; d. 5 May 1885 at Greenlawn; son of Benjamin and Betty Ballton

BALLTON, James S. * - 4 mos 5 days; d. 20 April 1880 at Greenlawn; son of Samuel Ballton

BALLTON, Jane J. - 8 mos 17 days; d. 17 June 1890 at Greenlawn; daughter of Charles H. Ballton

BANCROFT, Mrs. - funeral 11 December 1883 at Hempstead

BANCROFT, C. J. - d. 10 July 1882 at Windsor, Connecticut; formerly of Lloyd's Neck

BANKS, Edward - 19 y 7 m 17 d; d. 1 October 1889 at Northport; interment at East Northport; son of Michael Banks

BANKS, Sarah G. McDougall - 45 yrs 9 mos; d. 12 July 1883 at Huntington; wife of George B. Banks

BANVARD, Elizabeth - d. 7 December 1889 at Watertown, S. Dakota; wife of John Banvard

BARBER, Samuel - d. 21 April 1888 at Newtown Creek; killed in boiler explosion on tugboat

BARKER, Ellen Eliza - 65 yrs 18 days; d. 15 August 1887 at Long Swamp; interment at Green-Wood, Brooklyn; wife of Israel A. Barker

BARKER, Israel A. - 24 y 5 m 4 d; d. 19 September 1886 at Long Swamp; interment at Green-Wood, Brooklyn

BARNES, Anna Jane - 35 years; d. 31 October 1885 at Huntington Harbor

BARNES, Lizzie E. - 2y 7m 12d; d. 28 February 1879 at Cold Spring; daughter of Edward and Helen Barnes

BARNES, Rev. William Guthrie - d. 16 December 1884 at Fredericksburgh, Ohio; interment at Islip

BARNETT, Peter - d. 31 August 1885 at Hicksville; interment at Plain Edge

BARNEY, Benjamin - 90 yrs 8 mos; d. 29 March
1881 at Huntington
BARNEY, Eliza - 86 yrs 6 mos; d. 2 April 1885
at Huntington; interment at Weedsport,
Cayuga County, N. Y.; b. 2 July 1798 at
Nantucket, Massachusetts; m. 1816 to Samuel
Barney; moved to Cayuga County in 1836;
operated Underground Railroad station in
Cayuga County during 1840's; lived 4 years
in San Francisco, California, following the
Gold Rush; widow of Samuel Barney; mother of
David Barney of Huntington
BARNHART, Edith H. - 2 y 5 m 24 d; d. 5 Decem-
ber 1883 at Northport; daughter of Rev.
I. C. Barnhart, Minister at St. Paul's M. E.
Church, Northport
BARNUM, Peter C. - 72 years; d. 22 March 1889
at East Meadow; largest property owner in
Town of Hempstead
BARRETT, Clarissa - 87 yrs 6 mos; d. 19 May
1884 at Brooklyn
BARRETT, Edward S. - 15 mos 10 days;
d. 17 July 1885 at Centreport; son of Arthur
W. and Margaret Barrett
BARRETT, Freeman - 37 years; d. 10 July 1880
at Cold Spring
BARRETT, Olivia - 78 yrs 10 mos; d. 5 July
1884 at Cold Spring, widow of Artemas
Barrett
BARRETT, Selah B. - 20 yrs 9 mos; d. 24 Octo-
ber 1889 at Brooklyn; injured in accident on
the Fulton Ferry; crushed between ferry boat
and dock; funeral Cold Spring; interment at
Huntington; son of Dewitt C. Barrett
BARRETT, Susan A. - 44 years; d. 8 April 1878
at Cold Spring; wife of Dewitt C. Barrett
BARROWS, Isabella Gibson - d. 12 February 1885
at Huntington; wife of Rev. Napoleon
Barrows, Rector of St. John's Episcopal
Church, Huntington
BARTLES, Mrs. William - d. 23 January 1890 at
Island Trees; interment at Jerusalem
BARTLETT, Hannah - 17 yrs 6 mos; d. 27 Decem-
ber 1880 at Vernon Valley
BARTLETT, William O. - d. 23 September 1881 at
Yaphank; lawyer; wrote for N. Y.Evening Post

BARTO, Edmund L. - 54 yrs 10 mos; d. 15 March
1886 at New York City; died while working in
Brewster & Company factory; b. 1831 Amityville; to Huntington 1849; to New Haven,
Conn. 1860; to New York City 1876; carriage
maker by trade
BARTO, John - 80 years; d. 6 August 1882 at
Babylon
BARTO, Phebe M. - 29 y 10 m 24 d; d. 20 September 1885 at New York City; former resident
of Huntington
BARTOW, Mrs. B. P. - d. "last week" at Hempstead; 30 January 1885 paper
BARTOW, Eddie - 4 y 9 m 14 d; d. 16 June 1883
at West Neck
BARTOW, Luther C. - 68 years; d. 27 December
1884 at Northport
BARTOW, Morris - ca. 60 years; d. 25 March
1880 at Half Hollow Hills; killed by falling
tree
BARWICK, Harry H. - 4 y 3 m 12 d; d. 4 June
1888 at Brooklyn; interment at Huntington
BASSETT, William - 26 years; drowned 24 June
1879 off Cold Spring at Seawanhaka Boat Club
Regatta
BASSFORD, Amelia A. Seacord - 73 years;
d. 17 September 1884 at New York City;
interment at Green-Wood, Brooklyn; widow of
Byria W. Bassford
BATES, Alfred S. - 76 years; d. 17 October
1889 at Scarsdale, N. Y.; former resident of
Lloyd's Neck
BATES, Rev. Edmund O. - d. 8 May 1886 at
Brooklyn; b. 1808 Peekskill, N. Y.; M. E.
clergyman; pastor of many M. E. churches on
Long Island: North Hempstead Circuit 1842-
1843; Huntington 1852-1853; New York City
and Brooklyn after 1861; pastor of Mariners'
Church, Brooklyn
BATES, James * - 32 years; drowned 3 July
1879 at Glen Cove
BATTLEMAN, Harry E. - 3 y 2 m 15 d; d. 24 Oct-
tober 1884 at West Hills
BAUKNEY, child - d. Hempstead; fell into pail
of scalding water; child of John N. Baukney;
26 October 1883 paper

BAYARD, Kate - d. 16 January 1886 at Washing-
ton, D. C.; found dead in bed; daughter of
U. S. Secretary of State [Thomas F. Bayard]
BAYARD, Mrs. Thomas F. - d. 31 January 1886;
wife of U. S. Secretary of State
BAYLES, Ann - 61 y 1 m 3 d; d. 21 January 1880
at Port Jefferson; wife of James M. Bayles
BAYLES, Clarissa - 82 years; d. 23 September
1889 at Mount Sinai
BAYLES, Delia - d. 20 March 1887 at Oyster
Bay; daughter of Charles H. Bayles
BAYLES James M. - 74 years; d. 29 March 1889
at Port Jefferson; b. 18 January 1815; ship
builder by trade; founded J. M. Bayles & Son
1861; son of Elisha Bayles; husband of
Desire Ann Hawkins; father of James E.
Bayles, Samuel H. Bayles, G. Frank Bayles,
Mrs. A. Curtis Almy, Hamilton T. Bayles,
S. Taber Bayles and Havens P. Bayles
BAYLES, Joseph D. - drowned 28 August 1880 off
Cape Canaveral, Florida; swept overboard in
a storm; son of Joseph Bayles of Port Jeff-
erson
BAYLIS, Abram - 65 years; d. 29 November 1878
at East Norwich
BAYLIS, Ashton - 10 y 4 m 23 d; d. 9 September
1882 at Huntington; son of Daniel L. and
Cornelia Baylis
BAYLIS, Bertha F. - 25 yrs 4 mos; d. 7 July
1887 at Melville; wife of F. A. Baylis
BAYLIS, Catherine - 48 y 2 m 21 d; d. 13 March
1887 at Melville
BAYLIS, Daniel - 82 years; d. 5 December 1879
at Melville
BAYLIS, Elizabeth - 79 yrs 10 mos; d. 21 April
1885 at Melville
BAYLIS, Elizabeth - 92 years; d. 18 March 1888
at Jamaica; interment at Melville
BAYLIS, Florence - 20 y 10 m 4 d; d. 8 March
1890 at Melville suffocated by coal gas;
daughter of John Mann; wife of Smith K.
Baylis
BAYLIS, Frederick L. - 21 y 6 m 3 d;
d. 28 November 1890 at Half Hollows; son of
Jacob and Phebe M. Baylis
BAYLIS, Hannah - 92 years; d. 11 October 1882
at Greenpoint; widow of Thomas Baylis

12

BAYLIS, Henrietta - 42 years; d. 26 December 1882 at Melville
BAYLIS, Isaac Mills - 68 y 3 m 9 d; d. 10 February 1878 at Melville
BAYLIS, Jennie E. - 23 years; d. 14 November 1883 at Melville; daughter of Jacob Baylis
BAYLIS, Mehetable - 83 y 10m 4 d; d. 14 January 1881 at Old Fields
BAYLIS, Parmelia - 61 years; d. 7 January 1881 at Brooklyn; interment at Melville
BAYLIS, Phebe - d. 29 July 1880 at Melville; wife of Elias Baylis, Jr.
BAYLIS, Phebe M. - 50 y 10 m 11 d; d. 2 November 1887 at Half Hollow Hills; wife of Jacob Baylis
BAYLIS, Richard Montgomery - 54 y 2 m 17 d; d. 19 April 1882 at Huntington
BAYLIS, S. Josephine - 34 y 3 m 3 d; d. 16 February 1882 at Melville; wife of Oliver Baylis
BAYLIS, Sarah Elizabeth - 57 y 9 m 23 d; d. 19 December 1888 at Huntington; daughter of Henry and Hannah Sammis; wife of George Baylis
BAYLIS, Sarah J. - 6 mos 10 days; d. 19 August 1882 at Melville; daughter of Oliver and Josephine Baylis
BAYLIS, Smith C. - 37 y 5 m 29 d; d. 4 March 1883 at Farmingdale
BAYLIS, Smith K. - 24 y 10 m 17 d; d. 8 March 1890 at Melville; suffocated by coal gas; son of Jacob Baylis; husband of Florence Baylis, who also was suffocated; father of John Smith Baylis, age 15 months, who survived the coal gas; brother of Mrs. Frank Whitson of Syosset
BAYLIS, Townsend - 79 years; d. 11 May 1880 at Greenvale
BAYLY, George - d. 17 October 1888 at East Norwich
BAYLY, John - 69 years; d. 15 April 1887 at Jericho; brother-in-law of Jackson Tappen
BEACH, Mary E. - 3 1/2 years; 2 July 1880 paper; resident of Glen Cove; "Seawanhaka" fire on East River

BEACON, Mrs. Joe - d. "last week"; resident of Freeport; to be buried in St. George's Churchyard, Hempstead; trustees refused to allow burial and stopped funeral service; 3 March 1888 paper

BEATTY, Brazillai B. - 63 years; d. 10 May 1887 at West Hills

BEATTY, Cornelius - 77 years; d. 2 May 1883 at New York City; brother of Alfred Beatty

BEAVEN, Mary L. - 56 yrs 2 mos; d. 1 September 1883 at Cold Spring

BECKMAN, Peter J. - 40 years; d. 19 November 1887 at Astoria; jumped from window of house into street

BEDELL, Charlotte - 73 years; d. 26 May 1888 at New York City interment at Plain Edge; sister-in-law of Henry Bedell

BEDELL, Edward - d. 11 April 1883 at Baldwins; hit by railroad train

BEDELL, Harry - d. Patchogue; interment 4 February 1889 at Babylon; ran Babylon stage for many years

BEDELL, Moses - d. 15 July 1883 near Freeport; local Methodist preacher

BEDELL, Samuel - d. "this week" at Melville; 18 January 1890 paper

BEDELL, Stephen A. - d. saw mill accident at Greenpoint; 11 August 1888 paper; resident of Hempstead

BEDELL, Walter - funeral 5 June 1888 at Farmingdale

BEDFORD, Hannah - 73 y 2 m 7 d; d. 24 May 1882 at Huntington; interment at New Providence, New Jersey

BEEBE, infant - 17 days; d. 8 March 1880 at Brooklyn; child of Henry and Matilda Beebe

BEEBE, George - ca. 40 years; d. 23 June 1885 at Orient; overdose of laudanum taken for tooth ache

BEEBE, Hannah - 71 years; d. 15 August 1885 at Northport; wife of Lyman Beebe

BEEBE, Lyman M. - 79 y 2 m 8 d; d. 3 November 1887 at Northport; b. New London, Connecticut; ship pilot in New York Harbor; sailing master in famous yacht races; in charge of fleet of fishing vessels

BEEBE, Theophilus - 46 years; d. 6 February 1886 at Northport

BEEBE, Willie - 15 years; d. 7 July 1882 at Northport; son of Henry and Dora Beebe; interment at Green-Wood, Brooklyn

BEECHER, Henry Ward - d. 8 March 1887 [at Brooklyn]; [nationally important Congregationalist clergyman, abolitionist and political leader; brother of Harriet Beecher Stowe]

BEERS, Amelia - 79 yrs 5 mos; d. 24 July 1881 at Jamaica

BEERS, Emily H. - 14 y 8 m 2 d; d. 21 September 1884 at Huntington; daughter of W. S. Beers

BEERS, Harriet K. - d. 7 January 1889 at Brooklyn; widow of Nathan T. Beers

BEERS, James Edgar - 42 years; d. 21 June 1885 at Dix Hills; funeral at Comac

BEERS, John Henry - 67 years; d. 13 June 1885 at Huntington; son of Hawley Beers; brother of Edward Beers and Nathan Beers, both of Brooklyn, and Lucinda of Huntington; "money broker"; resident of Brooklyn; formerly of Cold Spring

BEERS, Lavinia Crook - d. 2 February 1889 at Brooklyn; wife of John Z. Beers

BEERS, N. T. - 74 years; d. 27 July 1887 at Brooklyn; Brooklyn businessman

BEERS, Nathan - 21 years; d. 29 July 1887 at Babylon; grandson of N. T. Beers

BEERS, Zenas - 87 y 10 m 12 d; d. 7 October 1879 at Dix Hills; active Methodist

BEHR, T. [Miss] - 6 years; d. 31 March 1890; funeral at Glen Cove

BEITLER, Joseph S. - 59 yrs 9 mos; d. 24 May 1885 at Huntington; noted horse trainer; operated Suffolk Driving Park

BELCHER, Thomas - d. Brooklyn from result of railroad accident at Jamaica; resident of Far Rockaway, formerly of Centreport; 14 April 1888 paper

BELKNAP, Jennet Lenox - 73 years; d. 26 December 1889 at New York City; daughter of Robert Maitland; widow of Aaron B. Belknap; mother of R. L. Belknap of Huntington

BELL, Mrs. - d. 22 December 1888 at Orange,
  N. J.; mother of Peter A. Bell of Hicksville
BELL, Mrs. A. V. A. - 83 yrs 18 days;
  d. 31 January 1890 at Long Swamp
BELL, Isaac - d. New York City; Cold Spring
  item; 26 January 1889 paper
BELL, John - 73 years; funeral 9 January 1881
  at Bayville
BELL, Thomas - d. 22 December 1889 at Mill
  Neck; "had charge of the Underhill property"
  at Mill Neck
BELLOWS, Isaac - 70 yrs 2 mos; d. 9 April 1882
  at Mount Sinai
BELLOWS, Nancy M. - d. 22 January 1887 at Good
  Ground
BELMONT, August - 74 years; d. 24 November
  1890 at New York City; interment at Newport,
  Rhode Island; b. Alzey, Germany; important
  banker, financier and political leader;
  father of August Belmont, Jr. of Hempstead;
  account of funeral in Hempstead column of
  6 December 1890 paper
BENJAMIN, Jehial - d. 22 January 1889 at
  Riverhead; "dropped dead"
BENJAMIN, Judah P. - d. [6 May 1884] at Paris,
  France; [Louisiana political leader; Confed-
  erate Secretary of War and] Secretary of
  State
BENJAMIN, R. H. - d. 26 April 1886 at River-
  head; President of Riverhead Savings Bank
BENJAMIN, Roselle - d. "last week" of typhoid
  fever Riverhead item; 18 October 1890 paper
BENEDICT Rev. T. N. - 68 y 6 m 16 d;
  d. 17 March 1886 at Miller's Place
BENNETT, Aaron B. - 2 July 1880 paper; resi-
  dent of Brooklyn "Seawanhaka" fire on East
  River
BENNETT, Alexander B. - 16 years; d. 1 Decem-
  ber 1881 at Amagansett; killed in block and
  tackle accident
BENNETT, Almy - 68 y 11 m 13 d; d. 28 February
  1885 at Oyster Bay Cove; wife of Nicholas
  Bennett
BENNETT, Amelia - d. 25 May 1887 at Brooklyn;
  interment at Cold Spring Harbor; wife of
  Abraham D. Bennett

BENNETT, Benjamin D. - 23 yrs 6 days;
   d. 12 August 1880 at Albany, New York;
   resident of Mount Sinai
BENNETT, Diedamia - 74 years; d. 17 November
   1890 at Centreport; found dead in her room;
   interment at Green-Wood, Brooklyn; widow of
   George I. Bennett; mother of G. H. R. Bennett, Mrs. Andrus Titus and Maria Bennett;
   sister of Seth R. Robins
BENNETT, Evelina D. - 2 July 1880 paper; resi-
   dent of Brooklyn "Seawanhaka" fire on East
   River; wife of Aaron B. Bennett
BENNETT, George S. - 41 y 8 m 16 d;
   d. 30 April 1881 at Oyster Bay
BENNETT, George W. - d. at Flatbush Insane
   Asylum, Flatbush; resident of Hempstead;
   4 January 1884 paper
BENNETT, Georgia A. - 19 y 10 m 16 d;
   d. 7 August 1882 at Long Swamp; daughter of
   Nathaniel Bennett
BENNETT, Henry - d. "one day this week" at New
   York City; interment at St. James; son of
   John Bennett; 5 June 1885 paper
BENNETT, Nathaniel T. - 62 y 11m 23 d;
   d. 15 June 1889 at Long Swamp
BENNETT, Sarah - 42 years; d. 11 August 1880
   at Oyster Bay
BENNETT, Thomas F. - d. 19 July 1883 at
   Hicksville; dropped dead in the street
BENNETT, Walter L. - 74 y 8 m 14 d;
   d. 29 October 1889 at Long Swamp; "suddenly"
BENNETT, Walter Leslie - 10 y 7 m 11 d;
   drowned 12 May 1886 at Cold Spring Harbor;
   son of George Bennett
BENT, Silas - 66 years; d. 26 August 1887 at
   Shelter Island; U. S. Naval officer; served
   with Perry's Expedition to Japan 1854;
   resident of St. Louis, Missouri
BENTLEY, James - d. Newark, N. J.; 16 August
   1890 paper; brother of A. Bentley of Port
   Jefferson
BERESHEIMER John - 55 years; d. 28 May 1879
   at College Point killed by lightning
BERGEN, infant - d. Flatlands; 25 October 1890
   paper; son of Mrs. J. V. Bergen of Flatlands; former resident of Echo

BERGEN, Leonard M. - d. 2 April 1885 at
Brooklyn; former resident of Hempstead
BERGLAND, Godfried - 25 years; drowned 20 Nov-
ember 1888 at Main Street Wharf, Greenport;
native of Sundswald, Sweden
BERKLEY, Celia * - 5 mos 11 days; d. 11 September 1889 at Huntington
BERNICHI, Felix - d. Weldon, N. C.; 24 Jan-
uary 1879 paper; killed by trained bear;
circus act had been at Huntington during the
fall of 1878
BERNINGER, Michael - 65 years; d. 19 July 1887
at Fresh Pond; lockjaw from pitchfork injury
BERNNIS, Edward - d. 11 September 1883 at Long
Island City; railroad accident
BERRY, Ellen J. - 36 y 6 m 12 d; d. 2 January
1886 at New York City
BERRY, John C. - 45 years; d. 2 October 1889
at New York City; former resident of Hunt-
ington
BERRY, Thomas - 70 years; d. 21 May 1884 at
Huntington
BERRY, Thomas W. - 48 years; d. 20 September
1882 at Huntington
BERTHOLF, Mrs. J. M. - funeral at Florida,
Orange County, N. Y.; sister of J. C.
Totten of Cold Spring; 29 May 1885 paper
BERTRAND, Charles - d. 3 March 1885 at Hicks-
ville; paralytic stroke
BERTRAND, Frederick - death recorded 15
January 1886 paper; resident of Plain Edge
BESCHOTT, Ferdinand - d. 23 July 1885 at Bres-
lau; Breslau postmaster; died sorting mail
BETSCHA, Mr. - death recorded 9 January 1885
paper; Hicksville item
BETTS, Burrell - 81 years; d. 26 May 1888 at
Oyster Bay
BETTS, C. Wyllis - d. "last week"; Southampton
item; 7 May 1887 paper
BETTS, George E. - 18 days; d. 11 January 1881
at New York City; son of George Betts
BETTS, John - 81 years; d. 19 December 1890 at
Huntington; "one of the first to enter into
the tailoring business in this village many
years ago"
BETTS, Susan - d. 11 November 1878 at Yaphank;
re-buried at Huntington 2 January 1880

BETTS, William - 83 years; d. 5 July 1884 at
   Jamaica; former law professor at Columbia
   University
BIALLA, Mr. - death recorded 11 December 1885
   paper; Northport item; father of John B.
   Bialla
BIERD, Harold Leroy - infant; d. 18 August
   1890 at Jericho; interment at Green-Wood,
   Brooklyn; son of William Bierd
BIGGS, child - d. "last week"; 30 March 1889
   paper; Riverhead item; child of Alden Biggs
BILLINGS, John - d. "forepart" of last week at
   Butter City, Montana; interment at Glen
   Cove; former resident of Cedar Swamp; 9 Nov-
   ember 1889 and 16 November 1889 papers
BIRCH, Joshua - d. "last week" at Jacksonville, Florida; yellow fever epidemic;
   former Long Island resident; 29 September
   1888 paper
BIRCH, Mary - 55 years; d. 7 November 1884 at
   Huntington
BIRCH, Mima - 91 years; funeral 24 February
   1886; Farmingdale item; 16 days short of
   92nd birthday
BIRCHELL, Henry - 31 years; d. 15 January 1885
   at Bethpage; killed in railroad accident;
   engineer of train which de-railed; interment
   at Hempstead
BIRDSALL, James - 87 years; d. 1 November 1883
   at Glen Cove; father of Hon. John Birdsall
BIRMINGHAM, Ellen - 44 years; d. 24 October
   1884 at Huntington
BISCHOPF, William - 17 y 3 m 8 d; d. 5 January
   1890 at Hicksville; interment Lutheran
   Cemetery, Middle Village
BISHOP, Mrs. - d. 19 February 1890 at Brooklyn; sister of Mrs. John Taylor of Greenlawn
BISHOP, Charles W. - 62 y 2 m 25 d; d. 24 Sep-
   tember 1884 at Northport
BISHOP, Fannie - 89 years; d. 2 February 1879
   at Northport
BISHOP, Henry - 74 years; d. 17 December 1888
   at Cold Spring; interment at White House,
   New Jersey
BISHOP, John C. - 63 y 1 m 25 d; d. 22 Decem-
   ber 1879 at Morrisania, N.Y.; interment at
   Huntington

BISHOP, John S. - drowned 13 July 1883 at
   Centre Moriches
BISHOP, Lawrence E. - 4 years; d. 26 April
   1887 at Northport
BISHOP, Lucinda - 63 years; d. 25 November
   1880 at Northport; wife of James Bishop
BISHOP, Maria H. - 79 y 3 m 22 d; d. 10 August
   1882 at Cold Spring; wife of Zebulon Bishop
BISHOP, Phebe E. - 35 y 4 m 21 d; d. 24 Octo-
   ber 1878 at Northport; wife of Roscoe Bishop
BLACHLEY, Bertha May - 10 years; d. 10 January
   1888 at Deer Park; daughter of Jarvis and
   Mary Ann Blachley
BLACHLEY, Henry - 80 years; d. 17 May 1882 at
   Half Hollow Hills
BLACHLEY, Isaac J. - 50 y 6 m 3 d; d. 16 June
   1885 at Dix Hills
BLACK, Jeremiah S. - 78 years; d. 19 August
   1883 at York, Pennsylvania; statesman, judge
   and Democratic party leader; served as U. S.
   Attorney-General [1857-1860] and U. S.
   Secretary of State [1860-1861]
BLAINE, Walker - 35 years; d. 15 January 1890
   at Washington, D. C.; son of U. S. Secretary
   of State James G. Blaine
BLAIR, Harry * - 6 days; d. 14 December 1890
   at West Hills; child of William Blair and
   Mrs. Sophia Spencer; wouldn't nurse and died
   from starvation
BLANCHARD, Henrietta C. A. - 47 y 9 m 9 d;
   d. 22 November 1886 at Brooklyn; interment
   at Northport; daughter of Scudder Bryant;
   wife of F. Loring Blanchard
BLASDALE, Dr. Charles - 50 years; d. 21 August
   1887 at Jericho; interment at Springfield,
   Massachusetts; native of France; former
   President of Queens County Medical Society
BLASIUS, Catherine H. - 23 years; d. 31 July
   1881 at Greenlawn
BLAZINS, Catherine - 67 y 11 m 21 d;
   d. 13 March 1883 at Mount Sinai; wife of
   John Blazins
BLESSING, Margaret - 83 years; d. 6 September
   1889; interment Calvary, Queens County
BLOOMINGDALE, Isidore - 2 July 1880 paper;
   resident of New York City; "Seawanhaka" fire
   on East River

BLOXOM, Edward - 3 mos 12 days; d. 12 August
   1882 at East Neck; son of Edward and
   Arabella Bloxom
BLOXSOM, Alice D. - 10 mos 22 days; d. 28 July
   1883 at Huntington; daughter of Harver
   Bloxsom
BLOXSOM, Agnes M. - 10 mos 25 days; d. 1 Aug-
   ust 1883 at Huntington; daughter of Harver
   Bloxsom
BLOXSOM, Edward - 3 mos 23 days; d. 22 January
   1887 at Huntington
BLOXSOM, Harvey - 77 y 11 m 24 d; d. 4 March
   1886 at Huntington
BLYDENBURGH, Ebenezer S. - 84 years;
   d. 20 November 1880 at Smithtown
BLYDENBURGH, Hamilton - 74 years; d. 17 Oct-
   ober 1884 at New York City; Smithtown
   native; wholesale grocer dealer
BLYDENBURGH, Julia A. - 86 yrs 1 mo; d. 9 Sep-
   tember 1884 at New York City; interment at
   Smithtown Branch
BLYDENBURGH, Ruth - 86 years; d. 17 March 1881
   at Stony Brook
BOCHBENDER, Chilles - funeral 16 October 1889
   at New York City; Hicksville item
BOCKUS, Jane - 76 years; funeral 14 October
   1888 at Oyster Bay; widow of Isaac Bockus;
   sister of John M. Sammis
BODIE, Eva - 18 mos; d. 29 May 1881 at New
   York City; interment at Northport; fell from
   tenement window; daughter of Henry Bodie
BODIE, Frederick - 3 years; d. 29 May 1881 at
   New York City; interment at Northport; fell
   from tenement window; son of Henry Bodie
BODIE, Henry - interment at Northport 2 Febru-
   ary 1888; resident of Greenpoint
BOGART, Mrs. Andrew - funeral 2 September 1889
   at Brookville
BOGART, Mrs. Vincent - d. 18 February 1889 at
   North Babylon; interment at Babylon
BOGERT, Mrs. - d. 23 May 1884 at Northport
BOGUE, Charles - 19 years; d. 11 August 1878
   at Brooklyn; railroad flagman at Fort Greene
   crossing; hit by train which cut off his
   legs
BOHEN, Kittie - d. 20 December 1890 at
   Brooklyn; "well known in Westbury"

BOLLER, Matilda - suicide at Woodside; 29 February 1884 paper; wife of Charles M. Boller

BOLLES, Mrs. Francis A. - d. at Scranton, Pa.; 14 April 1888 paper; interment at Riverhead

BOLTE, Henry - 27 years; d. 2 September 1883 at Springfield; railroad accident

BOMAN, Jane - 100 years; d. "this week" at Flushing; 19 January 1889 paper; aunt of Mrs. William Cobb of Westbury

BOOKBINDER, Hester - 28 yrs 1 day; d. 5 June 1884 at Greenlawn

BOORMANN, J. H. - 72 y 9 m 24 d; d. 12 March 1890 at Hicksville; interment Lutheran Cemetery, Middle Village

BOOTH, Mary - ca. 70 years; suicide 16 September 1884 at Southold

BOOTH, Nancy Monsell - 85 years; d. 29 July 1887 at Greenport; widow of William Chatfield Booth

BORJESON, Martin - ca. 36 years; drowned 13 June 1885 in Hempstead Harbor between Sea Cliff and Glen Cove; lost off yacht "Lena" of Knickerbocker Yacht Club; body floated ashore at Sea Cliff 23 June 1885

BORUM, Samuel - 40 years; drowned 9 September 1878 off Bridgeport, Conn. while sailing an oyster sloop; father of 12 or 14 children; resident of Five Mile River, Connecticut; formerly of Syosset

BOSSINGER, Ignatz - d. 15 July 1883 at Winfield; sunstroke

BOUTON, Eleanor M. - 85 years; d. 2 September 1881 at Huntington; widow of Amos Bouton; mother-in-law of William L. Jackson

BOWEN, John L. - d. 12 March 1888 at Yaphank; int. at Huntington; "peculiar" "eccentric" "looked upon as somewhat a tramp"; $5,000 savings found after death; account in 8 November 1890 paper about suit in Suffolk County Surrogate's Court over estate

BOWERS, Sarah M. - 74 yrs 8 mos; d. 5 November 1879 at St. Johnsland

BOWLES, Mr. - 75 years; d. 15 November 1882 at St. Johnland

BOYCE, child - funeral "last week" at Oyster Bay; interment at Mill Neck; 22 March 1890 paper; child of William Boyce

BOYD, Mrs. E. C. - 84 years; d. 27 July 1883
at Freeport; widow of E. C. Boyd of Brook-
lyn; mother of Mrs. James M. Crawford
BRADBURY, James W. - ca. 90 years; d. 25 Oct-
ober 1886 at Oyster Bay
BRADLEY, Daniel - ca. 100 years; d. 20 July
1889 at Poospatuck; American Indian
BRADLEY, Mary A. - 73 years; d. 18 March 1885
at Northport
BRADY, Ann - 42 years; d. 29 March 1881 at
Comac
BRAGAW, Julia - 61 years; d. 30 March 1884 at
Greenpoint; wife of Daniel Bragaw
BRAGAW, William - 80 years; d. "recently" at
Long Island City; son of Richard Bragaw, a
veteran of the Revolution; veteran of the
War of 1812; m. 6 January 1820 Miss Towns-
end; father and grandfather of Union sol-
diers in the Civil War; one son was prisoner
of Confederates at Andersonville, Georgia;
7 February 1879 paper
BRANDEGEE, J. C. - d. 14 December 1886 at
Brooklyn; former resident of Lloyd's Neck
BRANDEGEE, Jeannette Caroline - 74 years;
d. 19 July 1882 at Bayonne, New Jersey;
daughter of Andre Daniel Chastant; widow of
Jacob Brandegee
BRANDORSTEIN, child - infant; murdered 20 Dec-
ember 1883 at Woodhaven; son of Theresa
Brandorstein; infant murdered by his mother
BRANDT, August - drowned 10 May 1882 in Great
South Bay
BRANDT, Catherine - 64 years; d. 16 March 1884
at Woodbury
BRANDT, Theodore - suicide near Jericho;
20 June 1884 and 12 September 1884 papers
BRANDT, Willie K. - 2 y 7 m 19 d; d. 6 Septem-
ber 1882 at West Hills
BRANNIGAN, child - d. 22 March 1884 at
Hunter's Point; daughter of Johanna Branni-
gan; mother left 5 children alone in house;
this child starved to death
BRANT, Mrs. Leonard - 41 years 8 mos; d. 3 May
1890 at Hicksville; interment at Jerusalem;
widow who leaves 6 children

BRAUN, Augusta - 8 years 2 mos; d. 15 October
1888 at Hicksville of diphtheria; interment
at Westbury; daughter of Sebastian Braun

BRAZIER, Gussie E. [*?] - 9 mos 4 days;
d. 3 August 1884 at Huntington; daughter of
Charles and Georgiana Brazier

BRAZIER, Sarah E. * - 21 years 4 mos; d. 15
August 1885 at Huntington

BREEN, child - d. at East Meadow of diphtheria; interment 3 January 1888; child of
Patrick Breen

BREEN, Katie - 15 mos; d. 3 September 1887 at
Hicksville; daughter of Dennis and Maggie
Breen

BREMNER, Julia - 2 years; d. 28 March 1890
funeral at Oyster Bay Cove; daughter of
George Bremner

BRENTON, James E. - 49 years; d. 7 March 1884
at Jamaica; Editor of Long Island Democrat

BRENTON, James J. - 75 years; d. 13 August
1881 at Jamaica; Editor of Long Island
Democrat

BREWSTER, child - d. 6 September 1889;
Northport item; child of James Brewster

BREWSTER, Mrs. Richard - d. 27 February 1890
at Setauket; active member of Caroline
Episcopal Church

BRICKETT, William H. - 3 years; d. 7 September
1889 at Hicksville

BRINCKERHOFF, Daniel - 85 years; death
recorded 9 January 1885 paper; resident of
Manhasset

BRITT, Libbie Scott - d. 2 June 1880 at
Ravenswood; daughter of John Scott; wife of
J. W. Britt; interment at Huntington

BROCK, infant - d. 22 July 1878 at Huntington;
child of William Brock

BROOKS, Anna A. - 44 yrs 9 mos; d. 1 February
1880 at Haddam, Conn.; interment at Huntington

BROOKS, Laura M. - 9 months; d. 15 May 1882 at
Bridgeport, Conn.; interment at Huntington

BROSS, child - infant; d. 20 January 1889 at
West Islip; interment at Babylon; child of
Dr. William and Fannie Miller Bross

BROWN, child - interment 18 September 1889 at Westbury; daughter of Mr. and Mrs. Brown of Brooklyn

BROWN, Bridget - funeral 8 April 1890 at Glen Cove

BROWN, Mrs. Charles - funeral 19 December 1886 at Centreport; resident of Bridgeport, Conn.

BROWN, Charles E. - 33 yrs 20 days; d. 7 June 1887 at Huntington; found dead in bed; known to have heart trouble; son of John J. Brown

BROWN, Charles Franklin * - 4 months; d. 31 May 1887 at Greenlawn

BROWN, Daniel - 82 y 5m 13 d; d. 8 February 1882 at Northport

BROWN, Diodama E. - 45 yrs 3 mos; d. 2 April 1879 at Newark, N. J.; wife of Thomas F. Brown

BROWN, Elizabeth - 69 y 5 m 29 d; d. 2 January 1880 at Long Swamp

BROWN, Elizabeth G. - 82 years; d. 10 September 1884 at Huntington; widow of Stephen Brown

BROWN, Emma Southworth - 19 y 7 m 6 d; d. 11 April 1882 at Huntington

BROWN, George - 21 years; killed 2 May 1883 at New York City; accident at dock at foot of East 33rd Street; painting side of barge; crushed between barge and dock; son of John Brown of Huntington

BROWN, George F. - 1 year; d. 1 September 1884 at Long Swamp

BROWN, Mrs. Henry - d. 14 February 1886 at Half Hollows; interment at Mount Sinai

BROWN, Irving E. - 3 mos; d. 15 August 1884 at Long Swamp

BROWN, James - 80 years; d. 17 November 1883 near Freeport; Freeport resident; died on exposure on meadows in Hempstead Bay off Freeport

BROWN, James Monroe - 44 years; d. 29 January 1888 at Jamaica son of W. H. and Louisa Monroe Brown; husband of Margaret C. Anderson

BROWN, James R. - d. 20 January 1882 at Sinclairsville, N. Y.; former resident of Cold Spring

BROWN, Jemina - 82 y 5 m 2 d; d. 2 January 1888 at Huntington

25

BROWN, John - murdered 22 March 1888 at Port
Washington
BROWN, John H. * - 9 y 10 m 15 d; d. 12 Nov-
ember 1878 at Old Fields
BROWN, John J. - 5 mos; d. 1 October 1889 at
Long Island City
BROWN, Joseph - d. New Haven, Conn.; formerly
of Port Jefferson; interment 7 June 1890 at
Port Jefferson
BROWN, Julie E. - 34 y 7m 10 d; d. 22 November
1888 at Huntington; wife of George W. Brown
BROWN, Kateline E. - 47 years; d. 5 September
1886 at Cold Spring
BROWN, Margaret - 66 years; d. 21 March 1887
at Huntington; wife of James Brown of
Philadelphia, Pa.
BROWN, Martha - 46 years; d. 30 November 1879
at Huntington; wife of William Brown, Jr.
BROWN, Mary * - 105 years; d. 26 January 1883
at Brooklyn; interment at Huntington; b. a
slave in Monmouth County, N. J.; worked 65
years for Woodhull Ketcham family
BROWN, Mary - 83 years; b. 30 April 1883 at
Northport
BROWN, Mattie L. - 20 y 4 m 23 d; d. 29 Dec-
ember 1890; Hempstead item; wife of William
Brown
BROWN, Polly - 89 years; d. 20 April 1890 at
Rocky Point; widow of Joel Brown
BROWN, Samuel - 68 years; d. 31 October 1882
at Comac
BROWN, Samuel T. - 18 y 1 m 19 d; d. 30 Janu-
ary 1885 at Union, New Jersey
BROWN, Sophronia - 82 yrs 8 mos; d. 15 Novem-
ber 1880 at Miller's Place; widow of William
Brown
BROWN, Theresa - 54 years; d. 6 November 1886
at Dix Hills
BROWN, Thomas - 44 years; d. 5 April 1885 at
Huntington; interment at Brooklyn; served in
Union Navy during Civil War; with Admiral
Porter's fleet on Mississippi River during
Vicksburg Campaign
BROWN, Thomas - 53 years; d. 1 June 1885 at
Albany, N. Y.; interment at Huntington;
former resident of Huntington

BROWN, William - drowned 25 May 1884 at Glen Cove

BROWN, William C. - d. 22 July 1883 at St. James; former resident of Watertown, N. Y.

BROWN, William C. - 1 y 4 m 9 d; d. 19 January 1888 at Huntington; son of George and Julia Brown

BRUEN, Mary Ann - funeral 23 January 1889; Oyster Bay item

BRUNDAGE, Ethel - 1 y 10 m 20 d; d. 15 June 1886 at Brooklyn; interment at Huntington

BRUNDAGE, James H. - 79 years; d. 25 March 1881 at New York City; interment at Huntington

BRUSE, Emma D. - 38 yrs 11 mos; d. 11 June 1882 at New York City

BRUSH, Mr. - d. in Florida; yellow fever epidemic; former resident of Hicksville; 6 October 1888 paper

BRUSH, Mrs. - d. in Florida; yellow fever epidemic; former Miss Herbage of Hicksville; 6 October 1888 paper

BRUSH, child - infant; d. Woodbury; 20 April 1889 paper; child of Charles Brush

BRUSH, Ansel Ives - 49 y 8 m 16 d; d. 5 November 1884 at East Northport

BRUSH, Caesar * - 84 years; d. 30 October 1879 at Huntington

BRUSH, Caroline Jane - 75 years; d. 8 March 1880 at Clover Hill, New Jersey; widow of Jonas Platt Brush

BRUSH, David - 72 yrs 8 mos; d. 14 May 1879 at Woodbury

BRUSH, E. Amanda - d. 5 February 1886 at Greenpoint; interment at Huntington; native of Centreport; widow of David Brush, her sister's widower, whom she married ca. 1877

BRUSH, Mrs. Elijah - d. 28 February 1890 at Smithtown; interment at Hauppauge

BRUSH, Elizabeth - 69 years; d. 19 February 1879 at Woodbury; widow of David Brush; mother of Morris Brush

BRUSH, Elizabeth - 82 yrs 10 mos; d. 26 June 1885 at West Hills; widow of John R. Brush; maiden name was Elizabeth Carman; mother of Samuel Brush, Abner Brush, Rev. Jesse Brush, Dr. George W. Brush and Zophar Brush

BRUSH, George - 73 y 7 m 25 d; d. 19 May 1885
at Greenlawn; son of Zephaniah and Elizabeth
Brush; b. West Neck 1811; m. Amanda Sammis;
former resident of Cedar Swamp, Queens
County, and for past 33 years resident of
Old Fields

BRUSH, George Washington * - 3 yrs 1 mo;
d. 6 December 1880 at Huntington

BRUSH, Gilbert - 40 y 3 m 19 d; d. 21 Septmber
1880 at Greenlawn

BRUSH, Hannah Amanda - 67 yrs 2 mos;
d. 18 February 1882 at Greenlawn; wife of
George Brush

BRUSH, Harriet N. - 48 yrs 8 mos; d. 1 February 1890 at Greenlawn; interment at Huntington; daughter of Selah Bunce; wife of Frederick Brush; sister of Helen Bunce and Mrs.
David Bryant

BRUSH, Jacob S. * - 62 yrs 1 mo; d. 27 June
1886 at Huntington

BRUSH, Jeremiah - 68 y 5 m 20 d; d. 1 May 1888
at Sunken Meadow

BRUSH, John R. - 83 years; d. 17 November 1884
at West Hills; husband of Elizabeth Carman

BRUSH, John S. - 75 yrs 10 mos; d. 21 January
1890 at Comac; "old and respected citizen"

BRUSH, John T. - d. at New York City; interment 16 February 1879 at Smithtown; grandson
of Elijah Brush; resident of Florida

BRUSH, Julia E. * - 39 yrs 7 mos; d. 8 November 1881 at Huntington; wife of William
Brush

BRUSH, Louisa - 36 y 9 m 11 d; d. 11 May 1882
at West Hills; wife of David Brush

BRUSH, Louisa M. - 69 y 7 m 4 d; d. 8 July
1889 at Cold Spring; widow of Skillman Brush

BRUSH, Margaret - 66 y 9 m 19 d; d. 11 April
1881 at Comac; wife of John S. Brush

BRUSH, Marietta - 37 years; d. 6 October 1878
at Greenlawn; wife of Gilbert Brush

BRUSH, Mary A. - 78 yrs 26 days; d. 1 April
1889 at Northport interment at Huntington;
b. Glenwood; maiden name Mary A. Downing;
widow of James Madison Brush who she m.
1832; mother of 13 children; these surving
her: Thomas Henry Brush, James M. Brush,

28

BRUSH, Mary A. (continued)
George W. Brush, Gilbert Brush, Mrs. Sarah
Matthias and Mrs. Susie Walters
BRUSH, Mary E. - 47 y 9 m 11 d; suicide 21 May
1879 at Comac; wife of Joseph Brush
BRUSH, Matilda - 50 years; d. 7 February 1887
at Woodbury; interment at Cypress Hills;
wife of Joseph Brush
BRUSH, Matilda Monfort - 3 yrs 6 days;
d. 16 August 1885 at West Neck; daughter of
Charles E. and Ellie K. Brush
BRUSH, Philetus S. - 72 y 9 m 16 d; d. 16 Nov-
ember 1879 at Northport; interment at Comac
BRUSH, Rhoda Ann * - 70 years; d. 14 February
1889 at Huntington
BRUSH, Russell Van Cott - 2 years; d. 4 Febru-
ary 1881 at West Neck
BRUSH, Samuel - 74 y 1 m 6 d; d. 24 April 1881
at Old Fields
BRUSH, Sarah Gould - 63 y 1 m 4 d; d. 9 July
1884 at Huntington; widow of Thomas P.
Brush; mother of Thomas F. Brush, Mrs.
Hewlett J. Long, Mrs. Daniel Baylis and Mrs.
J. E. Morse
BRUSH, Sidney C. - 5 y 8 m 19 d; d. 9 July
1885 at Greenlawn; son of Frederick and
Harriet N. Brush
BRUSH, Skillman - 68 yrs 5 mos; d. 2 August
1884 at Greenlawn
BRUSH, Theodore S. - 37 years; d. 26 March
1878 at Clay Pitts
BRUSH, Webster Witmore - 7 y 3 m 23 d;
d. 18 January 1887 at Huntington; son of
Samuel J. and Phebe Brush
BRUSH, William - 22 y 9 m 29 d; d. 17 October
1879 at Brentwood; Constable for Town of
Islip
BRYAN, George B. - 2 months; d. 15 August 1881
at Cold Spring; son of Frederick and Ann
Bryan
BRYAN, Sybil O. B. - 37 y 1 m 10 d; d. 26 May
1879 at Middleville
BRYANT, child - 18 mos; d. 25 August 1890;
Port Jefferson item; child of Thomas Bryant
BRYANT, Elizabeth - 80 years; d. 18 April 1884
at Northport; widow of John Bryant

BRYANT, Jacob - 72 yrs 22 days; drowned 5
September 1889 in Centreport Harbor
BRYANT, Melancthon - 73 years; d. 6 May 1884
at Northport
BRYANT, Samuel - 93 years; d. 12 February 1878
at Old Fields
BRYANT, William Cullen - d. 12 June 1878 at
New York City; poet and newspaper editor;
biography and poetry review in 14 June 1878
paper
BRYAR, Edward K. - 77 years; d. 30 May 1890 at
West Neck; former New York City merchant;
"lived a retired life at his home at West
Neck for many years"
BRYAR, William R. - 32 yrs 15 days; d. 26 July
1878 at West Neck
BRYCE, Andrew - 60 years; d. "last week" at
Oyster Bay; 10 December 1887 paper
BRYCE, John W. - 70 years; d. 23 December 1889
at Jersey City, N. J.; newspaper editor;
resident of Harrison, N. J.
BUCHANAN, David - d. ca. 13 August 1882 at
Oyster Bay; found dead in house on 15 August
1882
BUCK, John - 25 years; d. 16 July 1885 at
Hopedale; hit by railroad train
BUCKINGHAM, Mrs. Charles - d. 9 January 1890
at Setauket
BUCKLEY, Patrick F. - skeleton found 4 December 1885 in woods near Valley Stream; had
been missing since April when he went to
Babylon; resident of New York City
BUELL, William A. - d. at Southold; 24 November 1888 paper; son of Dr. Matthew Buell; "a
wandering, shiftless character" who ended up
in the Yaphank poorhouse. Just prior to
death, received $30,000 bequest from rela-
tive. 24 August 1889 paper has involved
account of family dispute over estate and
account of Buell's life
BUFFETT, Adelia T. - 49 years; d. 29 December
1881 at Fresh Pond; wife of Chatfield E.
Buffett
BUFFETT, Caesar * - 83 years; d. 27 November
1880 at Oyster Bay; former slave of Mrs.
Benjamin Underhill

BUFFETT, Henry - 65 y 1 m 14 d; d. 5 March
1888 at Dix Hills; funeral at Elwood;
brother of Nathaniel Buffett and David
Buffett

BUFFETT, Joseph - 79 y 8 m 1 d; d. 30 May 1884
at Woodbury; interment at Huntington; son of
Eliphaz and Mary Buffett; b. Woodbury 29
September 1804; m. Sarah Sammis 1831; former
resident of Bayside ca. 1830

BUFFETT, Joseph H. - 8 y 1 m 28 d; d. 4 September 1882 at Melville; son of Ketcham and
Sarah J. Buffett

BUFFETT, Lillian E. - 26 years; d. 25 April
1889 at Elwood; funeral at Dix Hills; wife
of G. Henry Buffett

BUFFETT, Mary E. - 32 y 1 m 3 d; d. 23 September 1887 at Fresh Pond, daughter of
William F. and Nancy Buffett

BUFFETT, Nancy - 82 y 7 m 10 d; d. 16 April
1885 at Middleville; b. Islip 6 September
1802; daughter of Jarvis Rogers and Mary
Mowbray; widow of William P. Buffett,
m. 25 April 1825

BUGLAND, Mrs. - d. 22 September 1885 at
Hicksville

BUMSTEAD, Ann Elector - 37 years; d. 26 November 1879 at Oyster Bay Cove, wife of Jacob
Bumstead

BUNCE, Abram J. - 79 y 11 m 22 d; d. 19 August
1882 at Centreport

BUNCE, Albert "Captain" - 77 years; d. 5 February 1887 at East Neck

BUNCE, Annie - 25 years; d. 5 September 1886
at West Hills

BUNCE, Clifford M. - 2 y 1 m 22 d; d. 6 February 1889 at Queens

BUNCE, E. Stanton - 22 y 8 m 11 d; d. 7 October 1881 at Centerport

BUNCE, Ed A. - 33 years; d. Bridgeport, Conn.;
funeral 21 September 1890 at Port Jefferson

BUNCE, Eliza E. - 50 years; d. 16 April 1890
at Northport; wife of Albert S. Bunce;
maiden name Eliza E. Olmstead; resident of
Brooklyn before marriage

BUNCE, Elizabeth - 74 y 10 m 11 d; d. 30 December 1890 at Huntington

31

BUNCE, Elkanah - 83 y 4 m 15 d; d. 12 August
1888 at Centreport

BUNCE, Gloriannah Adeline - d. 21 December
1889 at New York City; interment at Cypress
Hills; daughter of Azel Lewis; widow of John
Bunce; half-sister of David Lewis of
Northport

BUNCE, Grace - 10 years; d. 23 December 1886
at Northport; daughter of Frank S. and
Hannah M. Bunce

BUNCE, H. Elizabeth - 30 y 7 m 20 d;
d. 26 August 1884 at Comac; wife of Edward
Bunce

BUNCE, Jeanette - 69 years; d. 27 February
1887 at Yaphank; funeral at Centreport;
widow of Albert Bunce

BUNCE, Jesse S. - 79 y 9 m 18 d; d. 25 October
1886 at Centreport

BUNCE, Joseph Titus - 81 y 4 m 29 d;
d. 10 September 1879 at Cold Spring

BUNCE, Luella M. - 19 y 8 m 16 d; d. 11 May
1887 at Northport; daughter of Fleet and
Louisa Bunce; overdose of morphine

BUNCE, Matilda - 80 y 1 m 11 d; d. 31 July
1887 at Northport; widow of Samuel E. Bunce

BUNCE, Mattie N. - 2 y 1 m 14 d; d. 22 April
1880 at Comac; daughter of E. A. and E. H.
Bunce

BUNCE, Rachel - 84 y 5 m 14 d; d. 24 September
1884 at Northport; widow of Matthew Bunce

BUNCE, Reuben T. - 8 y 5 m 20 d; d. 20 May
1880 at Cold Spring

BUNCE, Samuel Allen - 56 years; d. 6 June 1890
at Northport; grocer

BUNCE, Sarah - 96 years; d. 7 June 1883 at
East Neck; mother of Edward Bunce; grandmother of Mrs. I. B. Pedrick

BUNCE, Sarah A. - 29 y 6 m 27 d; d. 22 July
1879 at Centreport; wife of Elbert Bunce

BUNCE, Sarah Ophelia - 30 yrs 4 mos;
d. 29 June 1889 at City Island, N. Y.;
funeral at Centreport

BUNCE, Sidney - d. 23 December 1885 in Costa
Rica; resident of Babylon; died of fever
while visiting with friend in Costa Rica

BUNCE, Smith - d. 25 October 1886; funeral at
Centreport

BUNCE, Susan - 78 years; d. 16 June 1887 at Centreport

BUNCE, Sylvester - 69 year; d. 10 June 1887 at Northport

BUNKER, Dennis M. - d. 28 December 1890 at Boston, Massachusetts; "artist of ability"; parents residents of Garden City

BUNN, child * - 7 mos; d. 21 January 1886; Farmingdale item; child of Hannah E. Bunn

BUNN, Aaron * - d. 26 May 1889 at Westbury

BUNN, Abraham - drowned 7 February 1887 at Fur Pond, Shinnecock; fell through the ice

BURBANK, Mary E. - 54 years; d. 26 December 1888 at South Norwalk, Conn.; interment at Huntington

BURCH, Florence - funeral 20 June 1887 at Farmingdale; resident of Brooklyn; daughter of Alfred Burch

BURCH, Maria - 79 y 2 m 25 d; d. 23 November 1879 at Huntington

BURGER, John M. - ca. 40 years; d. 27 April 1890 at Mill Hill, Oyster Bay; interment at East Norwich

BURGESS, Henry A. - d. 7 May 1885 at Baxter Springs, Kansas; brother of F. W. Burgess of Huntington

BURK, Mary - 10 years; d. 8 November 1884 at Jamaica; clothes caught fire; daughter of John T. Burk

BURK, Robbie E. - 10 days; d. 19 August 1890; Port Jefferson item; son of Emmett Burk

BURKE, child - 8 mos; d. 1 February 1889; Hicksville item; interment at Hempstead; one twin of Mrs. Burke, sister of John Dauch

BURKE, Eliza - 85 years; d. 23 January 1887 at Eaton's Neck Light

BURKE, Mary - 18 years; d. 24 July 1883; hit by railroad train; resident of Greenpoint

BURKE, Mary A. - 66 years; d. 15 October 1889 at Port Jefferson

BURMACH, Felix - ca. 50 years; suicide by shooting 30 April 1890 at Central Park; interment at Bethpage; fur cap and glove maker

BURNER, William - 63 years; d. 4 May 1883 at Huntington

BURNETT, Whitfield - d. 19 October 1890 at "the River" Smithtown; funeral St. James

BURNHAM, Mr. - suicide 24 June 1884 at Yonkers, N. Y.; of Hotckiss, Burnham & Co., 36 Broad St., New York

BURNS, Mrs. - d. 1 February 1890 at Glen Cove

BURNS, Frank - 14 years; d. 9 May 1880 at Hauppauge

BURNS, Susannah - 72 y 6 m 18 d; d. 14 October 1885 at Huntington; widow of John Burns of Riverhead

BURR, Emma S. - 4 mos 4 days; d. 24 July 1889 at Comac; daughter of Lester H. and Mary Burr

BURR, Maurice A. - 61 years; d. 23 June 1884 at Smithtown Landing; funeral at Comac

BURR, Platt R. - 76 years; d. 5 October 1879 at Comac

BURR, Sarah Maria - 67 y 4 m 26 d; d. 3 November 1883 at Huntington; widow of William Burr

BURR, Smith - 83 y 6 m 14 d; d. 6 April 1887 at Comac; father of Carll Burr; raised trotting horses

BURR, Townsend H. - 76 y 1 m 9 d; d. 17 January 1890 at Brooklyn; interment at Huntington; b. Dosoris; son of Jarvis Burr; former resident of Cold Spring; founder 1849 of Cold Spring Baptist Church; shoe manufacturer in Cold Spring; later shoe merchant in Brooklyn

BURR, William - 66 y 9 m 14 d; d. 21 May 1880 at Huntington

BURRELL, H. H. - d. 27 November 1883 at Oyster Bay; sail maker

BURROWES, Sarah Daisy - 105 years; d. 7 February 1884 at New York City; b. New York City 1779, daughter of John Daisy and granddaughter of Philip Schuyler; m. John Nicholas Oakley Burrowes 1814

BURTIS, Fannie E. - d. 16 September 1885

BURTIS, Oliver D. - 78 years; d. 21 September 1887 at Syosset interment Green-Wood, Brooklyn; b. Hempstead; m. Rachel Smith; merchant tailor in Brooklyn

BURTT, William C. - 33 years; d. 17 July 1887
at Flushing; interment at Northport; dentist
in New York City

BUSHNELL, Hannah - 81 years; d. 15 December
1879 at Oyster Bay

BUTLER, Annie E. - 19 y 6 m 16 d; d. 22 July
1889 at Huntington

BUTLER, James - 75 yrs 5 mos; d. 14 March 1885
at Huntington

BUTLER, John S. - 77 yrs 3 mos; d. 29 September 1889 at Melville

BYRNE, Bridget - 60 years; d. 21 August 1881
at Huntington; widow of Michael Byrne

BYRNES, Robert B. - 29 years; d. 18 August
1879 at New Orleans, Louisiana; factory
accident; son of Mrs. Ellen B. Sammis

CAHILL, Julia - d. Adirondack Mountains from
consumption; funeral 22 September 1885 at
Babylon; niece of Walter Scudder; had gone
to Adirondacks to recover her health

CAIN, R[ichard] H. [*] - d. 17 January 1887;
funeral at Washington, D. C.; Bishop of
African Methodist Episcopal Church;
[Reconstruction congressman from South
Carolina]

CAIRE, Lewis Joslyn - infant; d. 13 February
1890 at Jersey City, N. J.; son of Lewis H.
and Emilie A. Caire

CALDER, Augusta Cella - 24 years; d. 27 October 1887 at Huntington; daughter of Donald
Calder

CALDER, Dorothy Annie - 5 y 3 m 11 d;
d. 22 May 1887 at Huntington

CALDER, Emily G. - 13 years; d. 28 February
1884 at Comac

CALDER, Walter D. - 6 months; d. 6 January
1884 at Comac

CALLAHAN, child - 5 months; d. 30 June 1886 at
Oyster Bay; child of William Callahan; in
bed with mother, who rolled over on it

CALLAHAN, Patrick - d. at Brighton Beach; hit
by railroad train; resident of Sheepshead
Bay; 3 September 1887 paper

CALVERT, Mr. - 72 years; d. 22 October 1888 at
Plain Edge

CAMPBELL, George - interment 27 December 1880
at Port Jefferson; former Suffolk Co. Clerk

CAMPBELL, Lockwood C. - 71 y 11 m 11 d;
d. 24 November 1881 at Fresh Pond

CAMPBELL, Mary - d. 13 April 1888 at Winnipeg,
Manitoba; wife of George H. Campbell; sister
of Rev. A. G. Russell of Oyster Bay

CANAVELLO, Antenette Delmonico - d. 15 March
1890 at Brooklyn; daughter of Peter Delmonico; wife of John P. Canavello

CANAVELLO, Rosa Delmonico - d. 19 January 1884
at Brooklyn; daughter of Peter Delmonico;
wife of Charles Canavello

CANNON, Bridget - 48 years; d. 20 August 1888
at Brooklyn; interment at Huntington

CANVAN, John J. - 73 years; drowned 22 January
1890 off Neversink, N. J.; ship pilot;
slipped and fell overboard; father of J. J.
Canvan of Hicksville

CANVAN, John Julius - 1 mo 10 days; d. 8 March
1889 at Hicksville; interment at Westbury;
son of John Canvan

CARDONA, John - 83 years; d. 15 January 1886
at Brooklyn; fell down flight of stairs into
cellar; interment at Huntington

CARLL, Aaron J. - 12 y 3 m 6 d; d. 27 December
1878 at Northport; son of Jesse and Anne E.
Carll; diphtheria

CARLL, Albert * - 33 years; d. 9 April 1890 at
Roslyn; interment at East Norwich

CARLL, Ann * - 87 years; d. 22 August 1890 at
Westbury; widow of Charles Carll; mother of
11 children; only one survives her; b. 14
February 1803 at North Hempstead; "one of
the founders of African Methodism in Westbury....It was in her house that Mt. Zion
AME Church was organized, June 26, 1887...
Mrs. Carll was always found in every movement that was for the up-building of her
race. She was a woman much beloved..."

CARLL, Charles S. * - 9 days; d. 22 July 1887
at Huntington

CARLL, David - 62 years; d. 27 December 1888
at Crescent City, Florida; brother of Jesse
Carll of Northport; famous City Island ship
builder; owned 60,000 orange trees in
Florida

CARLL, E. Gussie - 2 y 1 m 12 d; d. 19 December 1878 at Northport; daughter of Jesse and Anne E. Carll

CARLL, Egbert E. - 51 years; d. 5 April 1879 at Dix Hills

CARLL, Elbert - d. 8 October 1887 at Babylon; first Supervisor of Town of Babylon when Babylon was divided off from Huntington to become a separate town

CARLL, Elizabeth - 53 y 8 m 10 d; d. 19 April 1880 at Comac; wife of John Carll

CARLL, Fannie M. - d. 17 March 1886 at Brooklyn; funeral at Dix Hills; daughter of Oliver L. and Julia M. Carll

CARLL, Gertrude L. - 30 yrs 6 mos; d. 27 October 1878 at Comac

CARLL, Gilbert - 93 years; d. 3 September 1880 at Dix Hills

CARLL, Israel - 56 yrs 4 mos; d. 27 November 1878 at Northport

CARLL, Mary A. - d. 8 February 1885 at Comac; daughter of Silas Carll

CARLL, Mary A. - 78 years; d. 2 January 1889 at Brooklyn; interment at Huntington

CARLL, Richard U. - 61 y 2 m 14 d; d. 19 May 1884 at Northport

CARLL, Russell L. - 1 y 2 m 9 d; d. 13 August 1883 at Northport; hit in head by iron pin which fell from wagon; son of Jesse and Ann E. Carll

CARLL, Sarah - 93 y 2 m 16 d; d. 19 February 1881 at Huntington

CARLL, Sarah L. - 64 y 4 m 11 d; d. 30 November 1884 at West Hills; daughter of Richard Collyer; wife of Lemuel Carll

CARLL, Seraphina - 93 y 2 m 18 d; d. 28 November 1879 at Huntington; widow of Selah Carll

CARMAN, Bertha - d. 25 July 1890 at Hempstead; daughter of Isaac N. Carman

CARMAN, Caroline - 31 years; d. 25 February 1890 at New Castle; interment at Hempstead

CARMAN, Eva H. - 30 years; d. 18 February 1884 at St. James; wife of Joseph Carman

CARMAN, John F. - 3 mos 25 days; d. 13 April 1882 at Half Hollows; son of Clarence and Caroline Carman

CARMAN, Mrs. Samuel - d. 18 February 1888 at
   St. James
CARMAN, Sarah E. - 4 mos 1 day; d. 20 April
   1882 at Half Hollows; daughter of Clarence
   and Caroline Carman
CARMAN, Treadwell - ca. 74 years; d. 15 August
   1880 at Amityville
CARMAN, William A. - 59 years; d. 29 January
   1885 at West Hills
CARPENTER, Mrs. Charles - death recorded;
   Hicksville item; 13 November 1885 paper
CARPENTER, Dehlia - 42 years; d. 7 March 1878
   at Oyster Bay; wife of James Carpenter
CARPENTER, Sarah Ann - ca. 90 years; d. "last
   week" at Sea Cliff; 2 November 1889 paper
CARPENTER, Thomas H. - ca. 45 years; ship
   captain who "mysteriously disapperared"
   perhaps was murdered 18 November 1886 aboard
   schooner; body drifted ashore at Sea Cliff
   22 November 1886; see also: 28 May 1887
   paper
CARR, Amelia - 78 y 2 m 18 d; d. 30 May 1879
   at Long Swamp
CARR, Mary H. - 83 years; d. 25 August 1887 at
   Huntington; daughter of Israel Valentine;
   wife of William H. Carr
CARTER, Eliza * - 55 years; d. 17 April 1883
   at Huntington
CARTER, Jane - 76 yrs 10 mos; d. 19 July 1887
   at Centreport; wife of Robert T. Carter;
   mother of Rev. S. T. Carter
CARTER, Robert - 82 years; d. 28 December
   1889 at New York City; native of Scotland;
   "one of the most widely known laymen
   in the Presbyterian Church in the United
   States"; elder of Scotch Presbyterian
   Church, New York City; President Board of
   Foreign Missions; Vice-President American
   Bible Society; father of Rev. Samuel Carter
   of Huntington
CARTWRIGHT, Hannah M. - 73 y 10 m 11 d;
   d. 21 February 1888 at Shelter Island; wife
   of B. C. Cartwright; sister of David Tuthill
CARTWRIGHT, Mary W. - 46 y 8 m 7 d; d. 14 Oct-
   ober 1888 at Shelter Island; daughter of
   Lawrence V. B. and Mary S. Woodruff; wife of
   B. C. Cartwright

CARSON, Hannah - 86 years; d. 3 January 1879 at Greenlawn

CASE, Mrs. F. B. - interment 7 August 1890 at Commack; mother-in-law of Carll S. Burr

CASE, J. Wickham - d. 10 May 1886 at Southold; former Suffolk County Clerk; annotated and published Southold Town records

CASEY, James- 2 mos 11 days; d. 20 August 1882 at Huntington; son of John and Annie Casey

CASEY, Mary - 73 years; d. 10 October 1882 at Huntington; interment at Calvary Cemetery, Queens County

CASH, Joseph O. - d. 14 March 1890 at Comac

CASH, Mary Jane - 49 years; d. 23 March 1890 at Commack; widow of Joseph Cash

CASH, Thomas - 41 years; funeral 29 July 1890 at Oyster Bay; funeral was "one of the largest ever known in this village" [Oyster Bay]

CASHAW, infant - d. 6 October 1878 at Cold Spring; child of Thomas and Emma Cashaw

CASHAW, Mary E. - 1 yr 10 mos; d. 1 May 1878 at Oyster Bay; daughter of Thomas A. and Emma Cashaw

CASS, James - 67 years; d. 9 May 1890 at Greenlawn; interment at West Neck; father of Mrs. John Conklin

CASS, John - 17 days; d. 25 January 1881 at Cold Spring; son of Thomas and Mary E. Cass

CASS, Mary - 65 years; d. 11 January 1883 at Little Neck

CASSELL, Charles Henry * - d. "three weeks ago" in Washington Territory; brother of Mrs. William Henry Jackson of Westbury; 2 March 1889 paper

CASSIDY, Patrick H. - body found 24 January 1890 at Canarsie Landing stuck in mud of Jamaica Bay; resident of Flatlands

CATTANAC, W. Shaw - ca. 18 years; d. 21 September 1886 near Jamaica; died while riding on railroad train; interment at Hauppauge

CAUSE, Richard * - 109 years; d. 22 January 1887 at Glen Cove; b. at Westbury

CAVANAGH, Mary - 65 years; d. 14 July 1884 at Huntington

39

CHALMERS, David Bethune - 78 yrs 11 mos;
  d. 19 February 1885 at Centreport; interment
  at Commack; b. 28 March 1806 at New York
  City; husband of Ruth A. Burr
CHALMERS, George O. - 32 yrs 25 days;
  d. 19 March 1886 at Willard, [Seneca Co.],
  N. Y.; interment at Comac; b. 22 Febrary
  1854; son of David B. and Ruth Chalmers
CHAMBERLAIN, Stephen - drowned 1 July 1889 in
  Long Island Sound; fell overboard from
  steamboat "Connecticut"
CHAMBERS, Catherine - 79 years; d. 19 July
  1888 at Jersey City, New Jersey
CHAPIN, Sidney H. - d. 26 July 1890 at Glen
  Cove; interment at Green-Wood, Brooklyn; son
  of Rev. E. H. Chapin
CHAPMAN, Hannah R. - 31 yrs 2 mos; d. 16 Aug-
  ust 1880 at Jersey City, N. J.; interment at
  Huntington
CHAPMAN, John T. - 3 years; d. 30 November
  1881 at Jersey City, N. J.; interment at
  Huntington
CHAPPELL, Amanda - 45 y 3 m 14 d; d. 23 April
  1880 at Centreport; wife of Barney Chappell
CHAPPELL, Barney H. - 68 years; funeral 19 May
  1889 at Northport; son of Phebe Chappell of
  Centerport; brother of Mrs. Warren Rowland,
  who was killed in train wreck at South
  Norwalk, Conn., coming to funeral
CHAPPELL, Phebe A. - 86 years; d. 18 December
  1890 at Centreport found dead in her room
CHARLETON, Francis - 57 years; d. 21 April
  1882 at West Neck
CHATTERTON, Joseph M. - ca. 59 years;
  d. 26 January 1887 at Farmingdale;
  newspaperman; b. Germantown, Pennsylvania
CHENEY, Mrs. - d. 5 July 1890 at Sayville;
  mother of Editor of Sayville News
CHENEY, Elizabeth - d."last week" at Port
  Jefferson; daughter of Editor of Port
  Jefferson News-Letter; 17 October 1884 paper
CHESEBROUGH, Robert - 5 yrs 4 mos; d. 10 July
  1882 at Northport; son of Charles A. and
  Elizabeth Chesebrough
CHESHIRE, infant daughter - 3 mos; d. 18 Octo-
  ber 1879 at Oyster Bay; daughter of Luther
  and Lucinda Cheshire

CHESHIRE, child - 2 years; death noted; Oyster
Bay item; child of William Cheshire; 9 March
1889 paper
CHESHIRE, Betsy - 76 years; d. "this week" at
Syosset; 11 February 1888 paper
CHESHIRE, Deborah - 89 years; d. 1 July 1889
at Flushing; widow of Jeremiah Cheshire;
former resident of Huntington
CHESHIRE, George B. - 3 y 6 m 20 d; d. 30 Dec-
ember 1883 at St. Johnland; son of Wilber B.
Cheshire
CHESHIRE, Jeremiah - 72 y 3 m 4 d; d. 28 April
1889 at Greenlawn; interment at Oyster Bay
CHESHIRE, John W. - 1 y 10 m 24 d; d. 8 Sept-
ember 1880 at Middleville
CHESHIRE, Valentine - d. 18 December 1888 at
East Norwich; "suddenly"
CHICHESTER, John N. - 61 y 8 m 8 d; d. 1 December 1883 at West Hills; found dead in the
road
CHIPP, Charles J. - 77 years; d. 13 November
1890; funeral at Oyster Bay; interment at
New York City; b. 26 September 1813;
resident at Oyster Bay since 1865; Justice
of the Peace for Oyster Bay; biography in 15
November 1890 paper
CHRIST, Mrs. - death noted; Hicksville item;
9 January 1885 paper
CHRIST, Mrs. - "old woman"; d. 17 September
1886 at Jamaica; died from neglected
scalding wounds
CHURCH, Franklin P. - 1 month; d. 9 September
1880 at Huntington; son of Franklin and
Susie Church
CHURCH, George - 40 yrs 6 mos; d. 22 July 1886
at Sunk Meadow
CHURCH, Nancy - 45 years; d. 11 January 1890
at Fresh Pond
CHURCHILL, Mrs. - d. death noted; Smithtown
item; mother of Rev. J. A. Churchill of
Smithtown; 25 October 1890 paper
CISCO, Cecelia * - 1 year; d. 1 December 1887
at Huntington
CISCO, Ellen * - 65 years; d. 27 January 1884
at Cold Spring
CLAFFLIN, infant - 3 mos; d. 8 September 1879
at Centreport; child of Sanford Clafflin

CLAPP, child - death noted; Hempstead item;
daughter of Mr. Clapp; died of scarlet
fever; 13 February 1885 paper
CLARK, child - 11 years; d. 20 February 1888;
Smithtown item; daughter of J. Frank Clark;
died of scarlet fever
CLARK, Alonzo - d. 13 September 1887 at New
York City; medical professor College of
Physicians & Surgeons
CLARK, Eli D. - d. 13 December 1887 at New
Dorp, Staten Island; interment at Northport;
son of H. D. Clark, formerly of Northport
CLARK, Frances A. - 65 years; d. 24 December
1880 at Brooklyn; daughter of Gilbert
Carll; widow of Nathan Clark
CLARK, George A. - drowned "this week" in Lake
Champlain; steam tug "Little Nellie"
capsized; brother of Mrs. Dr. J. S. Cooley
of Glen Cove; 19 July 1890 paper
CLARK, Henry H. * - 79 years; d. 3 October
1886 at Centreport
CLARK, Jacob - d. 9 January 1880 at Water
Mill; hit by railroad train; resident of
Plainfield, New Jersey
CLARK, James - drowned at Norwalk, Conn.;
funeral at Huntington; 7 January 1881 paper
CLARK, James - 17 y 8 m 22 d; d. 25 September
1881 at East Northport; son of James and
Mary Isabella Clark
CLARK, John - 16 years; d. 16 October 1881 at
East Northport son of James and Mary
Isabella Clark
CLARK, John - 92 y 7 m 5 d; d. 1 August 1885
at Brooklyn; interment at Mt. Olivet,
Maspeth; native of Portsmouth, England;
grandfather of Joseph Irwin of Huntington
CLARK, Mary - 25 yrs 9 mos; d. 6 November 1878
at Cold Spring
CLARK, Nancy - d. 24 April 1888 at Head of
the River, Smithtown; interment at Stony
Brook
CLARK, Mrs. S. C. - d. 17 March 1886 at
Hempstead
CLARK, William - drowned 12 September 1881 in
Housatonic River, Connecticut
CLAUS, David - 60 years; suicide 30 September
1889 at Bowery Bay; took poison

CLAUS, Geshe R. - 46 years; d. 21 October 1888
at Hicksville
CLAUSING, Alfred - d. 27 October 1888 at Deer
Park; interment at New York City
CLEMENE, Mr. - death noted; resident of
Manetto Hill; 2 January 1885 paper
CLEMMENS, Elizabeth - 74 y 7 m 10 d;
d. 25 January 1890 at Plainview; interment
at Hicksville; "A touching as well a pretty
sight in the funeral procession was that of
the old lady's favorite mare 'Fannie' being
led behind the hearse covered with the black
lace shawl of her mistress. It was the wish
of Mrs. Clemmens that this should be, as she
was so fond of her horse."
CLEVELAND, James - 45 years; drowned 1 July
1882 in Long Island Sound off Huntington;
jumped off steamboat going to Greenport
CLIFFORD, Henry - drowned 19 January 1883 off
Fisher's Island ship collision
CLIFFORD, Jane - 72 years; d. 22 June 1888 at
Huntington
CLINCH, Ann Taylor - 86 years; d. 7 November
1880 at Smithtown; widow of James Clinch
CLINCH, Charles - funeral 15 June 1890
at St. James
CLOVER, Milton - d. 4 March 1889 at Fishkill
Landing, N.Y.; former resident of Oyster Bay
CLOWES, Sarah Hewlett - 89 years; funeral
26 March 1886 at Hempstead
CLUNE, Ellen - 3 y 2 m 17 d; d. 20 June 1882
at Melville; daughter of John and Mary Clune
CLUNE, Michael - 34 years; d. 6 February 1879
at West Neck
COCHRANE, Rev. - d. 22 February 1887 in New
Jersey; brother-in-law of Rev. S. T. Carter
COCK, George E. - resident of Manhasset;
d. "last week"; b. Manhasset 1816; Quaker;
Secretary of U. S. Insurance Company; father
of Benjamin Cock and George Cock; 31 August
1889 paper
COCKRELL, Sophia - 79 years 5 mos; d. 28 December 1883 at Lloyd's Neck
COCKS, William E. - 33 years; d. 5 April 1890
at Oyster Bay; interment at Brookville
CODDINGTON, Jesse P. - 21 y 6 m 12 d;
d. 12 June 1887 at Dix Hills

CODLING, Rev. Robert - d. 7 December 1884 in
Florida; M. E. preacher; stationed at Cold
Spring, Smithtown, Port Jefferson, Patchogue, Babylon, Islip, Woodbury (1859);
father of W. B. Codling of Smithtown
CODY, Kitty - death recorded; Oyster Bay item;
"horrible affair" involving Frank Dudgeon;
daughter of James Cody; 23 March 1889 paper
COE, Edwin - d. at Brooklyn; former resident
of Riverhead; interment at Riverhead; a
pilot on the East River; 13 November 1885
paper
COFFMAN, George - d. "a few days ago" at West
Jamaica; former resident of Riverhead;
24 July 1886 paper
COGER, George - 9 y 10 m 2 d; d. 2 March 1881
at Brooklyn
COGER, George - 3 years; d. 26 May 1890 at
Brooklyn; son of George and Martha Coger
COGER, John J. - 53 y 10 m 22 d; d. 12 Decem-
ber 1890 at Huntington Harbor; son of Will-
iam and Mary Ann Coger; brother of George W.
Coger of Brooklyn; Civil War veteran; former
resident of Brooklyn
COGER, Mary Ann - 82 yrs 7 mos; d. 24 Septem-
ber 1890 at Huntington Harbor; widow of
William Coger; mother of John Coger and
George W. Coger; sister of Mrs. Casper
Ritter; member of First Presbyterian Church,
Huntington
COGGSWELL, William Ireland - 3 mos 21 days;
d. 17 August 1884 at Huntington; son of
William L. and Helena M. Coggswell
COGSWELL, Lizzie Brush - 22 y 8 m 28 d;
d. 30 June 1887 at Huntington; daughter of
Thomas H. Brush; wife of John Cogswell
COLE, William - 52 y 11 m 12 d; d. 29 January
1882 at Middleville
COLEMAN, John - drowned in ship wreck off
Block Island, R. I.; resident of Gardiner,
Maine; 18 January 1884 paper
COLES, Butler - d. 23 October 1888 at New York
City; funeral at Oyster Bay; interment at
Glen Cove; son of Butler Coles, grandson of
Nathaniel Coles; b. 1831 Glen Cove; served
with 22nd N. Y. Vols. and Harris Light

COLES, Butler [continued]
Cavalry during Civil War; fought at Battles
of Antietam and Brandy Station

COLES, Frederick - 29 years; d. 16 February
1890 at Brooklyn; former resident of
Northport

COLES, Georgietta - 26 y 1 m 3 d; d. 7 January
1887 at Northport

COLES, Margaret J. - 20 y 7 m 18 d; d. 14 January 1888 at Cypress Hills; interment at
Huntington; former resident of Huntington

COLLIER, Jessie - 21 y 3 m 5 d; d. 15 June
1878 at East Northport

COLLIGAN, Katie Ellen - 1 m 21 d; d. 10 November 1888 at Huntington; died in bed; daugh-
daughter of William Colligan

COLLINS, child - 6 months; funeral at Comac;
16 October 1885 paper; child of John Collins

COLLINS, Samuel - d. 7 August 1879 at Oyster
Bay; accident at Smith's Brick Yard; head
nearly severed from body

COLLYER, Catherine - d. 1 February 1884 at
Laurel Hill, Queens County; poisoned;
daughter of Dennis Cowhey; wife of Thomas
Collyer

COLLYER, Charles - 78 y 3 m 17 d; d. 9 April
1878 at Manetto Hill

COLLYER, Mary/Maria L. - 53 yrs 7 mos;
d. 13 September 1879 at Jersey City Heights,
N. J.; widow of Henry Collyer

COLLYER, Minnie May - 3 y 5 m 12 d;
d. 19 April 1884 at Brooklyn; interment at
Huntington

COLLYER, R. L. - 28 days; d. at White Plains,
N. Y.; 11 February 1888 paper; son of
William A. and Annie B. Collyer

COLLYER, Thomas - d. 2 February 1884 at Laurel
Hill, Queens County; poisoned

COLT, Robert O. - d. 16 December 1885 at San
Francisco, California; interment at Babylon;
resident of West Islip; member of Babylon
Presbyterian Church; died while on a trip to
Australia

COLTON, Susan E. - 2 July 1880 paper; resident of Brooklyn; "Seawanhaka" fire on East
River

COLWELL, Mrs. - d. 7 February 1889; Westbury
item; interment at Calvary Cemetery, Queens
County; daughter is organist at St. Bridget's R. C. Church

COLYER, Charles - ca. 79 years; d. 9 April
1878 at Woodbury; son of Charles Colyer and
Mary Whitson; husband of Mary Van Wyck,
daughter of Richard Van Wyck, m. 1822;
b. Sweet Hollow 1799; moved to Woodbury in
1822 and lived in same house until his death

COLYER, Cordelia - 41 y 3 m 10 d; d. 18 April
1886 at Brooklyn; wife of John L. Colyer

COLYER, John - 83 y 3 m 2 d; d. 6 March 1880
at Brooklyn; formerly of Huntington

COLYER, Mary - 56 y 5 m 23 d; d. 6 March 1884
at Melville; widow of Charles W. Colyer

COMBES, Florence - 1 y 2 m 10 d; d. 3 June
1879 at Hoboken, New Jersey; daughter of
Edward and Phebe Combes

COMBES, John - 20 Years; d. 26 January 1879 at
Long Island City; son of John and Catherine
Combes; formerly of Dix Hills

CONANT, Fred H. - 37 y 7 m 27 d; d. 27 August
1884 at Pueblo, Colorado; son of William A.
Conant; former resident of Huntington

CONGDON, Timothy P. - 72 y 7 m 14 d; d. 6
January 1888 at Shelter Island

CONIN, Dennis - suicide 18 January 1885 at
Flatbush

CONKLIN, infant - d. 10 July 1886 at Centreport; child of Joseph Conklin

CONKLIN, child - 9 months; d. Newark, N. J.;
interment 30 June 1888 at Northport; son of
Philetus Conklin

CONKLIN, child - 10 years; d. "a few days
ago"; 14 June 1890 paper; interment at
Smithtown Landing; son of Warren Conklin

CONKLIN, Abel M. - 57 yrs 11 mos; d. 21 October 1887 at Oyster Bay; interment at Huntington; son of Abel Conklin and Mary Miller;
husband of Imogene Earle; b. 22 November
1829 at Huntington; druggist in New York
City and after 1880 in Oyster Bay

CONKLIN, Abigail M. - 69 yrs 10 mos;
d. 14 July 1882 at Dix Hills; wife of
Stephen Conklin

CONKLIN, Addie - 27 y 11 m 13 d; d. 1 July
1888 at Huntington daughter of Amos P. and
Emma L. Conklin; teacher in primary school
in Huntington

CONKLIN, Amanda - 82 y 2 m 17 d; d. 29 March
1886 at Brooklyn; widow of Brewster Conklin

CONKLIN, Amos P. - 44 years; d. 29 January
1881 at Huntington

CONKLIN, Angeline - 26 years; d. 27 March 1880
at St. Johnsland; wife of Charles Conklin

CONKLIN, Anna M. - 69 y 7 m 19 d; d. 28 January 1888 at Northport

CONKLIN, Benjamin - d. 14 April 1888 at Riverhead; fell 16 feet to ground inside a barn

CONKLIN, Buel - 47 years; d. 5 April 1882 at
Bocas del Toro, Chiriqui Lagoon, Colombia;
formerly of Cold Spring

CONKLIN, Cecilia R. - 22 y 9 m 19 d;
d. 27 April 1884 at Cold Spring; daughter of
R. M. Conklin

CONKLIN, Charles - 63 y 9 m 3 d; d. 17 January
1879 at Long Island City

CONKLIN, Charles R. - 36 y 5 m 2 d; d. 11 June
1886 at Brooklyn; interment at Huntington;
former resident of Huntington

CONKLIN, Clara A. - 6 mos 23 days; d. 1 August
1879 at Comac; daughter of Henry and Rosa
Conklin

CONKLIN, Rev. Cornelius - 77 yrs 7 mos;
d. 26 February 1888 at Stockton, New Jersey;
interment at Mount Pleasant, New Jersey; son
of Thomas W. Conklin

CONKLIN, D. H. - 70 years; d. 21 April 1880 at
Smithtown

CONKLIN, Daniel P. - 93 years; d. 1 May 1889;
funeral at Centreport

CONKLIN, Edward - ca. 60 years; d. "two weeks
ago" at City Island; 30 July 1880 paper

CONKLIN, Edward L. - 5 months; d. 20 October
1884 at Northport; son of John R. and Phebe
Conklin

CONKLIN, Elias * - 70 years; d. 6 December
1879 at Oyster Bay

CONKLIN, Eliza - 40 years; d. 24 July 1886 at
Brooklyn; former resident of Huntington

CONKLIN, Elizabeth - 1 year; d. 14 July 1890
at Cold Spring Harbor; daughter of Edward H.
and Millie Conklin

CONKLIN, Emma Nelson - 2 yrs 7 mos; d. 23 October 1886 at Huntington; daughter of Edward
T. Conklin

CONKLIN, Epenetus C. - 77 years; d. 14 September 1887 at Northport

CONKLIN, Eva Douglass - 4 years; d. 4 February
1887 at Huntington

CONKLIN, Ethel Bruce - 10 mos 9 days;
d. 25 August 1880 at Huntington; daughter of
James B. and Addie E. Conklin

CONKLIN, George W. - 54 years; d. Arlington,
New Jersey; 17 May 1890 paper

CONKLIN, Gilbert P. - 30 years; d. 13 February
1889 at Brooklyn

CONKLIN, Mrs. Hamilton - d. 31 May 1884 at
Northport

CONKLIN, Mrs. Hamilton - d. 22 August 1888 at
Northport

CONKLIN, Hannah - 72 years; d. 24 December
1882 at Huntington; wife of Jonas P. Conklin

CONKLIN, Harry - d. Jamaica; 7 September 1889
paper; father of 7 children; surviving are
David B. Conklin and Mrs. Thomas Cornell;
husband of Sabrina Valentine, Louise [---]
and Mary Hannah Hahden, who survives;
b. 10 January 1800 at Dix Hills; resident of
Jamaica since 1826; stage coach driver on
routes between Jamaica and Brooklyn and
Jamaica and New York City; long biography in
7 September 1889 paper

CONKLIN, Hattie N. - d. 18 October 1889 at
Oyster Bay; interment at Northport; wife of
Frank A. Conklin

CONKLIN, Henrietta S. - 62 years; d. 6 April
1886 at Babylon; interment at Huntington;
wife of William Conklin

CONKLIN, Ira - 76 y 11 m 3 d; d. 19 August
1882 at Huntington

CONKLIN, James B. - 37 yrs 11 mos; d. 13 December 1879 at Brooklyn

CONKLIN, Jane A. - 83 years; d. 14 May 1889 at
Brooklyn; widow of Ezra Conklin; mother of
Mrs. A. S. Higgins and Mary E. Conklin, a
school teacher in Huntington for many years

CONKLIN, Jeremiah W. - 59 yrs 10 mos; d. 27
January 1878 at Babylon; son of Platt
Conklin; deaf and dumb; teacher of deaf
CONKLIN, Jesse - d. 17 June 1885 at Babylon;
fell off dock and died of injuries from
fall; b. Half Hollows 1809; proprietor of
"American House" and "Castle Conklin" hotels
in Babylon
CONKLIN, Mrs. John - d. 26 October 1890 at
Patchogue; "quite suddenly"
CONKLIN, John A. - 33 y 2 m 20 d; suicide 14
March 1887 at Dix Hills; hung himself in a
barn; son of David B. and Sarah J. Conklin;
brother of George A. Conklin and Mrs.
Frances O. Soper
CONKLIN, Julia E. - 28 y 9 m 21 d; d. 12 Sept-
ember 1887 at Huntington; wife of Elbert
Conklin
CONKLIN, Lewis * - 46 years; d. 9 April 1889
at Port Jefferson; attacked his wife Grace
Conklin with an ax; son got involved to
protect mother; Grace then hit and killed
Lewis with the ax; interment at Mount Sinai;
father of Joseph Conklin and Annie S.
Conklin
CONKLIN, Lina Kelly - 46 years; d. 20 January
1883 at Algiers, Texas; wife of Charles
Conklin; native of St. Thomas, West Indies
CONKLIN, Maria L. - 45 years 7 mos;
d. 15 September 1882 at Huntington; wife of
Henry F. Conklin
CONKLIN, Maria Louisa - 2 y 8 m 16 d;
d. 23 May 1879 at Oyster Bay Cove; daughter
of George and Sarah Conklin
CONKLIN, Martha Wood - 59 yrs 11 mos;
d. 8 February 1882 at Elwood
CONKLIN, Mary - 76 yrs 9 mos; d. 5 July 1884
at Huntington; daughter of Matthias Davis
and Fanny Havens; widow of Strong Conklin
CONKLIN, Mary E. - 36 years; d. 25 June 1887
at Brooklyn
CONKLIN, Mary Elizabeth - d. 12 June 1888 at
Galva, Illinois; wife of Stephen A. Conklin;
left Huntington in 1856
CONKLIN, Mary J. - 46 y 11 m 2 d; d. 28 September 1878 at Williamsburgh

CONKLIN, Mary Jayne - 79 years; d. 15 November 1888 at Huntington; widow of Abel Ketcham Conklin

CONKLIN, P. B. - d. 30 May 1889 at Newark, New Jersey; interment at Northport; son of Alexander Conklin

CONKLIN, Peleg C. - 65 y 7 m 23 d; d. 11 June 1878 at Centreport

CONKLIN, Rebecca - 68 yrs 14 days; d. 29 December 1883 at Huntington

CONKLIN, Rebecca Ann - 80 years; d. 18 January 1884 at East Neck; widow of Titus Conklin

CONKLIN, Rebecca P. - 63 y 7 m 15 d; d. 14 January 1880 at Huntington

CONKLIN, Rosetta - 74 yrs 3 mos; d. 1 October 1889 at Glen Cove

CONKLIN, Ruth - 79 years; d. 14 November 1883 at Brooklyn; interment at Huntington

CONKLIN, Sarah - 40 y 3 m 11 d; d. Huntington; 24 November 1888 paper; wife of George Woodhull Conklin

CONKLIN, Sarah A. - d. 30 July 1886 at Melville; wife of George H. Conklin

CONKLIN, Seaman Rogers - 63 yrs 25 days; d. 9 January 1890 at Stamford, Connecticut; interment at Huntington; former resident of Huntington

CONKLIN, Strong - "aged"; d. "last week" at East Norwich; 5 May 1888 paper; b. Dix Hills; worked with trotting horses

CONKLIN, Strong - 82 y 2 m 3 d; d. 3 February 1890 at Huntington; b. Huntington 1807; seaman; active Methodist

CONKLIN, Titus - 84 y 8 m 24 d; d. 13 December 1885 at Riverhead; one of the organizers of the Congregational Church at Riverhead

CONKLIN, Willard C. - 7 y 6 m 3 d; d. 19 November 1879 at Brooklyn; son of James and Addie Conklin

CONKLIN, William - 30 years; d. 26 August 1887 at Union Course; hit by railroad train

CONKLIN, William - 69 y 8 m 14 d; d. 3 August 1890 at Babylon

CONKLIN, William C. - 77 y 9 m 13 d; d. 23 July 1883 at Vernon Valley

CONKLING, Roscoe - d. [18 April 1888 at New
York City]; [died from aftereffects of
exposure from being caught outside during
the Blizzard of 1888; U. S. Senator from New
York State 1867-1881; major Republican party
leader of the 1860's, 1870's and 1880's.]
editorial in 21 April 1888 paper about
Conkling and his political importance

CONLIN, Lucy J. - 1 year; d. 9 September 1882
at Cold Spring

CONLON, Martin - 20 y 4 m 21 d; d. 3 February
1889 at Northport; funeral at Huntington

CONNELL, Catharine - 52 years; d. 24 February
1878 at West Neck

CONNELL, Martin - 71 years; d. 29 February
1884 at West Neck

CONNERS, James - 14 years; d. Hempstead;
interment 16 January 1889 at Westbury

CONNERS, Kittie - 20 years; suicide 11 December 1890 at Roslyn; drowned herself in a
cistern; daughter of Luke Conners

CONNOR, Morris E. - d. 4 December 1887 at
Woodbury; interment at Brooklyn

CONNOR, William C. - d. 26 April 1881 at New
York City; New York County Clerk; New York
County Sheriff

CONNOR, Willie - 19 years; d. 15 July 1880 at
Brooklyn; formerly of Huntington

CONWAY, Henry - drowned 12 November 1883 off
New Haven, Conn. on barge which sunk in a
storm; body came ashore at Plum Island 14
November 1883; resident of Virginia

COOGAN, Nicholas - d. 10 December 1883 at Port
Jefferson; died from alcoholism

COOK, Ida - 35 years; suicide in Long Island
Sound; 22 January 1887 paper; jumped off
steamboat going to Bridgeport, Conn.; daughter of Walter Leek; widow of Rockwell
Cook; resident of Port Jefferson

COOK, Mary J. * -15 years; d. 27 January 1889
at Huntington

COOKE, child - d. Bradford, Pa.; 8 February
1884 paper; coasting [sledding] accident;
daughter of F. P. Cooke, formerly of Huntington

COOKE, Erastus - death recorded in 10 July
1885 paper; former judge in Kings County

COON, Michael - 79 years; d. 10 February 1885
at Hempstead

COOPER, Mr. - drowned 17 July 1880 in Long
Island Sound off Town Of Riverhead

COOPER, Mr. - death noted; Hicksville item; 2
January 1885 paper

COOPER, Cornelius P. - d. at Tenafly, N. J.;
7 October 1881 paper; Cold Spring item

COOPER, Ellen - 60 years; d. 4 October 1888 at
Hicksville; mother of Mrs. Sevin

COOPER, Joseph - d. "last week" in Florida;
10 March 1888 paper; funeral at Flatbush;
Westbury item

COOPER, Robert - d. 12 January 1884 at East
New York

COOPERS, Dennis - ca. 45 years; d. 14 August
1879 at East Moriches; hunting accident;
resident of Hoboken, New Jersey

COOT, Mrs. - d. 16 June 1887 at Riverhead;
mother of Mrs. Shuloff

CORBET, Henry - d. at New York City; fell from
elevated railroad train; interment 25 August
1885 at Elwood

CORBETT, Thomas - 88 years; d. 24 April 1882
at Comac

CORBIN, Thomas - 28 years; d. 13 October 1887
at New York City; suffocated from gas in
hotel room

CORCORAN, children - d. at Smithville South;
four children of Patrick Corcoran from
scarlet fever; 28 November 1884 paper

COREY, James H. - drowned 7 December 1888 in
Hempstead Harbor, Glen Cove, while duck
hunting; hotel keeper

CORNELIUS, Harriet D. - 34 years; d. 6 June
1890; interment at Hempstead; wife of F. C.
Cornelius

CORNELIUS, Lot - 79 years; d. 4 October 1878
at Locust Valley

CORNELL, Mrs. - interment 25 February 1889 at
Westbury; resident of Hempstead

CORNELL, Lydia A. - 70 years; d. 7 May 1890 at
Hempstead; widow of James Cornell; mother of
E. T. Cornell and C. E. Cornell; sister of
Mrs. Benjamin F. Rushmore; member St. Geor-
ge's Episcopal Church

CORNELL, Mary T. - 74 y 4 m 20 d; d. 20 May 1890 at Huntington; wife of George Cornell

CORNELL, William - 16 years; d. drowned while swimming 1 July 1890 at Babylon; interment at Huntington

CORSE, Stephen * - 60 years; d. 7 September 1887 at Little Neck; hit by railroad train

CORWIN, Daniel Arden - d. 31 October 1883 at Baiting Hollow

CORWIN, Edna May - 11 months; d. 21 March 1883 at Glen Cove; daughter of Willie M. and Carrie Corwin

CORWIN, Fred G. - d. 2 June 1890 at Fort Plain, N. Y.; son of Hubbard Corwin of Riverhead

CORWIN, Harrison - 71 years; d. 7 February 1888; Riverhead item

CORWIN, J. Frank - d. 13 February 1882 at Baiting Hollow

CORWIN, Mehitabel - interment "last week"; 15 October 1887 paper; wife of Nathan Corwin, Riverhead item

CORWIN, Nathan - 89 years; d. 21 April 1890 at Riverhead; one of the first merchants to do business in Riverhead; former Riverhead Town Clerk

CORWIN, Serepta - 51 yrs 11 mos; d. 3 June 1885 at Huntington; wife of A. Corwin

CORWIN, Wallace - 31 years; d. 28 February 1879 at Riverhead; fell down stairs; son of Nathan Corwin

CORWIN, William M. - d. at Brooklyn; interment 1 December 1887 at Riverhead; brother of James Barrett Corwin

COSINE, Julia A. - 76 years; d. 10 June 1887 at Huntington

COUBLER, infant - d. 8 January 1888; Plainview item; interment at Breslau

COULTER, child - interment 16 July 1890; Westbury item; child of Oliver Coulter

COURTNEY, child - 6 years; d. 27 September 1878 at Rockaway Inlet; daughter of John Courtney; boat carrying family swamped in Jamaica Bay; family moving by water from Bayport to Northwest Point on Jamaica Bay; lost furniture and all possessions

COVERT, Bernard - 77 years; d. 8 June 1882 at
Newburgh, New York
COVERT, Tessie - d. 6 March 1890 at Jamaica;
"victim of malpractice"; John Melville
Bassett charged
COVERT, William - ca. 28 years; thrown from
carriage out onto his head; funeral 31 Dec-
ember 1890; interment at Evergreens, Brook-
lyn; resident of East Williston
COWEN, James - 50-60 yrs; drowned 10 March
1890 at Glen Cove; employee of Duryea Starch
Works
COWHEY, Dennis - d. 19 January 1884 at Laurel
Hill, Queens County; poisoned
COWPERWAITE, child - 8 years; d. "last week"
at Brooklyn; 8 February 1890 paper; daughter
of Howard and Florence Crozier Cowperwaite
COX, Ann Eliza - d. 22 May 1888 at Brooklyn;
daughter of David B. Young; wife of Stephen
P. Cox
COX, Anna - 85 years; d. 13 July 1884 at
Woodbury; wife of Walter Cox
COX, Hannah * - "aged"; d. 9 December 1889 at
Glen Cove
COX, Henry * - drowned 27 July 1886 at Glen-
wood
COX, Samuel - d. 1 October 1890 at Sea Cliff;
interment at Cypress Hills
COX, Samuel S. - 65 years; d. 10 September
1889 at New York City; interment at
Green-Wood, Brooklyn; "well known statesman"
COYLE, Edward - drowned 6 April 1888 in
Nissequogue River at St. Johnland
COYLE, Ida May - 6 yrs 2 mos; d. 22 October
1888 at New York City; daughter of James H.
and Hannah J. Coyle
CRAFT, Henry - 73 y 5 m 16 d; d. 4 March 1882
at Northport
CRAFT, Mrs. William - d. "last week" at
Brooklyn; 2 April 1887 paper
CRAFT, William H. - killed 30 May 1883 in
Brooklyn Bridge disaster; resident of New
York City; Trustee of Willett Street M. E.
Church
CRAMPTON, Capt. - d. "last week" at Guilford,
Conn.; 17 Oct. 1884 paper; former captain of
sloop between Huntington and New York City

CRAWFORD, Charles - d. 30 May 1889; Greenlawn item; died from abscess in head; son of Elbert Crawford

CRAWFORD, Charles L. - killed 3 June 1887 at Bowery Bay Beach carriage accident; resident of Philadelphia, Pennsylvania

CRAYTON, Carrie Dusenbury * - 12 years; d. 23 February 1881 at Huntington

CREED, William - d. 19 September 1880 at East Rockaway; hit by railroad train

CRIPPEN, Sarah L. * - 15 y 7 m 26 d; d. 26 February 1883 at Huntington

CROFT, Mrs. Joseph - d. 20 January 1879 at Hunter's Point; fell dead in LIRR depot; resident of Glen Cove

CROMBLE, Fannie - d. 5 April 1889 at Woodhaven; funeral at Plainview; sister of Mrs. Grohman of Plainview

CROMWELL, Elizabeth - 74 y 4 m 23 d; d. 15 January 1882 at Melville

CROMWELL, Jeremiah - 88 yrs 8 mos; d. 22 July 1890 at Melville

CROMWELL, Maria S. * - 74 y 11 m 21 d; d. 16 June 1888 at Huntington

CRONE, Frederick - 75 years; d. 3 October 1890 at Glen Cove; resident of Glen Cove "for more than half a century"

CRONIN, Bridget F. - 82 years; d. 14 March 1890 at Huntington

CRONIN, Elizabeth - 78 years; d. 24 March 1889 at Little Neck

CROSS, George - 73 y 5 m 16 d; d. 26 April 1888 at Dix Hills

CROSS, Mrs. George - funeral 13 March 1890 at Comac; "an old and respected lady"

CROSSMAN, children - d. 8 August 1879 at Rockville Centre; two children of William Crossman; drank from can containing Paris Green

CROSSMAN, Alfred - 86 y 11 m 29 d; d. 21 March 1885 at Milton, Massachusetts

CROSSMAN, Franklin - 42 y 9 m 3 d; d. 25 June 1888 at West Neck; proprietor of West Neck Brick Yards

CROSSMAN, Mary G. - 68 years; d. 3 December 1878 at West Neck; widow of Gilbert Crossman

CROSSMAN, Mary Rushmore - 83 y 8 m 7 d;
d. 16 March 1884 at West Neck; widow of
Alfred B. Crossman; b. Half Hollow Hills
29 June 1800
CROSSMAN, Matilda C. - 49 y 1 m 17 d; d. 15
December 1880 at New York City; interment at
Huntington; wife of Jacob R. Crossman of New
Haven, Connecticut
CROSSMAN, Nathan - 91 y 6 m 3 d; d. 11 January
1885 at Milton, Massachusetts
CROSSMAN, Sarah - 79 yrs 28 days; d. 16 Decem-
ber 1882 at West Neck
CROSSMAN, Sarah Frost - 8 y 10 m 11 d;
d. 25 April 1888 at Griswold, Connecticut;
funeral at Huntington; daughter of Elwood
and Mary McKay Crossman
CROSSMAN, Silas C. - 49 years; d. 2 March 1882
at Frying Pan Shoals, N. C.; captain of
"Silas L. Wright" which sank in storm;
resident of Babylon
CROSSMAN, Smith B. - 70 years; d. 5 September
1883 at Jamaica; carriage maker; b. Half
Hollow Hills 1813
CROUPA, Winnie [male] - murdered 26 December
1890 at Bohemiaville; Frank Krulisch
murdered Croupa and mutilated the body
CROUSA, George W. - 22 y 9 m 5 d; d. 8 January
1888; Plainview item; interment at Bethpage
CROWELL, Jonathan - d. 1 September 1883 at
Patchogue
CROZIER, Delia B. - 60 y 10 m 17 d; d. 23 June
1886 at Brooklyn; interment at Huntington;
widow of Hiram J. Crozier
CROZIER, Hiram J. - 59 years; d. 6 March 1883
at Brooklyn; interment at Huntington; Uni-
versalist minister at Huntington ca. 1858-
1861
CROZIER, Jane E. - 78 y 10 m 28 d; d. 8 January 1878 at Brooklyn; mother of H. P.
Crozier
CUFF, Mary E. - d. "last week" at Hempstead;
20 September 1890 paper; interment at Flatbush; stricken with apoplexy on 8 September
1890; servant of Mrs. A. N. Selter of Hempstead
CUFFEE, infant - 4 days; d. 2 March 1885 at
Northport; son of Ira F. and Sarah Cuffee

CUFFEE, children [boy and girl] * - children
of John and Sarah Cuffee of Jamaica;
professional beggars for parents; died of
exposure; 8 January 1887 paper
CUFFEE, James H. * - 53 years; d. 3 June 1883
at Eaton's Neck; interment at Huntington
CUFFEE, William * - 113 years; d. 30 October
1883 at Plainfield, New Jersey
CUFFEY, Emeline * - d. about 2 January 1878
at Middle Island; died of exposure while
drunk; "paramour" of George Green
CUFFEY, Robert * - 9 years; found dead 24 February 1884 on Yaphank-Moriches Road; died of
exposure
CULVER, Henry - 56 years; found dead in his
wagon, Bushwick Avenue, Brooklyn; resident
of Pearsalls; 22 January 1886 paper
CUMMINGS, Martha - 23 y 5 m 18 d; d. 25 August
1879 at Woodbury
CUNNINGHAM, Miles - 72 years; d. "last week"
at Hauppauge; 16 December 1881 paper; native
of Ireland
CURRAN, Mrs. - d. 2 August 1890 at Brooklyn;
interment at Westbury; former widow of
Thomas Egan
CUSHING, John - 59 years; d. 13 June 1879 at
West Neck
CUSHING, John V. - 1 y 3 m 11 d; d. 25 June
1886 at West Neck
CUSHMAN, Earle - 72 years; d. 25 May 1883 at
Crab Meadow
CUSICK, James - 6 years; d. 17 July 1879 at
Bethpage; accident at Stewart's Brickyard;
son of James Cusick
CUTTING, Mary - 90 y 9 m 15 d; d. 24 March
1879 at Comac
DAILEY, Thomas - d. 7 April 1884 at College
Point; Secretary of College Point Savings
Bank
DAILY, youth - 16 years; drowned 11 August
1890 in Old Brick Kiln Pond, Jamaica;
resident of Flushing
DALEY, Nora - 16 years; d. 17 September 1889
at West Neck
DALLEY, Ann - 81 yrs 5 mos; d. 20 May 1882 at
Smithtown Branch

57

DALY, Jerry - 53 years; d. at New York City;
funeral 20 March 1890 at Northport; "for the
last twenty years he has made his home with
Arden Brown"

DANIELS, Mrs. William - d. "this week" at New
York City; 4 Febr. 1888 paper; former Miss
McGonigle of Hicksville

DANNAT, William H. - 73 years; d. 27 October
1889 at Exmouth, England; lumber merchant in
New York City; owned country estate at Hempstead

DARLING, Barnabas H. - 72 y 6 m 27 d;
d. 27 January 1886 at Smithtown; funeral at
Smithtown Landing

DARLING, Benjamin - d. 23 December 1888 at
Smithtown Landing

DARLING, Gilbert - d. 14 May 1883 at Stony
Brook; overdose of laudanum

DARLING, Hannah A. - 38 y 8 m 15 d;
d. 27 April 1885 at Huntington; wife of
Oscar Darling

DARLING, James - 89 years; d. 16 January 1889
at Smithtown Branch; funeral at Smithtown
Landing

DARLING, Mary J. - d. 29 April 1888; wife of
Jeremiah Darling; memorial bell given to
Presbyterian Chapel at Stony Brook;
14 December 1889 paper

DARLING, Samuel - suicide 5 January 1883 at
Glen Cove; jumped into path of railroad
train

DARLING, Sarah - 3 mos 20 d; d. 19 July 1885
at Huntington; daughter of Oscar Darling

DARLING, Mrs. Selah - d. 31 August 1890 at
Echo; funeral at Port Jefferson

DARLING, Walter - 77 or 79 yrs; d. 6 February
1886 at St. Johnland; funeral at Smithtown
Landing

DARLING, William - 84 years; d. 22 February
1890 at Port Jefferson

DAUCH, child - interment 24 January 1889;
Hicksville item; son of Mrs. Andrew Dauch;
her two remaining children died within a
week

DAUCH, Andrew - d. 11 January 1887 at Hicksville; smallpox; interment at Jerusalem

DAUCH, Joseph - d. 16 January 1889 at Hicks-
ville; interment at Jerusalem; son of Mrs.
Andrew Dauch
DAVIDS, Adelaide F. - 34 y 8 m 24 d; d. 9 Nov-
ember 1878 at Oyster Bay; wife of G. H.
Davids
DAVIDSON, children - two children of Joseph C.
Davidson of Pearsalls; died of diphtheria;
12 February 1887 paper
DAVIDSON, Anna - 1 year; d. 6 July 1888 at
Huntington
DAVIDSON, Harry S. - 9 yrs 18 days;
d. 27 March 1885 at Northport; son of H. H.
Davidson
DAVIDSON, John - 91 years; d. 26 December 1884
at Hempstead; medical doctor in Hempstead
for 60 years
DAVIS, child - 5 y 6 m 25 d; d. 3 August 1885
at Miller's Place; son of William and Ida
Davis
DAVIS, children - two children of N. W. Davis
died of dysentery; 24 August 1889 paper;
Port Jefferson item
DAVIS, Alonzo - d. 15 November 1887 at
Brooklyn; interment at Riverhead
DAVIS, Ann - 65 years; d. 30 April 1882 at
Mount Sinai
DAVIS, Mrs. Charles A. - 43 yrs 8 mos;
d. 10 May 1889 at Mount Sinai
DAVIS, Mrs. Charles G. - 36 yrs 20 days;
d. 19 September 1882 at Mount Sinai
DAVIS, Charles Homer - d. 14 February 1884 at
West Neck; son of Charles Davis
DAVIS, Charley L. - d. 25 January 1888;
Riverhead item; son of C. P. Davis
DAVIS, Clarissa - 79 y 7 m 25 d; d. 29 May
1883 at Mount Sinai; widow of Buel Davis
DAVIS, Daniel A. - 67 years; d. 27 August 1888
at Mount Sinai
DAVIS, Rev. E. B. * - 63 yrs 6 mos; d. 1 Jan-
uary 1881 at Huntington
DAVIS, Mrs. Edgar - 46 years; d. 4 March 1887
at Hicksville; funeral at Jericho
DAVIS, Ethel May - 2 y 11 m 1 d; d. 30 August
1885 at Mount Sinai; daughter of Elisha
Davis

DAVIS, Eugene T. - ca. 10 years; d. 7 September 1885 at Mount Sinai; son of Elisha E. Davis

DAVIS, George [Indian] - 46 years; d. 19 February 1881 at Shinnecock

DAVIS, Hiram - 69 years; d. 1 November 1884 at Kingston, N. Y.; native of Stone Ridge, Ulster County, N. Y.; father of Mrs. N. S. Ackerly of Northport

DAVIS, Israel J. - 70 years; d. 17 August 1888 at Bayonne, N. J.; interment at Port Jefferson; brother of Mrs. John D. Wells and Mrs. Daniel Jones

DAVIS, Mrs. J. Benjamin - 42 years; d. 24 December 1888 at Rocky Point

DAVIS, J. D. - interment 3 August 1884 at Hicksville; resident of New York City

DAVIS, Jefferson - d. 6 December 1889 at New Orleans, Louisiana; Confederate President; account of funeral 14 December 1889 paper; negative editorial 21 December 1889 paper

DAVIS, Joanna - 27 years; d. 15 August 1882 at Miller's Place

DAVIS, Joel - 77 y 6 m 6 d; d. 7 April 1883 at Mount Sinai

DAVIS, John * - d. 23 July 1880 at Glen Cove; born a slave in Virginia

DAVIS, L. Ray - 5 months; d. 16 August 1888 at Mount Sinai; son of Elisha E. and C. Elsie Davis

DAVIS, Lucinda * - 61 years; d. 28 August 1880 at Redding Centre, Conn.; resident of Miller's Place

DAVIS, M. Salome - 38 years; d. 14 January 1883 at Miller's Place; wife of Nathaniel T. Davis

DAVIS, Mary A. - 46 yrs 9 mos; d. 23 November 1886 at Eaton's Neck; wife of John Davis

DAVIS, Matilda - 34 years; d. 30 August 1884 at Miller's Place

DAVIS, Phebe - 55 years; d. 18 January 1884 at Ronkonkoma

DAVIS, Phoebe - found dead on floor at Lake Grove; "dead over a week"; 15 February 1884 paper

DAVIS, Sophrona - 68 yrs 11 days; d. 21 July 1886 at Miller's Place

DAVIS, Susan E. - 43 yrs 8 mos; d. 20 July 1887 at Mount Sinai

DAVIS, Sylvester R. - 75 years; d. 26 May 1887 at Miller's Place

DAY, James H. - 33 yrs 3 mos; d. 23 November 1884 at Northport

DAYTON, Charles B. - d. 24 August 1886 at East Hampton; medical doctor; died in office writing prescription; Army Surgeon during Civil War with 127 N. Y. Vols.

DAYTON, R. W. - 85 years; d. 28 December 1887 at Brooklyn; interment at Glen Cove; b. at Port Jefferson; captain of coasting vessels; resident of Glen Cove

DEAN, Fannie - 3 mos; d. 31 July 1887 at Dix Hills

DE BEVOISE, David D. - 2 July 1880 paper; resident of Brooklyn; "Seawanhaka" fire on East River

DEEGAN, Thomas - 45 years; d. 24 November 1883 at Long Island City; from burns received falling against stove

DE FOREST, Henry G. - 69 years; d. 18 November 1889 at Cold Spring Harbor; funeral at New York City; lawyer; son of Lockwood De Forest

DE FORREST, Frederick L. - 53 years; d. 15 January 1878 at Babylon; resident of New York City

DEGAN, Michael J. - 1 yr 2 mos; d. 14 July 1880 at Oyster Bay

DE GRAY, Emma - 30 years; d. 18 October 1889 at Cold Spring Harbor

DE GRAY, William - 64 y 4 m 24 d; d. 2 January 1878 at Huntington

DELAMATER, Cornelius H. - d. 7 February 1889 at New York City

DELANO, Mr. - drowned 17 July 1883 at Roslyn; brother of Mrs. Charles Haydock

DELMONICO, Charles - found dead in woods in Orange Mountains, N. J.; 18 January 1884 paper; [see also NYG&B Record January 1990]

DEMAREST, Phoebe Woolsey - 71 years; d. 25 January 1883 at Newark, N. J.; interment at Huntington; wife of Rev. James Demarest

DE MILT, Henrietta - 75 years; d. 12 January 1890 at Centreport; interment at Northport

DE MILT, J. B. - "old"; d. 28 April 1888 at
Amityville; found dead in his room; "old
retired sailor"

DE MOTT, James S. - 58 years; suicide by
jumping off ferry boat at New York City; 2
September 1889 paper; son of George De Mott;
resident of New Jersey

DE MOTT, John W. - 83 years; d. 26 February
1886 at Woodsburgh; held many offices in
Town of Hempstead government

DENAAN, Daniel - 4 1/2 years; d. at Jericho;
20 June 1884 paper; accident while at play

DENEEN, Michael - d. 10 August 1885 at Jericho

DENTON, Abigail A. - 65 y 11 m 7 d; d. 31 July
1885 at Cold Spring Harbor; wife of Andrew
J. Denton

DENTON, Elizabeth - 82 y 9 m 8 d; d. 1 April
1883 at Cold Spring Harbor; interment at
Huntington; widow of Israel Denton

DENTON, Mary * - 80 yrs 7 mos; d. 26 November
1881 at Woodbury

DENTON, Mary - 59 years; d. 13 October 1884 at
Cold Spring Harbor

DENTON, William * - 63 years; d. 11 April 1888
at Woodbury; "a respectable colored man"

DENTON, Willie - 3 y 11 m 22 d; d. 10 January
1878 at Oyster Bay

DE PEW, William H. - 48 years; d. 31 October
1887 at Brooklyn; son of John De Pew of
Poughkeepsie

DE PEYSTER, Fannie - 72 years; d. 4 January
1879 at East Norwich

DE PUY, Isabelle - 1 year; d. 20 July 1887 at
Amityville; daughter of Talbot and Frances
De Puy; died from teething remedy

DESILVEY, Luella Momeseta * - 1 year;
d. 8 September 1880 at Huntington

DE SILVIA, Clarence Ray * - 4 y 1 m 14 d;
d. 30 March 1885 at Huntington; son of Louis
and Mary A. De Silvia

DE SENDZEIMIR, Joseph - suicide 17 August 1881
at Amityville; cut his throat at wife's
grave

DE TURK, Ann Elizabeth - 71 years; d. 18 December 1890 at Commack; found dead in bed

DEUTCHER, Charles - 22 y 8 m 23 d; d. 5 May
1887 at Hicksville; funeral at Westbury

DE VEAU, Joshua M. - 75 yrs 2 mos; d. 23 July
1890 at Huntington Harbor; oysterman; kept
small store at Huntington Harbor; a "land-
mark of Huntington Harbor"

DE VINNE, Ambrose - 54 years; d. 24 October
1886 at Brooklyn

DE VINNE, Daniel - 90 years; d. 10 February
1883 at New York City; Methodist clergyman;
served at Huntington 1847-1848

DE WALL, Cornelius - 84 years; suicide 28 June
1886 at Port Washington; cut his own throat

DE WICK, Mrs. George N. - 42 years; d. 16 January 1890 at Port Jefferson; mother of ten
children, ages 19 years to 6 weeks

DEWICK, Lewis - 8 years; d. 1 July 1890 at
Amityville; interment at Port Jefferson; son
of George Dewick

DEXHEIMER, Elizabeth Margaret - 86 y 1 m 27 d;
d. 31 May 1890 at Hicksville; widow of
Christian Dexheimer; mother of Jacob E. Dexheimer; b. Munchein, Germany; immigrated to
USA in 1838; resident of Hicksville since
1849

DEY, William - 66 y 11 m 7 d; d. 22 January
1884 at Huntington

DIBBLE, Florence A. - 2 months; d. 13 August
1886 at Brooklyn

DICK, David H. - 67 years; d. 27 March 1883
at St. Johnland

DICKERSON, Alfred C. - 1 yr 7 mos; d. 8 January 1881 at Northport; son of Gilbert Dickerson

DICKERSON, Ebenezer - 87 yrs 10 days;
d. 30 July 1887 at Rocky Point

DICKERSON, Frank - 6 months; death noted;
interment at Northport; son of Gilbert Dickerson of Islip; [date of paper not copied]

DICKERSON, Mary E. - 70 years; d. 4 May 1883
at Woodville; wife of Benjamin Dickerson

DIETER, Mrs. A. W. - d. "last week" in
Florida; Smithtown item; [date of paper not
copied]; steamboat accident; boat capsized
and Mrs. Dieter seriously injured by hot
water from boiler

DILLER, Rev. [Alonzo P.] - d. [31 May 1889] at
Johnstown, Pennsylvania; killed in Johnstown
Flood along with wife and child; former

DILLER, Rev. [Alonzo P.] (continued)
assistant at St. Mary's Church, Brooklyn,
and "well known to a number of people of
Huntington"

DILLER, E. L. - d. 14 July 1880 at Randall's
Island; from burns suffered during
"Seawanhaka"fire on East River

[DILLER, Isaac] - d. [31 May 1889] at
Johnstown, Pennsylvania; killed in Johnstown
Flood; son of Rev. Alonzo P. Diller

DILLER, Rev. Jacob W. - 2 July 1880 paper;
"Seawanhaka" fire on East River

[DILLER, Marion] - d. [31 May 1889] at
Johnstown, Pennsylvania; killed in Johnstown
Flood; wife of Rev. Alonzo P. Diller

DILLER, William A. Muhlenberg - ca. 40 years;
d. 8 December 1880 at Elmira, New York;
funeral at Brooklyn

DILLON, Arthur S. - 4 mos 26 days; d. 7 July
1880 at Huntington; son of William J. Dillon

DIX, John A. - d. 21 April 1879 at [New York
City]; former Governor of New York State
[1872-1874]; had summer home at Westhampton

DOANE, Charles - 60 years; d. 7 November 1882
at St. James

DOANE, Mamie E. - funeral 10 December 1889 at
Riverhead; half-sister of D. Nelson Gay

DOANE, Mary E. - 63 years; d. 1 June 1890 at
Port Jefferson; mother of John C. Roe,
Charles F. Roe and Etta Doane

DOCHERTY, Catherine - found dead in a "filthy
house" at Union Course; 16 November 1883
paper

DOLAN, Fannie - 7 mos 10 days; d. 1 February
1879 at Northport; daughter of James and
Mary E. Dolan

DOLAN, James J. - 34 y 8 m 20 d; d. 2 October
1880 at Northport

DOLAN, Mrs. M. E. - funeral at Northport;
20 July 1883 paper

DONALDSON, Eliza - 8 y 11 m 4 d; d. 23 November 1879 at Hauppauge; daughter of Wallace
and Fannie Donaldson

DONLY, Mrs. - d. 31 December 1889 at New York
City; mother of Charles Donly of Farmingdale
and grandmother of Mrs. Samuel S. Stewart;
former resident of Hicksville

DONOHUE, Mrs. - d. 18 October 1889; interment
    at Hauppauge
DONOHUE, Patrick - 20 years; murdered at Sea
    Cliff; body found 11 September 1886;
    resident of Glen Cove
DONOVAN, Patrick - drowned 19 January 1883 off
    Fisher's Island; ship collision; resident of
    St. John, Nova Scotia
DORLAN, Charles - 10 years; d. 18 September
    1879 at Pearsalls; shot in gun accident by
    playmate
DORLAND, Bryant - drowned in Lake Ontario;
    1 January 1887 paper; former resident of
    Blue Point
DORLAND, William - drowned in Lake Ontario;
    1 January 1887 paper; former resident of
    Blue Point
DORLON, Valentine - 60 years; suicide 3 April
    1884 at Hempstead
DOTY, Ananias - 60 y 1 m 3 d; d. 8 July 1884
    at Woodbury; hit by railroad train; resident
    of Huntington
DOTY, Zebulon - 82 years; d. 8 January 1880 at
    Oyster Bay Cove
DOTZEIL, Jacob - d. 16 January 1885; fireman
    on train which de-railed at Bethpage; died
    from injuries received in wreck
DOUDICAN, Delia - 18 years; d. 24 October 1888
    at Islip; broke neck when fell off rear
    platform of railroad train and landed on
    tracks
DOUGALL, James - 78 years; d. 19 August 1886
    at Flushing; newspaper editor in Montreal
    and New York City
DOUGHERTY, Eliza - d. 18 October 1890 at
    Brooklyn; interment at Patchogue
DOUGHERTY, Mary - 40 years; d. 15 December
    1879 at Hauppauge; wife of Andrew Dougherty
DOUGLASS, Mrs. - death recorded 28 December
    1889 paper; resident of Sayville; well-known
    temperance worker throughout Suffolk County
DOW, Margaret A. - 53 y 11 m 19 d; d. 26 June
    1885 at Huntington; wife of Oliver Dow
DOWDEN, D. J. - d. Binghamton, N. Y.; 24 June
    1878 Binghamton paper; brother of James
    Dowden of Woodbury; [date of Long Islander
    not copied]

DOWDEN, Eliza - 66 years; d. 16 June 1880 at
Cold Spring; funeral at Huntington

DOWDEN, Patrick Joseph - d. 9 October 1890 at
Huntington; "pioneer Catholic"; moved from
Brooklyn to Babylon 1832 and to Cold Spring
1834; one of the founders of the Roman
Catholic Church in Huntington; father of
seven sons and three daughters

DOWLING, Michael - death recorded; Glen Cove
item; 29 January 1886 paper

DOWNING, Richard - 20 years; killed 8 June
1887 in construction accident at Brooklyn;
funeral at Oyster Bay; brother of C. M.
Downing

DOWNING, Susanna Maria - 75 y 3 m 4 d;
d. 18 February 1883 at Huntington; widow of
Ananias Downing

DOWNING, William L. - d. 23 November 1889 at
East Norwich; father of G. W. Downing

DOWNING, Mrs. William L. - d. 18 May 1889 at
East Norwich

DOWNS, young man - 18 years; d. 23 July 1889
at Riverhead; son of William Downs;
diphtheria

DOWNS, child - 9 years; d. 29 July 1889 at
Riverhead; son of William Downs; diphtheria

DOWNS, Charlotte P. - 61 years; d. 21 March
1883 at Glen Cove; widow of John P. Downs

DOWNS, Frank P. - 31 years; d. 22 November
1883 at Huntington; Bright's disease;
Editor of Suffolk Bulletin since 1881;
native of Huntington; had worked on newspapers in New York City

DOWNS, H. Maria - 65 y 2 m 14 d; d. 14 August
1887 at Centreport; daughter of Gilbert
Platt; widow of William T. Downs; mother of
Mrs. Emma Carter; resident of Huntington

DOWNS, Henry I. - 27 years; d. 18 May 1881 at
Huntington; overdose of morphine

DOWNS, Huldah - d. 11 April 1881 at Northville; clothing caught fire

DOWNS, John - d. 17 March 1882 at Riverhead

DOWNS, Sylvester - death noted; 1 January 1887
paper; Riverhead item

DOWNS, William T. - 36 y 6 m 17 d; d. 15 November 1884 at Huntington; carriage manufacturer

DOYLE, Eddie - d. 31 March 1890 at Hicksville; interment at Westbury; son of John W. Doyle

DOXSEE, Rev. Amos - death recorded 13 May 1881 paper by memorial resolutions from Teachers' Association

DRAKE, Fanny - 61 y 5 m 27 d; d. 7 June 1887 at Huntington; wife of John M. Drake

DRAPER, Eddie - d. "last week" at New York City; 10 November 1888 paper; Centreport item

DREW, Alexander - 48 years; d. 17 January 1885 at Huntington; Civil War Veteran; served with Ellsworth's Zouaves 1861 and later in Union navy. Was aboard U.S.S. "Cumberland" when it was sunk by C.S.S. "Merrimack" at Hampton Roads, Virginia, 1862

DREW, Louis M. - found in Hudson River off Fort Lee, New Jersey, 21 May 1879; resident of Hoboken, New Jersey; taught school in Huntington about 1849

DRIGGS, Egbert - 58 y 6 m 6 d; d. 30 January 1886 at Amityville; son of Abijah and Hannah Smith Driggs; suffered from severe inflammatory rheumatism since age 14; went blind in 1850; bed ridden since 1869; born East Northport 1828

DRIGGS, Hannah - 88 y 2 m 7 d; d. 13 March 1886 at Amityville; daughter of Melancthon Smith; widow of Abijah Driggs; married 1822; widowed 1831

DUDGEON, Mrs. Frank - d. 2 March 1888; resident of Locust Valley

DUFFY, Bridget - d. 19 March 1878 at Greenlawn; wife of Hugh Duffy, hired man of Warren Smith; fell dead headlong out of door into yard

DULCE, Charlotte - 69 years; d. 17 January 1890 at New York City; interment at Jerusalem; mother of Mrs. Brand; immigrated from Germany "about a year ago"

DUMPSON, Sarah Elizabeth - 38 years; d. 19 January 1886; Farmingdale item

DUNBAR, Emma - funeral 5 October 1886 at Smithtown

DUNHAM, Alvin - d. 15 December 1884 at Jamaica

DUNHAM, Mary E. - 61 years; d. 19 December
1886; Riverhead item; asked for glass of
water and then died
DUNN, Mrs. - d. 12 November 1889 at Queens;
interment at Cypress Hills
DUNN, J. Paris - d. 20 November 1889 at Sea
Cliff
DUNN, Julia - 47 years; d. 6 March 1889 at
Alms House [Yaphank]; resident of Huntington
DUNN, Thomas - d. 5 September 1884 at Nortport
DUNNING, Amelia - 87 years; d. 25 Febr. 1890
at Setauket; interment at Port Jefferson
DUPIGNAC, Charles - 11 weeks; d. at Farming-
dale; 3 October 1879 paper; smothered from
epilepsy
DURAND, Seneca - 76 yrs 6 mos; d. 21 September
1880 at Melville
DURYEA, child - d. 14 June 1887; Hempstead
item; son of Cornelius Duryea
DURYEA, Mrs. Cornelius - d. 17 June 1887;
Hempstead item
DURYEA, Edgar H. - 45 y 8 m 10 d; d. 3 June
1880 at Melville
DURYEA, Mrs. John R. - d. 9 August 1889 at
East Norwich
DURYEA, John W. - d. 14 June 1885 at Oregon,
Southold Town; Superintendant of Sunday
School, Presbyterian Chapel at Oregon
DURYEA, Margaret - 77 yrs 9 mos; d. 14 August
1887 at Plainview
DURYEA, Maria - d. at Babylon; funeral 31 May
1881
DURYEA, Nettie - infant; d. 12 September 1888
at Hicksville; daughter of Charles Duryea of
Newark, New Jersey
DURYEA, Peter - d. 17 September 1888 at Union-
dale; interment at Westbury
DURYEA, Sarah Jane - 51 y 3 m 16 d;
d. 30 March 1886 at Dix Hills; wife of
Egbert Duryea
DURYEA, Wright - d. 17 September 1889 at Glen
Cove; President Glen Cove Manufacturing
Company
DUSENBERRY, David Munson - 40 years;
d. 28 August 1884 at Huntington; interment
at Green-Wood, Brooklyn

DUSENBERRY, Edith C. - 12 y 2 m 2 d; d. 5 June
1886 at Huntington; daughter of Edward
Dusenberry

DUSENBERRY, Maude K. - 37 y 4 m 7 d; d. 2 February 1890 at New York City; widow of David
Dusenberry

DUVALL, Mr. - d. 8 September 1882; editor of
Riverhead News

DUVALL, Melissa * - 31 years; d. 5 May 1882 at
Huntington; wife of Floyd Duvall

DUVALL, Virginia M. * - 10 mos.; d. 14 May
1882 at Huntington; daughter of Floyd and
Melissa Duvall

DWYER, child - 5 years; d. 15 August 1879;
clothing caught fire; daughter of William
Dwyer

DWYER, Mary Low - 48 years; d. 13 December
1890 at Huntington; wife of William Dwyer

EARLE, Julius - d. 11 February 1882 at
Skaneateles Lake, New York

EATO, Mrs. Andrew * - d. 25 April 1890 at Glen
Cove

EATON, Mrs. - funeral "this week" at Patchogue; 16 February 1889 paper; sister of James
O. Terrell of Port Jefferson

EATON, Edward Henry - 20 yrs 4 mos; d. 8 December 1890 at Huntington

EATON, Mary - 62 yrs 5 mos; d. 9 June 1884 at
Mount Sinai

EBERLE, Edward A. - 14 yrs 6 mos; d. 17 October 1890 at Northport; interment at Comac

EBERLE, William James - 26 y 8 m 9 d;
d. 16 March 1890 at Northport; interment at
Comac

EBLEN, Thomas - 65 years; d. 6 December 1888
at Clarenceville; hit by railroad train
while crossing tracks in wagon

ECKERSON, Fannie A. - 49 years; d. 27 July
1890 at Huntington Harbor; wife of M. B.
Eckerson; raised flowers and plants in
extensive greenhouses; painter on porcelain;
had collection of rare china

ECKERSON, Fannie Bogert - d. 5 January 1886 at
Gainesville, Florida; interment at Hunting-
ton; daughter of M. Bogert and Fannie
Eckerson

ECKERSON, Kate Bogart - 26 y 3 m 25 d;
d. 25 September 1887 at Huntington; daughter
of M. B. Eckerson

EDDY, Herman - 20 years; drowned 28 June 1881
off Bridgeport, Conn.; body found by Capt.
T. B. Howell of Port Jefferson; son of J. H.
Eddy

EDEN, Catharine Elmore - 66 y 10 m 7 d;
d. 18 November 1890 at Huntington; wife of
William Eden; widow of Daniel Kingsley;
b. Smithtown; maiden name Bostwick

EDWARDS, Augustus - d. Middle Island; 15 November 1890 paper

EDWARDS, Bertha S. - 5 y 1 m 20 d; d. 26 December 1887 at Brooklyn

EDWARDS, Daniel - ca. 86 years; d. 17 March
1886 at Riverhead; former jailor at Suffolk
County Jail; native of Baiting Hollow

EDWARDS, Lewis A. - 68 years; d. 10 June 1879
at Orient; served in New York State Senate
1868-1869; b. Gardiner's Island 18 June 1811

EDWARDS, Sarah - 70 y 11 m 19 d; d. 6 February
1881 at Smithtown

EDWARDS, William J. - 2 yrs 22 days; d. 31
January 1888 at Brooklyn; son of Silas C.
Edwards

EGAN, Berry - d. 13 October 1886 at Evona, New
Jersey; son of Daniel and Emily B. Egan

EINHART, Mrs. - d. "a few days after" 24 October 1886; funeral at Long Island City;
mother of Matilda Einhart

EINHART, Matilda - funeral 24 October 1886 at
Long Island City

ELDER, Fred - funeral 28 November 1885 at New
York City; brother of Mrs. McCoskey Butts;
Babylon item

ELDRIDGE, children - two children of Henry
Eldridge died of scarlet fever; 13 February
1885 paper; Hempstead item

ELDRIDGE, Charles W. - 71 years; d. 10 January
1883 at Hartford, Conn.; formerly of Woodbury

ELDRIDGE, Ida C. * - 51 years; d. 16 June 1885
at Bay Shore; wife of William Eldridge

ELDRIDGE, William * - 50 years; d. 21 November 1882 at Islip; interment at Huntington

ELLIGER, George - 76 years; d. 22 February
1878 at Brooklyn; homeopathic physician in
Brooklyn and Philadelphia; treated many
Huntington people; native of Germany

ELLIOT, child - infant; interment 22 March
1889 at Westbury; son of Joseph Elliot

ELLIOTT, Elizabeth - 8 years; d. 1 January
1882 at Melville; daughter of James and
Fanny E. Elliott

ELLIOTT, Ethel - 6 years; d. 1 January 1882
at Melville; daughter of James and Fanny E.
Eliott

ELLIOTT, Fannie C. - 39 years; d. 9 January
1886 at Melville

ELLIOTT, James - d. 25 December 1887 at Hicks-
ille; fell dead at dinner table; funeral at
Plain Edge

ELLIOTT, William - 2 yrs 4 mos; d. 17 March
1885 at Huntington

ELLIS, David K. - 7 mos 17 days; d. 14 August
1886 at Vernon Valley; son of Thomas M. and
Sarah Ellis

ELLISON, James - 30 years; drowned 19 August
1887 at Bayville; upset row boat due to
epileptic fit

ELMENDORF, Sarah C. - 86 years; d. 5 December
1879 at Huntington

ELVERSON, Emma J. - 25 yrs 2 days; d. 18 September 1880 at Comac

EMERSON, H. F. - funeral 24 May 1886 at Glen
Cove

EMERSON, Martin - drowned 19 January 1883 off
Fisher's Island; ship collision

ENGEMAN, William A. - 44 years; d. 11 January
1884 at Brooklyn; proprietor of Brighton
Beach Race Course and Ocean Hotel at Coney
Island

ENGLEMAN, Adolph - 18 years; drowned 4 July
1884 at Woodside; resident of Sunnyside

ENGLISH, James E. - 77 years; d. 2 March 1890
at New Haven, Connecticut; former Governor
of Connecticut; War Democrat member of U. S.
House of Representatives during Civil War;
U. S. Senator from Connecticut 1875-1876

ERBEN, Henry - 84 years; d. 14 May 1884 at New
York City; builder of church organs

ERWOOD, Robert - d. 27 March 1878 at Babylon; found suffocated by gas in pit of gas house belonging to H. A. V. Post

ETZEL, Frank - 34 yrs 5 mos; d. 30 January 1890 at New York City; interment at Calvary, Queens County; brother of Jacob Etzel of Hicksville

EVANS, Thomas - 81 years 10 mos; d. 11 January 1882 at Huntington

FAGAN, Julia - 86 years; d. 8 October 1888 at Huntington

FAGAN, Peter - 83 y 8 m 12 d; d. 12 March 1884 at Huntington; worked 40 years at Crossman's Brickyards

FAGAN, William - 70 years; d. 13 March 1879 at Smithtown

FAGAN, William - 51 years; d. 12 January 1890 at New York City

FAIRCHILD, Mary E. - 32 years; d. 25 August 1883 at Cold Spring; interment at Newark, New Jersey

FAIT, Andrew - d. 13 June 1882 at Greenport

FANCHER, Nancy H. - 84 years; d. 31 May 1878 at Fairview, New Jersey; widow of Lysander Fancher; former resident of Huntington

FANNING, child - 6 years; d. 25 July 1890 at Glen Cove; son of John Fanning

FANNING, Lester - d. 1 December 1889 at Riverhead; former resident of Flanders

FARRAR, Benjamin - 82 years; d. 5 November 1886 at Northport

FARRINGTON, Frank - d. 1 September 1890; Glen Cove item; son of George Farrington

FAULKNER, Lester S. - d. 27 January 1890 at Canaseraga, N. Y.; funeral at Dansville, N. Y.; brevetted brigadier general in Union Army during Civil War

FAULKNER, Patrick - interment 10 April 1889 at Westbury; resident of Glen Cove

FAWCETT, Mrs. - d. 11 May 1889; funeral at New York City; mother of Leslie Fawcett; Hicksville item

FEEKS, Abijah S. - d. "one day last week"; 12 December 1884 paper; resident of New-bridge

FEEKS, Mrs. John D. - ca. 90 years; d. 7 February 1887 at Locust Valley; mother of Julius J. Feeks, Democratic politician

FELTHOUT, child - d. South Woodhaven; 18 February 1888 paper; diphtheria; child of John Felthout

FENN, Charles - 67 years; d. 24 December 1890 at East Meadow

FEORE, Thomas J. - 24 y 6 m 15 d; d. 16 January 1880 at Comac

FERRIS, Mrs. D. O. - d. 6 April 1883 at Bay Shore; wife of M. E. minister at Bay Shore

FERRIS Eleanor H. - d. 9 May 1887 at Brooklyn; wife of Rev. Daniel O. Ferris of South Second Street M. E. Church, Brooklyn

FERRY, Frank - d. Brooklyn; 19 May 1888 paper; music teacher; worked with Hicksville Brass Band

FIDELL, George - d. 12 May 1879 at Cow Bay; resident of Manhasset; killed by Edward Cook with an oar in fight over tresspass on oyster grounds

FIELD, Benjamin - 89 years; d. 9 February 1886 at Flushing; dropped dead at breakfast table

FIELD, Mary C. - ca. 80 years; d. 6 November 1881 at Greenport; killed in house fire

FIELDS, George - 82 y 4 m 12 d; d. 27 November 1884 at Dix Hills

FIELDS, Joel S. - funeral 27 March 1889 at South Comac

FIELDS, Luther - 75 years; d. 17 January 1890 at Middle Island; "found dead"; interment at Port Jefferson; woodchopper

FIELS, Frances Eliza - 71 y 2 m 18 d; d. 20 March 1889 at Huntington; widow of James Fiels

FIKE, infant - funeral 12 August 1888 at Farmingdale; child of H. Fike

FINN, Edward - 7 years; d. 26 August 1885 at West Neck

FINN, Henry - 82 years; d. 30 October 1883 at West Neck

FINN, James R. - 37 yrs 6 mos; d. 17 February 1886 at West Neck

FINNEGAN, John - drowned; body found on shore at Crescent Beach Grove [Glen Cove]; 12 February 1887 paper; resident of New York City

73

FINNEGAN, Mrs. John - d. November 1886; 12 February 1887 paper

FINNEGAN, Michael - 21 years; drowned 11 August 1888 in Northport Bay off Port Eaton; fell overboard from gravel schooner; interment at Huntington

FIRST, Henry C. - killed in oyster boat accident on the Chesapeake Bay; 16 November 1883 paper; resident of East Marion

FISCHER, Mr. - died in Queens County Jail; 2 June 1882 paper

FISHER, James - d. 23 April 1890 at Poughkeepsie, N. Y.; interment at Hauppauge

FISK, Clinton B. - d. 9 July 1890 at New York City; interment at Coldwater, Michigan; active M. E. layman; Union officer during Civil War; namesake of Fisk University, Nashville, Tennessee

FISK, Samuel - 85 years; d. 30 April 1882 at Crab Meadow

FITTING, child - d. 22 September 1887 at Westbury; interment at Hicksville; child of John Fitting

FITZGERALD, E. M. - d. 19 April 1884 at Long Island City; hit by railroad train; veterinary surgeon; resident of Greenpoint

FITZGERALD, William - 70 years; d. 26 December 1885 at Jamaica; fell getting off train and was run over; resident of Jamaica for 40 years

FLACHANS, John - drowned 10 August 1879 in a brook at Jamaica; saloon keeper and politician

FLANNIGAN, Thomas - 2 July 1880 paper; resident of New York City; "Seawanhaka" fire on East River

FLEET, children - d. 10 March 1890; interment at Crab Meadow; twin children of John Fleet

FLEET, Abram J. - 58 y 9 m 27 d; d. 30 January 1880 at Centreport

FLEET, Arnold - d. 7 February 1889 at Oyster Bay

FLEET, Mrs. Arnold - funeral 9 March 1886 at Oyster Bay

FLEET, Charles H. - 61 y 8 m 1 d; d. 7 May 1884 at Huntington; son of John and Phebe Fleet; dry goods merchant; native of Hunt-

74

FLEET, Charles H. (continued)
ington Harbor; at age 13 went to work for
Zophar Oakley; at 21 to John W. Smith of
Hempstead in drug business; then to T. K.
Hall of New York City in furniture business
and to J. S. Mott of Manhasset; returned to
Huntington in 1850 to open own business;
partner of Edward Conklin and Thomas Aitkin;
member of St. John's Episcopal Church,
Huntington
FLEET, David - 73 yrs 1 mos; d. 29 July 1878
at Long Swamp
FLEET, David C. - 42 years; d. 30 April 1885
at Long Swamp
FLEET, Frances - 62 years; d. 4 March 1884 at
Brooklyn; interment at Huntington; daughter
of Zebulon Fleet; former resident of
Huntington
FLEET, Laura A. - 30 y 2 m 3 d; d. 9 May 1890
at East Neck; interment at Crab Meadow; wife
of John P. Fleet; former resident of
Northport
FLEET, Mrs. Luke - d. 4 February 1885 at
Mineola; interment at Hempstead
FLEET, Mary Eliza - 13 y 5 m 5 d; d. 15 June
1883 at Huntington
FLEET, Richard L. - 10 mos 23 days;
d. 10 March 1890 at East Neck; son of
John P. and Laura A. Fleet
FLEET, Sarah - 87 years; d. 14 May 1878 at
Huntington; sister of Samuel Fleet; talented
writer
FLEET, Sarah P. - 78 y 1 m 4 d; d. 5 January
1887 at Long Swamp; widow of David Fleet;
sister of Caleb Hogan
FLEISCHMANN, Herman R. - 32 y 11 m 26 d;
suicide 4 October 1885 at Melville;
"newly wed"
FLEMING, Frederick - d. 9 February 1887 at
Locust Valley
FLEMMING, John - d. New York City; 7 January
1888 paper; suffocation from gas in hotel
room; interment at Mattituck; former resident of Riverhead
FLETCHER, Anderson - 79 years; d. 5 November
1884 at Northport

FLOOD, Robert F. - 23 years; d. 5 August 1888 at Greenlawn; jumped too soon off train; fell and was run over; Franciscan Brother known as "Brother Robert"

FLOYD, Benjamin - 96 years; d. 17 February 1887 at Old Field

FLOYD, John G. - 75 years; d. 6 October 1881 at Mastic

FLOYD, Miami - 85 years; d. 5 December 1880 at Smithtown; widow of John Woodhull Floyd

FLYNN, Mary Ann - 2 July 1880 paper; resident of New York City; "Seawanhaka" fire on East River

FLYNN, Timothy - 73 or 74 yrs; d. 16 March 1890 at Greenlawn or Northport; interment at Huntington; carpenter

FOLGER, [Charles J.] - 66 years; d. 11 September 1884 at Geneva, N. Y.; United States Secretary of the Treasury [under President Chester A. Arthur]

FOLKS, Huldah Emma * - d. 15 March 1890 at Smithtown; wife of James Folks, coachman for Mrs. J. Lawrence Smith; a "worthy colored lady"

FORAN, William G. - 39 y 11 m 19 d; d. 15 May 1889 at Long Swamp

FORCHER, George P. - 37 years; d. 28 July 1884 at Hicksville; resident of New York City

FORDHAM, Edward - drowned 22 November 1883 in Shinnecock Bay; resident of Southampton

FORDHAM, Lydia - 85 years; d. "last week" at Riverhead; 21 September 1889 paper

FORDHAM, Sarah - 70 y 3 m 15 d; d. 24 March 1883 at Westhampton; widow of Albert Fordham; interment at Speonk

FORDHAM, Thomas - d. Sag Harbor; 30 November 1883 paper; son of Sylvanus H. Fordham

FORGIE, infant - d. 26 July 1887; Hicksvile item; one twin child of George Forgie

FORKIN, Joseph - 15 yrs 11 mos; d. 19 November 1881 at Huntington; son of Michael and Bridget Forkin

FOSTER, Frank M. - 38 years; d. 4 June 1880 at New York City; interment at Setauket

FOSTER, Mrs. Nat W. - d. 15 October 1888; funeral at Riverhead

FOWLER, Hannah A. - d. 17 March 1886 at Paolo,
    Kansas; wife of P. P. Fowler; native of
    Huntington
FOWLER, Iantha Titus - 66 y 9 m 16 d;
    d. 6 September 1882 at Huntington
FOWLER, William - 67 yrs 1 mo; d. 9 February
    1881 at Southampton
FOX, Edward B. - 33 y 2 m 12 d; d. 20 May
    1889; funeral at Northport; son of John J.
    and Elizabeth Fox; brother of George Fox of
    Port Jefferson
FOX, Jessie - 5 yrs 5 mos; d. 13 February 1880
    at Northport; daughter of William Fox
FOX, John Jay - d. 29 May 1880 at Brooklyn;
    son of John J. Fox
FRANCIS, Ebenezer - 95 years; d. 7 August 1886
    at Cambridge, Massachusetts; father of Rev.
    Eben Francis, former Univeralist pastor in
    Huntington; grandfather of Mary F. Wood of
    Huntington
FRANCIS, John * - d. 1 December 1887 at East
    New York; fell from wagon and broke neck
FRANCIS, Lottie - 12 years; suicide 3 November
    1884 at Jamaica
FRANCIS, Rebecca - 54 years; d. 17 May 1880 at
    Centreport
FRANK, Edward - 6 mos; d. 26 July 1887 at
    Plainview; son of Robert Frank
FRANK, Julius - 2 July 1880 paper; resident of
    Whitestone; "Seawanhaka" fire on East River
FRANK, Robert - d. 27 December 1888 at Plain
    Edge; "brutally beaten by the Smiths last
    Spring"; interment at Hicksville
FRANKLIN, Dr. - funeral 12 March 1889 at Farm-
    ingdale; cremation at Mt. Olivet Crematory,
    Newtown
FRANKLIN, Hattie J. - d. 12 December 1887 at
    Oyster Bay; daughter of John Franklin
FRAZIER, Aaron * - 83 years; d. 13 April 1890
    at Huntington
FRAZIER, Abby Ann * - 56 years; d. 6 January
    1885 at Huntington
FRAZIER, Charity J. * - 70 y 3 m 3 d;
    d. 7 September 1885 at Huntington; wife of
    Aaron Frazier
FRAZIER, Charles T. * - 70 y 6 m 24 d;
    d. 3 November 1884 at Huntington

FRAZIER, Henry Jarvis * - 5 years; d. 24 December 1880 at Huntington

FRAZIER, James B. * - 26 yrs 3 mos; d. 7 June 1886 at Huntington

FRAZIER, Lauretta * - 26 yrs 7 mos; d. 6 June 1881 at Huntington

FREDERICKS, Louisa - ca. 9 years; d. 8 April 1884 at Breslau; burned in brush fire

FREDERICKS, Peter - 6 yrs 5 mos; d. 14 February 1887 at Jerusalem

FREMONT, John C. - 77 yrs 6 mos; d. 13 July 1890 in New York City; ["Pathfinder of the West"; Republican candidate for President 1856; Union general during Civil War]; biography in 19 July 1890 paper

FRENCH, Hannibal - d. 28 April 1889 at Sag Harbor; Sag Harbor postmaster

FREYTAG, Mrs.; d. Seaford; funeral 12 August 1887 at Plain Edge; sister of August Schaeffer

FROST, Gideon - 81 years; d. 25 February 1880 at Greenvale; interment at Matinnecock; Quaker who gave $500,000 endowment to Friends School at Matinnecock

FROST, Valentine - d. "suddenly last week" at Locust Valley; well-known farmer; 26 April 1890 paper

FRUEND, George E. - ca. 30 years; murdered 26 May 1884 at Dutch Kills by brother-in-law C. B. Waring

FRY, William T. - 71 yrs 6 mos; d. 21 September 1888 at Brooklyn; interment at Huntington

FUENFGELD, Mary Margarette - 2 mos 2 days; d. 7 August 1889 at Hicksville; daughter of Joseph Fuenfgeld

FULLER, Lawrence - d. 14 January 1884 at Jamaica; hit by railroad train; resident of Foster's Meadow

FULLER, William Henry - 62 y 2 m 28 d; d. 20 October 1886 at Huntington

FULTON, Vandevort B. - 14 yrs 11 mos; d. 12 September 1882 at Northport; son of William Fulton of Brooklyn

FUNFGELD, George - 56 years; d. 30 July 1887 at Hicksville

FURLONG, Jane S. - 9 months; d. 1 August 1885
at Comac; daughter of Francis J. and Eleanor
Furlong

GAINES, Laura A. - d. 21 March 1883 at Brooklyn; interment at Huntington; daughter of
Royal A. and Laura Gaines

GAINES, Laura W. - 57 years; d. 23 June
1883 at Brooklyn; widow of Royal A. Gaines

GAINES, Martha Robinson - 70 years; d. 2 March
1883 at Huntington; wife of Stephen W.
Gaines

GAINES, Samuel C. - 39 years; d. 15 August
1878 at Greenlawn; funeral at Huntington

GALE, Edward D. - d. 13 February 1882 at
Jamaica; Democratic politician in Queens
County

GALE, Samuel * - 34 years; d. 11 October 1878
at Oyster Bay

GALLOWAY, Charles - 6 months; d. 11 May 1890
at Jericho; interment at Hicksville; son of
William Galloway

GALLOWAY, William - 81 years; d. Walpole, New
Hampshire; interment 21 August 1887 at
Highland Mills, Orange County, N. Y.;
resident of Jericho

GALOW, George B. - 1 month; d. 18 March 1883
at Huntington; son of Fritz and Lena Galow

GALVIN, Catherine C. - 57 years; d. 5 August
1878 at Centreport

GANNON, William H. - 18 y 6 m 8 d;
d. 18 August 1880 at Huntington

GARDINER, Abbie A. - 51 y 8 m 7 d; d. 10 April
1883 at Cold Spring; wife of Warren Gardiner

GARDINER, Adeline - 77 years; d. 20 April 1884
at Northport

GARDINER, Almy - 78 y 2 m 27 d; d. 19 December
1886 at Cold Spring Harbor; widow of James
Gardiner

GARDINER, Emily C. -16 y 2 m 25 d; d. 8 May
1880 at Dix Hills

GARDINER, Fannie E. - 83 years; d. 28 March
1886 at Old Fields; widow of Joel B.
Gardiner

GARDINER, Jacob Brush * - 2 yrs 11 mos;
d. 20 December 1888 at Huntington;
diphtheria; son of John Gardiner

GARDINER, James - 79 yrs 15 days; d. 22 August
1883 at Cold Spring; native of Modestown,
Accomac County, Virginia; moved to West Neck
ca. 1828; oyster and clam business

GARDINER, John William * - 4 mos 1 day;
d. 4 March 1885 at Huntington; son of John
and Ann Gardiner

GARDINER, Margaret - 62 years; d. 2 August
1883 at Huntington

GARDINER, Maria M. - 72 y 11 m 5 d; d. 15 January 1883 at Vernon Valley; wife of Benjamin
Franklin Gardiner

GARDINER, Mary B. - 65 y 1 m 28 d; d. 21 May
1888 at Huntington; daughter of Augustin
Bryant; wife of George C. Gardiner; mother
of Mrs. Henry Brush

GARDINER, Mary E. - 28 y 8 m 11 d; d. 13 February 1878 at Centreport; wife of John H.
Gardiner

GARDINER, Mary Scudder - 59 y 10 m 8 d;
d. 13 November 1884 at Northport; wife of
William Gardiner

GARDINER, Mary V. - 67 y 10 m 10 d;
d. 21 March 1888 at Huntington; b. Long
Swamp; daughter of Josiah Smith; widow of
George Gardiner; mother of Joel S. Gardiner

GARFIELD, James A. - d. 19 September 1881 at
Long Branch, New Jersey; President of the
United States [1881]; [assassinated 2 July
1881 at Washington, D. C.]

GARRETSON, Garret R. - 74 years; d. 28 August
1887 at Flushing; famous seed grower

GARRITY, Mary - 65 years; d. 18 March 1886 at
West Hills

GARVEY, James - 42 yrs 6 mos; d. 11 July 1883
at West Neck

GARVEY, Johnnie - drowned 7 April 1889 at
Oyster Bay

GARVEY, Patrick - 52 years; d. 30 April 1883
at West Neck

GARVEY, Thomas - 49 years; d. 17 December 1878
at West Neck

GASKOIN, James - death recorded 17 April 1886
paper; resident of Brooklyn; former resident
of Manetto Hill; Hicksville item

GASSETT, child - 8 years; d. 11 August 1889;
Riverhead item; daughter of Harry Gassett

GASSNER, Conrad - 28 years; d. 16 March 1886
at Elmont; shot by mistake by his employer
John Kreischer who mistook Gassner for a
chicken thief
GASSNER, Mrs. George S. - d. 28 May 1888 at
St. Johnland
GATES, John Henry - 74 y 4 m 2 d; d. 4 May
1887 at Greenlawn
GATES, Martha S. - 8 m 23 d; d. 20 March 1885
at Greenlawn; daughter of Edward A. Gates
GEARTH, George - infant; d. 9 August 1887; son
of John Gearth
GENTRY, Abram M. - 63 years; d. 20 February
1883 at Huntington; interment in Texas;
native of Tennessee; Mexican War veteran
GEORGE, infant - d. 13 June 1878 at Huntington; child of Walter George
GEORGE, Augustus - 31 years; d. 28 June 1889;
hit by locomotive on Manhattan Beach Railroad while attending to switches; funeral at
Hicksville; husband of Mary Froechler;
nephew of Robert Purick of Hicksville
GEORGE, C. - ca. 80 years; found dead in woods
at Locust Valley; interment at Flatbush;
13 August 1880 paper
GEORGE, Walter K. - 4 mos 10 days; d. 10 January 1880 at Huntington; son of Walter George
GERARD, Alexander - d. 27 July 1883 at Setauket; fell off railroad bridge at Setauket
depot; resident of East Setauket
GERLACH, Willie - 11 years; drowned 2 June
1888 at Flushing; son of J. B. Gerlach
GERMAIN, Elisha - drowned 2 February 1880 off
Glen Cove; boat sunk in storm
GERMAIN, James - drowned 2 February 1880 off
Glen Cove; boat sunk in storm
GERMAINE, John - 66 years; d. 11 November 1887
at Glen Cove; engineer aboard "Henry Clay"
steamboat at the time of the infamous 1852
fire in Hudson River off Yonkers
GETTEY, Harry M. - ca. 25 years; found dead 24
January 1887 at Moriches; committed suicide
at his mother's grave
GIBSON, Elizabeth - 95 years; d. 27 December
1889 at Albany, N. Y.; widow of John Gibson;
mother of Isabella G. Barrows

GIESTLICH, Mrs. - murdered "last week" at
  Philadelphia, Pa.; 14 June 1878 paper;
  mother of Mrs. John Payne of Stony Brook
GIFFORD, William Lincoln - 6 weeks;
  d. 21 September 1884 at Oyster Bay
GILCHRIST, George - interment 30 December
  1885; Cold Spring item; "old resident" of
  Cold Spring
GILCHRIST, William E. - 32 years; d. 27 Dec-
  ember 1885 at Woodbury; interment at Brook-
  ville; native of East Norwich; nephew of
  William Velsor
GILDERSLEEVE, child - interment 12 November
  1888 at Comac; child of Sarah Gildersleeve
GILDERSLEEVE, Angeline - 57 y 5 m 13 d;
  d. 18 January 1889 at Long Swamp
GILDERSLEEVE, Ansel B. - 8 yrs 4 mos;
  d. 12 May 1887 at Huntington; son of Ansel
  B. and Sarah J. Gildersleeve
GILDERSLEEVE, Charles L. - 58 yrs 1 mo;
  d. 17 February 1879 at Vernon Valley
GILDERSLEEVE, Daniel - 86 years; d. 4 November
  1884 at Brooklyn; interment at Comac; "from
  excitement while in the act of voting";
  native of Comac
GILDERSLEEVE, Eliza - 77 y 3 m 5 d; d. at Long
  Swamp; 6 April 1883 paper
GILDERSLEEVE, Elizabeth H. - 78 yrs 5 mos;
  d. 13 June 1890 at Port Eaton; funeral at
  Northport; widow of Charles L. Gildersleeve
GILDERSLEEVE, George W. - 18 y 7 m 22 d;
  d. 15 May 1878 at Huntington
GILDERSLEEVE, James - 30 years; d. 21 Sept-
  ember 1887 at Brooklyn; interment at Comac;
  son of Smith and Elizabeth Gildersleeve;
  former resident of Woodbury
GILDERSLEEVE, Joel- 76 y 1 mo; d. 28 September
  1879 at East Northport
GILDERSLEEVE, Sarah A. - 81 yrs 3 mos;
  d. 18 April 1889 at Northport
GILDERSLEEVE, Sarah L. - d. 1 August 1880 at
  Brooklyn; interment at Comac; wife of Moses
  R. Gildersleeve
GILDERSLEEVE, Smith - 56 years; d. 14 May 1884
  at Woodbury; interment at Comac; son of
  David Gildersleeve; father of Mrs. Dewitt C.

GILDERSLEEVE, Smith (continued)
Barrett (by first wife); husband of Eliza-
beth Crum; b. Brooklyn 1827; Superintendant
of Brooklyn Gas Works; moved to Woodbury ca.
1866; Methodist
GILDERSLEEVE, Thomas W. - 75 y 2 m 5 d;
d. 25 March 1887 at Huntington; son of Jona-
than G. Gildersleeve; husband of Frances B.
Griffith for 53 years; father of Ansel B.
Gildersleeve and Mrs. Thomas Young;
Methodist
GILES, George W. - 28 years; d. 17 July 1885
at Brooklyn; funeral at Woodbury; native of
Woodbury
GILL, Annie - 19 y 7 m 6 d; d. 8 April 1888 at
Gold Coin City; interment at Westbury
GILL, Cornelius - 21 years; d. 7 April 1888;
Hicksville item; interment at Calvary Cem-
etery, Queens County
GILLETTE, Charles E. - d. at Sayville;
31 March 1888 paper
GILLIES, Grace Foster; d. 29 August 1890 at
Delhi, N. Y.; daughter of John Foster; wife
of P. M. Gillies, Editor of Delaware
Express; former resident of Huntington
GILLMORE, Q[uincy] A[dams] - d. "recently" at
Brooklyn; 5 May 1888 paper; interment at
West Point, N. Y.; Union general during
Civil War
GILMAN, John - 24 years; d. 28 July 1890 at
Westbury; died while on visit to brother
Robert Gilman of Westbury; resident of
New Jersey
GILROY, infant - d. 18 December 1878 at Brook-
lyn; child of James Gilroy of Long Swamp
GILROY, Jane - 1 yr 26 days; d. 19 December
1878 at Brooklyn
GLADDING, Franklin - badly decomposed body
found in Long Island Sound off Town of
Southold; resident of Providence, Rhode
Island; 14 July 1882 paper
GLANVILLE, Mrs. - d. "one day this week";
16 June 1888 paper; former resident of
Huntington
GLANVILLE, A. E. (Professor) - d. 14 December
1887 at Perth Amboy, N. J.; former resident
of Huntington

GLASSEY, William J. - 7 mos 19 days;
d. 27 June 1880 at Round Swamp; son of
Samuel and Margaret Glassey
GLOVER, Rev. Charles - d. 19 October 1883 at
Rye, N. Y.; brother of Rev. H. C. Glover;
former resident of Orient
GLOVER, Lydia A. - d. 27 June 1884 at Amity-
ville; wife of Rev. H. C. Glover
GLOVER, William - d. 18 June 1884 at Good
Ground; killed in scaffold collapse;
resident of Bellport
GLYNN, Bessie - 11 months; d. 16 August 1885
at Cold Spring
GOADER, Jane - suicide 23 April 1889 at
Brentwood; cut her throat with razor
GOLDEN, child - d. 23 January 1887 at Jamaica;
child of Daniel Golden; diphtheria; third
death in family within week
GOLDSMITH, Eliza F. - d. Newtown "recently";
17 September 1880 paper; wife of Rev. Dr.
Goldsmith, minister of Newtown Presbyterian
Church 1819-1854
GOOD, James - 27 years; d. 8 May 1878 at New
York City
GOOD, James E. - 76 years; d. 4 January 1889
at Greenlawn; found dead in bed
GOOD, John - d. 25 October 1888 at Woodbury;
"suddenly"
GOODE, Allen * - d. "last week" at Richmond,
Virginia; "a faithful old colored man" who
worked for Townsend Brothers of Oyster Bay;
died on visit to "his old home"; memorial
service at Oyster Bay [date of paper not
copied]
GORDON, infant - 2 days; d. at Lake Ronkon-
koma; 25 February 1888 paper
GORDON, John - d. 12 June 1878 at Sayville;
murdered by brother-in-law John Atkinson,
who was found to be insane
GORMAN, Thomas - interment "this week" at
Westbury; 25 January 1890 paper; resident of
Roslyn
GORRY, Maria E. - 40 years; death reported
12 July 1890 paper; Hempstead item; wife of
Christopher Gorry

GOTHARD, [Rev.] William - 75 years; d. 10 November 1883 at Brooklyn, E. D.; M. E. minister of New York East Conference; served in Queens and Suffolk Counties

GOTTKER, John A. - 68 years; d. 15 February 1880 at Brooklyn; interment at Dix Hills

GOTTKER, Julia - 38 yrs 6 mos; d. 2 December 1884 at New York City; interment at Comac; daughter of Samuel Soper

GOTTKER, Sarah - d. 23 April 1880 at New York City; interment at Dix Hills

GOUGH, John B. - d. [at Frankford, Pa.]; 5 March 1886 paper; temperance reformer

GOULD, Alexander - 49 years; d. 30 April 1885 at Birmingham, Conn.; interment at East Hampton

GOULD, Benjamin C. - 78 y 11 m 21 d; d. 20 October 1881 at Yaphank

GOULD, Edward - 71 years; d. 22 July 1878 at Smithtown

GOULD, Matilda W. - 71 y 9 m 5 d; d. 22 March 1885 at Jersey City, N. J.; interment at Huntington; wife of Ebenezer Gould

GOULD, Rebecca - 71 y 3 m 19 d; d. 9 April 1890 at Brooklyn; widow of David Gould

GOULD, Ruth - 98 y 10 m 14 d; d. 8 September 1884 at Huntington; daughter of David Sammis; widow of Conklin Gould

GOULD, S. N. - suicide by drowning at Bridgeport, Conn.; 30 July 1887 paper; Editor of Port Jefferson News Letter

GOULD, Sarah B. - 76 years; d. 7 June 1881 at Huntington

GOULD, William Reid - d. 30 December 1883; dealer in law blanks in New York City

GOUTHRIE, Theodore - 2 July 1880 paper; resident of New York City; "Seawanhaka" fire on East River

GRADY, Henry W. - d. 23 December 1889 at Atlanta, Georgia; Editor of the Atlanta Constitution

GRADY, Mrs. John - d. 28 September 1888 at Bayport; ate poison toadstools thinking they were wild mushrooms

GRAHAM, Michael J. - 68 years; flagman; hit by Union Elevated Railroad train at Brooklyn; 18 January 1890 paper

GRANT, General [Ulysses S.]- d. [at Mount Mc
   Gregor, N. Y.] 24 July 1885 paper; funeral
   8 August 1885 at Riverside Park, New York
   City, a legal public holiday; detailed
   account in 14 August 1885 paper
GRAY, Joseph - 57 years; funeral 24 March 1890
   at Glen Cove; Union veteran of Civil War;
   member Daniel L. Downing Post #365, G. A. R.
GRAY, Margaret * - 80 years; d. 15 November
   1887 at Jamaica
GRAY, Mary Edith - 2 July 1880 paper; resident
   of New York City; "Seawanhaka" fire on East
   River
GRAY, Samuel - 21 years; d. 8 December 1884 at
   Glen Cove; hunting accident; son of Joseph
   Gray
GREEN, Daniel * - 107 years; d. 27 February
   1882 at Yaphank; oldest ex-slave in Suffolk
   County; grandmother was an Indian; b. New-
   town 12 March 1775; survived by 90 year
   old wife
GREEN, George C. - 3 yrs 11 mos; d. 22 June
   1887 at Huntington; son of George Green
GREEN, Henry * - 93 years; d. 6 September 1888
   at Jericho; interment at Westbury
GREEN, John C. - funeral 9 June 1886 at Hunt-
   ington
GREEN, Julia - d. 10 May 1883 at Centre
   Island; interment at Cold Spring; daughter
   of Patrick Green
GREEN, Mary - 49 years; d. 18 October 1879 at
   West Neck
GREEN, Mrs. Patrick - d. 26 May 1890 at Centre
   Island; interment at Brookville
GREEN, William H. - 26 y 1m 8 d; d. 25 January
   1880 at Eaton's Neck; hunting accident
GRETSINGER, Eugene - 14 years; drowned 13 Feb-
   ruary 1887 at Garden City; choir boy at Gar-
   den City Cathedral; funeral at Garden City;
   resident of Brooklyn
GRIFFIN, Patrick - ca. 50 years; d. 1 September 1880 at Vernon Valley; found dead
GRIFFIN, Mrs. Patrick - d. 11 February 1885
   near Garden City; been drinking; died of
   exposure; froze to death

86

GRIFFIN, Thaddeus - d. "a year ago" at
Hempstead; 23 April 1887 paper; shot by
accident by Theus Taylor of Merrick in
shooting contest at Norwood; Taylor was to
shoot tin can off Griffin's head but missed;
Taylor acquitted of manslaughter after two
trials [see: Gritman, Thaddeus]
GRIFFING, Charey - 81 years; d. 8 December
1889 at New York City; interment at Mount
Sinai
GRIFFING, Charles Grant - d. at Shelter Is-
land; funeral 18 October 1887; shot himself
by accident while playing with gun
GRIFFING, Mrs. Cyrus - 69 years; d. 17 December 1888 at Port Jefferson
GRIFFING, Joseph - d. 5 April 1890; Woodbury
item; knocked out of wagon and run over;
brother of W. H. Griffing
GRIFFING, Lydia - funeral 3 July 1888 at
Riverhead
GRIFFING, Madison W. - 64 yrs 9 mos; d. 9 May
1878 at Huntington
GRIFFING, Maria S. - 59 yrs 11 mos; d. 11
August 1878 at Huntington; widow of Madison
W. Griffing
GRIFFING, Sidney L. - 82 years; d. 17 March
1889 at Bloomfield, N. J.; Riverhead item;
"one time a prominent and leading lawyer at
the Suffolk County bar"
GRIFFITH, Adeline - funeral 15 January 1888 at
Northport
GRIFFITH, Emma - 20 years; d. 7 April 1879 at
Vernon Valley
GRIFFITH, George - d. 26 April 1882 at City
Island; accident at David Carll's shipyard;
funeral at Port Jefferson; formerly of
Northport
GRIFFITH, Sarah - 70 years; d. 17 January 1884
at Middleville
GRIFFITHS, Sarah J. - 31 y 2 m 27 d;
d. 22 October 1878 at Vernon Valley
GRIGGS, Mrs. - funeral "this week"; interment
at Jamaica; 7 December 1889 paper; Northport
item
GRIMES, Ann - 83 years; d. 25 August 1889 at
Brookville; funeral at Hicksville; interment
at Westbury; widow of James Grimes

GRIMES, Thomas - death reported 2 January 1885
paper; Hicksville item
GRIMM, Frederick C. - d. at Morris Grove, Town
of Jamaica; 5 December 1881 paper
GRINDATT, William J. - ca. 26 years;
d. 11 October 1880 at Cold Spring
GRINSTED, Loretta - 38 y 11 m 17 d; d. 17 Aug-
ust 1881 at Huntington; wife of A. F. Grin-
sted of Orange, New Jersey
GRISWOLD, Frank W. - d. 27 December 1884;
resident of Riverhead
GRITMAN, Thaddeus - d. 22 April 1886 at
Hempstead; put whiskey bottle on head for
friend to shoot; friend missed and killed
Gritman; resident of Merrick [see: Griffin,
Thaddeus]
GRUNSPLANS, Michael - 60 years; suicide
2 February 1880 at Hicksville
GUITEAU, Charles J. - executed at Washington,
D. C.; 30 June 1882 paper; assassin of
President James A. Garfield
GUNDER, Mary - 75 years; d. at Brooklyn; 3
August 1883 paper; hit by railroad train
GUNTHER, Caspar - suicide 8 December 1888 at
South Glen Cove; hanged himself to nail
driven over doorway at his home
GURNEY, Marie Belle - 2 yrs 6 mos; d. 9 Nov-
ember 1881 at New York City; daughter of
Robert F. and Josephine F. Gurney
GURNEY, Mary Ella - 1 yr 9 mos; d. 18 April
1885 at Greenlawn; daughter of Robert F.
and Josephine Gurney
GURNEY, William - 57 years; d. 2 February 1879
at New York City; commander of 127 New York
Volunteers Civil War; father of Robert
Gurney of Greenlawn; b. Flushing 21 August
1821; long obit 7 February 1879 paper
GURNEY, William - 9 y 1 m 2 d; d. 9 February
1884 at Cold Spring Harbor; interment at
Rondout, N. Y.; son of John Gurney
GUTWEILER, Mr. - d. 27 January 1890 at New
York City; "prominent member of the Masonic
and Odd Fellows organizations"; father of
Rev. Gutweiler of Hicksville
GUTWEILER, Mrs. - d. New York City; 21 January
1888 paper; mother of Rev. E. Gutweiler of
Hicksville

GUTWEILER, Mary - d. 14 June 1889 at New York
City; sister of Rev. E. Gutweiler of Hicks-
sville
HACKETT, Alexander - d. 20 November 1890 at
Patchogue
HACKNEY, David A. - young man; d. 1 January
1888; Cold Spring Harbor item; died suddenly
while watering livestock; son of Robert W.
Hackney
HACKNEY, Robert W. - 66 years; d. 7 May 1888
at Cold Spring
HADDEN, John - drowned 15 July 1885 in Great
South Bay off Patchogue; resident of
Flushing
HADOCK, Henry - d. 30 July 1884 at Jericho
HAFF, Daniel - d. 26 February 1886 at South
Haven; b. Comac 1 April 1795; active Metho-
dist; long-time resident of Sayville; step-
father of John Wood; father-in-law of Rev.
T. M. Terry
HAFF, Gracie R. - 10 y 7 m 20 d; d. 18 Novem-
ber 1889 at Babylon
HAFF, Mattie - 5 years; death reported
24 April 1886 paper; Amityville item;
daughter of Silas Haff
HAFF, Smith - interment 12 March 1889 at
Hauppauge; former resident of Smithtown
HAFF, William - 73 years; d. 24 March 1886;
Amityville item
HAGGERTY, John - 64 years; d. 8 March 1881 at
Smithtown
HAGNER, Alexander - d. 7 April 1880 at Jamai-
ca; interment at Cypress Hills; Surrogate
of Queens County
HAHN, infant - 1 week; funeral 29 May 1889;
Hicksville item; child of John H. Hahn
HAHN, Henry - d. 20 August 1885 at Hicksville
HAINES, Miriam - 54 years; d. 5 February 1887
at Rockville Centre; had premonition that
she would die at 1:00 o'clock on that day
HALL, infant - d. 1 July 1878 at Setauket;
child of George Hall
HALL, Mrs. Colonel - d. 14 July 1883 at Glen
Cove
HALL, Edward S. - 40 years; d. 18 October 1889
at South Norwalk, Conn.; interment at Amherst,

89

HALL, Edward S. (continued)
Massachusetts; Principal of Huntington Union
School 1876-1884

HALL, John - 11 years; d. 3 April 1882 at
Northport; fell into a cistern; son of Seely
Hall

HALL, Lillian A. - 1 yr 2 mos; d. 21 October
1883 at Huntington; daughter of Henry Hall

HALL, Mrs. S. B. - d. 22 January 1888 at
Locust Valley

HALL, Scudder - 73 years; d. 23 December 1885
at Huntington; b. Cold Spring 1812; resident
of New York City ca. 1832-1857; in Huntington since 1857; father of George Hall,
William Hall, Emma Hall and Charles Hall

HALL, Susie C. - d. 28 December 1880 at New
York City; wife of William King Hall

HALL, Thomas J. - 77 y 3 m 17 d; d. 17 December 1883 at New York City; native of New
Hampshire; steamboat operator

HALLINAN, Jeremiah - 4 y 1 m 1 d; d. 21 February 1882 at Round Swamp

HALLINAN, Michael - 54 years; d. 28 May 1881
at Round Swamp

HALLOCK, Almira - ca. 72 years; d. 2 February
1880 at Northport; wife of James Hallock

HALLOCK, David Horace - d. 30 September 1887
at Southampton; son of M. W. Hallock

HALLOCK, Deborah - 75 y 11 m 5 d; d. 16 March
1878 at Northport; widow of Peter Hallock

HALLOCK, Electa A. - 74 y 1 m 2 d; d. 6 January 1879 at Miller's Place; widow of Philip
Hallock

HALLOCK, Elisha - d. 22 March 1882 at Franklinville; killed in accident loading hay
into barn

HALLOCK, Eliza - ca. 70 years; d. 24 January
1883 at Mount Sinai; widow of Richard
Hallock

HALLOCK, Elmira - 38 years; d. 30 January 1888
at New York City; resident of Rocky Point

HALLOCK, Elvin B. - drowned 26 October 1881
off Orient Point; schooner "P. M. Wheaton"
rammed and sunk near Gull Island

HALLOCK, Frances E. - 42 years; d. 29 July
1885 at Rocky Point; widow of James Hallock

HALLOCK, Mrs. George W. - d. 20 September 1888
   at Calverton
HALLOCK, Hannah - d. Blue Point; 9 November
   1883 paper; hit by railroad train
HALLOCK, Hannah W. - 67 yrs 5 mos; d. 25 May
   1879 at Jamaica
HALLOCK, Isaiah - 71 years; d. 11 February
   1882 at Riverhead; in wagon which was hit by
   railroad train
HALLOCK, J. F. -"old age"; d. 4 February 1887
   at Northville
HALLOCK, James - 81 yrs 9 mos; d. 4 May 1882
   at Smithtown Branch
HALLOCK, James - 79 y 6 m 2 d; d. 8 August
   1882 at Rocky Point
HALLOCK, Maria - 97 years; d. 7 September 1889
   at Atlanticville; fell down stairs; before
   accident had been very healthy and required
   a physician only once during her long life
HALLOCK, Mary - d. 24 December 1888 at Rocky
   Point; widow of James Hallock
HALLOCK, Minor - d. "last week" at Smithtown;
   25 September 1885 paper
HALLOCK, Victor - 40 years; d. 8 August 1887
   at Aquebogue; wagon accident
HALSEY, Mrs. - 94 years; d. "last week";
   Riverhead item; 8 January 1886 paper
HALSEY, Abraham - d. 3 May 1887 at Water Mill
HALSEY, Edward - 26 years; d. "recently" in
   Texas; Riverhead item; 2 November 1889
   paper; "was buying up horse stock in Texas"
HALSEY, Henry W. - d. 12 April 1887 at River-
   head
HALSEY, Sophia - d. 15 March 1886 at Bridge-
   hampton; clothes caught fire; widow of
   Oliver Halsey
HALSEY, Stephen L. - 65 yrs 14 days;
   d. 28 February 1890 at Smithtown; interment
   at Smithtown Landing; Superintendent of
   Smithtown Branch M. E. Sunday School
HALSEY, W. - drowned 10 August 1889 at Southampton
HALSEY, William R. - 8 y 11 m 17 d; d. 2 June
   1878 at Old Fields
HAMES, Henry * - 45 years; drowned 1 September
   1889 at Bridgehampton gathering water lilies
   on Long Pond

HAMILTON, Jessie E. - 46 y 10 m 16 d;
d. 18 June 1884 at Huntington; daughter of
Henry Funnell; widow of Viola Hamilton

HAMILTON, Robert Ray - drowned 24 August 1890
in Snake River, Yellowstone Park, Wyoming;
owned ranch in Bingham County, Idaho; involved in notorious divorce from Eva Hamilton

HAMILTON, William - 73 yrs 11 mos; suicide
16 March 1890 at Northport; shot himself in
the head; "an old sea captain"

HAMMOND, Emmett * - 22 years; d. 11 February
1889 at Setauket Bay; fell from rigging of
schooner "Louise"; resident of Huntington

HAMMOND, Frank E. - d. 23 July 1890 at Haverstraw, N. Y.; hit by railroad train; resident of Mount Sinai; interment at Mount
Sinai

HAMPTON, Zacheus - 83 years; d. 24 February
1888 at Smithtown Branch

HANCE, Joseph L. - 83 years; d. 10 March 1885
at Shelter Island; interment at Rumson, NJ

HANCOCK, General Winfield Scott - [d. 9 February 1886 at Governor's Island, N. Y.];
"flags at half mast" 10 February 1886;
editorial 19 February 1886 paper; Union
general in Civil War; Democratic candidate
for President 1880

HAND, Charles E. - ca. 88 years; death
reported 1 January 1887 paper; resident of
Amagansett; veteran of Mexican War; b. 1798

HAND, John - drowned 3 May 1878 off Crane Neck
Point when boat on way to City Island
capsized; resident of East Setauket

HANKINS, Carrie Tenbroeck - 29 y 9 m 21 d;
d. 21 January 1882 at Hempstead; interment
at Huntington; wife of Samuel M. Hankins

HANNAN, Sarah - d. 10 June 1890 at New York
City; interment at Green-Wood, Brooklyn;
mother of Mrs. Alec Taylor of Westbury

HANSELL, S. F. - d. 5 October 1890 at Philadelphia, Pa.; Philadelphia businessman;
summer resident of Huntington; father of
Mrs. Albert W. Palmer and Mrs. James B.
Dill

HANSEN, Capt. G. T. - drowned 3 February 1880
off Eaton's Neck; ship sunk

HARDING, George W. - ca. 25 years; d. 7 June
1882 at Patchogue; son of Rev. George R.
Harding

HARDWICK, Elizabeth A. - 60 y 8 m 14 d;
d. 16 November 1889 at Huntington

HARDWICKE, James H. - 65 years; d. 11 October
1885 at Huntington Harbor; found dead in
bedroom; interment at Cypress Hills

HARIGAN, Michael - d. 7 October 1889; former
resident of Hicksville

HARKINGS, Caroline J. - 42 years; d. 10 December 1885 at New York City

HARMAN, Elizabeth E. - 24 yrs 5 mos;
d. 18 December 1878 at Huntington

HARMON, Katie - 4 months; d. 29 August 1887 at
West Hills

HARNED, Amos - 84 y 7 m 23 d; d. 28 April 1880
at Comac

HARNED, Andrew J. - 54 yrs 4 mos; d. 24 April
1881 at West Hills

HARNED, Eunice - 84 years; d. 1 February 1881
at Huntington

HARNED, Joel - 88 years; d. 17 May 1879 at
West Hills

HARNED, Marietta - 51 y 7 m 14 d; d. 13 January 1882 at Smithtown; wife of J. B. Harned

HARNED, Minnie - 19 yrs 4 days; d. 19 March
1884 at Comac; daughter of Jacob and Francina Harned

HARNED, Ralph C. - 19 y 7 m 17 d; d. 24 May
1886 at Comac; son of Jacob and Francina
Harned

HARNED, Susan E. - 35 y 10 16 d; d. 28 May
1889 at West Hills; wife of Edward Harned

HARRIGAN, Edward - 53 years; drowned 22 September 1882 off Lloyd's Neck; interment at
West Neck

HARRINGTON, Christopher - 81 years;
d. 24 October 1886 at Comac

HARRIS, Maria - 76 years; d. 7 January 1881 at
Huntington

HARRIS, Mary Youngs - 5 mos 21 days;
d. 28 July 1879 at Huntington; daughter of
William and Jennie Youngs Harris

HARRIS, William - 15 years; drowned 25 August
1883 in Jamaica Bay, near Canarsie; son of
Robert Harris of Brooklyn, E. D.

HARRIS, Rev. William Logan - 69 years; death
reported 10 September 1887 paper; [d. at
Brooklyn]; funeral at New York City; inter-
ment at Woodlawn Cemetery, New York City;
native of Ohio; Bishop of M. E. Church
HARRISON, Hannah Hewlett - 86 years;
d. 14 October 1884 at Cold Spring Harbor;
daughter of Divine and Anne Hewlett; widow
of Thomas Harrison
HART, Emma - infant; interment 9 August 1887
at Brookville; daughter of John Hart of
Jericho
HART, John - 21 years; d. 2 September 1883 at
Springfield; railroad accident
HARTFORD, Henry - d. 13 August 1886; killed in
LIRR accident; breakman on train
HARTMAN, A. - funeral 15 October 1886 at
Hicksville
HARTOUGH, John H. - 36 yrs 18 days; d. 26 Oct-
ober 1883 at Huntington Harbor
HARTT, Adam Arden - 76 yrs 1 mo; d. 2 March
1883 at Huntington
HARTT, Alanson - d. "last week"; 25 September
1886 paper; resident of Jericho
HARTT, Celsus M. - 21 y 3 m 12 d; d. 3 March
1885 at Brooklyn; funeral at Northport; son
of Joseph B. and Phebe Hartt
HARTT, Clarence N. - 9 mos 2 days; d. 19 Dec-
ember 1889 at Northport; son of Henry W. and
Ada W. Hartt
HARTT, Clark - d. 23 June 1878 at Rio de Jan-
eiro, Brazil; officer in U. S. Navy; former
resident of Huntington
HARTT, Ezra - 82 years; d. 6 April 1886 at
Port Jefferson
HARTT, Fanny - 8 years; d. 2 September 1884 at
Northport
HARTT, Hannah - 49 y 11 m 6 d; d. 28 April
1888 at Huntington
HARTT, Hannah A. - 55 years; d. 13 September
1879 at Northport; wife of Erastus Hartt
HARTT, Henry Clay - d. 7 July 1882 at Phila-
delphia, Pa.; funeral at Northport; son of
Joel Hartt
HARTT, James F. - 82 yrs 3 mos; d. 23 August
1879 at Northport

HARTT, Jennie - 5 y 7 m 4 d; d. 23 August 1884
at Northport; daughter of David G. and
Armenia Hartt
HARTT, Capt. Joel - 55 y 10 m 17 d; d. 16 July
1882 at Northport
HARTT, John - death reported in Kansas; Long
Swamp item; 2 April 1887 paper; m. Abigail
Smith; son-in-law of James Smith
HARTT, Samuel P. - 75 years; d. 4 February
1879 at Northport
HARTT, Samuel S. - 13 yrs 3 days; d. 21 June
1881 at Northport; son of J. Fordyce Hartt
HARTT, Sarah * - 73 years; d. 22 April 1890
at Oyster Bay; interment at Pine Hollow;
"large congregation of white and colored
people" at funeral; "she was held in high
esteem"; long-time employee of Townsend
Underhill family
HARTT, Sophia E. - 62 yrs 4 mos; d. 13 Novem-
ber 1881 at Crab Meadow; wife of Charles S.
Hartt
HARTWIG, Charles - ca. 60 years; found dead
23 January 1880 at Hicksville; dead several
days when found in house
HARWARD, George C. - murdered 28 August 1880
at Brooklyn
HASBROOK, Charles - 2 July 1880 paper;
resident of Sag Harbor; "Seawanhaka" fire
on East River
HASBROOK, Josiah - 2 July 1880 paper; resident
of Sag Harbor; "Seawanhaka" fire on East
River
HASKELL, J. C. - drowned 19 January 1883 off
Fisher's Island; ship collision; resident of
East Boston, Massachusetts
HASTINGS, Hugh J. - d. 12 September 1883;
thrown from carriage "some days ago" at Long
Branch, New Jersey; Editor of Commercial
Advertiser
HATFIELD, Patrick - 68 years; d. 31 May 1890
at Hoboken, N. J.; resident of Hicksville
1859-1870
HATFIELD, Thomas - 82 years; d. 22 November
1887 at Hicksville
HATHAWAY, Philip B. - d. 23 September 1889 at
New York City; "well known criminal lawyer"

HATTEL, child - 17 months; funeral 18 May 1890
at Riverhead; daughter of Carl Hattel

HAUPTMAN, Fritz - d. 31 January 1889 at
Hinsdale; found dead in bed

HAUSER, Conrad - 49 years; d. 25 July 1879 at
Bayport; hit in head with a stone during a
fight

HAUSER, Margaretta - 42 years; d. 1 November
1889 at Hicksville; wife of August Hauser

HAUSER, Thaddeus V. - 6 months; d. 4 December
1882 at Melville; son of Thaddeus and Louisa
Hauser

HAVENS, Stratton M. - death reported 1 January
1887 paper; resident of Shelter Island

HAWK, Mary Jane - 57 years; d. 11 March 1886
at Northport

HAWKINS, child - 7 years; drowned 13 June 1878
at Islip; son of J. C. Hawkins; fell overboard

HAWKINS, Mrs. - d. 7 November 1890 at Patchogue

HAWKINS, Cecilia - 48 years; d. 13 March 1890
at Port Jefferson; sister of Mrs. C. H.
Davis; resident of Mount Sinai

HAWKINS, Chauncey - 2 July 1880 paper; resident of Brooklyn; "Seawanhaka" fire on East
River

HAWKINS, Cynthia - 49 years; murdered 1 October 1887 at Islip by son Francis Asbury
Hawkins; widow of Franklin Hawkins; long
account of son's criminal trial in 10
December 1887 paper

HAWKINS, Ebenezer - suicide 31 March 1880 at
South Setauket

HAWKINS, F. Asbury - executed by hanging
11 December 1888 at Riverhead for murder of
mother; first execution in Suffolk County
since 1854; interment at Islip

HAWKINS, Gilbert - 14 y 2 m 21 d; drowned
7 July 1883 at Northport; son of Gilbert
Hawkins

HAWKINS, Hannah A. - 35 yrs 6 mos; d. 20 October 1879 at Fresh Pond; wife of Gilbert
Hawkins

HAWKINS, Matildia - 80 yrs 9 mos; d. 12 September 1882 at Mount Sinai

HAWKINS, Nathaniel T. - 69 y 3 m 10 d;
d. 30 August 1882 at Newburgh, New York;
former resident of Mount Sinai
HAWKINS, Octavius Henry * - 4 mos 16 days;
d. 22 July 1885 at Huntington
HAWKINS, Mrs. Sylvester - d. 20 February 1890
at Port Jefferson
HAWKINS, Thomas - drowned in Long Island Sound
from sinking of schooner "Mary Hamilton";
4 January 1884 paper; resident of Stony
Brook
HAWKINS, William - 94 years; d. "last week" at
Stony Brook; 20 December 1878 paper
HAWKINS, William - 66 years; d. 28 April 1884
at Lake Grove
HAWLEY, Edward M. - d. 4 December 1878 at
Brooklyn; infant son of Oscar F. and Sarah
C. Hawley
HAWLEY, Sarah C. - d. 6 December 1878 at
Brooklyn; wife of Oscar F. Hawley, Jr.;
interment at Miller's Place
HAWTHORNE, Robert H. - 83 years; d. 8 November
1889 at Ridgewood, New Jersey
HAWXHURST, Abram - d. 26 April 1886 at Oyster
Bay
HAWXHURST, Allen - 82 years; d. 23 April 1879
at Oyster Bay
HAWXHURST, George - 2 yrs 8 mos; d. 2 March
1880 at Oyster Bay; son of John Hawxhurst
HAWXHURST, Mary - 15 years; funeral "this
week"; Oyster Bay item; 25 February 1888
paper
HAYDEN, Joel B. - d. Reading, Pennsylvania;
14 May 1887 paper; former resident of
Hempstead
HAYES, Lucy Webb - 56 years; d. 25 June 1889
at Fremont, Ohio; [First Lady of the United
States 1877-1881]; wife of ex-President
Rutherford B. Hayes
HAYNES, child - death reported; Oyster Bay
item; 15 February 1890 paper; child of
Nathaniel Haynes
HAYS, Catherine - 39 y 9 m 2 d; d. 14 May 1888
at Huntington
HAYS, George - 16 years; d. 22 July 1880 at
East Setauket; mistaken for an animal and
shot

HAZELDINE, Edith Ann - 9 years; drowned
14 July 1887 at Sunk Meadow Creek, St. Johnland; daughter of Ella Frances Hazeldine
HAZELDINE, Ella Frances - 28 years; drowned
14 July 1887 at Sunk Meadow Creek, St. Johnland; daughter of Laura Skidmore
HAZZARD, Mary E. - 32 years; d. 3 March 1885
at Brooklyn; wife of Charles Hazzard
HEARTT, Platt - 76 years; d. 14 December 1885
at Babylon
HEASLEY, Arthur - 15 years; drowned 18 May
1890 in Long Island Sound, off Dosoris when
boat upset; body recovered 6 June 1890;
funeral at Glen Cove; interment at Locust
Valley; son of James Heasley
HEATH, Mrs. - d. 1 March 1886; Hicksville item
HEBERER, Elizabeth - 54 y 10 m 16 d; d. 13 May
1887 at Hicksville
HEDGES, Edwin - d. 8 May 1881 at New York
City; son of Judge Hedges
HEGEMAN, Catherine - funeral 2 March 1889 at
Greenvale; widow of James Hegeman; mother of
Edward Hegeman
HEGEMAN, Clinton B. - disappeared 12 December
1885; body later found; either suicide or
murder; interment 14 May 1886 at Glen Cove;
resident of Greenvale
HEGEMAN, Everett - suicide 7 October 1888 at
Brookville; shot himself in the head; son of
William Hegeman; grandson of Daniel Hegeman
HEGEMAN, Rem - 70 years; d. 16 February 1888
at Melville
HEICHER, Martin - d. 2 December 1884; hit by
railroad train near Garden City; resident of
Hempstead; formerly of Hicksville
HEIDINGSFELDER, Mr. - d. 29 March 1889 at
Breslau; found dead in the road; husband of
Margarette Heidingsfelder
HEIL, John - 55 years; d. 21 August 1887 at
Hollis; hit by railroad train
HEISCHMAN, Mrs. - d. 7 May 1889; Hicksville
item; interment at Brooklyn; mother of Mrs.
Grandilenard
HELGANZ, Henry - suicide 2 November 1884 at
New Lots
HELISH, John - 18 years; drowned 7 August 1881
off Islip in Great South Bay

HELMS, child - infant; d. 15 March 1889 at
Woodbury; son of Charles A. Helms
HELMS, Royal P. - 7 mos 24 days; d. 4 October
1881 at Woodbury; son of Charles A. and
Elizabeth Helms
HEMPSTEAD, Clement - d. 26 August 1888 at
Riverhead
HENDERSON, Mrs. - funeral 22 November 1884 at
Velsor Graveyard, Woodbury [perhaps this is
Cornelia Velsor who m. 1832 Joseph Hender-
son]
HENDERSON, Katie V. - 6 yrs 14 days;
d. 25 November 1878 at Huntington; daughter
of Charles Henderson
HENDRICKS, [Thomas A.] - d. 25 November 1885
at Indianapolis, Indiana; Vice President of
the United States; [U. S. Senator from Indi-
ana 1863-1869; Governor of Indiana 1873-
1877; elected U. S. Vice President under
Grover Cleveland in 1884]
HENDRICKSON, infant - d. 8 December 1880 at
Northport; child of Daniel Hendrickson
HENDRICKSON, child * - funeral 15 March 1885;
child of James Hendrickson of Winfield
HENDRICKSON, Abigail Chichester - 62 years;
d. 27 July 1879 at Hinsdale; daughter of Asa
Chichester of West Hills; wife of George W.
Hendrickson
HENDRICKSON, Catherine - d. 10 August 1883;
found dead in bed; sister of John C. Hen-
drickson of Queens
HENDRICKSON, Charles - d. 5 September 1885 at
Brooklyn; former resident of Woodbury; blind
HENDRICKSON, Chester A. - 1 mo 19 days;
d. 24 January 1890 at Huntington
HENDRICKSON, Daniel D. - d. 6 December 1884 at
Queens
HENDRICKSON, Mrs. Edward - funeral 15 February
1888 at Oyster Bay
HENDRICKSON, Emma - 35 years; d. 23 May 1882
at Yaphank; interment at Northport; daughter
of Samuel Costello; wife of David Hendrickson
HENDRICKSON, George - 12 y 10 m 4 d;
d. 25 November 1887 at Mexico, N. Y.; fell
off fence while balancing on top; interment

99

HENDRICKSON, George (continued)
at Huntington; son of A. W. Hendrickson,
formerly of Huntington

HENDRICKSON, George W. - 67 years; d. 17 August 1879 at Jamaica; fell down stairs;
brother-in-law of Mrs. George A. Scudder

HENDRICKSON, Irene Thompson - d. 11 January
1889 at Jamaica; interment at Westbury;
daughter of Edward and Hannah Tompkins;
wife of Stephen Hendrickson

HENDRICKSON, Mrs. J. A. - 48 years;
d. 28 March 1885 at Mexico, N. Y.; interment
at Huntington

HENDRICKSON, Jason - 70 years; d. 11 July 1890
at Hempstead

HENDRICKSON, John - 56 years; suicide 14 September 1878 at Babylon; shot at wife and
neighbor girl, then killed himself

HENDRICKSON, Julie - 4 yrs 6 mos; d. 29 April
1882 at Mt. Pleasant, Westchester Co.;
daughter of Elbert Hendrickson; interment at
Huntington

HENDRICKSON, Mary E. - 40 y 4 m 14 d;
d. 16 February 1878 at Huntington; wife of
Coles Hendrickson

HENDRICKSON, Mary L. * - 2 y 11 m 12 d;
d. 17 May 1886 at Centreport

HENDRICKSON, Phebe Ann - 71 years; d. 2 March
1878 at Old Westbury; daughter of Isaac
Whitson of West Hills; wife of A. A. Hendrickson

HENDRICKSON, Samuel * - d. "recently" at South
Jamaica; 28 March 1884 paper

HENDRICKSON, Samuel J. - d. 8 November 1890;
Farmingdale item

HENDRICKSON, Sarah C. -"elderly lady";
d. 25 May 1887 at Hempstead; fell into a
well; mother of Mrs. William F. Conklin

HENGLE, Anna - 44 years; d. 14 November 1889
at Central Park; wife of W. F. Hengle

HENNESSY, Thomas - 78 years; d. 28 July 1890
at Brooklyn

HENNESY, Mrs. - d. "this week" at New York
City; 21 June 1890 paper; mother of Charles
Hennesy of Centerport

HENRY, Hannah E. - 25 y 9 m 6 d; d. 14 July
    1881 at Brooklyn; kerosene explosion; inter-
    ment at Cold Spring; daughter of Benjamin
    Doty
HENRY, Maria Matthews - 52 years; d. 10 July
    1887 at Northport
HENRY, Patrick - d. 27 January 1880 at Hicks-
    ville; died from result of fight
HENSLEY, child - death reported; Oyster Bay
    item; 14 August 1885 paper; son of James
    Hensley
HENTZ, John - d. 1 March 1890 at Hempstead;
    established Queens County Sentinel ca. 1855;
    ran hotel for many years; brother of Mrs.
    Robert Seabury and Mrs. A. J. Spooner
HERBAGE, Mary - 74 yrs 10 mos; d. 5 January
    1890 at Hicksville; interment at Utica, NY;
    mother of Elijah Herbage and Henry Herbage
HERBERT, Mrs. - 81 years; d. 19 November 1884
    at Hicksville; widow
HERBERT, C. H. - d. 16 September 1882 at
    Hicksville; hit by railroad train; resident
    of Jericho
HERFORT, Catherine - 33 yrs 2 mos; d. 18 Janu-
    ary 1887 at Hicksville; daughter of Andrew
    Sevin; wife of Andrew Herfort
HERMON, child - 11 months; d. 6 July 1887;
    interment at Hicksville; son of Henry Hermon
    of Westbury
HERRMANCE, Daniel - 50 years; d. 11 October
    1887 at Chicago, Illinois; former ticket
    taker at LIRR depot in Hempstead
HERZOG, child - 4 mos 19 days; interment
    19 January 1890 at Hicksville; daughter of
    Fred Herzog
HERZOG, Mrs. F. - 65 years; d. 4 March 1885 at
    Hicksville
HERZOG, Freddie - 2 y 5 m 23 d; d. 14 January
    1890 at Brooklyn; interment at Hicksville;
    son of Fred Herzog
HERZOG, Mrs. Henry - ca. 60 years; d. 22 Sept-
    ember 1880 at Lower Melville
HESTER, Henry - d. 9 February 1885; resident
    of Astoria

HEWEY, Betsey - ca. 80 years; funeral "last
week" at Glen Cove; 22 March 1890 paper;
"well and favorably known throughout the
community"

HEWLETT, Alfred J.- 84 years; d. 5 August 1889
at Yaphank; interment at Cold Spring; many
years insane; former resident of Cold Spring

HEWLETT, Elizabeth - 84 years; d. 17 March
1890 at Hempstead; "very eccentric character"; "lived for the past fifty years in an
old hut" "always wore an old faded green
dress and carried an old umbrella"; many
years ago "she was a village belle"

HEWLETT, Hester A. - d. 11 July 1890 at Washington Square, Hempstead; cancer; recently
had operation in Brooklyn for its removal
but operation was unsuccessful; wife of
Oliver Hewlett

HEWLETT, Jacob C. - 79 y 3 m 5 d; d. 28 December 1879 at Cold Spring

HEWLETT, Maria Hartsfield - 36 years;
d. 14 January 1885 at Wilmington, North
Carolina

HEWLETT, Julia - 77 years; d. 17 July 1886 at
Woodbury; daughter of John V. Hewlett

HEWLETT, Margaret - 80 years; funeral 1 February 1889 at Oyster Bay; widow of C. Hewlett

HEWLETT, Mary - 97 years; d. 3 January 1887 at
Roslyn; interment at Woodsburgh; widow of
George Hewlett; long time resident of East
Rockaway

HEWLETT, William H. - d. 27 June 1887 at
Brooklyn; interment at Hempstead

HICKS, Benjamin - 94 years; d. at Manhasset
Valley; 28 December 1883 paper

HICKS, Elizabeth T. - 86 years; d. 21 December
1889 at Westbury; mother of Benjamin D.
Hicks; "well known and wealthy Quaker lady";
"active interest in charitable and philan-
thropic undertakings"

HICKS, Mrs. James - death reported 8 January
1886 paper; Hicksville item

HICKS, Mary - 50 years; interment 30 May 1889
at Westbury; daughter of Joshua Titus; wife
of Jacob Hicks

HICKS, Theodora - infant; d. 6 March 1888 at
Woodbury; interment at Jericho; daughter of
Theodore and Rachel Hicks

HICKS, Thomas * - d. 6 February 1889 at Binghamton, N. Y.; interment at Islip; died in
Chronic Insane Asylum

HIGBEE, Harriet - 75 yrs 7 mos; d. 22 August
1888 at Centreport; mother of Roger Higbee

HIGBEE, Richard - 63 years; d. 3 March 1888 at
Babylon

HIGBIE, Edna - 85 yrs 8 mos; d. 16 April 1883
at East Northport; widow of Richard S.
Higbie

HIGBIE, Maria/Marion - 91 years; d. 22 December 1884 at Northport; widow of Jonas Higbie

HIGBIE, Prudence - 85 years; d. 25 August 1890
at West Islip; mother of Benjamin S. Higbie;
grandmother of Babylon Town Supervisor Richard Higbie

HIGBIE, William A. - 11 mos 12 days;
d. 8 February 1885 at Huntington; son of
Altimont S. and Nettie A. Higbie

HIGGINS, Charles - 79 years; d. 30 August 1889
at Yatesville, Conn.; interment at Walling-
ford, Connecticut; former resident of Huntington; father of A. S. Higgins

HILDEBRAND, Leopold - d. 26 August 1884 at
Glen Dale; hit by railroad train

HILDRETH, Capt. - 42 years; drowned 16 September 1883 in Atlantic Ocean; washed overboard from schooner "Gracie N." during storm
while sailing north from Georgetown, South
Carolina; wife is resident of Good Ground

HILDRETH, Susan J. - 34 yrs 6 mos; d. 14 February 1881 at Water Mill; daughter of Nathan
Hildreth

HILL, George - 67 years; d. 6 February 1888 at
Riverhead; son of Phineas and Sarah Hill;
native of Huntington; local M. E. preacher

HILL, John - drowned 12 March 1888 in Huntington Bay; tried to get ashore from barge
during Blizzard of 1888; 31 March 1888 paper
has account of finding body on Eaton's Neck

HILL, Walter B. - 78 y 6 m 5 d; d. 15 July
1890 at West Hills ; involved in aboltionist
movement before Civil War; active in Republican Party and West Hills M. E. Church

HINDS, Charles T. - 54 years; d. 11 June 1890
  at Elwood
HINES, child - 3 years; d. 19 August 1888 at
  Jericho; child of Michael Hines
HINES, Eugene - ca. 28 years; suicide 18 May
  1885 at Setauket; hung himself in a tree
HINES, Mrs. Michael - 89 years; d. 30 November
  1888 at Jericho; interment at Westbury
HOAGLAND, Catherine - 84 years; d. 26 November
1880 at Brookville
HOBAN, Mary - 85 years; d. 16 September 1881
  at Huntington; widow of Richard Hoban
HOBAN, Patrick - 65 years; d. 17 May 1882 at
  Huntington
HOBERG, Johanna - 37 years; suicide 11 May
  1886 at Manor; took rat poison
HODGETT, child - interment 7 January 1888 at
  West Hills; body brought from Michigan for
  burial; grand-daughter of Henry Beare
HODGETTS, Charles W. - 6 months; d. 12 August
  1881 at Woodbury
HODGETTS, Stephen F. - funeral 7 March 1886 at
  West Hills; resident of Detroit, Michigan
HODINGER, Barbara - 74 years; d. 7 April 1884
  at Breslau
HOE, James C. - 67 years; d. 12 September 1880
  at East Moriches
HOECH, child - 11 months; d. 4 July 1887;
  Hicksville item; son of Mr. Hoech
HOEL, Edward - 35 years; d. 27 July 1878 at
  Farmingdale
HOFFMAN, Ernest - d. "about 8 months ago";
  Hicksville item; 18 June 1887 paper
HOFFMAN, Frank - 70 years; d. 17 February 1884
  at Hicksville
HOFFMAN, Jacob - d. 15 March 1886 at Brooklyn;
  former resident of Hicksville
HOGAN, young girl - d. 21 January 1888 at Bath
  Beach; accidentally shot by brother
HOGAN, Belle - 6 y 10 m 30 d; d. 20 January
  1888 at Greenlawn; daughter of William and
  Edith Hogan
HOGAN, Bessie - 4 mos 20 days; d. 17 July 1889
  at Greenlawn; daughter of George W. Hogan
HOLBROOK, Goldney Platt - d. 31 July 1890 at
  Brooklyn; interment at Huntington; son of
  Arthur C. and Belle Holbrook

HOLDEN, Lillian Rhodes - 1 yr 2 mos;
   d. 18 April 1880 at Chicago, Illinois;
   interment at Huntington
HOLDEN, Lillie J. - d. 14 September 1885 at
   New York City
HOLDEN, Randall - 74 years; d. 17 July 1883
   at Huntington
HOLDEN, Sarah Rhodes - 77 years; d. 18 July
   1890 at Huntington; widow of Randall Holden;
   grand-daughter of General William Allen
HOLLAND, William - 84 years; drowned 27 March
   1887 at Great Harbor, Fisher's Island;
   native of Yarmouth, England
HOLLER, John - d. at Brooklyn; 16 March 1889
   paper; had been found badly frost bitten
   while lying in the road at Woodbury
HOLLER, John H. - 55 yrs 26 days; d. 26 Novem-
   ber 1883 at Huntington
HOLLEY, George A. - 59 y 7 m 23 d; d. 16 June
   1884 at Rocky Point
HOLLIS, Esther - d. 23 November 1887 at New
   York City; widow of Rev. William McAllister
HOLLIS, William E. - d. "a few days ago"; 25
   February 1881 paper; lawyer in Brooklyn
HOLLY John H. * - 38 y 1 m 17 d; d. 17 August
   1883 at Huntington
HOLMES, Abram L. - 80 years; d. 19 September
   1888 at Cold Spring
HOLMES, Edward - 70 yrs 9 mos; d. 21 March
   1879 at Cold Spring
HOLMES, Elizabeth - 43 y 9 m 12 d; d. 12 Febr-
   uary 1885 at Cold Spring; blood poisoning;
   wife of William Holmes
HOLMES, Mary Ann - 65 years; d. 3 October 1881
   at Cold Spring; widow of Edward Holmes
HOLMES, Mrs. M. L. - d. 8 May 1885; Hempstead
   item
HOLMES, William - 25 years; drowned 22 March
   1882 off Rye Point
HOMAN, Bradford - ca. 74 years; d. 24 September 1880 at Yaphank; resident of Cold Spring
HOMAN, Henry Lewis - 10 mos 17 days;
   d. 15 July 1889 at Cold Spring; son of
   William Homan
HOMAN, John D. - 1 y 2 m 23 d; d. 22 July 1889
   at Port Jefferson; son of L. B. Homan

HOMAN, S. Havens - 62 years; d. 25 November
1879 at Mount Sinai

HOMAN, Sarah W. - 87 y 1 m 26 d; d. 28 October
1883 at Mount Sinai

HOPKINS, George W. - 53 y 6 m 24 d; d. 21 June
1887 at Mount Sinai

HOPKINS, Maria - 87 y 6 m 19 d; d. 30 November
1880 at Miller's Place; widow of Samuel
Hopkins

HOPPER, Clara M. H. - 37 years; d. 11 August
1878 at Chelsea, Mass.; wife of Alonzo
Hopper

HOPPER, John - 77 years; d. 5 November 1884 at
Huntington; hatter; native of Newtown

HORNBY, Alexander - 78 years; d. 9 May 1888;
hit by railroad train at Brentwood

HORNE, Rev. J. W. - d. 6 September 1884 at
Southport, Conn.; hit by railroad train;
former pastor of Babylon M. E. Church

HORSEY, Samuel F. - 65 years; d. 22 May 1888
at Oyster Bay; native of Exeter, England

HORTON, Mrs. - d. 9 December 1890; funeral at
Jericho; interment at Cold Spring; mother of
Albert Horton

HORTON, Albert - funeral 29 August 1886 at
Hicksville

HORTON, Alfred P. - 79 years; suicide at
Patchogue; took poison; 15 June 1889 paper;
Cold Spring item

HORTON, Adeline - 18 years; d. 11 January 1888
at Port Jefferson

HORTON, Mrs. Calvin - 82 years; death reported
12 February 1887 paper; resident of Riverhead; same paper reports death of Mrs. Horton's daughter at Bay Shore

HORTON, Eliza Sanford - 84 years; d. 24 June
1888 at Lebanon Springs, N. Y.; mother of
Dr. H. D. Horton of Huntington

HORTON, George E. - 9 mos 19 days; d. 12 July
1889 at Cold Spring

HORTON, Dr. Heman B. - 59 years; d. 21 September 1890 at Huntington; medical doctor;
b. New Lebanon, Columbia County, N. Y.
6 October 1831; graduated 1858 Berkshire
Medical College, Pittsfield, Mass.; Army
doctor during Civil War at Washington, D. C.

HORTON, Dr. Heman B. (continued)
and Alexandria, Va.; post-war career at
Eden, Albany and Kinderhook, N. Y.;
established medical practice at Huntington
in 1871

HORTON, Justus E. - d. 4 March 1884 at
Greenport; father of Schuyler B. Horton

HORTON, Sarah A. - 27 years; d. 23 September
1888 at Brooklyn

HOUGHTON, C. Harry - suicide "week before
last" at Boston, Mass.; 10 December 1880
paper; former resident of Port Jefferson

HOUSER, George - 60 years; d. 12 July 1880
at Hicksville

HOUSER, John - 23 years; d. 24 July 1883;
hit by railroad train; resident of
Greenpoint

HOWARD, Adaline - 55 y 5m 24 d; d. 15 March
1880 at West Neck; widow of Virgil Howard

HOWARD, Clarence - 6 years; d. 17 March 1887
at New Haven, Conn.; son of Harold and
Gertie Howard

HOWARD, Clarence G. - 20 y 8 m 22 d;
d. 27 December 1879 at West Neck; son of
Farnam L. Howard

HOWARD, Earle H. - 1 year; d. 26 September
1881 at West Neck; son of Eugene Howard

HOWARD, Ethel B. - 1 y 5 m 3 d; d. 9 September
1879 at West Neck; daughter of Warren N. and
Amelia M. Howard

HOWARD, Frank - d. 21 April 1889 at Port Jefferson; interment at New York City

HOWARD, Mamie - d. 8 December 1889 at Brooklyn; wife of James Howard; daughter-in-law
of Mrs. Maria Smith of Centreport; former
resident of Centreport

HOWARD, Richard C. - 14 months; d. 11 August
1885 at West Neck; son of Eugene H. and
Caroline A. Howard

HOWARD, Rev. Robert Theus - 68 y 8 m 14 d;
d. 16 January 1885 at Cold Spring; rector of
St. John's Episcopal Church, Cold Spring; b.
Charleston, S. C. 2 May 1816; Episcopal
clergyman at St. Stephen's, Charleston and
Prince George Winyah, Georgetown, S. C.;
after Civil War served churches in Fonda,

HOWARD, Rev. Robert Theus (continued)
Gloversville and Staten Island, N. Y. before
coming to St. John's; biography 6 February
1885 paper
HOWARD, Sarah Elizabeth * - d. 12 January
1890 at Oyster Bay
HOWARTH, Elizabeth - 70 y 6 m 20 d; d. 8 Nov-
ember 1885 at Greenlawn
HOWARTH, Hezekiah - 70 yrs 10 mos; d. 9 August
1887 at Greenlawn
HOWATT, Mary - 39 years; d. 19 July 1885 at
Greenvale; funeral at Cold Spring; daughter
of Elbert Burr; wife of William Howatt
HOWE, Hiram W. - funeral 5 January 1890 at
Gravesend with interment at Cypress Hills;
"famous horseman and road house keeper"
HOWELL, Mrs. Rev. Frank G. - d. "last week" in
Ohio; 22 September 1888 paper; Riverhead
item
HOWELL, Hampton F. - d. "recently" at River-
head; 5 February 1886 paper; left large sum
of money to M. E. Church Missionary Society
HOWELL, Harvey - d. 21 December 1879 at
Bridgehampton
HOWELL, James S. - 4 y 1 m 21 d; d. 13 Febr-
uary 1886 at Northport; son of J. H. and
Hannah T. Howell
HOWELL, John - drowned 24 October 1888 off
Chatham, Massachusetts; washed overboard
from schooner near Cape Cod during storm;
memorial service 4 November 1888 at Northport M. E. Church
HOWELL, Lucretia Jane (Nancy) - suicide
10 February 1887 at Aquebogue; drowned
herself in a well; wife of John Frank Howell
HOWELL, Selah - 51 years; d. 18 December 1881
at Northport; former resident of Port Jefferson
HOWELL, Selah * - 28 yrs 10 m; d. 13 September 1882 at Huntington Station; hit by
railroad train
HOWITT, William - 47 yrs 5 mos; d. 31 July
1878 at Cold Spring
HOYLAHAN, Annie - 5 years; d. 23 May 1879 at
Whitestone Point; dress caught fire at clam
bake; daughter of Michael Hoylahan

HOYT, Mr. - interment at Hauppauge 6 July
1881; resident of Queens
HOYT, Andrew J. - 64 y 9 m 8 d; d. 11 December
1884 at Huntington Harbor
HUBBARD, Emma - d. 5 September 1886 at Amity-
ville; killed by horse which bit and tramp-
led on her; interment at Islip; daughter of
John O. Hubbard
HUBBARD, Susan - d. 25 January 1888; Northport
item
HUBBS, Mrs. Amos - d. 24 February 1889 at
Jericho; interment at East Norwich
HUBBS, Arden - 62 years; d. 23 July 1878 at
Farmingdale
HUBBS, Catharine J. - 75 yrs 5 mos;
d. 12 October 1882 at Smithtown Branch
HUBBS, Charles F. - 27 y 8 m 11 d; d. 12 March
1879 at Huntington
HUBBS, Ellis - 49 y 1 m 2 d; d. 18 June 1880
at Cold Spring
HUBBS, George F. - 61 y 4 m 3 d; d. 6 February
1888 at Comac
HUBBS, James H. - 81 yrs 1 day; d. 12 July
1890 at Northport
HUBBS, Jane E. - 53 years; d. 28 February 1884
at Huntington; daughter of Richard D. Berry;
wife of Samuel Hubbs with whom she ran the
Suffolk Hotel since 1875
HUBBS, John - 69 y 3 m 4 d; d. 28 March 1889
at Cold Spring; brother of Samuel Hubbs
HUBBS, Jonas - ca. 75 years; d. 13 May 1883 at
Hauppauge
HUBBS, Platt R. - 77 y 5 m 8 d; d. 13 August
1884 at Long Swamp; interment at Comac;
father of Mrs. Andrew I. Smith
HUBBS, Ruth - 71 y 10 m 8 d; d. 31 August 1881
at Northport; widow of Alfred Hubbs
HUBBS, Susan - 64 years; d. 25 August 1881 at
Northport
HUBBS, Mrs. William - d. 25 July 1890 at
Northport
HUDSON, Anna A. - 52 yrs 10 mos; d. 1 February
1883
HUDSON, Carll S. - d. 16 February 1887 at
Greenlawn; son of William S. and Mary A.
Hudson

HUDSON, Claudius W. - 2 yrs 7 mos;
    d. 8 September 1890 at Huntington; funeral
    at Greenlawn; interment at East Northport;
    son of William S. and Mary A. Hudson
HUDSON, Capt. Horan - 81 y 3 m 14 d;
    d. 20 July 1881 at Miller's Place
HUDSON, John E. - 32 y 5 m 21 d; d. 16 January
    1881 at Middleville
HUDSON, John L. - 5 months; d. 25 March 1883
    at Greenlawn; son of William S. and Mary
    Hudson
HUDSON, Sylvanus - d. 25 October 1888 at
    Yaphank; "old resident" of Port Jefferson
HUGHES, Burr - 26 years; killed in ship
    explosion off Sands Point; 5 December 1884
    paper
HUGHES, Christopher - 30 years; killed in ship
    explosion off Sands Point; 5 December 1884
    paper
HULBURD, Hiland R. - 2 July 1880 paper;
    resident of New York City; "Seawanhaka" fire
    on East River
HULEU, Louis F. - 75 y 10 m 12 d; d. 29 July
    1885 at Huntington
HULL, Judith F. - d. 16 May 1889 at Danbury,
    Connecticut; widow of Isaac P. Hull; sister
    of John F. Wood of Huntington
HULSE, Ellsworth - ca. 21 years; d. 11 Decem-
    ber 1881 at Port Jefferson; son of Daniel
    Hulse
HULSE, George T. - d. 17 February 1879 at
    Baiting Hollow; lockjaw
HULSE, John E. - d. 17 March 1889 at Port
    Jefferson
HULSE, Mrs. Selah - d. 2 March 1889 at Port
    Jefferson
HULTS, Mary E. - 63 years; d. 14 May 1890 at
    East Meadow; funeral at Hempstead; wife of
    Abram Hults
HUMISTON, Frank - 31 years; d. 27 November
    1888 at Bridgeport, Conn.; funeral at Port
    Jefferson; interment at Patchogue; native
    of Port Jefferson
HUNT, George - d. 13 July 1880 at Rye, N.Y.;
    hit by railroad train
HUNT, Harry L. - 4 months; d. 29 April 1887 at
    Brooklyn; son of George and Hattie Hunt

HUNT, William L. - drowned 16 September 1889
at Oyster Bay; probable suicide; interment
at Hempstead; resident of Ridgewood
HUNTER, James * - 80 years; d. 17 April 1889
at Huntington
HUNTER, Rossie * - 15 yrs 3 mos; d. 7 August
1880 at Smithtown
HUNTING, Rev. James M. - 87 years; d. 13 May
1882 at Jamaica; Presbyterian minister at
Bridgehampton; native of Sag Harbor
HUNTTING, Charles H. - 50 years; d. 25 Febr-
uary 1881 at Jamaica; interment at Smithtown
Branch
HUNTTING, James R. - d. 13 February 1882 at
Bridgehampton; whaling captain; former
supervisor Town of Southampton
HUNTTING, Jonathan W. - 77 years; d. 9 January
1890 at Southold; "one of the prominent men
of Southold Town"; father of Dr. J. G.
Huntting of Huntington
HUNTTING, Joseph R. - 84 years; d. 16 November
1880 at Smithtown Branch

HUNTTING, Malvina A. - 73 y 9 m 5 d;
d. 28 August 1880 at Southold; wife of
Jonathan W. Huntting
HURD, Gertrude - 60 years; d. 4 April 1885 at
Huntington; daughter of Jacob Westervelt;
wife of Arthur T. Hurd
HURRELL, Mary - 85 years; d. 24 March 1889 at
East Norwich
HUSTED, Seymour L. - 76 years; d. 13 June 1887
at Brooklyn; Brooklyn business leader
HUTCHINSON, John P. - drowned March 1887 at
Port Jefferson; body found 7 August 1887 at
Mount Sinai; interment 8 August 1887 at
Mount Sinai
HUTTON, Mrs. J. A. - d. "this week" at Lake-
ville; 17 May 1890 paper; "dropped dead
...from heart disease"
HYDE, E. C. - 74 yrs 6 mos; d. 29 May 1879 at
Warrensville, Illinois
HYDE, Isaac - d. 14 April 1885 at Hempstead
INGAILS, John - 63 years; d. 8 June 1885 at
Northport

INGERSOLL, Mrs. - d. 13 January 1890 at
Brooklyn; interment at Livingston, N. Y.;
mother of William Ingersoll of Northport
INGERSOLL, Thomas - drowned 20 January 1889
off Cape Hatteras, N. C.; schooner "Allie R.
Chester", owned by Jesse Carll of Northport,
sunk off Hatteras
INGLEY, Dosis [?] - suicide 7 August 1884 at
Amityville
INGLIS, Gracie - 15 years; d. 18 April 1883 at
Fresh Pond
INMAN, John - d. 8 February 1886 at Riverhead;
resident of Baiting Hollow
IRELAND, David Elwood - 32 y 6 m 3 d;
d. 19 January 1887 at Huntington
IRELAND, Derrick - 80 y 8 m 11 d; d. 17 Decem-
ber 1880 at Long Swamp
IRELAND, George - 69 years; d. 23 September
1886 at Comac
IRELAND, Harriett - 74 y 8 m 7 d; d. 6 April
1878 at Long Swamp; wife of Derrick Ireland
IRELAND, Havens - 79 years; d. 1 November 1884
at Brooklyn
IRELAND, Herbert L. - 35 y 7 m 16 d;
d. 7 April 1887 at Huntington
IRELAND, Isaac C. - 68 y 10 m 8 d; d. 30 Aug-
ust 1888 at Huntington Station; suddenly
while on hay wagon; resident of Melville
IRELAND, Jacob - 70 years; d. 4 May 1885 at
Old Fields
IRELAND, John O. - d. at Greenport; 20 July
1883 paper; fell dead in ice cream parlor;
father of Dr. Tredwell L. Ireland
IRELAND, Martha Collyer - 42 years; d. 16 May
1882 at Brooklyn; wife of John H. Ireland
IRVIN, Alex - d. 25 November 1884; son of
Richard Irvin of Northport
IRVIN, Richard - 88 years; d. 4 July 1888 at
Oyster Bay; commission merchant in New York
City; native of Glasgow, Scotland; father of
Richard Irvin, Mrs. James A. Burden,
Rev. William Irvin and Mrs. George G. Gray
IRVING, Charles - 32 years; d. 24 December
1879 at Orient; killed in ship accident;
interment at Albany, New York
IRVING, George Tappen - d. 10 January 1887 at
Flushing

IRWIN, Ann - d. 24 April 1881 at Riverhead;
found dead in bed
IRWIN, Clara James - d. 15 November 1889 at
Brooklyn; wife of Frank Irwin; former
resident of Centreport
IRWIN, Clarence F. - 18 years; d. 30 November
1886 at Huntington; son of Joseph and Martha
Irwin
IRWIN, Mary A. - 75 yrs 1 mos; d. 18 January
1890 at Centreport; interment at Brooklyn;
mother of James Irwin of Brooklyn; resident
of Centreport since 1858
IVENS, Ann Maria - 68 years; d. 17 June 1890
at Northport; widow of Zenias Ivens
IVENS, Zenias - 64 yrs 7 mos; d. 28 November
1885 at Northport
JACKSON, child * - 6 months; found 10 June
1887 on railroad track at Hempstead
JACKSON, Ann Elizabeth * - 49 years;
d. 28 March 1882 at Huntington; wife of
Henry D. Jackson
JACKSON, Clarence H. * - 2 mos 25 days;
d. 17 October 1881 at Huntington; son of
Aaron and Keziah Jackson
JACKSON, Elizabeth * - 15 y 8 m 12 d;
d. 26 October 1890 at Jericho; interment at
Westbury; daughter of Henry Jackson
JACKSON, Harry - 12 years; d. 26 December 1886
at Little Neck; killed playing with a
pistol; son of Henry Jackson
JACKSON, James * - 20 years; interment 13 Nov-
ember 1889 at Lakeville; hunting accident at
Great Neck; son of James Jackson of Douglas-
ton
JACKSON, John - 104 yrs 27 days; d. 11 Febr-
uary 1878 at Tianna, near Good Ground
JACKSON, Josiah W. - 1 y 5 m 6 d; d. 19 Febr-
uary 1879 at Woodbury
JACKSON, Joyce - 24 years; d. 7 May 1887 at
South Dix Hills; wife of Edward Jackson
JACKSON, Julia * - 78 y 1 m 7 d; d. 31 January
1879 at Huntington
JACKSON, Julia * - 1 yr 9 mos; d. 12 September
1881 at Huntington; daughter of Aaron
Jackson

JACKSON, Julia V. * - 2 mos 21 days; d. 6 October 1881 at Huntington; daughter of Jeffrey and Tamar Jackson

JACKSON, Keziah G. * - 38 years; d. 12 January 1889 at Huntington

JACKSON, King - d. "last week" in New Jersey; 8 March 1890 paper; former resident of Westbury

JACKSON, Lillie - 11 years; d. 7 July 1887; Hicksville item; interment at Westbury; daughter of Anselm Jackson

JACKSON, Phebe - 84 years; d. 1 January 1879 at Huntington; widow of Douglas Jackson

JACKSON, Phebe - d. at Locust Valley; funeral 26 November 1889 at Westbury; widow of Jacob Jackson; mother-in-law of I. C. Thorne

JACKSON, Tamer - 42 yrs 9 mos; d. 2 June 1884 at Huntington

JACKSON, Thomas - d. "last week" at Brooklyn; 15 September 1888 paper; uncle of Sidney W. Jackson of Jericho

JACKSON, Thomas E. - d. at St. Louis, Missouri; 21 September 1889 paper; killed in a prize fight

JACKSON, Timothy F. - ca. 69 yrs; d. 14 August 1881 at Flushing; Quaker; native of Jericho

JACOBS, Christian - d. 16 December 1886; interment Lutheran Cemetery, Middle Village; lived near Farmingdale

JACOBS, Emma - 17 yrs 6 days; d. 17 February 1878 at Huntington

JACOBS, Randal Smith - 3 months; d. 26 July 1886 at Huntington

JAGGER, Sarah P. - 59 yrs 3 mos; d. 22 February 1881 at Southampton

JAGGER, William - ca. 65 years; d. 9 April 1890 at Jericho; Ketcham & Jagger "in the cider business"; "Jericho loses ones of its most respected citizens"

JAMES, David - d. 6 April 1885; Northport item

JAMES, Irena - 69 y 1 m 12 d; d. 12 January 1890 at Cold Spring Harbor

JAMES, William - 2 yrs; d. 30 August 1882 at Cold Spring; son of David J. and Alma James; scarlet fever

JAMES, Willis - 81 years; d. 6 April 1885 at Northport

JANSEN, Joseph - suicide 16 October 1885 at
  Amityville; jumped in front of railroad
  train; patient at Long Island Home; resident
  of Long Island City
JANSSEN, Elizabeth - 13 years; d. 5 August
  1882 at St. Johnland; daughter of Herman and
  Amelia Janssen
JARRETT, Sarah O. - 50 years; d. 4 April 1878
  at Northport
JARVIS, children * - d. 30 October 1883 at
  Merrick; poisoned by Paris green; two
  children of Moses Jarvis
JARVIS, Aaron - 73 years; d. 11 February 1881
  at Northport
JARVIS, Almeda Brush - 83 y 6 m 24 d;
  d. 11 January 1890 at Huntington; wife of
  P. C. Jarvis for nearly 60 years; mother of
  S. Lee Jarvis and Joseph R. Jarvis
JARVIS, Ann - 71 yrs 3 mos; d. 9 February 1880
  at Huntington; wife of Jonathan Jarvis
JARVIS, Carlton - 73 y 3 m 20 d; d. 7 July
  1878 at Melville
JARVIS, Elizabeth - 79 years; d. 23 April 1887
  at Huntington
JARVIS, Emily A. - 43 y 3 m 17 d; d. 27 March
  1888 at Huntington; wife of Joseph R. Jarvis
  whom she m. 1867; born Huntington 9 December
  1844, daughter of James and Mary Horton
JARVIS, Esther - 78 yrs 5 mos; d. 14 July 1878
  at Cold Spring
JARVIS, Fanny * - 80 years; d. 18 July 1888 at
  Huntington; wife of Aaron Jarvis
JARVIS, Hannah - 74 yrs 7 mos; d. 20 November
  1884 at Northport; widow of Aaron Jarvis
JARVIS, Henry - 83 y 6 m 4 d; d. 24 May 1882
  at Centreport
JARVIS, Ira - 50 y 2 m 11 d; d. 22 July 1889
  at Centreport; native of Cold Spring; Civil
  War veteran
JARVIS, Irena - 52 years; d. 14 July 1878 at
  Northport
JARVIS, John A. - d. 11 August 1889 at Setau-
  ket; interment at Port Jefferson
JARVIS, John H. - 49 yrs 8 mos; d. 25 August
  1886 at East Norwich; native of Melville; in
  milk business in Brooklyn and later a
  policeman in New York City

JARVIS, John J. - 25 y 5 m 15 d; d. 4 November 1879 at Huntington

JARVIS, Jonathan - 50 y 4 m 4 d; d. 1 May 1887 at Melville

JARVIS, Letty - 69 yrs 9 mos; d. 2 November 1884 at West Hills; widow of William Jarvis; mother of Jonathan Jarvis, Jackson Jarvis and Mrs. Alexander Gardiner

JARVIS, Lydia Ann * - 25 yrs 10 mos; d. 27 December 1883 at Smithtown Branch

JARVIS, Margaret - 76 y 5 m 3 d; d. 25 July 1887 at Centreport; mother of Ira Jarvis

JARVIS, Martha L. * - 20 years; d. 8 April 1885 at Northport

JARVIS, Mollie - 3 yrs 8 mos; d. 8 December 1878 at Westfield, New Jersey

JARVIS, Moses - 83 y 11 m 7 d; d. 23 September 1890 at Huntington Harbor; "suddenly"; deacon of Second Presbyterian Church; 60 years a resident of Centreport Cove

JARVIS, Samantha - 80 y 1 m 24 d; d. 29 July 1886 at Huntington; widow of Edward Jarvis

JARVIS, Woodhull - 79 y 1 m 6 d; d. 1 June 1890 at Melville

JAYNE, Mrs. - funeral 14 July 1886 at Northport

JAYNE, Jane - 65 years; d. 23 December 1883 at Brooklyn

JAYNE, Richard - 62 y 10 m 16 d; d. 18 Febr. 1888 at Cold Spring; veteran of both Mexican and Civil War; famous for participation in running and walking contests

JAYNE, Stephen - 74 years; d. 5 March 1887 at Huntington

JAYNE, Whitman - 86 yrs 9 mos; d. 11 November 1886 at Smithtown

JEFFREY, child * - 11 months; murdered 1 August 1883 at Smithtown; child of George Jeffrey and Dolly Pollard; father threw child across room; child hit the wall and broke its neck

JEFFREY, Reuben - d. at Brooklyn; 21 December 1889 paper; "prominent Baptist clergyman"

JENKINS, Derwood C. * - 4 mos 12 days; d. 16 December 1888 at Huntington

JENKINS, Frederick N. - 7 weeks; d. 17 April
1883 at Cold Spring; son of Samuel and
Abigail A. Jenkins

JENKINS, Henry - 3 mos 13 days; d. 10 February
1889 at Huntington; son of Samuel and Mary
B. Jenkins

JENKINS, John - 77 years; d. 28 June 1881 at
Huntington

JENKINS, Mary - 70 y 11 m 3 d; d. 17 December
1878 at Cold Spring

JENKINS, Mary Ann * - funeral 7 February 1889
at Oyster Bay; found dead in bed; wife of
William Jenkins

JENKINS, Rev. William - funeral 15 May 1886 at
Plainview; former pastor of Manetto Hill
M. E. Church

JENNINGS, Jessup T. - 86 years; d. 16 April
1885 at Green's Farms, Connecticut

JENNINGS, Richard - d. 15 February 1881 at
Patchogue

JERVIS, John B. - 89 years; d. at Rome, N. Y.;
16 January 1885 paper; native of Huntington;
born John B. Jarvis; son of Timothy Jarvis;
famous civil engineer builder of canals and
railroads; namesake of Port Jervis, N. Y.

JESSUP, Fanny - d. "a few days ago" at Southampton; 17 December 1887 paper; fell dead
while walking in her room; widow of Zebulon
Jessup

JEWELL, M. E. - 32 years; d. 17 September 1879
at Comac; daughter of Zebulon Whitman; wife
of James Jewell

JEWETT, Charles - 71 years; d. 3 April 1879 at
Norwich, Connecticut; temperance lecturer

JODRY, George - 93 years; d. "last week" at
Yaphank Almshouse; 10 August 1883 paper;
resident of Southampton; veteran of Napoleon's Grand Army of France

JOHNS, Percival - d. 24 April 1886; Oyster Bay
item; struck by lightning while planting
potatoes; resident of Bayville

JOHNSON, Mrs. - death reported; 2 January 1885
paper; Hicksville item

JOHNSON, child - drowned 15 June 1886 at
Riverhead; child of widowed Mrs. Johnson

JOHNSON, child - d. at Hempstead; 3 December
1887 paper; diphtheria; child of Edmund
Johnson

JOHNSON, triplets * - d. 3 July 1889 at
Jericho; "they failed to live"; triplets of
Mrs. William Johnson

JOHNSON, Mr. - d. "last week"; Glen Cove item;
30 August 1890 paper; brother of Joseph
Johnson of Glen Cove

JOHNSON, Abiatha - 81 y 10 m 21 d; d. 28 Jan-
uary 1888 at Huntington Harbor; son of
Samuel and Mary Hartt Johnson; husband of
Abigail Jarvis; father of Reuben Johnson,
Ida Johnson, Jarvis Johnson and Matilda
(Mrs. John R.) Scudder; native of Hunting-
ton; captain of coastal vessels on Long
Island Sound; keeper of Lloyd's Neck Light-
house

JOHNSON, Abraham Lawson - 5 y 7 m 14 d;
d. 1 March 1884 at Cold Spring; son of
Charles Johnson

JOHNSON, Alexander S. - 78 y 3 m 12 d;
d. 20 August 1887 at Huntington Harbor; son
of Samuel C. and Mary S. Johnson; native of
East Neck; owner of ship yard; lumber dealer

JOHNSON, Ann - 77 y 4 m 11 d; d. 24 June 1888
at Huntington; widow of Alexander Johnson

JOHNSON, Carl M. - drowned 25 October 1890 at
Glenwood; body found "last week" at Glen
Cove; 15 November 1890 paper

JOHNSON, Carll - suicide at Linden, N. Y.;
jumped from a railroad train; resident of
Jamesport; 9 February 1883 paper

JOHNSON, Charles - d. 9 July 1887; Cold Spring
Harbor item

JOHNSON, Clarence - 1 mo 23 days; d. 4 April
1885 at Huntington Harbor; son of Oscar
Johnson

JOHNSON, Rev. Daniel Van Mater - d. 20 Novem-
ber 1890 at Brooklyn with interment at
Green-Wood; Episcopal clergyman; rector of
St. Mary's Church, Brooklyn; long-time
visitor to Huntington; recently preached at
St. John's, Huntington; funeral attended by
sixty Episcopal clergymen, many from Long
Island and Brooklyn

JOHNSON, Elias B. * - 24 y 2 m 14 d; d. 16
October 1878 at Huntington

JOHNSON, Elizabeth * - 32 years; d. 3 January
1878 at New York City; interment at Huntington; widow of James Johnson; former
resident of Huntington

JOHNSON, Elizabeth - 75 y 5 m 27 d;
d. 15 January 1882 at Lloyd's Neck;
wife of George R. Johnson

JOHNSON, Emiline - interment "this week" at
Atlantic City, N. J.; 5 February 1886 paper;
widow of Nelson Hicks of Jericho; mother of
Theodore S. Hicks

JOHNSON, Emily F. - 28 y 1 m 24 d; d. 7 April
1878 at Huntington; wife of George R.
Johnson

JOHNSON, George - d. 19 April 1889 at Mineola; funeral at Freeport; interment at
Jericho; brother of James Johnson; resident
of Plain Edge "sent to the [Mineola] insane
asylum recently"

JOHNSON, George C. * - 1 yr 7 mos; d. 6 March
1885 at Huntington; son of George and Ruth
Johnson

JOHNSON, George R. - d. 12 May 1880 at Galveston, Texas; interment at Huntington

JOHNSON, George R. - 83 yrs 2 mos; d. 8 November 1884 at Lloyd's Neck

JOHNSON, Hannah (Indian) - murdered 18 February 1879 at Bay Shore; probably by husband
Ephraim Henry Johnson *

JOHNSON, Harriet - 79 years; d. 3 April 1889
at Plain Edge; wife of George Johnson

JOHNSON, Harriet J. - 23 days; d. 9 November
1890 at Huntington

JOHNSON, Henry M. - drowned 28 June 1881 off
Bridgeport, Conn.; resident of New York
City; body found by Capt. T. B. Howell

JOHNSON, Jane A. - 52 yrs 4 mos; d. 19 October
1882 at Northport; widow of Alexander
Johnson

JOHNSON, Julia * - over 80 years; d. "last
week" at Hempstead; 9 November 1889 paper;
burned by hot stove

JOHNSON, Lillie A. * - 5 mos 5 days;
d. 18 July 1885 at Huntington; daughter of
Merritt Johnson

JOHNSON, Mary - 84 years; d. 26 May 1881 at
Huntington; interment at Comac
JOHNSON, Peter - 44 years; d. 15 April 1880 at
Middleville
JOHNSON, Raymond - 1 y 2 m 9 d; d. 2 August
1878 at Huntington; son of Oscar and
Caroline Johnson
JOHNSON, Russell - 8 mos 2 days; d. 12 July
1889 at Huntington
JOHNSON, Rev. Samuel F. - d. 24 April 1886 at
Rockville Centre; interment at Hempstead;
M. E. clergyman; born Hempstead 2 June 1828;
son of Stephen Johnson; m. daughter of
Joseph Smith of Merrick; school teacher in
early career; joined New York East Confer-
ence M. E. Church 1851; served: Middle Is-
land & Selden, Amagansett, Riverhead, James-
port, Cutchogue, Huntington, Westhampton,
Moriches, Amityville, East Norwich, Far
Rockaway, Foster's Meadow, Woodsburgh, Ros-
lyn & Searingtown, Oyster Bay, Flatlands,
Stony Brook & Setauket as well as churches
in Connecticut; retired ca. 1884
JOHNSON, Sarah * - d. 19 October 1890 at
Brooklyn; interment at Westbury; former
employee of Mrs. William Rushmore
JOHNSON, Theodore * - d. 21 July 1886 at
Brooklyn; dropped dead while playing music
at a picnic; musician; resident of Oyster
Bay
JOHNSON, William * - 94 years; d. "last week"
at Yaphank Almshouse; 10 August 1883 paper;
resident of Southampton
JOHNSON, William - 63 yrs 7 mos; d. 2 January
1886 at Comac
JOHNSON, Rev. William H. - d. 26 August 1878
at Brooklyn; city missionary of the Eastern
District of Brooklyn
JOHNSON, William H. - funeral 29 December 1886
at New York City; interment at Cypress
Hills; proprietor of Suffolk Driving Park
JOHNSON, Capt. William S. - 57 yrs 11 mos;
d. 14 March 1878 at Huntington
JOHNSTON, Francis E. - ca. 70 years;
d. 26 January 1887 at Half Hollows; died
sitting in chair

JOHNSTON, Rebecca - 68 years; d. 13 April 1880 at Flushing; widow of Alexander Johnston

JOHNSTON, Robert H. - 76 years; d. 18 February 1890 at Oyster Bay; interment at Cypress Hills; former clerk in New York City Police Court

JOHNSTON, Sarah Ann - 62 y 4 m 11 d; d. 21 September 1880 at Oyster Bay

JONES, infant - 3 months; 2 July 1880 paper; "Seawanhaka" fire on East River; child of Charity Jones

JONES, Adrianne - 27 years; d. 1 February 1886 at Brooklyn

JONES, Alwilda * - 28 years; d. 9 May 1888 at New York City

JONES, Amelia - d. 19 September 1888; funeral at Setauket; aunt of Mrs. Charles P. Randall

JONES, Anna Lanton - d. 25 July 1882 at New Rochelle, N. Y.; daughter of Cyrus and Sarah M. Lanton; wife of Samuel Van Wyck Jones

JONES, Annie Bailey - d. 5 July 1882 at New York City; daughter of Theodorus Bailey; wife of Walter R. T. Jones

JONES, Anthony * - d. 23 January 1887 at Dutch Kills; from injuries received when hit by railroad train

JONES, Charles H. - 77 y 2 m 17 d; d. 23 January 1882 at Cold Spring; son of John and Hannah Hewlett Jones

JONES, Dorothy A. - 92 years; d. 7 May 1885 at Cold Spring Harbor; widow of David Jones

JONES, Edward Mitchell - 65 y 5 m 27 d; d. 2 November 1887 at Lloyd's Neck; exhaustion from boat upsetting while hunting; interment at Cold Spring Harbor; son of Walter Jones; born Cold Spring Harbor 10 May 1822; whaler and master of sailing ships; see 5 November 1887 paper for long obit

JONES, Frank - drowned in ship wreck off Block Island, R. I.; 18 January 1884 paper

JONES, Frank S. - 27 yrs 6 mos; d. 4 March 1881 at Wichita, Kansas; son of James P. and F. A. Jones; former resident of Huntington

JONES, George - 42 years; body found on beach at Fire Island; Swedish sailor; 14 August 1878 paper

JONES, Isaac H. - 82 years; d. 13 October 1887
   at Woodbury; former factory superintendent
   at Cold Spring Harbor
JONES, Israel Baldwin - 94 years; d. 1 October
   1886 at Brooklyn; interment at Huntington;
   born at Dix Hills; son of James Jones
JONES, Lucy Dumont - 26 years; d. 17 June 1886
   at Bath-on-Hudson, N. Y.; daughter of Van
   Gasbeck Dumont; wife of William H. Jones;
   resident of Woodbury
JONES, Martha - 66 years; d. 12 November 1884
   at Dix Hills
JONES, Nora Scudder - d. 7 June 1886 at Cold
   Spring; daughter of Henry G. Scudder; widow
   of John H. Jones
JONES, Samuel W. - 59 y 3 m 7 d; d. 8 February
   1878 at Huntington; son of William Jones
JONES, Sarah - d. 29 July 1879 at Babylon;
   widow of Edmund Jones of Colchester,
   Connecticut; mother of Israel C. Jones
JONES, Shepard Smith - funeral 30 October 1889
   at Setauket; featured as violin player in
   W. S. Mount's painting "Power of Music"
JONES, Theodosius Bailey - 15 years;
   d. 27 March 1879 at Concord, New Hampshire;
   son of W. R. T. Jones
JONES, Thomas B. - 68 years; d. 4 September
   1887 at Northport; son-in-law of P. V. B.
   Stanton; father of William J. Jones, Frank
   B. Jones and Hazel Seymour; born at Jamaica;
   resident of Brooklyn; President of Nassau
   Fire Insurance Company
JONES, Townsend Howard - 1 y 9 m 19 d;
   d. 19 February 1884 at Brooklyn; son of
   Townsend and Katharine H. Jones
JONES, Walter Dumont - 10 mos 2 days;
   d. 12 August 1882 at Bath-on-Hudson, N. Y.;
   son of William H. and Lucy D. Jones
JONES, Walter Restored - 61 years; d. 28 Dec-
   ember 1884 at Woodbury; son of William H.
   Jones; father of William H. Jones of Albany,
   N. Y. and Mrs. O. J. Woodhull of San Anto-
   nio, Texas; marine insurer and ran shipping
   business; between New York and Cuba and the
   West Indies

JONES, William Edward - 65 y 9 m 11 d;
    d. 20 January 1890 at Cold Spring Harbor;
    son of John H. Jones and Lucretia Hewlett
    Jones; brother of John D. Jones, Walter R.
    T. Jones, Townsend Jones, Samuel A. Jones,
    Mrs. C. B. Moore and Mrs. Charles P. Stew-
    art; merchant in Cold Spring Harbor; school
    trustee; trustee of St. John's Episcopal
    Church
JONES, William T. - 37 y 8 m 18 d; d. 19 July
    1889 at Huntington
JORDAN, Wilhelmina - 58 years; d. 25 August
    1886 at Centreport
JOY, Joshua R. - d. 30 April 1883 at Wilming-
    ton, North Carolina; interment at Huntington
JOYCE, John - 65 years; d. 29 December 1879 at
    Dutch Kills; hit by railroad train
JUDD, Frank L. - d. "suddenly" at Southold;
    funeral 30 August 1890 at Riverhead
KAGAAN, Mary A. - 35 years; d. 9 March 1884 at
    Cold Spring; child birth; wife of James
    Kagaan
KAHL, Conrad - drowned 24 November 1889 at
    Centre Island; small boat upset
KALER, David H. - 34 y 7 m 12 d; d. 13 August
    1889 at Cold Spring Harbor
KALLY, John W. - 15 years; d. 19 July 1882 at
    Cold Spring Harbor; interment at Huntington;
    son of William Kally
KANE, William L. - 6 m 15 d; d. 15 August 1885
    at Cold Spring ; son of William and Luella
    Kane
KANGETER, John - 60 years; d. 13 January 1882
    at Huntington
KARTS, Mr. - washed overboard from "U.S.S.
    Tallapoosa" off Lloyd's Neck; body found off
    Glen Cove 23 August 1882; interment at
    Oyster Bay
KASULKY, Clarence - 3 years; d. 26 June 1887
    at Queens; fell into tub of scalding water
KATHMANN, Frederick H. - 51 years; d. 14 June
    1889; interment at East Northport; Civil War
    veteran; member Samuel Ackerly Post GAR;
    former hotel proprietor
KAULT, child - 9 years; d. "past week" at
    Hempstead; 21 August 1886 paper; son of Mr.
    Kault

KAY, Janet - 79 years; d. 21 November 1889 at
Hicksville

KAYLOR, James A. - 2 y 2 m 25 d; d. 15 Febru-
uary 1885 at Cold Spring; son of James A.
and Laura Kaylor

KEALEY, John - 76 years; d. 2 November 1881 at
Pigeon Hill

KEENAN, Christopher - d. 14 June 1887 at West
Islip; kicked by horse

KEENE, Louie - 1 y 6 m 4 d; d. 20 September
1881 at Cold Spring; child of G. Shepard and
Sarah Louise Keene

KEENE, Robert - 71 y 9 m 14 d; d. 14 October
1887 at Cold Spring Harbor

KEIFE, George - 10 years; d. 1 October 1888 at
Queens; wagon accident; son of Antoine
Keifer

KEIL, Miss - 20 yrs 5 mos; d. "this week" at
Island Trees; 2 July 1887 paper; resident of
New York City

KEISLING, Josephine - 11 years; d. 28 June
1887 at Hicksville; daughter of Charles
Keisling; diphtheria

KELL, boy - 5 years; d. 6 May 1887 at
Plainview; interment at Bethpage

KELLINGTON, Mr. - interment 1 September 1888
at East Northport; resident of Brooklyn;
formerly of Comac

KELLINGTON, Mrs. - d. "three weeks before
husband"; 8 September 1888 paper; Northport
item

KELLOGG, Amanda - 59 years; d. 13 April 1882
at Middleville; wife of Frederick Kellogg

KELLUM, Cecelia - 31 years; d. 17 September
1885 at Huntington

KELLUM, George - 27 years; d. 10 January 1886
at Babylon; epileptic; found dead in bed

KELLUM, George M. - 36 y 7 m 22 d; d. 24 March
1884 at Long Swamp

KELLUM, Jane W. - 59 yrs 6 mos; d. 5 March
1885 at Long Swamp

KELLUM, Lillian F. - 23 y 1 m 20 d;
d. 5 December 1889 at Long Swamp

KELLUM, Philip - d. 18 November 1885
at Babylon

KELLY, Elizabeth - d. "last week" at Hempstead; 27 March 1885 paper

KELLY, George B. - d. 3 December 1890; funeral at Patchogue; interment at Waverly

KELLY, James - d. "a few days ago"; 3 August 1889 paper; "killed by the cars" on his way home to New Jersey; Oyster Bay item

KELLY, James - suicide 19 March 1890 at St. James

KELLY, John - 50 years; found dead on barn floor; 6 February 1885 paper; "General Island Notes: Queens County"

KELLY, John J. - 1 year; d. 11 July 1880 at Oyster Bay; son of James and Mary Kelly

KELLY, Michael - murdered 12 September 1887 at Bayside; beaten to death by son-in-law John Brown, a soldier at Willet's Point

KELP, Henry C. - 20 years; drowned at Orient; 10 September 1880 paper

KELSEY, Conklin - 58 y 11 m 6 d; d. 8 April 1884 at Huntington

KELSEY, Harriet E. - 55 years; d. 6 May 1888 at New York City

KELSEY, Joel S. - 83 years; d. at St. John-land; 23 July 1887 paper; former resident of Huntington

KELSEY, John H. - 40 years; d. 2 April 1884 at Queens; interment at Huntington

KELSEY, John H. - 30 y 6 m 23 d; d. 15 May 1887 at Huntington

KELSEY, Loretta - 78 years; d. 2 December 1878 at Cold Spring

KELSEY, Margary E. - 61 years; d. 18 February 1887 at Dix Hills

KELSEY, Mary E. - 23 years; d. 1 May 1881 at Centreport

KELSEY, Rebecca C. - 10 months; d. 23 September 1884 at Humboldt, Nebraska; daughter of Rev. Joel and Elizabeth Kelsey

KELSEY, Sarah V. - 83 yrs 10 mos; d. 12 November 1884 at Vernon Valley

KELSEY, William - 7 months; d. 16 July 1885 at Huntington; son of William H. and Katie Kelsey

KELSEY, William S. - 42 years; d. 2 April 1884 at Huntington

KELSEY, Woodhull S. - 71 years; d. 11 May 1883 in Brooklyn; son of Platt Kelsey; father of Mrs. Ira Youngs; shipbuilder in Huntington

KELSO, Nathaniel - 1 y 6 m 8 d; d. 28 October
1879 at Greenlawn; son of Nathaniel K. and
Mabel Suydam Kelso

KEMMLER, William - executed 6 August 1890 at
Auburn, N. Y.; "first electricide in his-
tory"; in electric chair at Auburn State
Prison for murder of common law wife

KEMPEL, John - suicide 6 September 1881 at
Jamaica; murdered wife and committed suicide

KEMPSTER, James - 78 y 11 m 29 d; d. 29 April
1883 at Mt. Sinai

KEMPSTER, William H. - 7 years; d. 27 January
1886 at Mt. Sinai; son of William and
Kessiah Kempster

KENNEDY, girl - 3 years; d. 28 September 1886
at Jericho

KENNEDY, Lawrence - suicide 27 November 1888
at Sag Harbor; took rat poison

KENNEY, James - d. "last week" at Manor; railroad engineer killed in railroad wreck;
18 January 1884 paper

KENNY, Edward - 31 years; drowned 11 September
1883 at Greenport

KENT, Michael - drowned 19 January 1883 off
Fisher's Island; ship collision; resident of
St. John, Nova Scotia

KEOCH, Margaret - d. 15 October 1886 at Hicksville

KEOUGH, John - 61 yrs 7 mos; d. 15 January
1887 at Hicksville

KERBS, August William - 7 mos 8 days;
d. 19 August 1890 at Hicksville; son of
August Kerbs

KERN, Margaret - d. "last week" at Herricks;
interment at Lutheran Cemetery, Middle
Village; 26 July 1890 paper; resident of
Newtown

KERNAN, Patrick - ca. 70 years; found dead
13 August 1879 at Glen Cove

KERNITZ, Charles - 30 years; d. 24 November
1889 at Long Island City; Editor of Long
Island Beobachter

KERPS, girl - d. 16 October 1886 at Hicksville; daughter of August Kerps

KERR, Mr. - ca. 47 years; d. 15 February 1881
at New York City; resident of Williamsburgh;
father of H. D. Kerr of Northport

KETCHAM, infant - 1 mo 16 days; d. 9 August
   1879 at Northport; daughter of Brewster
   Ketcham
KETCHAM, infant - d. 5 July 1889 at Northport;
   son of Brewster Ketcham
KETCHAM, A. Mulford - 83 years; d. 11 October
   1885 at Brooklyn; funeral at Northport; long
   time merchant in Northport; deacon of Northport Presbyterian Church for 51 years
KETCHAM, Abel - 80 years; d. 27 May 1887 at
   Patchogue; funeral at Riverhead; resident of
   Riverhead
KETCHAM, Mrs. Abel - d. "two weeks ago";
   21 May 1887 paper; Riverhead item
KETCHAM, Abial - 84 y 4 m 6 d; d. 14 January
   1885 at Huntington; killed in house fire;
   son of Jacob and Hannah Ketcham; b. Bread
   and Cheese Hollow 8 September 1800; brother
   of Carll Ketcham of Elwood, Ira Ketcham of
   Babylon, Andrew Ketcham of Moriches and Mrs.
   Phebe Buffett of Elwood
KETCHAM, Rev. Alfred - d. "a few days since"
   at Vineland, N. J.; 10 April 1885 paper;
   brother of A. Mulford Ketcham of Northport;
   pastor of Babylon Presbyterian Church 1839-
   1848
KETCHAM, Amelia - 77 years; d. 26 August 1881
   at Northport; widow of Stephen Ketcham
KETCHAM, Carll - 73 years; d. 28 April 1890 at
   Greenlawn; found dead in his room
KETCHAM, David C. - 80 years; d. 23 December
   1889 at Montclair, New Jersey
KETCHAM, Eliphalet - 65 years; d. 2 February
   1880 at Riverhead; brother of Jacob Ketcham
   and Zophar Ketcham
KETCHAM, Eliza A. - 86 y 5 m 12 d; d. 12 Dec-
   ember 1882 at Northport
KETCHAM, Elizabeth A. - 46 y 10 m 26 d;
   d. 24 March 1890 at East Orange, N. J.;
   daughter of Woodhull Ketcham
KETCHAM, Emily A. - d. 8 March 1887 at
   Plainfield, N. J.; wife of Rev. Kneeland
   Ketcham
KETCHAM, Ezekiel - 83 years; d. 29 November
   1879 at Elwood
KETCHAM, Ezra F. - 62 years; d. 22 October
   1882 at Flushing; interment at Huntington

KETCHAM, Francis D. - 65 y 7 m 7 d; d. 23 July 1885 at San Jose, California; father-in-law of L. L. Nattigar; b. Huntington 16 December 1818; went to California in 1849; returned and m. Anne Lefferts 1853 at Huntington; to California 1854; County Assessor 1856-1860, Trinity County, Calif.; wheelwright Humbolt County, Calif. 1865; moved to San Jose 1872

KETCHAM, Franklin - funeral 18 July 1886 at Farmingdale

KETCHAM, Hannah - 87 yrs 10 mos; d. 26 March 1884 at Northport

KETCHAM, Hannah - 79 years; d. 22 October 1884 at Northport; widow of Jesse Ketcham

KETCHAM, Henrietta - 1 year; d. 24 June 1880 at Middleville; daughter of Ellsworth B. and Eva C. Ketcham

KETCHAM, Henry S. - 58 y 3 m 14 d; d. 27 November 1882 at Huntington Harbor

KETCHAM, Ida Louise - 34 y 2 m 6 d; d. 22 February 1888 at Brooklyn; interment at Huntington; daughter of Woodhull Ketcham

KETCHAM, Isaac H. - 34 y 1 m 9 d; d. 19 August 1881 at Melville; son of Isaac H. Ketcham

KETCHAM, Jacob - 79 years; d. 22 January 1881 at Huntington

KETCHAM, James - 50 years; d. month of December 1885 at Patchogue

KETCHAM, John - 83 y 3 m 22 d; d. 24 December 1880 at Huntington

KETCHAM, John W. - 36 y 1 m 2 d; d. 28 October 1883 at West Hills

KETCHAM, Joseph - d. 9 December 1880 at Amityville; run over by wagon after being thrown out

KETCHAM, Lucinda - 56 years; d. 3 August 1882 at Dix Hills; wife of Ira Ketcham

KETCHAM, Mary - 55 y 4 m 14 d; d. 30 September 1879 at Brooklyn; interment at Comac

KETCHAM, Mary - 87 years; d. 8 October 1887 at Brooklyn; widow of Stephen Ketcham

KETCHAM, Mary - 90 yrs 9 mos; d. 15 October 1887 at Melville; Melville native; daughter of John Everett; widow of Joel Ketcham; mother of Nathaniel Ketcham and Mrs. Isaac Ireland

KETCHAM, Phebe - 77 y 1 m 26 d; d. 16 May 1879 at Northport

KETCHAM, Phoebe Ann - 73 years; d. 6 June 1878 at South Paw Paw, Illinois; wife of Jeremiah Ketcham

KETCHAM, Raymond - 2 months; d. 30 December 1886 at Northport; son of Henry E. and Minnie Ketcham

KETCHAM, Ruhama C. - 76 yrs 10 mos; d. 14 August 1884 at Northport

KETCHAM, Ruth - 64 y 10 m 10 d; d. 13 April 1885 at Half Hollow Hills; wife of Isaac Ketcham

KETCHAM, Sarah - 82 years; d. 14 January 1885 at Huntington; killed in house fire; wife of Abial Ketcham; sister of Scudder Hall

KETCHAM, Smith R. - 67 years; d. 24 August 1886 at Fresh Pond

KETCHAM, Susan - 76 y 9 m 10 d; d. 11 December 1880 at Northport; widow of Daniel Ketcham

KETCHAM, Theodore - 80 years; d. 10 February 1883 at West Neck

KETCHAM, William W. - 5 mos 3 days; d. 26 June 1883 at Middleville; son of Ellsworth E. and Eva C. Ketcham

KETCHAM, Willie H. - 1 y 7 m 24 d; d. 11 September 1882 at Comac; son of William H. and Emma J. Ketcham

KETCHAM, Woodhull - 63 years; d. 4 November 1880 at Brooklyn; interment at Huntington

KEUNEMUND, John - 28 years; d. 29 January 1881 at Babylon; gun accident

KIERNAN, Patrick - d. 6 January 1886 at New York City; kicked by horse; resident of Brookville

KIETH, Charlie - d. 27 December 1885 in Costa Rica; died of fever; resident in Costa Rica "past few years"; former resident of Babylon

KILFOYLE, Margaret - 81 years; d. 29 September 1884 in Huntington

KING, Alexander - 23 y 4 m 5 d; d. 25 April 1878 at Cold Spring

KING, Edward - 77 years; d. 19 December 1879 at Arshamamoque, near Greenport in house fire; brother of Mrs. Jonathan Miller

KING, George - d. 21 October 1888 at St. Johnland; found dead in room at St. Johnland
Institution

KING, Hester A. - 33 yrs 10 mos; d. 13 April
1886 at Rochester, N. Y.; interment at
Huntington; daughter of John and Mary
Thompson; wife of Manuel King; b. Huntington
1852

KING, Lewis - 31 years; suicide 13 February
1880 at Jamaica; son of Richard King;
grandson of Governor John A. King; great-
grandson of Rufus King

KING, Richard - 87 years; d. 16 May 1890 at
Centreport; interment at Northport

KING, S. Helena - 1y 10 m 12 d; d. month of
September 1885 at Miller's Place; daughter
of Albert N. and Isabel N. King

KING, W. L. - ca. 30 years; suicide 29 September 1884 at Jamesport

KINNEY, Elizabeth - 66 years; d. 24 October
1879 at Cold Spring

KINSELLA, Patrick J. - 20 years; d. 12 January
1890 at New York City; interment at Westbury; son of Charles and Mary Kinsella;
grandson of Mrs. Daniel Kinsella

KINSELLA, Thomas - d. 11 February 1884 at
Brooklyn; Editor of Brooklyn Eagle; b. 1832
in Ireland

KIRBY, Charles T. - 1 yr 3 mos; d. 17 November
1880 at Northport; son of James and Hattie
Kirby

KIRBY, Emma - 18 years; suicide 13 May 1878 at
Ronkonkoma; took overdose of laudanum

KIRK, Lizzie - 50 years; d. 31 October 1884 at
Winfield; hit by railroad train

KIRK, Mary N. - 52 years; d. 24 March 1884 at
Huntington

KISSAM, Charles - 64 y 8 m 28 d; d. 13 November 1879 on East River, New York City on
board his vessel; resident of Centreport

KISSAM, George - d. 15 December 1889 at Brook-
lyn; son of Dr. Daniel Whitehead Kissam;
brother of Mrs. Rev. Charles Sturges of
Huntington; uncle of S. S. Kissam of
Greenlawn; m. Elizabeth W. Rose of Trenton,
N. J. who d. 1852; 2nd m. Phebe Ryerson,

KISSAM, George (continued)
daughter of Jacob Ryerson; former resident
of Huntington

KISSAM, George - d. "this week" at Port Jefferson; 15 November 1890 paper; Greenlawn
item

KISSAM, John O. - 73 y 7 m 14 d; d. 12 December 1887 at Greenlawn

KISSAM, Robert - death reported 15 December
1882 paper; wagon accident; resident of Glen
Cove

KLAUS, Gottleib - d. 3 November 1889 at
Hicksville; interment at Plain Edge

KLEIN, Hannah - suicide 11 September 1884 at
Jamaica; wife of Joseph Klein

KLEINMAN, Bertha - suicide at Quogue; 30 November 1883 paper

KLING, Frederick - 71 years; d. 21 February
1878 at Comac

KNAPP, Frederick - 50 years; suicide 12 September 1883 at Jamaica; Union veteran of
Civil War

KNAPP, Shepard F. - d. 25 December 1886;
New York City businessman; summer resident
of Babylon

KNEELAND, Harvey L. - d. 30 April 1878 at
Cambridge, Massachusetts; agent for
Fuller, Warren & Company

KNIGHT, George T. - 62 years; d. 17 January
1887 at Brooklyn; interment at Huntington

KNOOP, Louise - 54 years; d. 3 June 1886 at
Cold Spring Harbor

KNOWLES, Mr. - funeral 25 October 1886 at
Cypress Hills; father of William Knowles;
Hicksville item

KNOWLES, Mrs. - d. 30 October 1886 at New York
City; mother of William Knowles of Hicksville

KNOX, child - death reported 15 May 1885
paper; child of Rev. W. W. Knox of Bayonne,
New Jersey

KNOX, Rev. John P. - 71 years; d. 2 June 1882
at Newtown

KNUTTEL, Frederick - d. 29 January 1887 at
Hicksville; funeral at Jerusalem

KORN, George H. - 19 years; d. 19 November 1884 at Southold; hunting accident; son of John Korn

KOSKE, John - d. [prob.] at Jamaica; 30 November 1889 paper; "over-indulgence in Polish whiskey"

KOVLER, William - 60 years; d. 28 October 1890 at Central Park; found dead in bed

KRACK, Elizabeth - 54 y 10 m 27 d; d. 14 February 1889 at Hicksville; interment at Westbury; wife of Joseph Krack

KRAEMER, Ernest - 80 years; d. at Amityville; 16 April 1887 paper; long-time resident of Hicksville

KREBS, John - d. 4 February 1885 at Hicksville; trackman of LIRR; injury on the job resulted in blood poisoning

KROHEL, John - d. 15 January 1879 at Syosset; wagon accident caused when horses became frightened by railroad train; resident of Oyster Bay

KUNTS, Rosa Matilda - 6 years; d. 19 January 1889 at Hicksville; interment at Brooklyn; daughter of Louis Kunts

LABORT, James - d. 22 January 1883 at Manor; froze to death

LAHWAN, Lawrence - drowned 29 August 1885 at Northport; upset small boat during a drunken fight

LAIN, Robert B. - ca. 40 years; body washed ashore at Smith's Point 26 July 1879; captain of steamer "Langshaw"

LAMPHEER, Delia - 45 years; d. 5 June 1879 at East Moriches; clothing caught fire

LANDEN, Mathilda - drowned 14 July 1883 at Rockaway Beach

LANDWEHR, Henry - suicide 25 February 1881 at Babylon

LANE, David E. - 9 years; d. 11 April 1888 at East Hartford, Conn.; son of Davis E. and Adrienne E. Lane

LANE, Davis V. - 86 years; d. 13 April 1886 at Huntington; father of Mrs. F. W. Burgess; b. 16 April 1800 in Maine

LANE, Hannah - 75 yrs 8 mos; d. 17 April 1886 at Centreport

LANE, Nancy - 80 years; d. 29 January 1890 at
Huntington; widow of Davis V. Lane; mother
of Davis E. Lane, Mrs. F. W. Burgess, Henry
Lane and the late Mrs. Ollie Velsor; former
resident of Wayne, Maine

LANE, Mrs. Rev. O. C. - d. 20 June 1888;
Riverhead item

LANE, Oliver - d. 25 March 1884 at Riverhead;
thresher machine accident

LANE, William L. - 6 months; d. 15 August 1885
at Cold Spring

LANMAN, Frederick - 55 years; d. 11 August
1888 at Glenwood; fire onboard steamboat
"Bay Ridge"

LARRABEE, Charrie Jane - 58 years; d. 20 March
1882 at Huntington; wife of Robert Larrabee

LARRABEE, Elizabeth - 1 yr 1 mo; d. 28 May
1880 at Oyster Bay; daughter of George
Larrabee

LARRABEE, Gamaliel - 88 years; d. 5 September
1878 at Oyster Bay; father of E. W. Larrabee
and Robert Larrabee

LA RUE, George B. - d. 4 December 1885 at
Broadhead Bridge, Ulster County, N. Y.;
interment at Goshen, N. Y.; station agent at
Syosset

LATTEN, Joseph - d. 10 January 1890 at Newtown; former resident of Oyster Bay

LAUCK, infant - d. 13 May 1885 at Hicksville;
child of Albert Lauck

LAUCK, John Philip Adam - d. 22 April 1889 at
Hicksville; interment at Westbury; Proprie-
tor of Germania Hall; b. Nassau on the
Rhine, Germany 22 August 1822; immigrated to
USA 1853; to Hicksville 1860

LAURIE, Mary - funeral 19 April 1886; Oyster
Bay item

LAVELL, infant - death reported 10 October
1884 paper; child of David Lavell of
Hicksville

LAVELLE, Bessie - 11 months; d. 16 August 1885
at Cold Spring; daughter of Joseph J. and
Annie Lavelle

LAVELLE, David - ca. 25 years; d. 12 November
1885 at Westbury; fell off railroad train

LAVELLE, David (continued)
and run over at Baiting Hollow; still alive,
he was put on westbound train; funeral at
Hicksville
LAWLER, Patrick - d. 12 January 1887 at Whitestone; thrown from wagon by frightened horse
LAWRENCE, Edward A. - 52 years; d. 4 June 1883
at Bayside; son of Effingham Lawrence;
12 years Supervisor of Town of Flushing;
3 terms in New York State Assembly; 2 terms
in New York State Senate; President of
Queens County Agricultural Society
LAWRENCE, Mrs. Jarvis - d. 25 September 1888
at Cold Spring
LAWRENCE, John W. - 91 years; d. 28 December
1888 at Flushing; Member U. S. House of
Representatives from Long Island 1843
[d. 20 December 1888 and served in Congress
1845-1847 per Biographical Directory of the
American Congress 1774-1971]
LAWRENCE, Joseph E. - d. "short time ago" at
Flushing; 2 August 1878 paper; newspaper
editor in California during Gold Rush;
Editor of Flushing Journal; interment at
Bayside
LAWRENCE, Leonard W. - 93 years; d. 30 August
1887 at St. Johnland
LAWRENCE, Mrs. Leonard W. - 95 years;
d. 30 June 1889 at Smithtown
LAWRENCE, Thomas - 65 years; d. 16 February
1884 at Flushing; former Supervisor of Town
of Flushing
LAWRENCE, William S. - 58 y 6 m 5 d;
d. 1 March 1883 at New York City; suffocated
when gas light went out in room at Putnam
House hotel; resident of Huntington
LAWS, J. Benjamin - 83 yrs 1 mo; d. 23 July
1887 at Rocky Point
LEAMY, Michael - 54 years; d. 26 February 1888
at Long Swamp
LEAYCRAFT, Richard - 50 years; d. 2 February
1878 at Brooklyn; former resident of Huntington
LEE, George H. - 19 y 7 m 11 d; d. 8 November
1879 at Huntington; son of S. O. Lee
LEE, Jackson - d. 16 July 1886 at Calverton;
hit by railroad train; resident of Waverly

LEE, Mary - 24 years; 2 July 1880 paper;
"Seawanhaka" fire on East River
LEE, S. - d. 20 February 1888 at Riverhead
LEE, Samuel B. - 88 y 1 m 20 d; d. 20 March
1880 at New Village
LEEK, Halsey S. - 3 y 7 m 12 d; d. 12 June
1882 at Cold Spring; son of Stephen T. and
Fanny Leek
LEET, child - 5 years; drowned 3 February 1890
at Great Neck; drowned in barrel of spring
water
LEFEVRE, William - 60 years; d. at Yaphank;
15 August 1884 paper; hit in face with an
iron by woman he was living with; died of
lockjaw; resident of East Hampton
LEFFERTS, Henry C. - 67 y 1 m 28 d;
d. 8 December 1889 at Brooklyn
LEFFERTS, Henry H. - 31 y 1 m 25 d;
d. 18 December 1887 at Brooklyn; interment
at Huntington
LEFFERTS, Jarvis S. - 73 y 11 m 26 d;
d. 24 May 1882 at West Neck
LEFFERTS, Samuel H. - 87 y 8 m 23 d;
d. 10 October 1882 at Centreport
LEGGETT, Mrs. Abraham - suicide "two weeks
ago" at New Bridge, N. J.; 26 October 1883
paper; former resident of Centreport
LENTILHON, Mrs. - d. 3 January 1890 at Oyster
Bay; interment at New York City; daughter of
Edward Sevan
LEONARD, Mary - ca. 60 years; d. 21 June 1887
at Yaphank; former resident of Huntington
LEONARD, Thomas - 26 years; d. 19 August 1883
near Gravesend; struck by lightning
LEONARD, Thomas F. - 15 years; d. 6 July 1888
at West Neck; son of John Leonard
LEONARD, William - 20 years; d. 11 January
1878 at West Neck; scarlet fever
LESTER, Thomas S. - d. "two weeks ago"; 6 Nov-
ember 1885 paper; "eccentric and wealthy
resident of Southold"
LEUTH, George - d. 6 December 1888 at Wood-
haven; hit by rapid transit train; interment
at Jerusalem; son of Peter Leuth; husband of
Alice Carpenter; b. 5 September 1854 at
Brooklyn; former resident of Hicksville

135

LEUTH, Mrs. Peter - 60 y 5 m 10 d; d. 24 May
1887 at Hicksville

LEVALLY, Gilbert - d. 29 March 1886 at
Riverhead

LEVERICH, Henry S. - 80 years; d. 3 March 1885
at Newtown; commission broker in New York
City; b. at Newtown June 1804

LEVI, George * - d. 6 July 1887; Glen Cove
item; resident "of the Landing"

LEWIS, infant - 2 days; d. 14 January 1884 at
Northport; son of Franklin and Anna A. Lewis

LEWIS, child - 3 years; d. at Oyster Bay Cove;
24 April 1886 paper; son of George Lewis

LEWIS, infant - 6 months; d. 7 August 1888 at
Oyster Bay; child of Frederick Lewis

LEWIS, Abigail C. - 80 yrs 3 mos; d. 15 December 1883 at Northport; widow of Solomon C.
Lewis

LEWIS, Anne - d. 20 February 1880 at Lansingburgh, New York; wife of William B. Lewis

LEWIS, Daniel - 88 years; d. 5 January 1881 at
East Norwich

LEWIS, Dio - 63 years; d. 28 May 1886 at
Yonkers, N. Y.; medical doctor and health
and diet reformer; former resident of
Smithtown; b. at Auburn, N. Y. 3 March 1823

LEWIS, Egbert S. - 65 y 8 m 16 d; d. 19 Novem-
ber 1887 at Northport; son of Joseph C.
Lewis and Sarah Scudder; father of Eva
Carman, Frank Lewis, Alvin Lewis, Joseph C.
Lewis, Egbert Lewis, Fannie Mills and Sara
Selleck; sea captain; "well known among
coasting sailors"

LEWIS, Epenetus - 76 years; d. 23 June 1887 at
Westbury; interment at Green-Wood, Brooklyn;
b. at East Meadow 11 January 1811

LEWIS, Frances - 45 yrs 5 mos; d. 25 July 1889
at Huntington; daughter of Daniel Smith

LEWIS, Frances R. - 50 yrs 9 mos; d. 11 August
1887 at Northport; wife of Egbert G. Lewis

LEWIS, George - 24 years; suicide 11 June 1885
at Locust Valley; placed himself on railroad
tracks to be run over by train; funeral at
Huntington

LEWIS, Henry - 2 yrs 8 mos; d. 1 August 1879
at Oyster Bay Cove; son of George and Ella
Lewis

LEWIS, Henry Francis - 60 years; d. at Brooklyn; funeral 3 January 1889 at Northport; brother of Joseph Lewis and Egbert S. Lewis

LEWIS, Henry L. - 32 years; d. 17 August 1889 at Buffalo, N. Y.; son of Walter L. and Margaret E. Lewis

LEWIS, James W. - 18 yrs 5 mos; d. 4 April 1889 at Huntington

LEWIS, Joseph * - ca. 52 years; suicide 27 February 1885 at Jericho; hanged himself

LEWIS, Lillie May - 5 years; d. [perhaps 20] September 1879 at Oyster Bay; [recorded as 30 September 1879 in 26 September 1879 paper]

LEWIS, Lizzie S. - 25 y 7 m 21 d; d. 14 June 1881 at Northport; wife of Joseph C. Lewis

LEWIS, Mary - d. 20 January 1890 at Westbury; interment at Green-Wood, Brooklyn; mother of Wilbur R. Lewis

LEWIS, Mott - 29 y 7 m 28 d; d. 1 June 1882 at Huntington

LEWIS, Peter - d. 23 June 1888; funeral at Hempstead; merchant in Hempstead

LEWIS, Phebe - 66 y 7 m 19 d; d. 9 January 1888 at Northport; wife of Joseph S. Lewis

LEWIS, Phebe - 38 yrs 24 days; d. 28 July 1888 at Huntington

LEWIS, Phebe F. - 64 years; d. 5 September 1884 at Northport

LEWIS, Sarah Scudder - 91 y 2 m 20 d; d. 6 February 1887 at East Neck

LEWIS, Sarepta - 73 yrs 6 mos; d. at Cold Spring; 8 January 1887 paper

LEWIS, Warren B. - funeral 18 August 1890 at Centreport; interment at Northport

L'HOMMEDIEU, child - 7 years; d. 10 January 1884 at Head of the River, Smithtown; diphtheria; daughter of John L'Hommedieu

L'HOMMEDIEU, Alden - 75 years; d. 25 September 1888 at St. James

L'HOMMEDIEU, Mrs. Charles - 73 years; d. 17 February 1890 at Smithtown Landing; mother of George L'Hommedieu of Centreport

L'HOMMEDIEU, Coles - 44 y 5 m 5 d; d. 26 April 1889 at Comac

L'HOMMEDIEU, Mrs. J. L. - d. 2 August 1890 at
Old Field; interment at Setauket; daughter
of Charles Jayne; resident of Brooklyn
L'HOMMEDIEU, Samuel - 79 years; d. 21 March
1884 at Smithtown Branch
LILLIS, Mr. - drowned at Norwalk, Connecticut;
7 January 1881 paper; funeral at Huntington
LIMBERG, Charlotte Christina - 64 years;
d. 4 April 1888 at Hicksville; wife of
Frederick Limberg
LINCK, Henry - 66 years; d. 13 April 1888 at
Hicksville
LINCOLN, Abraham - 16 years; d. 5 March 1890
at London, England; son of Robert T. Linc-
oln; grandson of President Abraham Lincoln
LINCOLN, Florence H. - d. "last week"; 23 Nov-
ember 1889 paper ; interment at Cohasset,
Massachusetts; Farmingdale item
LINDSAY, Alice - 83 y 9 m 10 d; d. 27 May 1886
at New York City; resident of Huntington
LINDSAY, William - 82 y 1 m 2 d; d. 18 April
1886 at New York City
LINDSTEAD, Leo - 6 months; d. 28 July 1889 at
Crab Meadow; son of Theodore and Albertina
Linstead
LINNINGTON, Stephen - 70 years; d. at Brooklyn
(at his "city home"); 6 March 1885 and 20
March 1885 papers; summer resident of Cold
Spring; cigar merchant in Brooklyn; native
of New Lots
LIPPOLD, Carl H. - 35 years; suicide 21 Sept-
ember 1889 at New York City; shot himself in
the head
LIVINGSTON, Mrs. - d. at Babylon; 17 October
1884 paper; daughter of Elbert Carll; wife
of editor of South Side Signal
LIVINGSTON, Julia Augusta - death reported
12 December 1884 paper; daughter of James
Boggs and Sarah Lloyd Broome; descendant of
James Lloyd, proprietor of the Manor of
Queens Village, Lloyd's Neck; wife of Lewis
Livingston; resident of Rhinebeck, N. Y.
LLOYD, John Henry - d. 10 November 1888; son
of Henry and Caroline B. Lloyd
LOCKE, John D. - d. 28 November 1883 at
Whitestone; tinware manufacturer

LOCKE, Mrs. Richard - d. 23 March 1890; funeral at Smithtown Branch

LOCKITT, John - 59 yrs 5 mos; d. 29 July 1878 at Brooklyn; meat-packing business in Brooklyn; land owner in Huntington; native of England

LOCKWOOD, infant - d. 21 September 1886 at Oyster Bay; child of Edward Lockwood

LOCKWOOD, Carrie - d. at Woodhaven; 12 October 1889 paper; daughter of Rev. Lockwood, formerly of Melville; schoolteacher

LOCKWOOD, Henrietta A. - 2 days; d. 12 September 1879 at New York City

LOCKWOOD, James H. - 65 y 9 m 28 d; d. 28 August 1884 at Cold Spring

LOCKWOOD, Robert H. - 81 years; d. 13 May 1889 at Woodbury; funeral at Cold Spring; brother of James H. Lockwood; son-in-law of John Stillwell; brother-in-law of William Stillwell

LOCKWOOD, Sarah - 20 years; d. 11 February 1878 at Oyster Bay; daughter of Joseph Lockwood

LOCKWOOD, William G. - 68 years; d. 1 September 1880 at Brooklyn; interment at Huntington

LOEHWING, Alfred - 21 y 11 m 24 d; d. 6 January 1890 at Hicksville; graduate of New York College of Pharmacy

LONG, Frank - d. 25 August 1889 at New York City; funeral at Oyster Bay; interment at Cedar Swamp

LONGBOTHAM, Henry - suicide 10 May 1881 at Selden

LOPER, Abraham L. - 29 years; d. 9 November 1886 at Montauk Point; gun accident; resident of Amagansett

LOPER, Annie M. - 3 yrs 2 mos; d. 21 August 1887 at Northport; daughter of William H. and Carrie A. Loper

LOPER, Charles S. - 70 years; d. 1 December 1884 at Riverhead; director of Murray Hill Bank, New York City

LOPER, John - murdered; 5 March 1880 paper; resident of Sag Harbor

LORD, Grace - d. 27 May 1885 at Boston, Massachusetts; killed by falling derrick; sister of Thomas Lord; former resident of Huntington

LORD, Thomas - 84 y 11 m 20 d; d. 9 February 1879 at New York City

LOTT, John A. - d. 20 July 1878 at Flatbush; judge of Supreme Court; President of Long Island Bible Society

LOWNDES, Edward - d. 5 August 1887 at Rowayton, Connecticut

LOWNDES, Ruth - d. 2 June 1890 at Centreport; funeral at South Norwalk, Connecticut; widow of William Lowndes; mother of Mrs. Jarvis, Sylvia Lowndes, Ruth Lowndes, William Lowndes, Allison Lowndes and Ellison Lowndes

LOWRY, Corrinna C. - d. 12 September 1890 at Melville

LOWRY, Edwin - 13 y 9 m 6 d; d. 30 October 1882 at Melville; son of J. J. Lowry

LUCE, Mrs. Hallock F. - d. at Northville; 25 February 1887 paper; choked to death at supper; daughter of Lewis Young

LUDLAM, Robert Feeks - 86 years; d. 8 September 1890 at Oyster Bay; father of Alfred Ludlam and Mrs. E. P. Golden

LUDLAM, Samuel - d. 25 January 1889 at Oyster Bay; interment at Mill Neck

LUDLOW, Judith Ann - d. September 1886; 13 November 1886 paper; resident of Jamaica

LUDLOW, William H. - 70 years; d. at Oakdale [death date not copied]; husband of Frances Nicoll; brother-in-law of William Nicoll; father of Nicoll Ludlow, William Ludlow and Frank Ludlow; Commissioner on Prisoners during Civil War; large landowner; New York State political figure

LUDLUM, George - d. September 1882; 28 March 1884 paper; son of Henry Ludlum

LUDLUM, Henry - 86 years; d. November 1883 at Centre Island; 28 March 1884 paper; father of George Ludlum; grandfather of James H. Ludlum

LUDWIG, King of Bavaria - death reported; 3 July 1886 paper

LUPTON, Josiah B. - 4 yrs 3 mos; d. 1 August
1885 at Miller's Place; son of John D. and
Emma A. Lupton

LUPTON, Josiah H. - 34 y 7 m 20 d; d. 21 June
1881 at Miller's Place

LUSH, Catherine A. - 70 years; d. 30 September
1890 at Hempstead; mother of Carman R. Lush
and Mary E. Bedell

LUX, John - 59 years; d. 30 December 1884 at
Babylon

LUYSTER, Mrs. Charles - d. 6 June 1890 at
Brookville; found dead in churchyard, just
having left the parsonage after visiting
family of Rev. Sewicks; resident of Glen
Cove

LUYSTER, Mrs. Daniel - funeral 21 April 1890;
niece of Richard C. Colyer; resident of
Brookville

LYNCH, Mr. - murdered at New York City in a
saloon by Thomas Shanessy of West Neck
Brickyards; 1 May 1885 paper

LYNCH, child - interment "this week" at
Westbury; 19 January 1889 paper; child of
Peter Lynch of Roslyn

LYNCH, children - children of Peter Lynch of
Roslyn; "buried three of his children" within one week; final one interred 30 January
1889; 2 February 1889 paper; Westbury item

LYMAN, Clara Jane - 4 mos 12 days; d. 9 September 1885 at Huntington Harbor

LYNDE, Mary - 45 years; d. 3 January 1878 at
Glen Cove

LYONS, Ann Maria - 68 years; d. 17 June 1890
at Northport

LYONS, Daniel - murdered 12 February 1890 at
Brooklyn by brother-in-law John McGuinness,
who was found not guilty by reason of self-
defense; 19 July 1890 paper

LYONS, Frank - d. 19 April 1884 at Long Island
City; hit by railroad train; proprietor of
Greenpoint and New York Express; resident of
Greenpoint

LYONS, Thomas - 55 years; d. 10 January 1888
at Setauket

LYONS, Thomas Henry - 24 years; d. 14 June
1879 at Stony Brook; found dead in barn

141

LYSTER, Charles - death reported 14 June 1890
paper; resident of Brookville; formerly of
Woodbury

MAC GEUHY, James - 18 years; drowned 2 June
1879 at Shelter Island; son of Robert Mac
Geuhy

MACGREGOR, Andrew J. - 52 y 8 m 13 d;
d. 15 October 1886 at Crab Meadow

MAC GREGOR, Caroline - death reported 24 April
1886 paper; resident of Oyster Bay Cove

MACK, Bridget - drowned at Hay Beach, Greenport about 1 April 1878; interment at Southold; wife of Daniel T. Mack of East Marion;
"deranged"

MAHAN, Celia K. - 55 y 4 m 4 d; d. 21 June
1887 at Cold Spring Harbor; wife of George
Mahan

MAHAN, Fanny Reamer - 28 yrs 11 mos;
d. 10 March 1885 at Cold Spring; wife of
John Mahan

MAHAN, Lizzie - 14 yrs 1 mos; d. 13 March 1889
at Northport

MAHAR, Robert - murdered 8 July 1884 at
Mineola

MAHAR, Thomas - d. 4 September 1885 at Hicksville; fell dead while robbing a chicken
coop

MAHON, James - 50 years; d. 9 June 1884 at
Northport

MAHON, Samuel - 32 years; drowned 26 May 1888
at New London, Conn.; sailor on schooner
from Cold Spring

MAHONEY, Elizabeth - 75 years; d. 15 May 1878
at Oyster Bay; wife of Daniel Mahoney

MALLOY, Edward W. - 16 yrs 4 mos; d. 1 April
1878 at Northport

MALLOY, Jesse - 21 y 10 m 25 d; d. 15 August
1881 at Northport; son of William H. and
Adelia Malloy

MALLOY, Josephine A. - 7 y 1 m 16 d; d. 2 August 1884 at Northport; daughter of William
H. and Adelia Malloy

MALONE, John - drowned 5 July 1887 off Center
Island

MALONEY, James - interment 20 November 1889 at
Westbury

MALONEY, Margaret - 2 July 1880 paper; resident of New York City; "Seawanhaka" fire on East River

MANEY, Belle - d. "recently" in China; 27 February 1880 paper; see: MC KIEGE Isabella

MANLEY, Maria M. - 82 y 3 m 20 d; d. 13 February 1888 at Fresh Pond; interment at New Brunswick, N. J.; wife of John A. Manley

MANN, Anna H. - 20 y 11 m 17 d; d. 28 August 1883 at Huntington; adopted daughter of William Mott

MANN, Harry - ca. 10 years; drowned 28 September 1883 at Smithtown; funeral at Comac

MANN, Henry - d. 25 March 1886 at Syosset

MANN, Mrs. Jacob - d. 26 February 1885 at Hicksville

MANN, Josephine - 36 yrs 2 mos; d. 9 March 1879 at Smithtown

MANN, Mamie - 7 years; d. 14 August 1889 at Hicksville; "alcoholic poisoning"; given a little whiskey to settle upset stomach, she drank herself an overdose from whiskey bottle; daughter of Jacob Mann

MANN, William - 67 years; d. 11 December 1881 at Lloyd's Neck; interment at Setauket

MANNIE, Sarah - interment 28 June 1885 at Northport; niece of Elkanah Soper; resident of Brooklyn

MANNING, Robert S. - suicide "a few days ago" in New Jersey; 2 July 1880 paper

MANNY, Dennis - d. 22 July 1879 at Brooklyn; yellow fever

MANNY, Loretta - 3 months; d. 7 July 1887 at Huntington; daughter of Corenelius J. and Mary J. Manny

MANSON, Edwin C. - 28 y 3 m 2 d; d. 3 December 1883 at Brooklyn; interment at Huntington; grandson of Jonathan Jarvis

MARAN, Thomas - 18 years; d. 10 January 1879 at Glen Cove; coasting accident; struck head on bridge abutment

MARBLE, John - funeral 8 October 1889 at Bethpage

MARCY, John S. - d. 3 May 1885 at Brooklyn; former member of New York State Legislature from Suffolk County; former president of

143

MARCY, John S. (continued)
  Suffolk County Agricultural Society;
  resident of Riverhead
MARGOT, Frank - d. 24 October 1889 at Bethpage
  Junction; run over by railroad train; inter-
  ment at Westbury
MARSH, Cornelia Edith - 3 y 5 m 20 d;
  d. 13 February 1879 at New York City;
  daughter of Dr. E. T. T. Marsh
MARSH, John - 1 yr 5 mos; d. 22 August 1884 at
  New York City; interment at Huntington
MARSH, Mamie E. - 4 mos 4 days; d. 14 August
  1882 at Long Swamp; daughter of John and
  Emma E. Marsh
MARSHALL, Edwin Madison - 2 y 9 m 6 d;
  d. 26 November 1878 at Brooklyn; grandson
  of Thomas F. Marshall
MARSHALL, Martha Grant - 5 years; d. 18 Decem-
  ber 1878 at Brooklyn; niece of Thomas F.
  Marshall; formerly of Huntington
MARSHALL, Mary A. - 62 y 6 m 4 d; d. 22 Sept-
  ember 1885 at Miller's Place
MARSHALL, Thomas F. - 58 years; d. 21 July
  1885 at Brooklyn; interment at Cypress
  Hills; pilot on East River ferry boats;
  former resident of Huntington
MARTIN, Maggie - 7 years; d. 28 June 1885 at
  Brooklyn; ate pickles colored by copper
MARTIN, Norman Melville - 6 mos 18 days;
  d. 3 July 1881 at New York City; son of
  Louis and Susan Martin
MARTIN, Patrick - d. at Hauppauge 4 July 1879
  paper
MARTLING, George F. - 35 years; d. 18 February
  1885 at New York City; former resident of
  Huntington
MARTLING, Vincent - 75 years; d. 6 February
  1886 at East Norwich
MASSAKER, William - d. 5 December 1890 at
  Oyster Bay
MASSET, Elizabeth - 49 yrs 5 mos; d. 13 Sept-
  ember 1889 at New York City; interment at
  Calvary Cemetery, Queens County; sister of
  Mrs. August Fleischbein of Hicksville
MATEAR, William J. - 37 years; d. 5 December
  1880 at New York City; interment at North-
  port

MATHEW, Sarah H. * - 33 years; d. 10 February
1889 at Dix Hills
MATTDEUX, Isaac - 17 years; d. 28 April 1884
at Manhasset; killed by a young colt; son of
William Mattdeux
MATTHEWS, Chief Engineer - d. near Long Beach;
29 May 1886 paper; struck by lightning;
engineer for Long Beach Waterworks
MATTHEWS, Emily Caroline - d. at Brooklyn;
interment 4 March 1890 at Hempstead; wife of
Smith Matthews; former resident of Hempstead
MATTHEWS, Mrs. Harmon - d. 2 September 1890 at
Syosset; "an elderly lady"
MATTHEWS, James - ca. 30 years; drowned 14
July 1882 at Northport
MATTHIAS, Herman - d. 1 June 1880 at Hicks-
ville; resident of Syosset
MATTHIAS, Washington W. - 43 years; d. 9 March
1885 at Northport
MAURER, Philip - death reported 20 July 1883
paper; resident of Huntington
MAXIM, Mrs. John - 64 years; d. 9 March 1886
at Plain Edge
MAXWELL, Celia Gardner Alexander - d. 16 Octo-
ber 1888 at Aix-les-Bains, France; daughter
of George W. Alexander; wife of Henry W.
Maxwell; involved in charity work in Brook-
lyn; resident of Brooklyn; summer resident
of Huntington; b. Fairmount, Westchester
County, N. Y. in 1857
MAXWELL, Isabella - d. "about 3 weeks ago" at
Dublin, Ireland; 29 September 1882 paper;
sister of James Maxwell
MAY, Benjamin S. - died of typhoid fever;
27 February 1885 paper; resident of Manetto
Hill
MAY, John - d. 10 August 1884 near Manhattan
Beach; killed in railroad accident; former
resident of Hicksville
MAY, Louisa - 19 yrs 9 mos; d. 9 May 1887 at
Plainview; consumption; daughter of Francis
May
MAYBEE, Annie - 39 years; murdered 17 November
1883 at Brookville; daughter of Garrett
Maybee

MAYBEE, Mrs. Garrett - 71 years; murdered
  17 November 1883 at Brookville
MAYHEW, infant * - d. 14 February 1889 at Dix
  Hills; child of James Mayhew
MAYHEW, Ann * - 74 years; d. 17 April 1889 at
  Westbury
MAYHEW, Oscar Frank [*?] - d. 28 August 1890
  at Westbury
MAYHEW, Prince Albert- 32 years; d. 1 Septem-
  ber 1889 at Westbury
MAYHEW, Sarah * - 33 years; d. 10 February
  1889 at Dix Hills
MAYNARD, William - d. "last week" at River-
  head; 30 November 1889 paper; an "old
  citizen"
MAYNZ, Jeanette - suicide 20 January 1886 at
  Amityville; hanged herself; inmate of Long
  Island Home
MC ALLISTER, Rev. William - d. 3 January 1880
  at New York City; M. E. minister with the
  New York East Conference
MC BRIEN, Julia - 7 yrs 4 mos; d. 24 June 1886
  at East Neck; daughter of William and
  Bridget Mc Brien
MC CAFFREY, Patrick - found in well 29 April
  1886
MC CARTNEY, Maria - 32 years; d. 6 December
  1888 at West Neck
MC CARTY, James - 28 yrs 6 mos; d. 16 March
  1887 at Mineola; resident of Hicksville
MC CARTY, Thomas - 24 yrs 6 mos; d. 19 June
  1887; Hicksville item; son of James Mc Carty
MC CAULEY, Annie - 3 yrs 3 mos; d. 20 December
  1884 at Huntington
MC CAULEY, Isaac H. - 61 years; d. 26 September 1879 at Chester, Pennsylvania; brother
  of Rev. Thomas Mc Cauley of Chester, Pa.;
  lawyer at Chambersburg, Pennsylvania
MC CAULEY, Patience M. - d. 12 December 1889
  at Vernon Valley; "death resulted from old
  age"
MC CAUSLAND, Mary A. - 22 years; d. 17 August
  1878 at Comac; interment at New York City
MC CLELLAN, General [George B.] - d. 29 October 1885 at [Orange, N. J.]; [Union general
  during Civil War; Democratic candidate for
  President 1864; post-war Governor of N. J.]

MC CLURE, Thomas - given up for lost; 27 November 1885 paper; left on ship for Charleston, S. C. on 10 October 1885; never heard from again; resident of Riverhead

MC CLOUD, James - suicide 8 May 1881 at Breslau

MC COHN, Minnie - 18 years; d. 20 July 1890 at Floral Park; grand-daughter of Washington Smith of Centerport

MC CONNELL, Garrie G. - 9 months; d. 1 August 1888 at Centreport

MC CORD, Mrs. Thomas - 40 years; d. 8 March 1888 at Hicksville; funeral at Plain Edge

MC CORMICK, Peter - murdered 22 June 1884 at Long Island City by Patrick Kiernan

MC COUN, "Ex-Vice Chancellor" - 93 years; d. 18 July 1878; interment at Oyster Bay; father of Charles Mc Coun; judge; vice-chancellor of First Circuit 1831; justice of Supreme Court Second District 1847; resident of New York City

MC COUN, Joseph - d. 9 June 1886 at Oyster Bay

MC COUN, Mary - d. 4 February 1885 at Oyster Bay

MC COY, Jane - 12 years; drowned 23 July 1878 at Great Neck; resident of Mineola

MC CUE, Patrick - 50 years; d. 15 February 1878 at Jamaica; hit by railroad train while walking on tracks; resident of East New York

MC CULLOCH, David S. - 1 y 9 m 3 d; d. 23 October 1889 at Brooklyn; son of David Mc Culloch

MC CULLOCH, David Scott - 6 mos 27 days; d. 17 July 1887 at Brooklyn

MC CULLOCH, Eddie - 6 y 7 m 4 d; d. 14 July 1881 at Huntington; son of David and Catherine Mc Culloch

MC CUSKER, Mrs. - 80 years; d. 23 June 1889; Westbury item; mother of Rev. J. J. Mc Cusker

MC DERMOTT, John - 22 yrs 11 mos; d. 27 February 1888 at Brooklyn

MC DONALD, James - suicide 30 May 1882 at East Patchogue

MC DOUGALL, Rev. James - 87 yrs 7 days; d. 24 March 1888 at Brooklyn; son of Hugh

MC DOUGALL, Rev. James (continued)
Mc Dougall; m. Julia Ann Kitchel 1833;
father of Mrs. Dr. Banks; b. Newark, N. J.
16 March 1805; graduated Princeton College
1830; "stated supply" for Presbyterian
churches in Virginia and West Va.; served in
Huntington 1836-1854 and Freeport 1856-1862;
retired from ministry in 1862; funeral at
Huntington conducted by Rev. Carter of First
Presbyterian, Rev. Putnam of Second Presbyterian and Rev. Peck of St. John's Episcopal
MC EVOY, Mrs. Dennis - 56 years; d. 2 April
1880 at Oyster Bay
MC FARREN, Mrs. Robert - d. at New York City;
funeral 12 April 1885 at Comac
MC GARRICK, Frank - d. 17 July 1884 at New-
town; hit by railroad train
MC GINNIE, James - 25 years; d. "about a month
ago" at Memphis, Tennessee; stepped on
broken electric light wire; funeral 12
November 1888 at Huntington; native of West
Neck
MC GOVERN, John - 2 July 1880 paper; resident
of New York City; "Seawanhaka" fire on East
River
MC GREGOR, Mary E. - 64 y 5 m 2 d; d. 20 February 1888 at New Haven, Conn.; widow of
Henry Mc Gregor; former resident of Cold
Spring
MC INTYRE, A. P. - death reported 19 July 1890
paper; Editor of the Long Island City
Tribune
MC KAY, James Thomson - 47 years; d. 20 May
1890 at Huntington; son of Duncan Mc Kay;
wrote short stories, poems and magazine
articles for "Century", "Lippincott's" and
"Atlantic Monthly"; b. New York City
22 January 1843; lived in Huntington since
1850; lost sight in one eye from a child-
hood accident; gradually lost sight in other
eye and went totally blind; sister Margaret
read and wrote for him after he became blind
MC KENNA, Peter - 55 y 1 m 6 d; d. 13 January
1889 at Huntington
MC KEON, James - d. 30 January 1882 at Islip;
fell between cars on railroad train

MC KIEGE, Isabella - 25 y 8 m 21 d; d. 29 December 1879 at Shanghai, China; interment at Northport 29 March 1880   see: MANEY Belle

MC KITTRICK, James - drowned in Long Island Sound with sinking of the "Mary Hamilton"; 4 January 1884 paper; resident of St. James

MC LEAN, child - drowned 30 January 1878 at Roslyn; fell through the ice; son of P. B. Mc Lean

MC LOUGHLIN, Michael F. - 38 years; d. 2 August 1885 at Northport; New York City alderman 1883

MC MANN, James - 50 years; d. 26 October 1889 at Huntington; interment at Westbury

MC MENOMY, Elizabeth J. - 61 y 8 m 18 d; d. 25 May 1885 at Long Swamp

MC MILLEN, Andrew - 3 mos 9 days; d. 17 August 1887 at East Northport; son of Andrew C. and Helen Mc Millan

MC NAMA, Rachael - 87 y 1 m 9 d; d. 31 January 1890 at Melville

MC NAMARA, Thomas - 31 years; d. at Brooklyn; funeral 5 December 1890 at Central Park; son of Cornelius Mc Namara; native of Central Park

MC QUEEN, Andrew - d. 20 October 1889 at Oyster Bay; father of James Mc Queen

MC QUEEN, Maynard - 4 yrs 7 mos; d. 2 February 1880 at Oyster Bay; son of James and Julie Mc Queen

MC SWINEY, Helena B. - 37 years; d. 3 March 1879 at Huntington

MC TOYE, Harry D. - 13 years; drowned 13 February 1887 at Garden City; choir boy at Garden City Cathedral; resident of Brooklyn

MC VAY, Sarah - 62 years; d. 17 January 1885 at Miller's Place

MEAD, Warren - d. 13 July 1880 at Rye, N. Y.; hit by railroad train

MEAD, William - 57 y 7 m 14 d; d. 14 February 1882 at Brooklyn; former resident of Lloyd's Neck

MEADE, Clara Forsyth Meigs - 68 years; d. 5 February 1879 at Huntington; widow of Capt. Richard W. Meade, U. S. N.; interment at Philadelphia, Pa.

MEAGLE, child - 10 months; murdered 28 September 1885 at Maspeth; drowned in a drain on Grand Street, Maspeth, by its father, Henry Meagle

MEDAB, Sarah Elizabeth * - 21 yrs 7 mos; d. 21 November 1881 at Huntington

MEET, Sarah * - d. at Roslyn from injuries sustained when hit by railroad train 31 December 1878 while lying on track during a fit; 10 January 1879 paper

MEIS, Mrs. John - 52 years; d. 29 April 1890 at Hicksville; mother of Mrs. Henry Rence

MEISCHEIN, child - death reported; 14 August 1886 paper; when child died its mother Catherine Meischein of Manorville attempted suicide

MELTON, Emma - d. 11 May 1878 at Lakeland; overdose of opium; wife of H. Ben Melton

MELVILLE, Mary - 32 years; d. 12 November 1885 at Williamsburgh

MENKING, Frederick G. - 72 y 7 m 13 d; d. 27 June 1885 at Huntington

MERCHANT, Edward - suicide 2 March 1888 at Breslau; shot himself

MERCLE, Oscar - ca. 24 years; suicide ca. 8 November 1885 at West Babylon

MERRIAM, William W. - d. "two or three weeks ago" at Southampton; 9 February 1889 paper; left $80,000 to U. S. government in his will; eccentric school teacher who once taught at Melville; heir to part of Merriam-Webster dictionary fortune

MERRIFIELD, Edward - 28 years; d. 3 July 1880 at Brooklyn; interment at Huntington

MERRIFIELD, Nancy - 62 y 8 m 23 d; d. 5 January 1886 at Brooklyn; interment at Huntington

MERRILL, Mary S. - 3 y 10 m 6 d; d. 17 September 1888 at New York City

MERRITT, Coles - death reported; 23 March 1889 paper; "aged and respected resident of East Meadow"

MERRITT, Fowler - 77 years; d. 14 February 1888 at Huntington; native of New York City

MERRITT, John E. - 49 years; d. 15 April 1890 at Bayville; steamboat captain

MERRITT, Julia - 68 y 7 m 8 d; d. 23 February
1884 at Huntington; wife of Fowler Merritt
MERRITT, Rebecca - d. 23 February 1884 at
Bayville; mother of Daniel Merritt
MERRITT, Sally M. - 73 years; d. 28 December
1886 at Tarrytown Heights, N. Y.; interment
at Huntington
MERRY, Anna J. * - 10 months; d. 6 September
1884 at Huntington; daughter of Elijah Merry
MERRY, Martha A. * - 3 mos 17 days;
d. 14 September 1887 at Huntington
MERRY, William H. * - 6 mos 12 days;
d. 14 March 1890 at Huntington
MESSMER, William - d. "last week" at Hempstead; 23 August 1890 paper; carriage
accident; horse ran off; Messmer thrown from
carriage and broke neck
METZ, John - killed at North Babylon when barn
collapsed; 5 October 1883 paper
METZER, Miss - 22 years; drowned 27 July 1890
at Lackawaxen, Pa.; resident of Glen Cove
MEYER, child - 6 years; d. at New York City;
diphtheria; interment 23 May 1888 at
Jerusalem; daughter of Henry Meyer;
niece of Mrs. John Dauch
MEYER, Lewis - d. 27 August 1884 at Winfield;
butcher; froze to death in ice box
MEYERS, Theodore - 35 years; d. 23 December
1890 at Hempstead; blind musician
MIDDLETON, Rev. Dr. - funeral 11 July 1888 at
Glen Cove; Episcopal clergyman; rector of
St. Paul's at Glen Cove; Archdeacon of
Queens County
MILES, Charles E. - d. 20 July 1883 at Baby-
lon; Superintendent of Kerosene Bureau of
Brooklyn Fire Department
MILES, Mary M. - 66 y 11 m 19 d; d. 23 Novem-
ber 1890 at Huntington; mother of Rowland
Miles and Mrs. Edgar Hallock; former resi-
dent of Northport
MILLER, Anna M. - 15 y 6 m 15 d; d. 11 Febru-
ary 1885 at Mount Sinai
MILLER, Annie - d. at Hempstead; interment
2 November 1889 at Plain Edge; former
resident of Manetto Hill

MILLER, C. Ophelia - 69 years; d. 20 January
1888 at Miller's Place; widow of Edwin N.
Miller

MILLER, Frank - 15 years; drowned 1 September
1889 at Bridgehampton in Long Pond while
gathering water lilies; resident of Amagansett

MILLER, Frederick - 45 y 3 m 7 d; d. 17 March
1884 at Mount Sinai

MILLER, George - d. 21 October 1883 at Riverhead; former Suffolk County judge

MILLER, Mrs. George - d. "two weeks" before 21
October 1883; 9 November 1883 paper

MILLER, George W. - 19 years; d. 16 February
1890 at Oyster Bay Cove; interment at Cold
Spring

MILLER, Henry - murdered June 1888 at Coney
Island; Jockey James Stone sentenced to be
hanged for murder; 28 December 1889 paper

MILLER, Herbert - 2 yrs 1 mo; d. 16 October
1890 at Northport; son of John Miller

MILLER, Horace A. - 65 years; d. 12 November
1878 at East New York; hit by railroad
train; father of Mrs. Moreland Conklin;
flour dealer; resident of East New York
since 1855

MILLER, James - 5 months; d. 8 May 1889 at
Cold Spring

MILLER, John - 73 years; d. 19 November 1884
at Brooklyn; resident of Port Jefferson

MILLER, Mrs. John - d. 26 November 1890 at
Patchogue

MILLER, John H. - 73 years; funeral 27 April
1885 at West Islip; interment at Babylon

MILLER, Mrs. Jonathan - 80 years; d. 19 December 1879 at Arshamamoque, near Greenport;
killed in house fire; sister of Edward King

MILLER, Laura - 82 years; d. 11 October 1882
at Smithtown Branch

MILLER, Maria - 47 years; d. 19 October 1887
at Oyster Bay Cove

MILLER, Mary R. - 30 y 2 m 8 d; d. 12 September 1887 at Huntington; daughter of Isaac
and Mary Brown; wife of John Miller; native
of Hauppauge

MILLER, Smith - 58 yrs 2 mos; d. 1 May 1881 at
Oyster Bay

MILLER, Stella - 3 years; d. 25 January 1889
  at Huntington; daughter of John Miller;
  granddaughter of Isaac Brown
MILLINGTON, Samuel F. - 61 yrs; d. 19 August
  1882 at Greenlawn
MILLS, Ann Eliza - 51 y 6 m 23 d; d. 18 June
  1880 at Huntington; wife of J. Thomas Mills
MILLS, Caroline - 66 y 1 m 9 d; d. 8 July 1889
  at Fresh Pond
MILLS, Charles E. - 56 years; d. 19 July 1886
  at Philadelphia, Pa.
MILLS, Clarissa H. * - 95 years; d. 19 August
  1885 at Brooklyn; interment at Huntington;
  mother of George A. Mills and Isabella
  Simms; b. Jerusalem South 2 July 1790;
  60 years a resident of Huntington
MILLS, E. S. - 3 mos; d. 8 July 1880 at
  Smithtown; daughter of J. B. Mills
MILLS, Emily C. - 67 years; d. 17 March 1884
  at Smithtown; wife of William H. Mills
MILLS, Henry - interment 30 December 1890 at
  Port Jefferson; resident of Setauket
MILLS, Horatio W. - 2 July 1880 paper;
  resident of Smithtown; "Seawanhaka" fire on
  East River; son of Wickham Mills
MILLS, John E. - 49 y 8 m 22 d; d. 28 December
  1879 at Fresh Pond
MILLS, Jonas D. - 86 y 8 m 20 d; d. 30 January
  1882 at Hempstead; interment at Smithtown
MILLS, Mary C. - 80 yrs 4 mos; d. 21 June 1881
  at Hempstead; wife of Jonas D. Mills
MILLS, Richard D. - ca. 70 years; d. 1 Febru-
  uary 1884 at Ronkonkoma
MILLS, Sidney * - 70 years; d. 23 August 1890
  at Northport; "a worthy colored resident";
  "a conscientious and consistant Christian"
MILLS, Mrs. Thomas - d. 5 December 1887 at
  Oyster Bay
MILTENBERGER, Anton - d. 14 June 1887 at
  Hempstead; blood poisoning
MILTENBERGER, Henry - 10 days; d. 25 September
  1889 at Westbury; interment at Hempstead;
  son of Antonia Miltenberger
MINDERMAN, William - 24 years; suicide 13 Oct-
  ober 1890 at Hicksville; shot himself

MINOR, Mrs. - d. 30 November 1887 at Oyster
Bay; "one of the oldest residents of this
village"

MINOR, Sarah T. - 60 years; d. 6 June 1889
at Oyster Bay; interment at Oyster Bay Cove;
wife of Ezra Minor

MITCHELL, Edward E. - 81 years; d. at Flushing; 27 July 1889 paper; son of Rev. Edward
Mitchell; business partner of A. T. Stewart

MITCHELL, Elijah - d. 16 March 1887 at
Brooklyn; interment at Oyster Bay

MITCHELL, John - drowned in sinking of
schooner off Eaton's Neck; 1 May 1885 paper;
resident of South Brooklyn

MITCHELL, Nancy * - 89 years; d. 9 April 1881
at Sunken Meadow

MITCHELL, Patrick - drowned in sinking of
schooner off Eaton's Neck; 1 May 1885 paper;
resident of South Brooklyn

MITCHELL, Rev. Silas * - "over 80" years;
d. "this week" [date of paper not copied];
pastor of "colored church at Lakeville";
well known in Oyster Bay; formerly pastor of
African M. E. Zion Church in Oyster Bay and
served elsewhere on Long Island, Connecticut, Rhode Island and the Hudson River
Valley

MITCHELL, Warren - 84 years; d. 15 January
1888 at Manhasset

MOISES, Eugene - 24 years; d. 5 January 1881
at Oyster Bay

MONFORT, Anne E. - 59 y 10 m 9 d; d. 16 September 1887 at Woodbury; daughter of Walter
Cox; widow of Obadiah V. Monfort

MONFORT, Clarence - 8 mos; d. 25 July 1881 at
Oyster Bay; son of Franklin P. and Frances
A. Monfort

MONFORT, Elbert - d. 23 December 1889 at
Syosset; "old resident"

MONFORT, Emma P. - 29 y 2 m 3 d; d. 23 December 1881 at Jamaica; interment at Huntington; daughter of Mrs. M. P. Tappen; wife of
Henry A. Monfort

MONFORT, Garret - d. 11 November 1889 at
Hempstead; Hempstead merchant with "Monfort
& Hammond"

MONFORT, Garrett - 54 years; d. 3 January 1878 at Glen Cove

MONFORT, Mrs. George - d. "last week" at Brooklyn; 1 January 1886 paper; interment at Brookville; daughter of Henry Bayles of Oyster Bay

MONFORT, Frank - d. suicide 19 November 1887 at East Norwich; took arsenic

MONFORT, Ida - 23 years; drowned 18 August 1888 at Oyster Bay; funeral at Glen Cove; sister of George Monfort

MONFORT, Madeline - 3 y 7 m 16 d; d. 19 December 1881 at Jamaica; daughter of Henry A. and Emma Monfort; interment at Huntington

MONFORT, Mrs. Madison - funeral "this week"; 12 April 1890 paper; interment at Brookville; sister of Andrew J. Luyster

MONFORT, Mary - d. 25 September 1890 at Woodbury; daughter of Francis Wicks; wife of Samuel V. Monfort; former organist at Huntington M. E. Church; secretary of Mite Society, Woodbury M. E. Church

MONFORT, Obadiah V. - 63 yrs 2 mos; d. 5 January 1885 at Woodbury; from leg injury received in railroad accident; son of William Monfort; husband of Elizabeth Cox; native of Black Stump, Flushing

MONILAWS, Catharine Ann - 51 years; d. 12 August 1890 at Oyster Bay

MONROE, Frankie - 9 months; d. 3 July 1886 at St. Johnland

MOODY, Peter C. - d. 19 April 1888 at Huntington

MOON, Mrs. Joseph - d. 9 July 1889; Riverhead item; stomach cancer; daughter of Isaac Winters

MOON, Sarah - 60 y 3 m 7 d; d. 30 May 1888 at West Neck

MOORE, infant - d. 18 January 1889 at Brooklyn; interment at Port Jefferson; child of Charles L. Moore; grandchild of Mrs. Samuel Emmons

MOORE, Mrs. - d. 17 November 1889 at Queens; interment at Plattsburg, Canada; "one of our oldest residents"; mother of Mrs. Foster

MOORE, Mrs. - d. 3 December 1890; Westbury item; mother of Clara Moore

MOORE, Alfred - d. 16 September 1878 at West
     Islip; fell down dead; resident of Orange,
     New Jersey
MOORE, Catharine - 2 yrs 11 mos; d. 11 August
     1886 at Cold Spring Harbor; daughter of
     Thomas Moore
MOORE, Daniel - 2 July 1880 paper; resident of
     New York City; "Seawanhaka" fire on East
     River
MOORE, Mrs. Rev. W. H. - d. 29 June 1886; wife
     of rector of St. George's Church, Hempstead
MORGAN, Benjamin - d. 3 May 1886 at Northport
MORLEY, Rev. - d. 14 September 1890 at Hicks-
     ville; interment at Cypress Hills; former
     M. E. pastor at Hicksville
MORLEY, Mary - d. 6 March 1890 at Hicksville;
     interment at Cypress Hills
MORRELL, Joseph S. - d. 12 November 1886 at
     Mineola; found dead in the road; resident of
     New Haven, Connecticut
MORRIS, Mrs. - d. 14 November 1889 at New York
     City; fractured skull when she fell from
     stairs at elevated railroad station; mother-
     in-law of Rev. A. G. Russell of Oyster Bay;
     resident of Princeton, New Jersey
MORRIS, John - 54 y 11 m 28 d; d. 5 January
     1887 at Huntington
MORRIS, Merides - d. 11 September 1883 at New
     York City; injured in railroad accident at
     Long Island City
MORRIS, Miles - murdered 24 July 1880 at Sag
     Harbor
MORRIS, Richard - 82 years; d. 3 May 1882 at
     Huntington
MORRIS, Thomas - 70 years; d. 4 June 1878 at
     New York City in 6th Avenue Car; unclaimed
     body buried in public ground; family
     identified clothing and photograph at
     morgue; re-interment at Black Stump;
     resident of Great Neck, where he was
     employed for 20 years by Benjamin Hicks
MORRIS, Winifred - 38 years; d. 19 May 1882 at
     Old Fields; sister of Stephen Morris
MORRISON, James E. - death reported 18 June
     1887 paper; Oyster Bay item; son-in-law of
     C. J. Chipp

MOTT, child - d. 6 August 1890 at Mount Sinai;
daughter of Ellsworth Mott
MOTT, infant - d. at Mount Sinai; 16 Aug. 1890
paper; daughter of Everett and Joanna Mott
MOTT, Mrs. Connell [? Cornell] - d. 12 July
1890 at Old Westbury; interment at Westbury;
sister of Benamin Albertson and Hicks
Albertson
MOTT, Mrs. George A. - d. 15 February 1888 at
Brooklyn; interment at Northport
MOTT, Jacob - funeral 16 October 1889 at
Westbury; nephew of Cornell Mott; resident
of Glenwood
MOTT, James - 77 years; d. 15 March 1889 at
Glenwood
MOTT, Maggie May - 10 y 6 m 19 d; d. 5 March
1885 at Comac; daughter of William J. and
Mary C. Mott
MOTT, Margaret Bronson - 8 mos 18 days;
d. 9 August 1882 at Huntington; daughter of
Henry G. Mott
MOTT, Mary - 62 y 7 m 10 d; d. 18 November
1887 at Northport; widow of James S. Mott
MOTT, Oliver - d. 22 May 1883 at Hempstead
MOTT, Phebe - 90 years; d. 22 November 1880 at
Melville
MOTT, Ruth - 65 years; d. 28 August 1888 at
Melville; sister of Jesse Mott
MOTT, Susie - d. 19 July 1888; Farmingdale
item
MOTT, William - funeral 16 October 1889 at
Hicksville
MOTT, William E. - 51 yrs 2 mos; d. 25 December 1883 at Huntington
MOTTER, Samuel - ca. 55 years; d. at Millersburg, Pennsylvania; article "A Blasphemer's
Awful Death" in 19 February 1886 paper
MOWBRAY, Jarvis Rogers - d. 28 July 1886;
funeral at Islip; interment at Bay Shore;
son of Eliphalet Mowbray; physician at
Islip; held various offices in Town of Islip
government
MULCAHEY, Mrs. Patrick - d. 24 September 1887
at Glen Cove; found dead in cistern
MULFORD, Albert G. - 68 y 8 m 12 d; d. 27 June
1881 at Northport

MULFORD, Edward - 65 years; d. 6 June 1890
near Sing Sing, N. Y.; interment at Patchogue; on way to Sing Sing Prison to serve
term for aggravated assault when he suddenly
died on the railroad train; resident of
Patchogue; "He was a hard case"

MULFORD, Mrs. Henry - funeral 21 June 1884 at
Northport

MULFORD, Henry C. - 7 mos 18 days; d. 12 August 1885 at Northport; son of Henry D. and
Carrie E. Mulford

MULLANE, John H. - d. 13 January 1887; Hicksville item

MULLEN, Thomas - 53 years; d. 30 October 1883
at West Neck

MULLER, Mrs. - d. 12 January 1886 at Hicksville; went to milk cow; didn't return and
was found dead in barn

MULLINGS, Fannie A. - 38 years; d. 24 January
1889 at East Norwalk, Conn.; daughter of
J. M. Drake of Huntington; wife of Charles
A. Mullings

MUNCY, Elizabeth - 86 years; d. at Babylon;
interment 21 December 1885; mother of
Jesse Muncy of North Babylon

MUNSELL, James - 59 y 5 m 16 d; drowned
3 September 1882 at Mount Sinai

MUNSELL, Julia E. - 33 y 2 m 10 d; d. 13 February 1887 at Northport

MUNSON, Lillie - "committed suicide a few days
ago"; interment 28 May 1890 at Westbury;
daughter of Levi Munson; resident of Flower
Hill

MURDOCK, William - 65 y 3 m 16 d; d. 6 February 1881 at Center Moriches

MURE, Charles L. - 81 years; d. 3 December
1882 at St. Johnland

MURPHY, Ann - 51 years; d. 10 August 1882 at
Laurelton, Cold Spring

MURPHY, Catharine - 61 yrs 6 mos; d. 19 February 1880 at Melville

MURPHY, John M. - 23 years; d. 15 August 1884
at Waterbury, Jerauld County, Dakota Territory [now South Dakota]; killed by harbonic
acid gas while working in well; former resident of Huntington

MURPHY, Joseph - 5 yrs 5 mos; d. 30 December
1882 at Melville
MURPHY, Thomas - 61 years; d. 4 February 1883
at Huntington
MURPHY, Thomas - 11 mos 13 days; d. 30 July
1884 at Melville
MURPHY, Thomas - 31 y 6 m 6 d; d. 7 April 1888
at Melville
MURRAY, E. Walton - 31 years; d. 2 March 1880
at Woodbury
MURRAY, Edward - 12 y 2 m 18 d; d. 12 August
1878 at Little Neck
MURRAY, James - 31 years; d. 20 May 1889 at
Cold Spring; internal injuries received
"last fall" while loading sand onto schooner
at Rockaway; captain of schooner "Mary
Bird"; son-in-law of Edward Clark
MURRAY, John Milton * - 21 years; d. 26 June
1880 at Artist Lake; escaped from Suffolk
County Lunatic Asylum; shot and killed while
attacking a family
MURRAY, John V. - body found 9 August 1886
near Jamaica; fell off railroad train while
drunk; resident of Long Island City
MUSANTE, Rosa - 1 1/2 years; d. 29 August 1889
at Plainview; interment at Westbury;
daughter of Andrew Musante
MYERS, Albert W. * - 2 mos 16 days; d. 9 March
1883 at Huntington; son of Elbert Myers
MYERS, Caroline - d. 11 December 1888 at Woodbury; funeral at Hicksville; daughter of
Louis H. Myers
MYERS, Christopher - d. at Long Island City;
11 January 1890 paper; killed by falling
brick wall
NAIRNE, Thomas H. - 38 years; suicide 7 July
1884 at New York City
NAUMANN, Josephine - infant; d. 27 December
1890 at Hicksville; interment at Hempstead
NEALE, William - d. 10 February 1883 at Cold
Spring; suddenly of cerebral hemorrhage;
interment at Brooklyn
NELSON, Alfred - 1 yr 4 mos; d. 4 April 1880
at Oyster Bay; son of Alfred and Emma Nelson
NELSON, Edward - 26 years; d. 9 November 1888;
Oyster Bay item

NELSON, George - funeral 11 September 1887 at
   Oyster Bay
NELSON, William - 70 years; d. 24 May 1879 at
   Oyster Bay Cove
NESBITT, William - d. 25 November 1885 at
   Riverhead; stomach cancer
NEVIUS, Mrs. John - d. 31 October 1889;
   Northport item
NEVIUS, John F. - d. at New York City; funeral
   18 February 1888 at Northport; former
   resident of Crab Meadow
NEWINS, Georgianna * - 8 months; d. 23 July
   1887 at Huntington
NEWINS, Mrs. Joseph * - d. 29 April 1889 at
   Northport; "found dead in her bed"
NEWINS, Joseph M. * - 1 y 4 m 1 d; d. 15 July
   1889 at Huntington
NEWMAN, Henry S. - 60 y 9 m 9 d; d. 20 Novem-
   ber 1890 at Cold Spring Harbor; captain of
   coastal vessel "E & I Oakley"; born at Ocean
   Grove, N. J. 1830; resident of Cold Spring
   Harbor since 1858
NEWMAN, James L. - 24 y 4 m 11 d; d. 23 Febru-
   ary 1886 at Cold Spring Harbor
NEWTON, Ellen C. - 38 y 6 m 11 d; d. 27 Novem-
   ber 1880 at Huntington; wife of Emmett B.
   Newton
NEWTON, Elsie - d. 14 May 1888 at Northport;
   "suddenly of apoplexy"; wife of Edwin S.
   Newton
NEWTON, John W. - d. 22 December 1887 at West-
   hampton; gun accident; resident of Speonk
NEWTON, Sarah N. - 23 y 4 m 22 d; d. 14 August
   1880 at Smithtown Branch
NEWTON, William R. R. - 4 yrs 7 mos; d. 9 Oct-
   ober 1879 at Huntington; son of William R.
   R. Newton
NICHOLAUS, August - "killed lately" at Baby-
   lon; 19 October 1883 paper; accident at
   Belmont's farm
NICHOLLS, Laurietta H. - 29 years; d. 31 Aug-
   ust 1884 at Brooklyn
NICHOLS, Dr. Elias S. - 81 years; d. 4 Novem-
   ber 1880 at Smithtown; medical doctor
NICHOLS, George W. - 47 years; d. 2 June 1889;
   son of Gideon and Susan Nichols; husband of
   Rhoda A. Nichols; native of Cold Spring

NICHOLS, John - 68 years; d. 30 May 1879 at
Brooklyn; interment at Woodbury
NICHOLS, John F. - 23 yrs 3 days; d. 2 June
1882 at Brooklyn; son of Gideon and Susan
Nichols; interment at Huntington
NICHOLS, Percy Arthur - 14 months; d. 4 Janu-
ary 1887 at Northport; son of Oscar M. and
Ann Nichols
NICHOLS, Robert - 68 y 5 m 12 d; d. 14 August
1885 at Centreport
NICHOLS, Sarah E. - 19 y 8 m 10 d; d. 1 Sept-
ember 1887 at New York City
NICHOLS, Susan - 67 y 7 m 7 d; d. 22 February
1889 at Brooklyn; wife of Gideon Nichols (m.
1838); b. Red Mills, Patterson, Westchester
Co., N. Y. in 1822; mother of 14 children;
active Methodist; former resident of Cold
Spring; moved to Brooklyn in 1874; [Note:
Town of Patterson is in Putnam County, not
Westchester County]
NICHOLS, William T. - 70 y 4 m 11 d;
d. 11 January 1880 at Northport
NICKERSON, Charles - 40 years; d. 11 December
1889 at New York City; fell from platform
and was run over by elevated railroad train;
resident of Brooklyn
NICKERSON, Elsie - 5 mos 4 days; d. 4 Septem-
ber 1879 at Northport; daughter of Herman
Nickerson
NICKERSON, Herman - 29 yrs 3 mos; d. 6 June
1879 at Northport
NICOLL, Glorianna - d. 7 October 1888; item
from Sag Harbor Express; burned when lamp
caught clothing on fire; sister of Dr. S. B.
Nicoll
NICOLL, Sarah Greenly - 90 years; d. 30 Decem-
ber 1887 at Islip; widow of William Nicoll
NIGHTINGALE, Carolyn Ethel - 1 y 10m 11 d;
d. 6 May 1880 at Babylon; daughter of Rev.
James C. and Julia St. John Nightingale
NINE, Mary E. - 47 years; d. 23 February 1886
at Brooklyn; wife of John Nine
NOAK, Michael - drowned 22 May 1887 at Lake
Ronkonkoma
NOBLE, Kate P. - d. 5 September 1880 at Hemp-
stead; wife of Rev. Dr. Noble of Washington,
D. C.; mother of four ministers

NOON, B. F. - funeral 3 November 1889 at
Farmingdale
NORMAN, Carl - 37 years; d. at Islip;
26 October 1883 paper; fell from roof
NORTHROP, William - death reported 25 May 1889
paper; Port Jefferson item; resident of
Bridgeport, Connecticut
NORTON, Mrs. - funeral 6 April 1887 at St.
Patrick's R. C. Church, Glen Cove
NORTON, Capt. Albert - 85 years; d. 8 November
1888 at Mount Sinai
NORTON, Charlotte F. - 70 yrs 6 mos;
d. 21 June 1882 at Mount Sinai
NORTON, Elisha - 83 yrs 6 mos; d. 13 April
1885 at Mount Sinai
NORTON, Henry - d. 14 August 1889 at Glen
Cove; brother of James Norton
NORTON, John - drowned 19 January 1883 off
Fisher's Island; ship collision; resident of
Nova Scotia
NORTON, Sidney S. - d. at Port Jefferson;
28 August 1886 paper; former Supervisor of
Town of Brookhaven
NOSTRAND, Annie Smith - 5 mos; d. 19 July 1885
at Smithtown; daughter of Jacob and Sarah
Nostrand
NOSTRAND, Hannah - 86 yrs 2 mos; d. 20 March
1884 at Smithtown
NOSTRAND, Isaac - 70 years; suicide 15 Novem-
ber 1878 at Brooklyn; took laudanum and then
went to barn and cut his throat; father-in-
law of Moses Gildersleeve; resident of
Hempstead
NOTT, Maggie - 11 years; d. 4 March 1885 at
Comac; daughter of William Nott
NOWELL, Hannah M. - 67 years; d. 7 July 1887
at Huntington
NOYES, Stephen (Indian) - "died lately";
3 September 1887 paper; "noted desperado";
"half breed Shinecock Indian"; resident of
Flushing
NUGENT, Ellen Clune - 43 years; d. 9 December
1884 at Half Hollows
NUGENT, Julia - 85 years; d. 26 December 1887
at Half Hollow Hills
NUN, child - drowned 30 January 1878 at
Roslyn; fell through ice; son of A. Nun

NUNGANSER, Jacob - suicide 25 May 1884 at East
Williamsburgh; hanged himself in a tree;
resident of New York City
OAKES, child - 7 years; d. 9 July 1878 at
Babylon; killed by bolt of lightning; son of
Platt Oakes
OAKES, Edward - d. 5 April 1881 at Stony
Brook; found dead in bed; postmaster
OAKES, Esther C. - 65 yrs 2 mos; d. 4 November
1883 at Stony Brook; widow of Nathan Oakes
OAKLEY, Abbie - 60 y 11 m 23 d; d. 18 February
1890 at West Hills
OAKLEY, Rev. Charles M. - 66 years; d. 16 Feb-
ruary 1882 at Northport; Presbyterian min-
ister; b. 2 July 1815 at New York City;
educated at Union Theological Seminary 1838-
1839; ordained 1842 while serving church at
Nyack, N.Y.; served at Millville, N.J.,
Philadelphia, Pa., Port Richmond, S.I., N.Y.
and North Germantown, N. J. before coming to
Long Island to serve at Melville ca. 1853-
1867 and Amagansett ca. 1867-1880; his wife
was a native of Cape May County, New Jersey
OAKLEY, Charlotte B. - 86 y 4 m 18 d;
d. 17 April 1887 at Huntington; widow of
Z. B. Oakley
OAKLEY, Eliphalet W. - d. 18 February 1890 at
Babylon; found dead in bed; son of Eliphalet
W. Oakley; owned flour and feed mill at
Babylon
OAKLEY, Ezra - 67 y 9 m 15 d; d. 4 April 1881
at West Hills
OAKLEY, George W. - 31 years; d. 3 August 1882
at Northport
OAKLEY, Harriet - 73 yrs 11 mos; d. 19 April
1882 at West Hills
OAKLEY, Harriet N. - 64 y 4 m 5 d; d. 14 May
1880 at Brooklyn; interment at West Hills;
wife of Whitson Oakley
OAKLEY, Isaac K. - 83 years; d. 6 September
1885 at Salisbury Mills, N. Y.; President
Quassaick National Bank of Newburgh
OAKLEY, James M. - funeral 18 April 1887 at
Jamaica
OAKLEY, Jane - 89 y 11 m 13 d; d. 28 September
1882 at West Hills; widow of Solomon Oakley

OAKLEY, Jesse - 84 years; d. 24 August 1883 at
West Hills

OAKLEY, Marian - 6 mos 29 days; d. 27 July
1879 at Brooklyn; daughter of Samuel J. and
Marian Oakley

OAKLEY, Sarah C. - 5 mos 26 days; d. 11 August
1882 at West Hills; daughter of Zebulon E.
and Hannah Oakley

OAKLEY, Sarah G. - d. 20 June 1879 at New York
City; interment at Jamaica; daughter of I.
Youngs Whitson; wife of Solomon Oakley

OAKLEY, Whitson - d. 20 April 1890 at Brooklyn; interment at West Hills; son of Solomon
Oakley; grandson of Isaac Whitson; father of
Solomon Oakley and George Oakley; native of
West Hills; ran stage line in Brooklyn;
important horse dealer who supplied horses
to most of the horse car systems in Brooklyn
and New York

OAT, Mary J. - 51 y 6 m 7 d; d. 16 March 1882
at Huntington; wife of George Oat

OATES, William E. - 33 years; d. 2 May 1879 at
Huntington

OBERLY, William - suicide 9 October 1883 at
New York City; took Paris Green

O'BRIEN, children - d. at Brooklyn from diphtheria; 21 January 1888 paper; Hicksville
item; 2 children of Patrick O'Brien

O'BRIEN, Florence - 7 yrs 6 mos; d. 26 May
1888 at Hicksville; interment at Calvary
Cemetery, Queens County; son [sic] of
Patrick O'Brien

O'BRIEN, Sybil B. - 37 years; d. 26 May 1879
at Middleville; see: Sybil O. B. Bryan

O'BRINE, Julia - 85 years; d. 19 June 1883 at
Huntington

O'CONNER, Margaret - 88 years; d. 23 March
1887 at Westbury

O'CONNOR, Hannah - 60 years; d. 3 August 1882
at Northport

O'CONNOR, Morris - 68 years; d. 4 December
1887 at Woodbury

O'DONNELL, James - found dead 16 March 1890 at
Smithtown; under horse sheds at Upper Dock,
Smithtown; "day laborer at St. Johnland"

O'DONNELL, Helen B. - 27 years; d. 2 September
1884 at Brooklyn

O'DONNELL, Margaretta E. - 49 y 10 m 18 d;
d. 9 August 1885 at Northport; wife of John
O'Donnell

OEFLIN, Margaret - 73 yrs 11 mos; d. 27 September 1888 at Hicksville; interment at
Westbury

OGLER, William - 60 years; d. 22 November 1888
at Centreport; interment at Camden, N. J.

O'HARA, child - 4 years; death reported from
croup; child of Michael O'Hara; Hicksville
item; 22 June 1889 paper

O'KEEFE, Lizzie - 14 years; d. 13 June 1883 at
Greenlawn

OLCOTT, James - d. 18 December 1890 at Huntington; "respected young man"

OLDS, Delia A. - 39 years; d. 2 April 1879 at
Centreport

OLDS, Mary L. - 34 years; d. 18 August 1883 at
Northport; wife of George Olds

OLMSTEAD, Freddie W. - 6 y 5 m 12 d; d. 6 January 1887 at Northport; son of John Olmstead

OLMSTEAD, Rev. Miles N. - d. 30 July 1885;
minister at Woodbury 1860-1861

ONDERDONK, Adrian - d. 16 March 1888 at Flower
Hill

ONDERDONK, Henry - ca. 82 years; d. 22 June
1886 at Jamaica; antiquarian researcher and
local historian; b. Manhasset 1804; graduate
of Columbia 1827; professor at Union Hall
Academy, Jamaica; author of Revolutionary
Incidents of Queens County, Bibliography of
Long Island, etc.

ONDERDONK, Henry M. - d. 2 September 1885 at
Hempstead; son of Bishop Benjamin T.
Onderdonk; newspaper editor in Ohio and
Hempstead; publisher of Hempstead Inquirer
1870-1885; vestryman at St. George's Church,
Hempstead

ONDERDONK, William H. - d. 11 December 1882 at
New York City; former judge of Queens
County; resident of Great Neck

O'NEIL, James - 2 mos 7 days; d. 18 July 1885
at Huntington; son of John and Catharine
O'Neil

O'NEIL, Jeremiah - 20 years; d. 29 December
1887 at Hunter's Point; hit by railroad
train; resident of Woodside

OPPECK, Katharine A. B. - 4 mos 17 days;
d. 2 September 1890 at Huntington

O'REILLEY, Mary - d. 15 December 1888 at New
York City; nurse to M. B. Eckerson family

ORR, Mr. - d. 24 July 1887 at Chicago,
Illinois; husband of Lizzie Miller of
Whitestone

ORR, Henry - d. 29 October 1883 at Woodside;
hit by railroad train

ORTH, Agnes K. - 45 y 7 m 12 d; d. 17 January
1889 at Comac

OSBORN, Rev. T. S. - d. at Norwalk, Conn.;
24 March 1888 paper; interment at Riverhead

OSWALT, John - d. 24 April 1888 at Farmingdale; lived in South Carolina and Virginia;
"strong abolitionist" forced to move North
because of his views on slavery; [1870
census index lists birthplace as S. C.]

OSWELL, James - 40 years; d. "this week" at
Flushing Bay; 13 August 1887 paper; struck
head on rock while diving; stationed with
U. S. Army at Willett's Point

OTTENDORFER, Anna - d. "a few days ago" at New
York City; 18 April 1884 paper; owner of the
Staats Zeitung

OUSTERMAN, David - suicide 17 July 1881 at
East Rockaway; hanged himself

OVERTON, George E. - 38 years; d. 20 January
1881 at Southampton

OVERTON, Franklin - d. 15 April 1887 at
Peconic; former Supervisor of Town of
Southold

OVERTON, Julia - 70 years; d. 27 September
1890 at Port Jefferson; sister of Abby
Meserolk

OVERTON, Mary - d. at "State Normal School"
[nothing more]; interment 15 April 1888 at
Riverhead [see next]

OVERTON, Mary - d. "recently" at Oswego,
N. Y.; 23 June 1888 paper; Riverhead item;
daughter of Fanny Overton; resident of
Riverhead

OVERTON, William H. - 60 years; d. 6 January
1889 at Mount Sinai; interment at Mount
Sinai; at supper table of his sister Mrs.
Harriet Marchay; resident of New York City

PAHDE, Mrs. - d. 8 September 1888 at Hicksville; widow of J. Pahde

PAHDE, John - d. at Hicksville; 15 January 1887 paper; [see next]

PAHDE, John Henry - funeral 16 January 1887 at Hicksville

PAINE, Mrs. Henry Martin * - interment 25 March 1888 at Westbury

PAINTER, Jasper - death reported; 19 June 1886 paper; Glen Cove item

PALMER, Albert - d. "this week" at Boston, Massachusetts; 28 May 1887 paper; Oyster Bay item

PALMER, Rev. E. H. - d. "last week" at Baiting Hollow; 9 August 1890 paper; pastor of Baiting Hollow Congregational Church

PALMER, Mary E. - 53 years; d. 31 December 1883 at Brooklyn, E. D.; interment at Huntington; daughter of John and Jane Weatherill; wife of Walter Palmer

PARISH, Alice - 15 y 7 m 2 d; d. 10 November 1879 at Cold Spring

PARISH, Isaac - 62 years; d. 11 February 1890 in New Jersey; interment at Oyster Bay; nephew of Richard L. Parish of Oyster Bay

PARKER, Mrs. Frank - d. 21 November 1885 at Babylon; interment in Connecticut

PARKER, John S. - d. 2 February 1888 at Poughkeepsie, N. Y.; husband of Emily Ketcham of Huntington

PARKINS, John - suicide 28 July 1885 at Glen Cove

PARKS, Alexander - 67 years; d. 10 December 1883 at Flushing; Town of Flushing Tax Collector; Village of Flushing Trustee

PARRISH, Sarah - 55 years; d. 28 December 1880 at Oyster Bay; wife of Richard L. Parrish

PARSON, Merry A. - 48 years; d. 15 September 1881 at East Hampton

PARSONS, infant - d. 20 October 1890 at Patchogue; one twin of Mrs. S. Parsons

PARSONS, Jeremiah T. - d. 10 March 1882 at Amagamsett; merchant and postmaster

PARSONS, Josie - d. 14 October 1887 at Peeksill, N. Y.; wife of William Parsons

PASFIELD, Bide Lee [or Rida Lee] - 20 y 7m
    21 d; d. 9 June 1890 at Cold Spring; daugh-
    ter of William G. and Mary L. Pasfield
PASFIELD, Mary Libbie - 35 yrs 6 mos; d. at
    Brooklyn; 20 April 1883 paper; interment at
    Cypress Hills; daughter of Thomas Gilder-
    sleeve; wife of William G. Pasfield
PATRICK, Chela F. - d. 2 April 1890 at Centre
    Island; interment at Cedar Springs (Catholic
    Cemetery); [note: perhaps Cedar Swamp ?];
    Oyster Bay item
PATTERSON, Sarah Davis - 85 years; d. 27 April
    1890 at Plainview; fell down dead; mother of
    Margaret Patterson and Mary Patterson
PAULDING, Hiram - 81 years; d. 20 October 1878
    at West Neck; Rear Admiral, United States
    Navy; [long career in U. S. Navy; supported
    construction of John Ericcson's Monitors for
    Union Navy during Civil War; see Dictionary
    of American Biography]
PAULDING, Mary - 1 yr 9 mos; d. 31 July 1890
    at West Neck; daughter of Hiram and Virginia
    Paulding
PAYNE, Ellen - d. 13 January 1888 at River-
    head; wife of B. K. Payne
PAYNE, John H. - 58 y 8 m 11 d; d. 24 December
    1878 at Huntington
PAYNE, Margaret E. * - 85 years; d. 6 April
    1889 at Brooklyn; interment at Westbury;
    mother of Mrs. S. A. Thompson; b. Amity-
    ville 4 January 1804; active in AME Church
PAYNE, Sarah * - d. 11 December 1889 at Saga-
    more Hill, Oyster Bay; interment at Stony
    Brook
PEARSALL, Amelia A. - 59 years; d. 24 February
    1887 at Amityville; interment at Huntington;
    formerly Mrs. Amelia A. Waterbury
PEARSALL, David - 75 years; d. 21 September
    1887 at Rockville Centre; full through trap
    door into cellar
PEARSALL, Helen - funeral 12 April 1887 at
    Glen Cove; daughter of James B. Pearsall
PEARSALL, Jonas - 64 y 3 m 15 d; d. 13 Sept-
    ember 1878 at Huntington
PEARSALL, Oliver - d. 31 December 1884 at
    Norwood, Town of Hempstead; from finding his
    dog dead

PEARSALL, Phebe Ann - 68 y 1 m 17 d;
  d. 23 February 1889 at Huntington; daughter
  of Jacob Bedell; wife of Daniel Pearsall
PEARSON, Elizabeth - 76 years; d. 28 December
  1886 at Northport
PEARSON, Henry - 89 years; d. 11 March 1888 at
  Plainview; interment at Westbury [also
  called Peter Peasen]
PEASEN, Peter - [see Henry Pearson]
PEASER, Frank - 5 months; d. 27 January 1889
  at Hicksville; son of Peter Peaser;
  interment at Westbury
PEASER, Powell - funeral 21 November 1890
  at Westbury; suicide: hanged himself
PEASER, Riley - d. 3 January 1890 at
  Greenvale; interment at Westbury
PECK, Israel - 66 y 10 m 13 d; d. 30 October
  1881 at Southold; father of Mrs. J. G.
  Huntting
PECK, J. Milnor - d. 14 September 1882 at New
  York City; elevator accident; resident of
  Flushing
PECK, Lily - 1 month; d. 15 January 1886 at
  Hoboken, N. J.; daughter of W. Edward and
  Lily Peck
PECK, Lily Rogers - d. 19 December 1885 at
  Hoboken, N. J.; interment at Huntington;
  daughter of Thomas P. Rogers; wife of W. Ed-
  ward Peck (m. 1880); b. Factoryville, N. Y.
PECK, Robert - 60 years; d. 17 January 1888 at
  Hunter's Point; employee of LIRR; hit by
  railroad train
PEDEN, Thomas - 18 years; d. 15 March 1885 at
  Shelter Island
PEDRICK, B. - 82 years; death reported 24 Aug-
  gust 1883 paper; father of I. B. Pedrick of
  East Neck; resident of Hauppauge
PEDRICK, Eugenie G. - 2 yrs 10 days; d. --
  April 1882 at East Neck; daughter of I. B.
  and Eugenie Pedrick
PEDRICK, Reumah Adeline - 45 years; d. 19 Jan-
  uary 1880 at Baltimore, Maryland; interment
  at Hauppauge; wife of Emmet Pedrick; former
  resident of Hauppauge

PENDERGAST, James - d. 2 June 1879 at Fall
River, Massachusetts; brother of Michael
Pendergast

PENDERGAST, Kate - 28 years; funeral 3 August
1890 at Oyster Bay

PENDERGAST, Mary - 5 yrs 10 mos; d. 12 June
1879 at Huntington; daughter of Michael and
Mary Pendergast

PENDLETON, George H. - d. 24 November 1889 at
Brussels, Belgium; U. S. Representative and
Senator from Ohio; Democratic candidate for
Vice President 1864; diplomat; served as
U. S. minister to Germany

PENDLETON, Maria Lash - d. 2 March 1889 at
Brooklyn; wife of George H. Pendleton;
former resident of Woodbury

PERKINS, C. L. - d. 17 May 1887 at Paris,
France; funeral 14 June 1887 at Glen Cove

PERKINS, H. W. - d. 14 January 1890 at Nassau,
W. I. [Bahamas]; owner of schooner yacht
"Niwana"; Port Jefferson item

PERROTT, Ann M. - 66 y 11 m 12 d; d. 31 October 1887 at Northport; widow of John W.
Perrott

PERRY, Dr. Stephen - 75 y 3 m 14 d; d. 9 November 1885 at Northport

PERRY, Mrs. Stephen - d. 7 August 1886 at New
York City; interment at Northport; widow

PETERS, child - 14 months; d. 10 October 1888
at Hicksville; son of August Peters

PETERS, infant - 2 mos 24 days; d. 6 February
1890 at Hicksville; son of August and
Christina Peters

PETERS, John H. - 55 years; d. 1 January 1881
at East Norwich

PETERS, Mary - 55 yrs 5 mos; d. 16 December
1880 at Centreport; widow of John Peters

PETERS, Moses - 85 years; d. 20 July 1886 at
West Hills

PETERS, Sarah Ann - 57 years; d. 12 June 1887
at Woodbury; daughter of Josiah Walters;
widow of John H. Peters; resident of East
Norwich

PETERSON, Ellen - 48 years; d. 10 September
1885 at Eaton's Neck

PETERSON, Emily - 11 years; d. 26 November
1880 at Glen Cove; kerosene lamp fire

PETERSON, Phoebe - d. 19 October 1890 at
Wheatley; wife of William Peterson

PETTENGER, Dorothy - 70 y 3 m 19 d; d. 17 November 1878 at Brooklyn

PETTIT, Lewis E. - 76 years; d. 31 May 1890 at
Hempstead; shoemaker; lost leg six years ago
when hit by railroad train at Garden City

PETTIT, Townsend - 72 years; d. 5 August 1886
at Hempstead

PETTUS, Stephen - murdered 23 November 1889 at
New York City; official of Brooklyn Elevated
Railway; wealthy Brooklyn businessman;
Pettus "ruined" widow Mrs. Hannah R. South-
worth by drugging her and then "betrayed and
disgraced" her; Mrs. Southworth murdered
Pettus to revenge herself

PETTY, Henry - drowned after falling overboard
from schooner "Mary C. Decker"; Port Jefferson item; 29 December 1888 paper; "resident
of the Southside"

PHAROAH, David (Indian) - 40 years; d. 18 July
1878 at Montauk; son of Eleazer and Aurelia
Pharoah; half-brother of Stephen Pharoah;
son-in-law of William Flower; "King of the
Montauks"

PHAROAH, Stephen (Indian) - 57 years;
d. 6 September 1879; funeral at Freetown,
East Hampton; interment at Montauk; "King
of the Montauks"

PHAROAH, William H. (Indian) - drowned 3 September 1885 at Port Jefferson; son of the
"late King of Montauk"

PHELPS, Dora - ca. 33 years; d. 24 June 1880
at Riverhead; widow of Frederick O. Phelps

PHELPS, Isaac - found dead in boat 3 August
1883 at Greenport; resident of Middletown,
Connecticut

PHILLIPS, Charles - 82 y 8 m 11 d; d. 9 January 1884 at Mount Sinai; Mount Sinai postmaster

PHILLIPS, Frank - 9 years; d. 19 December 1889
at Brooklyn; bitten by dog two months ago;
died from hydrophobia in "horrible agony"

PHILLIPS, George S. - 82 yrs 8 mos; d. 13 January 1881 at Smithtown

PHILLIPS, James - body found "last week" at
Orient; 14 July 1882 paper

171

PHILLIPS, Wendell - d. [at Boston, Mass.];
8 February 1884 paper; noted abolitionist
PIERSON, Edwin H. - 7 days; d. 9 September
1888 at Greenlawn; interment at Huntington;
son of Casper H. and Lottie E. Pierson
PIKE, Ann - 81 y 5 m 19 d; d. 15 July 1881 at
Mount Sinai; widow of Jonathan Pike
PILLOLS, Edwards - d. 26 June 1888 at Oyster
Bay
PINE, Merwin - 15 years; d. 19 October 1889 at
Freeport; blood poisoning; son of P. Wesley
Pine
PINE, Samuel M. - 67 years; d. at Hempstead;
2 April 1880 paper
PINKHAM, Lydia - d. "last week" at [Lynn,
Massachusetts]; 1 June 1883 paper; manu-
facturer of patent medicine
PITT, Mrs. M. L. - interment 31 October 1890
at Hempstead; wife of George E. Pitt; resi-
dent of Brooklyn
PIXLEY, Adelia - 57 years; d. 7 March 1888 at
Centreport; found dead in bed
PLACE, Edward - d. 21 January 1887 at Astoria;
served in Union Navy during Civil War;
native of Huntington (b. 1840)
PLACE, Jeremiah - 70 y 9 m 15 d; d. 15 May
1884 at Huntington
PLACE, Joshua B. - 45 y 3 m 19 d; d. 6 March
1883 at Huntington; thimble manufacturer
PLACE, Martha A. - 51 yrs 10 mos; d. 20 March
1882 at West Hills; wife of Edward Place
PLACE, Nelson - 73 years; d. 27 January 1878
at Brooklyn; Huntington native (b. 1805) who
moved to New York City with parents during
his youth; shipping merchant; equipped
vessels for the California Gold Rush
PLACE, William A. * - 26 years; drowned
24 September 1879 at Greenport; boating
accident off Conkling's Point
PLATT, Abigail - 86 years; d. 1 March 1883 at
North Dix Hills; mother of Mrs. C. C. Tappen
and Mrs. Zophar Ketcham
PLATT, Dannie - 8 years; d. 13 December 1885
at Bayville; son of Frank Platt
PLATT, Eben G. - 59 years; d. 21 April 1888 at
Galveston, Texas; former resident of Huntington

PLATT, Edward - ca. 20 years; d. 28 August
1885 at Hauppauge; broke neck in fall from
carriage; interment at Smithtown Branch; son
of Eugene Platt
PLATT, Elias - d. 27 December 1890 at Smith-
town Branch; former Supervisor of Town of
Smithtown; elder at Smithtown Branch
Presbyterian Church
PLATT, George W. - 82 years; d. 3 April 1881
at New York City
PLATT, Harry George - 21 y 8 m 16 d;
d. 6 December 1886 at New York City; inter-
ment at Green-Wood, Brooklyn; son of Henry
C. and Jennie D. Platt
PLATT, Mary - 23 years; d. 19 May 1884 at
Smithtown
PLATT, Perry - 5 years; d. 14 April 1890 at
Smithtown; son of Edward Platt
PLATT, Silas Watts - 70 y 2 m 8 d; d. 8 Dec-
ember 1881 at Smithtown
PLATT, William H. - d. 27 August 1890 at
Yaphank; interment at Sayville; resident of
Northport; veteran of Mexican War
POMEROY, Caroline - 69 yrs 7 mos; d. 21 July
1880 at Smithtown; interment at Comac; widow
of Cyril B. Pomeroy
POMEROY, Cyril B. - 71 yrs 6 mos; d. 22 June
1880 at Comac
POPENHAUSEN, Conrad - funeral at College
Point; 28 December 1883 paper
POND, Isaac - 37 years; d. at Northfield,
Connecticut; 30 October 1886 paper
POOLE, Carrie Southard - 26 years; d. 14 July
1886 at Brooklyn; interment at Woodbury;
wife of Charles Poole
POOLE, Charles - 18 days; d. 30 July 1886 at
Woodbury; son of Charles Poole
POST, Ella - 23 yrs 6 mos; d. 5 June 1886 at
Farmingdale; interment at Bethpage; wife of
Samuel Post
POST, Harriet W. - d. 11 March 1878 at Tren-
ton, New Jersey; interment at Huntington;
widow of Richard B. Post
POST, J. Birdsall -23 years; funeral 13 Octo-
ber 1890 at Hempstead; son of Birdsall Post;
bookkeeper in father's store; member of

173

POST, J. Birdsall (continued)
Enterprise Hose Company; member of St.
George's Episcopal Church

POTTER, Done * - 55 years; d. 2 June 1890 at
South Dix Hills; fell into well on George
Field's farm; funeral at Greenlawn

POTTER, Mrs. Edward [*?] - funeral 9 May 1888
at Oyster Bay; funeral held at A. M. E. Zion
Church

POTTER, Emeline - 54 years; d. 21 September
1881 at Oyster Bay

POTTER, Gilbert - d. 18 March 1883 at
Williamsburgh

POTTER, Hugh - 70 years; d. 25 December 1890
at Hempstead

POTTER, Pierpont - 90 years; death reported
8 January 1886 paper; Clerk to Queens County
Board of Supervisors for 52 years

POWELL, Amy - 98 years; d. 15 December 1883 at
Manetto Hill; wife of Richard Powell

POWELL, Charles - "aged"; d. at East Meadow;
6 April 1889 paper; Woodbury item

POWELL, Rev. Charles W. - 54 years; d. 27 February 1888 at Southampton; funeral at Bay
Shore; M. E. clergyman serving M. E.
churches in Connecticut 1859-1874 and on
Long Island from 1874 to death; served
Flatlands 1874-1875; East New York 1876-
1878; Bay Shore 1879-1881; Flatbush 1882-
1884; Northport 1885-1886 and Southampton
since 1887; native of Burlington, N. J.

POWELL, Charles W. - d. 2 February 1890 at
Brockville, Ontario; resident of Amityville;
former Town of Babylon Tax Collector

POWELL, Deborah - 96 years; d. 24 February
1889 at Babylon; interment at Plain Edge;
mother of Mrs. Jesse Conklin

POWELL, Eddie - 11 years; drowned 1 August
1878 at Hempstead Reservoir; son of Robert
T. Powell, Hempstead postmaster

POWELL, Ephraim - d. 28 May 1879 at Mannetto
Hill

POWELL, Ephraim - d. 9 January 1880 at Manetto
Hill

POWELL, Mrs. Isaac - 58 years; d. 19 March
1886 at Amityville

POWELL, Jane - 72 yrs 10 mos; d. 18 October
1882 at West Hills; wife of Andrew Powell
POWELL, Jane A. - 61 years; d. 14 April 1881
at Cold Spring
POWELL, John J. - d. 16 December 1886 at
Farmingdale
POWELL, Mary L. - 11 y 1 m 10 d; d. 7 February
1888 at Huntington; daughter of George and
Susan D. Powell
POWELL, Phebe M. - 82 years; d. 19 February
1878 at Cold Spring
POWELL, Richard - 82 yrs 4 mos; d. 16 May 1890
at Westbury; "loved and respected by all who
knew him"
POWELL, Silas - 75 yrs 5 days; d. 2 November
1885 at Brooklyn
POWERS, Frank - 21 years; d. at St. Louis,
Missouri; 21 December 1889 paper; son of
James Powers, formerly of Hempstead; many
relatives living in Towns of Hempstead and
North Hempstead
POWERS, Patrick - ca. 45 years; suicide 1 Sep-
tember 1883 at Cold Spring
POWERS, Robert D. - 44 years; d. 1 January
1887 at Huntington; died sitting in a chair;
resident of West Neck; formerly of Brooklyn
PRATT, infant - 2 months; d. 5 March 1889;
Westbury item; child of Sidney Pratt
PRATT, Daniel - d. 19 June 1887 at Boston,
Massachusetts; famous eccentric
PRATT, Dannie - 8 years; d. 13 December 1885
at Bayville
PRATT, Lendall F. - 78 years; d. 8 November
1884 at Mineola; jumped from 3rd floor
window of Mineola Insane Asylum; resident of
Hyde Park
PRAY, John - 87 years; d. 22 April 1890 at
Hempstead; father of Elias Pray
PRICE, Mrs. - d. 18 June 1888; Smithtown item
PRICE, Artemus M. - 69 years; d. 9 December
1878 at New York; former resident of Oyster
Bay
PRICE, Thomas - 58 yrs 6 mos; d. 15 October
1882 at Northport
PRIDGETT, William A. * - 4 days; d. 31 May
1887 at Huntington

175

PRIME, Claudius B. - 59 years; d. 3 July 1878
at Huntington; stomach cancer

PRIME, Ebenezer W. - 22 yrs 11 mos; d. 13 August 1878 at Huntington; son of Henry R.
Prime

PRIME, Emma - 73 years; d. 14 April 1886 at
Huntington; daughter of Abraham and Sarah
Cotrel; widow of Edward Y. Prime; b. Flat-
bush 25 January 1813

PRIME, Henry R. - 73 years; d. 27 December
1886 at Huntington; son of N. S. Prime;
grandson of Benjamin Y. Prime

PRIME, Rufus - 79 years; d. 15 October 1885 at
Huntington; interment at Green-Wood, Brook-
lyn; son of Nathaniel Prime and Cornelia
Scudder; husband of Augusta Temple Palmer
(m. 1828); father of Fred E. Prime, Temple
Prime, Charles S. Prime and Cornelia Prime;
b. New York City 28 January 1806; former
Wall Street banker who retired to live in
Huntington in 1858

PRIME, Rev. S. Irenaeus - d. 18 July 1885;
Presbyterian clergyman; son of Rev. Nathaniel Scudder Prime; grandson of Dr. Benjamin
Youngs Prime; great-grandson of Rev. Ebenezer Prime

PRINCE, Mrs. George - d. 31 March 1890 "near
Boston"; funeral at Jericho; daughter of
Solomon Jackson of Jericho; "leaves a nine
day old child"

PRINCE, Hattie - d. 26 February 1880 at Santa
Fe, New Mexico; daughter of Dr. S. Russell
Childs; wife of L. Bradford Prince, Chief
Justice of New Mexico

PRINCE, John D. - 74 years; d. 27 October 1888
at Flatbush; father of George S. Prince of
Jericho; memorial notice from Dutch Reformed
Church of Flatbush in 10 November 1888 paper

PRINCE, Margaret - 56 years; d. 21 May 1879 at
Syosset

PRINCE, William - d. 18 December 1880 at
Washington, D. C.; son of the late William
Prince of Flushing; captain U. S. Army

PRINGLE, James E. - ca. 70 years; d. 15 March
1886 at Fresh Pond, Queens County; hit by
railroad train; resident of London, England

PROUL, Mr. - d. "recently"; 23 October 1886
paper; uncle of Mrs. George W. Burr of
Comac; resident of New York City

PROVOST, Sarah C. - 67 yrs 23 days; d. 6 November 1889 at Oyster Bay Cove; widow of Rev.
James C. Provost

PRYOR, Elizabeth - death reported 15 December
1888 paper; sister of Stephen Rushmore of
Westbury

PUGH, child - death reported 31 August 1883
paper; son of Editor Pugh of Long Island
City Courier

PUTNAM, Jay Van Vliet - infant; d. 28 August
1883 at Huntington; son of Rev. B. Van Vliet
and Ella Putnam

QUACKENBOSS, Mary E. - 59 y 4 m 19 d;
d. 24 December 1887 at New York City;
interment at Huntington; daughter of Joseph
Sammis; 1st husband was Mr. Silkworth (m.
ca. 1850); after Silkworth's death, she ran
his wire business; Huntington native

QUARLES, John Francis * - 39 years; d. "last
week" at Flushing; 6 February 1885 paper;
"colored lawyer"

QUIGLEY, child - 3 years; d. at Long Island
City; 16 April 1887 paper; choked to death
on a coffee bean; daughter of James Quigley

QUINN, Margaret - 9 mos 13 days; d. 27 September 1882 at Lloyd's Neck; daughter of Thomas
and Margaret Quinn

QUINN, Michael - d. at Woodside; 27 July 1883
paper; hit by railroad train after saving
life of woman on the tracks

QUINN, Samuel H. - drowned 5 August 1883 at
Far Rockaway; resident of New York City

RACKLIFFE, H. M. - d. 22 (or 31) May 1886 at
Corinna, Maine; former resident of Smithtown
Branch; M. D. graduate of Dartmouth College

RAIL, Alfred (Thomas per 13 December 1890
paper) - d. 24 November 1890 at Floral Park;
hit by railroad train while crossing tracks

RAINAN, Augusta - 2 July 1880 paper; resident
of Jersey City, N. J.; "Seawanhaka" fire on
East River

RALSTON, Edith - 3 y 2 m 27 d; d. 24 December
1879 at New Village; daughter of Christopher
A. and Mary M. Ralston

RALSTON, Gracie - 3 years; d. 27 August 1885 at Melville

RAMSBOTHAM, James - d. 13 August 1887 at Baldwins; victim of carriage accident on 7 August 1887

RAND, Helen - 10 years; d. 17 December 1887 at Lawrence; hit by stray bullet fired by neighbor at a bird; daughter of George C. Rand

RANDALL, Samuel - 78 years; d. 12 March 1888 at Middle Island; heavy barn door blew over on him during Blizzard of 1888

RANDOLPH, Lewis F. - 49 years; d. 22 February 1886 at Comac

RANGER, Samuel - d. 28 February 1881 at East Hampton

RAPELYEA, Beltha - d. 16 April 1889 at Oyster Bay; "violent hemorrhage from the lungs"; wife of Simon Rapelyea

RAPPOLD, Frederick - 4 years; d. at Brooklyn; 19 July 1890 paper; shot in gun accident by 7 year old brother George Rappold

RAPPYLEE, Susie E. * - 1 yr 7 mos; d. 22 May 1881 at Huntington

RAUSCHER, Barbara - 2 July 1880 paper; resident of New York City; "Seawanhaka" fire on East River

RAUSCHER, Kate - 2 July 1880 paper; resident of New York City; "Seawanhaka" fire on East River

RAY, Maria A. - 36 y 7 m 22 d; d. 1 June 1890 at Brooklyn; interment at Huntington; widow of Dr. Joseph Ray

RAYNOR, Andrew - d. 18 May 1890 at Bridgeport, Conn.; interment at Port Jefferson; son of Mrs. Edward Whittie; former resident of Port Jefferson

RAYNOR, J. Minor - d. 21 October 1882 at Greenport; gun accident

RAYNOR, Mary - 45 years; d. at Freeport; 11 June 1887 paper; choked after swallowing part of her false teeth

RAYNOR, William - d. 27 May 1885 at Mattituck; brakeman on railroad train; hit by low bridge while riding on top of railroad car

READDY, Patrick - 78 years; d. 2 November 1883 at Huntington

REARDON, Ellen - d. 20 March 1889 at Roslyn;
interment at Westbury

RECKENBELL, George E. - d. 8 May 1885; Hempstead item

REDDY, Ferdinand - 50 years; d. 7 February
1889 at Alms House [?Yaphank]

REDFIELD, Sarah S. - 83 years; d. 16 August
1882 at Cold Spring Harbor; interment at
Green-Wood, Brooklyn

REDMON, child - 4 years; d."recently" at
Unionville, Town of Hempstead; poisoned by
London Purple; son of George R. Redmon;
19 August 1881 paper; [note: Unionville
located in Town of Jamaica per 1873 map]

REDWOOD, Orville - 12 years; d. 6 May 1888 at
Smithtown; "suddenly"

REED, A. A. - d. 19 July 1882 at Roslyn;
interment at Manhasset; hotel keeper; Sea-
side House, Rockaway Beach; Jamaica Hotel,
Jamaica; Nassau House, Oyster Bay; and
Mansion House, Roslyn

REED, Margaret - d. 14 October 1889; Hicksville item; interment at Calvary Cemetery,
Queens County

REED, Mary - 2 July 1880 paper; resident of
New York City; "Seawanhaka" fire on East
River

REEGAN, Alfred - found dead 16 August 1881 at
Northwest, Suffolk County [Town of East
Hampton]

REEVE, infant - 1 year; d. 23 July 1880 at
St. Johnsland; child of Smith Reeve

REEVE, George I. - d. "last week" at Aquebogue; 10 May 1890 paper; "respected citizen
and farmer"

REEVE, Harrietta A. - 64 years; d. 11 April
1886 at Brooklyn; wife of Egbert Reeve

REEVE, Perry Belmont - 1 y 6 m 7 d; d. 9 July
1886 at Brooklyn; son of Egbert Reeve

REEVE, Sarah A. - 34 years; d. 7 February 1886
at Brooklyn

REEVES, Egbert A. - 1 year; d. 31 August 1884
at Brooklyn

REEVES, Immanuel - found drowned in Northport
Harbor; 26 November 1887 paper

REEVES, Jason E. - 18 yrs 6 mos; d. 6 September 1890 at Sunk Meadow
179

REGENSBURY, Irving S. - infant; d. 29 August
1888 at Melville; son of Samuel Regensbury
of New York City
REGENT, child - d. 19 November 1880 at Yaphank; lockjaw; son of Henry Regent
REHBERG, Dora - 73 yrs 10 mos; d. 5 January
1890 at Hicksville; wife of Martin Rehberg
REIKHERT, Mary Ryan - "young lady"; d. "suddenly" "this week" at New York City;
12 March 1887 paper; adopted sister of Mrs.
McMenomy; wife of Charles G. Reikhert;
former resident of Long Swamp
REILLY, Catherine - 72 years; d. 13 January
1884 at Northport
REILLY, Elizabeth S. - 16 days; d. 27 July
1886 at Brooklyn; interment at Huntington
REILLY, Miles - ca. 24 years; drowned 2 Sept-
ember 1883 at Oyster Bay
REINBOLD, infant - d. 16 April 1889 at Hicks-
ville
REINHARDT, Amanda - d. 13 October 1890 at
Hempstead; interment at Westbury; daughter
of Louis Reinhardt
REINHOLD, Ida - 10 months; d. 30 October 1886
at Hicksville; daughter of John and Rosa
Reinhold
REINSCH, Ernest - 27 years; suicide 5 February
1879 at Island Trees
REMSEN, Mrs. Abraham - "aged"; funeral 11 Jan-
uary 1888 at Oyster Bay
REMSEN, Ann - 88 years; d. 24 January 1890 at
Mill Hill, Oyster Bay; mother of John Rem-
sen; 60 years a member of Brookville
Reformed Church
REMSEN, Jackson - funeral 2 October 1887 at
Brookville; Jericho item
REMSEN, James S. - 76 years; d. 28 August 1887
at Jamaica; hotel owner at Rockaway Beach
and Jamaica
REMSEN, John - d. 14 October 1888 at East
Norwich; funeral at Brookville; Oyster Bay
Town Clerk for over 30 years
REMSEN, Phebe E. - 50 years; d. 26 January
1888 at South Norwalk, Conn.; interment at
Norwalk, Connecticut
REMSEN, William D. - 68 years; d. 2 July 1890;
funeral at Oyster Bay

RENNA, Mr. - d. 28 October 1885 at Hicksville;
"one of Hicksville's oldest residents"

RENTON, Margaret - 57 years; d. at New York
City; 31 May 1890 paper; interment at
Woodbury

REUBMANN, Annie - 40 years; d. 5 April 1878 at
Syosset

REYNOLDS, Albert - 8 mos 14 days; d. 24 July
1881 at Huntington

REYNOLDS, Peter - 49 years; d. 21 September
1889 at New York City; stabbed with a
carving knife in fight

RHINELANDER, William C. - d. "a few weeks ago"
at New York City; 19 July 1878 paper; grandfather of Mrs. John A. King, who inherited
$9,000,000 and wants to give the old King
Mansion to the Village of Jamaica

RHODES, Catherine - d. 11 September 1890 at
Lawrence; interment at Hempstead; widow of
Henry E. Rhodes; former resident of Hemp-
stead

RHODES, Charles - murdered 10 May 1887 at
Hummocks Island, Hempstead Bay, by Jesse
Abrams; resident of Oceanville

RHODES, William - d. 17 December 1878 at
Hicksville; thrown from wagon; resident of
Smithville, Town of Hempstead

RICE, Charles - 16 years; d. 22 October 1886
at West Hills

RICE, Gloriana - 84 yrs 9 mos; d. 29 July 1878
at Babylon; widow of David Rice of Comac

RICE, Richard S. - 39 years; d. 31 August 1887
at Dix Hills; former resident of Killyman,
County Tyrone, Ireland

RICH, George H. - 10 y 10 m 18 d; d. 4 April
1884 at Northport; son of George and Linie
Rich

RICHARD, Adolph - d. 4 August 1879 at Shelter
Island; baker; died of heat exhaustion at
Manhanset House; 125 F. in bake shop; he
drank ice water and sat in ice house and
died as a result

RICHARDS, Martin - d. 9 December 1884 at
Hempstead; hit by railroad train; resident of Old Westbury

181

RICHARDSON, Henry C. - 52 years; d. 7 August 1878 at Brooklyn, E. D.; died in a hardware store; resident of Hempstead; formerly of Huntington

RICHARDSON, Lemuel S. - ca. 63 years; d. 30 September 1879 at Brooklyn; retired president of Mackrell and Richardson Manufacturing Company; native of New York City (b. 1816)

RICHTER, John - ca. 15 years; drowned at Babylon; 24 October 1884 paper; resident of Breslau

RICKS, child - d. at Whitestone; 15 January 1887 paper; son of Anthony Ricks; this child and unnamed nephew of Anthony Ricks both died of diphtheria

RIDDLEBERGER, Harrison H. - 46 years; d. 24 January 1890 at Woodstock, Virginia; former U. S. Senator from Virginia [1883-1889]

RIDLEY, Edward - 69 years; d. 31 July 1883 at Gravesend; dry goods merchant on Grand Street, New York City

RIGGS, Edward S. - 10 y 4 m 4 d; d. 9 November 1878 at Huntington

RIGGS, John T. - 52 y 1 m 3 d; d. 24 July 1889 at Huntington

RIGGS, Martha - 30 years; d. 18 June 1879 at Comac; wife of Timothy Riggs

RIGGS, Samuel B. - 68 yrs 4 mos; d. 3 December 1879 at Huntington

RILEY, Thomas - 38 years; d. 5 June 1881 at Dix Hills; kicked by colt

RIPLEY, Henry E. - 82 years; interment 21 April 1886 at Brooklyn; Oyster Bay item

RITCH, George - F. J. Ritch & Sons dry goods store closed 13 November 1889 because of his death; Port Jefferson item

RITCHIE, child - interment 2 February 1890 at Locust Valley; son of Charles Ritchie; Glen Cove item

RITTER, Joseph - 5 yrs 9 mos; d. 29 June 1882 at Northport; interment at Huntington; son of Ferdinand Ritter

RITTER, Frederick L. - 7 days; d. 7 October 1879 at Huntington; son of Casper H. and Louise Ritter

ROAT, Mrs. George W. - d. 14 March 1889 at
Riverhead; daughter of Rev. Azel Down

ROBBINS, infant - d. 31 May 1886 at Huntington; son of William I. and Sarah E. Robbins

ROBBINS, Archie B. - 6 y 1 m 25 d; d. 29 June
1880 at Northport; son of Benjamin T. and
Helen A. Robbins

ROBBINS, Elizabeth - 43 y 1 m 13 d; d. 1 June
1879 at East Northport

ROBBINS, Joseph S. - 30 yrs 3 mos; d. 25 July
1883 at New York City

ROBBINS, Rachael Titus - 71 years; d. 18 October 1888 at Woodbury; interment at Jericho;
wife of Edward Robbins

ROBBINS, Walter - 36 years; d. 7 January 1886
at Jericho

ROBINS, Mrs. William - d. 15 May 1881 at
Brooklyn; carriage accident; sister of
Edward Carll

ROBINSON, Andrew * [see Robinson, Manley *] -
drowned 17 December 1890 when boat capsized;
body found in Northport Harbor 14 March 1891

ROBINSON, Henry - d. 12 April 1886 at Westbury; interment at Moriches; brakeman on
railroad train; fell off car and was run
over; m. widow of William N. Terrill

ROBINSON, Manley * - 19 years; drowned 17 December 1890 at Northport; out in harbor in
small boat during storm; recently moved to
Northport from Virginia

ROBINSON, Sadie E. - 31 y 10 m 12 d;
d. 1 February 1890 at Northport; daughter
of John Smith; husband died "six months ago"

ROBINSON, Rev. William L. - d. "last week" at
Good Ground; 9 August 1890 paper

RODMAN, John - d. at Locust Valley; 31 May
1890 paper; father of Mrs. Wright Remsen;
Oyster Bay item

ROE, Agnes - 18 years; drowned 15 July 1885 in
Great South Bay off Patchogue; resident of
Patchogue

ROE, Clarissa H. - 64 y 8 m 2 d; d. 22 February 1880 at Huntington

ROE, James P. - 70 y 7 m 1 d; d. 5 February
1888 at Huntington

ROE, Keturah - 85 years; d. 8 December 1880 at
Huntington

ROE, Sarah Ann - 68 y 11 m 8 d; d. 26 December
1889 at Huntington; wife of Thomas Smith
Roe; "member for many years of the Second
Presbyterian Church"

ROGERS, child - 19 months; d. 2 October 1887
at Bridgehampton; drowned in bath tub;
daughter of Alfred Rogers

ROGERS, Amelia - 86 years; d. 10 July 1886 at
Brooklyn; interment at Huntington; native of
Half Hollow Hills

ROGERS, Cornelia - 52 years; d. 16 October
1885 at Huntington; invalid for many years

ROGERS, David - 76 yrs 11 mos; d. 26 April
1884 at Cold Spring; interment at Green-
Wood, Brooklyn; son of Jacob and Elizabeth
Rogers; survived by second wife and three
children; b. Cold Spring Harbor 29 May 1807

ROGERS, Eliza L. - 42 yrs 16 days; d. 17 June
1890 at Huntington; wife of Moses R. Rogers

ROGERS, Elliott Stanley - 8 mos 24 days;
d. 9 October 1889 at Huntington; son of
Frank W. and Mary B. Rogers

ROGERS, Halsey - suicide 20 June 1882 at
Westhampton

ROGERS, Hannah - 85 yrs 7 mos; d. 17 October
1880 at Brooklyn; interment at Northport;
widow of Joshua Rogers

ROGERS, Harriet - 74 years; d. 8 July 1880 at
New York City; interment at Huntington;
widow of Theodore Rogers

ROGERS, Henry T. - 21 years; d. 11 January
1883 at Worcester, Massachusetts; son of
Rev. C. S. Rogers

ROGERS, Ida - d. 29 October 1887 at Riverhead;
daughter of Halsey Vail; wife of William
Rogers; resident of Peconic

ROGERS, Jacob - 79 y 3 m 9 d; d. 15 December
1880 at Elwood

ROGERS, Jarvis H. - 25 yrs 8 mos; d. 6 February 1880 at Manetto Hill

ROGERS, Jennie M. T. - 25 years; d. 7 June
1886 at Bayone City, N. J.; interment at
Huntington

ROGERS, Louis E. - 32 yrs 9 mos; d. 31 March
1890 at Santa Fe, New Mexico; interment at
Huntington; son of Isaac Rogers; widower of

184

ROGERS, Louis E. (continued)
Mary Seacord; "learned the carriage trade"
and had "fine large factory" on Main Street;
member of First Presbyterian Church; went to
New Mexico for health

ROGERS, Lydia - 90 y 6 m 3 d; d. 17 June 1884
at Huntington; daughter of Abel Brush; widow
of Conklin Rogers; mother of Hannah Kelsey,
Alma Rogers, Stephen C. Rogers, Isaac
Rogers, George Rogers and Laura Lefferts;
native of Woodbury

ROGERS, Mabel - 8 months; d. 14 November 1889
at Bayonne, N. J.; daughter of Theodore
Rogers

ROGERS, Maria - 55 years; d. 17 April 1883 at
Cold Spring; wife of Henry Rogers

ROGERS, Maria L. - 61 y 8 m 10 d; d. 27 July
1879 at Huntington; wife of Stephen C.
Rogers

ROGERS, Mary Frances - d. 26 July 1878 at
Jersey City, N. J.; wife of William E.
Rogers; formerly of Huntington

ROGERS, Mary Seacord - 30 yrs 9 mos; d. 26
February 1890 at Santa Fe, New Mexico;
interment at Huntington; wife of Louis E.
Rogers; active worker at First Presbyterian
Church; went to New Mexico with husband for
health

ROGERS, Dr. Melancton - 83 years; d. 25 June
1880 at Covington, Kentucky

ROGERS, Moses - 93 y 11 m 19 d; d. 14 April
1878 at Huntington; son of Zebulon Rogers

ROGERS, Rev. Moses - 93 yrs 10 mos; d. 25 August 1887 at Fresh Pond; funeral at Comac;
local preacher of the M. E. Church; native
of Clay Pitts

ROGERS, Nina - 32 years; d. 4 March 1881 at
Brooklyn

ROGERS, Phebe B. - 85 years; d. 18 June 1889
at New York City; wife of Thomas P. Rogers

ROGERS, Phineas - 92 years; d. 26 March 1878
at Dry Brook, Town of Chemung, [Chemung
County], N. Y.; native of Fresh Pond (b.
November 1786); m. 1807 at Huntington to
un-named wife who d. 4 March 1872, age 87;
War of 1812 veteran, serving on Long Island;

ROGERS, Phineas (continued)
settled in Chemung County (then Tioga
County) 1817; Commissioner of Deeds for
Tioga County, prior to creation of Cheming
County; member of the Baptist Church for
fifty years; father of 12 children, 10
residents of Chemung and vicinity

ROGERS, Robert - 55 years; d. 7 April 1883 at
Middletown, N. Y.; native of Fresh Pond;
formerly of Huntington

ROGERS, Robert B. - d. 8 August 1888 at Greenlawn; brother of Mrs. William H. Hogan of
Greenlawn; resident of Brooklyn

ROGERS, Samuel E. - 68 years; d. 13 October
1887 at Yaphank; funeral at Northport

ROGERS, Stephen C. - 68 y 10 m 3 d; d. 6 Sept-
ember 1885 at Huntington; son of Conklin and
Lydia Rogers; brother of Hannah Amelia
Kelsey, Alma Rogers, Isaac Rogers, George
Rogers and Mrs. J. B. Lefferts; native of
Cold Spring b. 29 October 1816; m. Maria L.
Rogers 26 December 1838; hotel keeper at
Suffolk Hotel; postmaster; Huntington Town
Clerk; Huntington Town Supervisor 1867,
1874-1883; Suffolk County Clerk; long obit
in 11 September 1885 paper

ROGERS, Warren - 53 yrs 2 mos; d. 16 April
1878 at Cold Spring

ROGERS, William - 71 y 3 m 7 d; d. 22 April
1886 at Elwood; interment at Woodlawn
Cemetery, New York City

ROHRBACH, Charles Henry - 13 y 10 m 5 d;
d. 1 February 1888 at Hicksville; son of
Hartman Rohrbach

ROHRBACH, Henry - 62 y 2 m 20 d; d. 24 January
1890 at Hicksville; immigrated to USA from
Germany at age 19; resident of Hickville for
past 35 years; m. 1847 Martha K. Wagner, who
d. ca. 1865; m. Mrs. Elizabeth Gable, widow;
father of six children by first wife

ROHRBACH, Mrs. Henry - funeral 26 January 1887
at New York City; former resident of
Hicksville

ROLLAND, Joseph E. - 1 y 2 m 24 d; d. 12 March
1886 at Brooklyn; son of Charles H. and Emma
J. Rolland

ROLPH, Reuben - 65 y 5 m 28 d; d. 11 January
1879 at Sparta, Virginia; former resident of
Huntington
ROME, Ann - 93 years; d. 1 November 1880 at
West Hills
ROME, George - 80 y 6 m 4 d; d. 15 May 1879 at
Brooklyn; interment at West Hills
ROME, Jane - 72 years; d. 11 May 1885 at West
Hills
ROOMANFENGEL, Charles - killed at Long Island
City by falling brick wall; 11 January 1890
paper
ROOSON, Henry B. - 58 years; d. 7 March 1888
at Smithtown Branch
ROOT, Mrs. D. C. - d. 12 August 1889 at Oyster
Bay; interment at Colchester, Connecticut
ROPES, Ripley - 70 years; d. 18 May 1890 at
Brooklyn; "was one of the most prominent men
in political, business and social circles of
Brooklyn and leaves a large fortune"
ROSE, Louis - suicide 30 May 1885 at Queens;
hanged himself
ROSE, Susan M. - 5 y 10 m 28 d; d. 15 Septem-
ber 1886 at Long Swamp; daughter of William
and Catherine Rose
ROSE, W. Brewster - 69 yrs 11 mos; d. 27 April
1881 at Brooklyn; interment at Northport
ROSELLE, Harriet A. - 68 y 11 m 29 d;
d. 23 January 1890 at Huntington
ROSELLE, James - 73 y 9 m 23 d; d. 15 June
1890 at Huntington
ROSELLE, Katie A. - 2 years; d. 6 December
1887 at Huntington; daughter of James
Roselle
ROSELLE, Mary H. - 17 months; d. 6 December
1887 at Huntington; daughter of James
Roselle
ROSEMAN, Frank - 44 years; d. 9 October 1880
at Yaphank
ROSENGREEN, S. B. - d. 6 January 1884 at
Corona; resident of Brooklyn
ROSS, Amelia Ruland - d. 15 December 1878 near
Patchogue; kerosene lamp explosion; daughter
of Mrs. Augustus Rice; wife of Eugene Ross
(m. 16 November 1878)
ROUKE, Catharine - d. 6 April 1884 at Flushing

ROWELL, Rev. Moses - 69 y 5 m 20 d; d. 2 February 1886 at Miller's Place

ROWLAND, Catherine A. - 60 years; d. 3 March 1887 at Greenlawn; wife of Charles Rowland

ROWLAND, Clarissa A. - 51 y 5 m 9 d; d. 16 April 1881 at Mount Sinai; wife of Lewis M. Rowland

ROWLAND, Eliza A. - 75 years; d. 16 June 1885 at Miller's Place; widow of Jeremiah Rowland

ROWLAND, Emily - d. 18 May 1889 at South Norwalk, Connecticut; hit by railroad train; funeral at Five Mile River, Connecticut; wife of Warren Rowland; sister of Mrs. David Wood of Greenlawn

ROWLAND, George W. - 1 yr 12 days; d. 28 February 1881 at Brooklyn; son of Charles H. and Emma J. Rowland

ROWLAND, Henry W. - d. 20 January 1885 at Jamaica

ROWLAND, Joseph - death reported 30 November 1883 paper; resident of Setauket

ROWLAND, Lewis M. - 58 y 2 m 8 d; d. 23 August 1886 at Mount Sinai

ROWLAND, Lora - 4 yrs 10 m; d. 7 March 1885 at Eaton's Neck; daughter of Edward and Frances Rowland

ROWLAND, Mary A. - 23 y 7 m 1 d; d. 16 April 1887 at Mount Sinai

ROWLAND, Richard W. - 66 y 5 m 25 d; d. 7 February 1889 at Eaton's Neck; "suddenly"; interment at East Northport; husband of Mary E. Rowland; father of Carrie D. Rowland

ROWLAND, Susan T. - 63 y 2 m 15 d; d. 16 November 1878 at Huntington; wife of Smith Rowland

RUDYARD, Mary A. - 79 years; d. 27 February 1879 at Oyster Bay

RUEGER, Mrs. Andrew/Cornelius - d. 17 September 1888 at Hicksville; interment at Westbury

RUGG, Clarissa - 60 years; d. 26 July 1884 at Bridgehampton; mother of murderer Charles H. Rugg

RULAND, child - d. at Middle Island; 27 December 1890 paper; son of Wallace Ruland and former Flora Rogers

RULAND, Mrs. Charles - d. 5 October 1888 at
Smithtown; interment at Hauppauge
RULAND, E. Emeline - 58 yrs 7 days; d. 7 June
1882 at Northport; wife of Darius B. Ruland
RULAND, Frederick C. - 3 years; d. 1 December
1878 at Huntington; son of Samuel Ruland
RULAND, Margaret E. - 5 y 11 m 12 d; d. 18
November 1878 at Huntington; daughter of
Samuel Ruland
RULAND, Mary W. - 7 years; d. 9 December 1878
at Huntington; daughter of Samuel Ruland
RULAND, Richard - d. 25 October 1890 at
Patchogue
RULAND, Samuel C. - 43 y 5 m 11 d; d. 7 Decem-
ber 1878 at Insane Asylum, Yaphank;
interment at Huntington
RULAND, Samuel H. - 9 y 3 m 20 d; d. 22 Novem-
ber 1878 at Huntington
RUNCIE, Johnnie - drowned 21 June 1888 near
Rockville Centre; son of John T. and Amelia
Runcie
RUSCO, George P. - 29 y 6 m 28 d; d. 28 Sept-
ember 1888 at Huntington
RUSCO, John P. - infant; d. 23 July 1882 at
Lloyd's Neck; son of George P. Rusco
RUSHMORE, Edmund - 72 years; d. 26 January
1890 at Westbury; brother of Stephen Rush-
more
RUSHMORE, Dr. Edwin C. - d. 4 February 1885 at
Hempstead; medical doctor found dead in his
office; native of Hempstead
RUSHMORE, Mrs. Elbert - d. 16 December 1878
at Hempstead; asphyxiated by coal gas
RUSHMORE, John - d. 17 November 1890 at
Jericho; interment at Westbury
RUSHMORE, Stephen - 76 years; d. 13 January
1890 at Westbury; father of Howard Rushmore
of Westbury and Edward Rushmore of Plainfield, New Jersey
RUSHMORE, Rev. Stephen - 73 years; d. 12 May
1890 at Hempstead; M. E. clergyman; "one of
the oldest ministers in the New York East
Conference"; native of Hempstead; appren-
ticed to Zophar Ketcham, harnessmaker;
entered M. E. ministry in 1843 and served
until retirement in 1883; last charge was
Newbridge, Town of Hempstead

RUSHMORE, Thomas - 70 years; d. 30 April 1878
at Roslyn; deaf; hit by railroad train while
crossing tracks

RUSSELL, Christina - 56 yrs 5 mos; d. 22 January 1890 at Hicksville; wife of Henry Russell; mother of Matilda Reuberg of Chicago,
Illinois

RUSSELL, Thomas - 68 years; d. 16 April 1888
at Islip

RUSZITS, John - d. 18 October 1890 at St. James; interment at Staten Island; "million-
aire furrier"

RYDER, Henry - 51 years; d. 25 January 1889 at
Shelter Island; killed by falling piece of
lumber while working on windmill

SAILSBURY, Mrs. Edward - d. 11 January 1879 at
Farmingdale; fell into a well

SALATA, Mrs. Samuel - suicide 11 August 1889
at Greenport; hanged herself

SALOAM, Ann - 75 y 7 m 26 d; d. 23 July 1889
at Northport

SALMON, Mrs. A. M. - d. 14 November 1886;
mistakenly took morphine thinking it was
quinine; resident of Peconic

SALVANO, Alexander - murdered "last Easter
Sunday" at Brooklyn by Nicolo Frezza;
26 July 1890 paper

SAMISON, Miss - 73 years; d. 6 September 1884
at Rocky Point

SAMMIS, infant - 2 months; d. 26 July 1885 at
Northport; son of Charles F. and Alice E.
Sammis

SAMMIS, Alexander - 70 y 1 m 20 d; d. 24 August 1880 at Huntington

SAMMIS, Alexander T. - d. 22 January 1884 at
Babylon

SAMMIS, Almira - 73 years; d. 16 December 1885
at Huntington; wife of Jesse Sammis

SAMMIS, Anna Eliza - 50 y 4 m 15 d; d. 8 March
1889 at Huntington; wife of Stephen Sammis

SAMMIS, Benjamin Jarvis - 75 yrs 5 days;
d. 13 June 1885 at Huntington

SAMMIS, Bertram Oakley - 1 yr 7 mos;
d. 29 January 1882 at Brooklyn; interment
at Huntington; son of Royal A. and Julia S.
Sammis

SAMMIS, Charity - 77 yrs 7 mos; d. 24 November
1880 at Huntington; widow of Alexander
Sammis

SAMMIS, Charles - d. 17 December 1884 at
Mineola; son of Seaman Sammis

SAMMIS, Charles - d. 13 September 1889 at
Oyster Bay; interment at Brookville

SAMMIS, Cora - d. 11 February 1879 at New York
City; abortion; grand jury indicted Frank
Cosgrove "betrayer" and Bertha Burger,
abortionist, for Cora's death 28 February
1879 paper; Burger sentenced to 12 years in
prison for death "by malpractice" 18 April
1879 paper; funeral at Northport; daughter
of Henry Sammis; teacher at Northport M. E.
Sunday School

SAMMIS, Daniel B. - 53 yrs 23 days;
d. 23 November 1887 at Huntington

SAMMIS, Daniel G. - 72 years; d. 29 August
1885 at Fresh Ponds

SAMMIS, Edith L. - 1 y 1 m 4 d; d. 2 August
1884 at Huntington; daughter of Joseph and
Lillian Sammis

SAMMIS, Eliza - 71 y 7 m 19 d; d. 31 May 1884
at Woodbury; accidental overdose of opium
used as medicine; widow of George Sammis;
resident of Huntington

SAMMIS, Ellen B. - 71 y 6 m 14 d; d. 27 August
1890 at Huntington

SAMMIS, Frank C. - 23 y 3 m 16 d; d. 8 June
1881 at West Neck; son of Edgar Sammis

SAMMIS, George - 77 years; d. 7 April 1879 at
Huntington

SAMMIS, George Fletcher - 8 yrs 9 mos;
d. 15 May 1885 at Brooklyn

SAMMIS, Gertie E. - 2 y 9 m 15 d; d. 16 October 1880 at Huntington; daughter of George
A. and Juliet Sammis

SAMMIS, Hannah - 86 y 10 m 19 d; d. 4 March
1889 at Huntington; mother of Stephen Sammis
and William H. Sammis

SAMMIS, Hannah C. - 78 years; d. 9 May 1889 at
West Neck; daughter of Thomas and Naomi
Fleet; widow of Lewis Sammis; native of East
Neck

SAMMIS, Henrietta Marion - 3 mos 22 days;
d. 27 April 1886 at West Neck; daughter of
W. Woodhull and Louisa S. Sammis
SAMMIS, Henry D. - 25 days; d. 5 March 1879 at
Huntington; son of Joseph H. and Phebe M.
Sammis
SAMMIS, Isabella E. - 30 y 5 m 6 d; d. 12 Feb-
ruary 1889 at Flushing; funerals Flushing
and Huntington; daughter of Henry Crawford;
born Limerick, Ireland; sister of John W.
Crawford of Flushing; wife of Henry S. Sam-
mis who she m. 2 October 1879 at John Street
M. E. Church, New York City; active Metho-
dist involved with John Street M. E. and
Huntington M. E. Churches
SAMMIS, Israel - d. 27 January 1879 at Baby-
lon; War of 1812 veteran
SAMMIS, Jacob - 72 years; d. 23 March 1883 at
Centreport
SAMMIS, James M. - 69 years; d. 24 April 1883
at Pleasant Valley, Dutchess County, N. Y.
SAMMIS, Jesse Fleet - 81 yrs 4 mos; d. 26 Dec-
ember 1880 at West Neck
SAMMIS, Joel - 63 years; d. 16 April 1879 at
New York City
SAMMIS, John S. - 78 years; d. 19 November
1883 at Arlington, Duvall County, Florida;
Huntington native who moved to Florida in
1828
SAMMIS, Jonathan - d. 8 March 1888 at Babylon;
civil engineer and surveyor
SAMMIS, Joseph - 64 y 11 m 1 d; d. 14 Septem-
ber 1884 at Frog Pond; found dead in the
road; son of Joseph and Betsy Sammis
SAMMIS, Joseph E. - 37 years; d. 20 February
1888 at South Oyster Bay; funeral at Brook-
lyn; construction accident; fell off roof of
hotel under construction; former resident of
Huntington
SAMMIS, Leman - d. at Mineola; 21 March 1884
paper; proprietor of Prairie House in
Mineola
SAMMIS, Libbie - 22 years; death reported
1 May 1886 paper; Hicksville item
SAMMIS, Louisa - 41 y 1 m 19 d; d. 17 February
1888 at West Neck; wife of William Woodhull
Sammis

SAMMIS, Louisa R. - 7 mos; d. 13 August 1881
at Huntington; daughter of Joseph H. and
Phebe M. Sammis

SAMMIS, Louisa S. - 6 y 2 m 28 d; d. 24 September 1886 at Brooklyn; daughter of Royal
and Julia Sammis

SAMMIS, Lucinda - 87 years; d. 5 October 1890

SAMMIS, Madeline P. Kellum - 24 years;
d. 25 October 1882 at Huntington; wife of
Joseph E. Sammis

SAMMIS, Mary - 55 y 6 m 7 d; d. 30 September
1881 at Centreport; wife of Jacob Sammis

SAMMIS, Mary A. - 51 years; d. 8 April 1882 at
New York City; interment at Huntington; wife
of Philander P. Sammis

SAMMIS, Mary A. - 74 years; d. 14 August 1884
at Northport; widow of Nathaniel Sammis

SAMMIS, Mary Elizabeth - 55 yrs 8 days;
d. 22 April 1884 at Huntington; daughter of
Carman Smith; wife of Joseph Sammis

SAMMIS, Mary I. - 78 years; d. 29 October 1880
at Huntington

SAMMIS, Melancthon Smith - 69 years; d. 8 January 1887 at Huntington; blind

SAMMIS, Mortie - 1 y 10 m 28 d; d. 4 February
1880 at Northport; son of Mortimer and
Lizzie Sammis

SAMMIS, Nelson - 65 y 6 m 28 d; d. 3 September
1878 at Huntington; son of Jonas Sammis

SAMMIS, Dr. O. K. - victim of "Narraganset"
disaster; body came shore at Waterford,
Conn. 27 June 1880; 16 July 1880 paper;
resident of Deer Park

SAMMIS, Phebe - 89 y 5 m 19 d; d. 3 November
1882 at West Neck; widow of Elbert Sammis

SAMMIS, Philander J. - 72 yrs 19 days;
d. 10 January 1890 at New York City

SAMMIS, Richard - 74 years; d. 3 January 1878
at West Neck

SAMMIS, Mrs. Richard - 83 y 4 m 14 d;
d. 20 June 1888 at Huntington; daughter of
Mr. Eversely of Norwalk, Connecticut

SAMMIS, Sarah A. - 18 y 5 m 9 d; d. 3 June
1880 at Northport; daughter of Rinaldo
Sammis

SAMMIS, Sarah Frances - d. 6 January 1888 at
New York City; daughter of Walter and
Lucinda Sammis
SAMMIS, Susan M. - 70 yrs 4 mos; d. 8 January
1880 at West Neck
SAMMIS, Walter L. - 16 yrs 4 mos; d. 12 July
1889 at Huntington; son of Daniel B. Sammis
SAMMIS, William A. - 62 y 9 m 13 d; d. 22 Feb-
ruary 1878 at West Neck
SAMPSON, Lizzie - 18 years; d. 7 September
1885 at Eaton's Neck
SAMSON, Hattie Louie - infant; d. 4 January
1881; daughter of John and Annie Samson
SANDERSON, Ann - 61 years; d. 10 January 1884
at Northport
SANDHUSEN, Mabel - 1 y 5 m 7 d; d. 19 November
1889 at New York City; interment at Hunt-
ington
SANDS, Mr. - interment 17 April 1889 at
Westbury; resident of Brooklyn
SANDS, Benjamin F. - 9 mos 26 days; d. 21 July
1879 at Huntington
SANDS, Phebe * - d. "several weeks ago" at
Port Washington; 2 January 1885 paper
SANDS, Samuel S. - d. 21 March 1889 at Garden
City; horse riding accident while hunting;
interment at Hempstead
SANFORD, Mary A. - 81 y 8 m 11 d; d. 19 April
1889 at Northport; widow of David H. Sanford
SANXEY, Annie E. - 43 years; d. 5 May 1882 at
Huntington Depot; wife of R. S. Sanxey
SATTERLY, infant - d. 16 April 1885 at Mount
Sinai; child of Thomas Satterly
SATTERLY, Caroline S. - 75 y 6 m 19 d;
d. 11 August 1884 at Mount Sinai
SATTERLY, Luther M. - 74 yrs 8 mos; d. 3 June
1882 at Mount Sinai
SATTERLY, William - d. 25 February 1890 at
Mattituck; funeral at Setauket; former owner
of Setauket Grist Mill
SAUER, Matilda - 41 years; d. 1 March 1889 at
South Oyster Bay; interment at Jerusalem
SAUTER, infant - 7 months; d. 25 August 1887;
Hicksville item; child of Louis Sauter
SAWTELLE, Hiram - decapitated body found 15
February 1890 near Lebanon, Maine

SAWYER, Van Buren - 8 years; drowned 31 May
1878 at Riverhead in Peconic River; pushed
from boat by Edward Stone

SAXTON, Brewster H. - 60 years; d. 16 July
1888 at Patchogue

SAXTON, Mrs. Caleb - suicide 31 July 1890 by
taking Paris Green; interment at Bethpage;
widow of Caleb Saxton

SCHACKWERTY, child - 1 year; d. 1 March 1890
at Mineola; interment at Woodhaven; child of
Joseph Schackwerty

SCHAEFER, Caroline - 85 years; murdered 8 October 1887 at Breslau; long time neighborhood
feud led to her murder by George Galebain, a
neighbor; wife of Beyer Schaefer

SCHAEFFER, Barbara - d. 8 February 1888 at
Hicksville; funeral at Plain Edge

SCHALER, Adolph - 22 y 5 m 11 d; d. 9 November
1882 at Melville

SCHARSINSKY, youth - ca. 15 years; drowned at
Babylon; 24 October 1884 paper; resident of
Breslau

SCHEIDWEILER, Christina - 26 years; murdered
29 January 1887 at Breslau; wife of Philip
Scheidweiler

SCHEIDWEILER, Philip - 78 years; murdered 29
January 1887 at Breslau

SCHEILER, Charles - d. 6 June 1887 at Long
Island City

SCHENCK, infant - 9 mos; d. 16 November 1878
at Oyster Bay; son of William and Isabella
Schenck

SCHENCK, Edna - 7 mos; d. 12 May 1880 at
Oyster Bay; daughter of William and
Isabella Schenck

SCHENCK, George P. - 40 years; d. 17 February
1887 at Manhasset

SCHENCK, Rev. Noah - 59 years; d. 4 January
1885 at Brooklyn; rector of St. Anne's
Episcopal Church

SCHENCK, Sarah - 90 years; d. 18 September
1880 at Syosset

SCHEUER, Maggie - 17 years; d. 1 April 1887 at
Farmingdale

SCHLIEMAN, child - 2 y 5 m 20 d; d. 26 May
1888 at Hicksville; dau. of August Schlieman

SCHLING, Charlotte - 26 y 4 m 9 d; d. 6 April
1881 at Huntington; wife of Nicholas Schling
SCHLING, Mary A. - 31 y 1 m 15 d; d. 17 April
1890 at Huntington; wife of Nicholas Schling
SCHLOTTER, Mary - 14 years; d. 1 October 1889
at Jamaica; hit by railroad train while
crossing tracks
SCHMIDT, John Jacob - 68 years; d. 16 July
1890 at Hicksville; father of Mrs. Conrad
Weickman; resident of Hicksville for 40
years
SCHMIDT, Louis - murdered 28 June 1880 at
Amityville
SCHNEPF, Adam - 5 y 1 m 10 d; funeral 27 Aug-
ust 1888 at Hicksville; son of Martin and
Pauline Schnepf
SCHNEPF, Willie - d. 17 January 1889 at
Hicksville; son of Martin Schnepf
SCHOFIELD, Frank * - 9 years; d. 14 September
1888 at Babylon; shot himself while playing
with a pistol; son of Rachel Schofield;
nephew of Harriet Gardiner
SCHOLEPEL, Henry - drowned 4 July 1887 off
Glen Cove Landing; resident of Mamaroneck,
N. Y.
SCHNEIDER, Frederick - d. 18 September 1887 at
Breslau
SCHRABER, George - d. "about 3 weeks ago" at
Port Jefferson; killed in L. I. R. R.
accident; 19 October 1883 paper
SCHREINER, Horace - 2 July 1880 paper;
"Seawanhaka" fire on East River
SCHRIEFER, Augusta Marie - 22 y 11 m 11 d;
d. 12 January 1890 at Hicksville; interment
at Hempstead; daughter of Charles Keisling;
wife of Henry Schriefer; mother of Dora
Schriefer and Henrietta Schriefer; b. Brook-
lyn 30 January 1867
SCHUCHMAN, Henry - 64 yrs 8 mos; d. 17 May
1890 at Hicksville; interment at Hempstead;
husband of Christina Schnepf; native of
Guttenberg, Germany; resident of Hicksville since 1855
SCHUFELD, James - killed at Long Island City
when a brick wall fell; 11 January 1890
paper

SCHULER, Anton William - 2 yrs 3 mos;
d. 20 November 1890 at Arlington, N. J.;
interment at Central Park; diphtheria; son
of Anton Schuler; grandson of Peter Nibbe
SCHULER, Hattie Maud - d. 2 July 1890 at
Arlington, N. J.; interment at Central Park;
daughter of Anton Schuler; granddaughter of
Peter Nibbe
SCHULER, Ida Margaretta - 4 years; d. 19 Nov-
ember 1890 at Arlington, N. J.; interment at
Central Park; diphtheria; daughter of Anton
Schuler; granddaughter of Peter Nibbe
SCHULTZ, Mrs. Carl - 60 years; d. at Hicks-
ville; funeral 25 February 1882
SCHULTZ, John - body found "a few days ago" in
Flushing Bay; 26 July 1890 paper; resident
of Brooklyn; possible murder
SCHULTZE, Lena - d. 28 August 1889 at Meadow
Brook; interment at Hempstead
SCHUMAN, Frederick - drowned in Long Island
Sound, just off shore; body found at Crane
Neck Beach; 8 December 1888 paper; Port
Jefferson item; resident of South Norwalk,
Connecticut
SCHWARTING, Ada - 3 years; d. 2 September 1887
at Eaton's Neck; daughter of Charles and
Mary Schwarting
SCHWARTING, John P. - 9 months; d. 27 August
1887 at Eaton's Neck; son of Charles and
Mary Schwarting
SCHWARTZ, Mary - 5 yrs 9 mos; d. 17 August
1880 at Huntington; daughter of Joseph and
Mary Schwartz
SCHWEIZER, Joseph - 4 y 9 m 11 d; d. 21 Janu-
ary 1881 at St. James
SCOTT, Annie - ca. 14 years; d. 2 August 1885
at Miller's Place
SCOTT, James - 85 years; d. 18 March 1886 at
Cold Spring; ship carpenter during 1830's
and 1840's
SCOTT, Jane - 85 y 2 m 9 d; d. 28 September
1878 at Brooklyn; interment at Huntington;
widow of Thomas Scott of Old Fields
SCOTT, Jessie M. - 70 years; d. 3 August 1890
at Syosset; sister-in-law of John Cooke
SCOTT, Margaret - 75 years; d. 13 March 1881
at Miller's Place

SCOTT, Capt. O. H. - 49 y 5 m 17 d;
d. 20 February 1878 at Centreport;
consumption
SCRIPTURE, Maude A. - 12 yrs 8 mos; d. at
Brooklyn; 20 November 1885 paper
SCUDDER, Anne Cornelia - 61 years; d. 16 April
1884 at East Neck; daughter of Henry and
Elizabeth Hewlett Scudder; wife of Henry G.
Scudder
SCUDDER, Augustus H. - 69 yrs 5 mos;
d. 11 March 1888 at Huntington
SCUDDER, David Conklin - 80 y 4 m 21 d;
d. 17 June 1878 at Huntington
SCUDDER, Elizabeth - 70 y 9 m 19 d; d. 17 Nov-
ember 1890 at Huntington; daughter of Asa
Chichester; wife of George A. Scudder (m.
1845); b. West Hills 29 February 1820;
member of Univeralist Church
SCUDDER, Frances T. - 81 years; d. 26 March
1887 at New York City; widow of Solomon C.
Scudder
SCUDDER, Hannah B. - 67 yrs 4 mos; d. 12 March
1888 at Huntington; widow of Augustus H.
Scudder
SCUDDER, Henry G. - 67 years; d. 27 January
1886 at Huntington; carriage accident; horse
bolted and upset carriage; passengers thrown
out; son of Isaiah and Rhoda Jarvis Scudder;
father of Gilbert Scudder of Santa Fe, New
Mexico, Henry G. Scudder of New York City,
Hewlett Scudder of Huntington and Nora J.
(Mrs. John H.) Jones of Woodbury; grocery
dealer in New York City; retired to Hunt-
ington in 1872
SCUDDER, Henry J. - 61 years; d. 10 February
1886 at New York City [interment at Northport; member of U. S. House of Representatives 1873-1875; lawyer in New York City]
SCUDDER, James L. - 45 years; d. 5 May 1881 at
Huntington
SCUDDER, Jane A. - 72 y 11 m 7 d; d. 16 August
1878 at Huntington; widow of Israel Scudder
SCUDDER, Joel S. - 48 y 6 m 14 d; suicide
29 June 1879 at Huntington
SCUDDER, Jonas - 60 years; d. 3 January 1879
at Almshouse, Yaphank; former resident of
Northport

SCUDDER, Lillie A. * - 2 months; d. 12 August
    1885 at Huntington; daughter of Alonzo
    Scudder
SCUDDER, Lydia M. - 50 y 2 m 28 d; d. 3 March
    1888 at Huntington
SCUDDER, Mary E. - 22 y 4 m 2 d; d. 23 January
    1882 at New York City; daughter of Henry J.
    and Louisa H. Scudder
SCUDDER, Phebe - 88 years; d. 15 February 1888
    at East Neck; daughter of Gilbert and
    Abigail Scudder
SCUDDER, Polly - 84 years; d. 23 May 1884 at
    Northport
SCUDDER, Rebecca Bennett - 43 y 8 m 25 d;
    d. 27 June 1882 at Huntington
SCUDDER, Reuben R. - 43 y 11 m 15 d;
    d. 18 September 1881 at Huntington
SCUDDER, Ruth - 80 years; d. 28 April 1887 at
    Huntington
SCUDDER, Samuel S. - 80 years; d. 14 December
    1887 at Woodbury; funeral at Huntington; son
    of Jesse Scudder; native of Crab Meadow; ran
    hotel in Huntington for 20-25 years; ran
    stage line during 1850's to railroad at
    Hicksville and Syosset and to steamboats at
    Cold Spring Harbor
SCUDDER, Sarah Ann - 82 years; d. 15 October
    1886 at West Hills; interment at East North-
    port; former resident of Northport
SCUDDER, William C. - 68 y 2 m 20 d;
    d. 24 April 1886 at Huntington; wife found
    him dead in the barn
SCUDDER, William Murray - 30 years;
    d. 30 March 1881 at St. Augustine, Florida;
    interment at Huntington; son of Henry G.
    Scudder
SCUDDER, Wilmot - d. 9 February 1885 at
    Riverhead; former Suffolk County Clerk
SEACORD, Daniel F. - 28 years; d. 20 October
    1886 at San Diego, California; interment at
    Green-Wood, Brooklyn; went to California to
    regain health, but died there of consump-
    tion; former resident of Huntington
SEACORD, Henrietta Jarvis - 90 years;
    d. 3 March 1881 at New York City; interment
    at Brooklyn; widow of Daniel Seacord; former
    resident of Smithtown

SEAMAN, Mr. - drowned in sinking of "Mary Hamilton" in Long Island Sound; 4 January 1884 paper; resident of "a south side locality"

SEAMAN, child - d. 9 April 1885 at Hempstead; child of Henry Seaman

SEAMAN, infant [illegitimate] - murdered by mother Susie Seaman and grandmother Mary E. Seaman and buried in the cellar at Oyster Bay; 23 July 1887 paper

SEAMAN, Adeline [*?] - d. 2 January 1890 at Brooklyn; interment at Westbury; sister of Rev. James Seaman of Cold Spring Harbor

SEAMAN, Eddie V. - 4 y 5 m 21 d; d. 15 December 1885 at Brooklyn; son of Edward and Esther Seaman

SEAMAN, James - d. 8 May 1882 at Flushing; rope walker killed in accident when rope broke

SEAMAN, John - ca. 19 years; d. 8 September 1882 at Northport; hit by railroad train; resident of Jericho

SEAMAN, Joseph - 3 yrs 5 mos; d. 23 July 1890 at Westbury; interment at Hempstead; son of James Seaman

SEAMAN, Judith A. - 55 y 2 m 4 d; d. 31 January 1880 at Half Hollow Hills; wife of Jesse N. Seaman

SEAMAN, Laura * - 17 years; d. 25 January 1889 at Cold Spring Harbor; interment at Westbury; daughter of Rev. James Seaman

SEAMAN, Lizzie - 39 years; d. 4 October 1878 at East Meadow; widow of Valentine M. Seaman

SEAMAN, Mary - "old"; funeral 23 January 1887 at Westbury; widow of Jacob Seaman

SEAMAN, Maria A. - 88 y 2 m 21 d; d. 8 July 1883 at Cold Spring

SEAMAN, Mrs. Oliver - 79 years; d. at Plain Edge; funeral 20 March 1887 at Jericho (Friends' Meeting); mother John T. Seaman

SEAMAN, Platt - 42 years; d. 19 February 1888 at Lower Melville

SEAMAN, Ruth K. - 10 mos 29 days; d. 24 March 1880 at Brooklyn; interment at Huntington; daughter of Edward and Esther Seaman

SEARING, Dr. - d. 8 January 1888 at Hempstead

SEARING, Charles V. - 35 years; d. 3 June 1889
at Oyster Bay
SEARING, Silas - 60 years; d. 25 October 1879
at Oyster Bay
SEARLES, Joshua [*] - d. at Oyster Bay;
9 April 1887 paper
SEARLES, Mrs. Joshua * - funeral 25 May 1886
at Oyster Bay; wife of "colored local
preacher"
SECOR, Hannah A. - 46 y 10 m 21 d; d. 25 June
1880 at Centreport; wife of John W. Secor
SEELY, Rebecca C. - 75 years; d. 12 January
1878 at Oyster Bay
SEGELKEN, Annie - 24 y 6 m 18 d; d. 15 June
1887 at Hicksville; daughter of Ernest
Hoffman; wife of John Segelken
SELLS, Joseph Henry * - 24 years; drowned 27
February 1890 at Old Field, Brookhaven Town;
subject to fainting spells; had a spell and
drowned in 18" of water; son of Jerry and
Martha Sells
SEINS, Esther - d. 15 September 1879 at Hemp-
stead; shot in a quarrel by Mrs. Lena
Vogelson
SEVIN, infant - d. 22 March 1886 at Hicks-
ville; child of Philip Sevin
SEVIN, Adam - d. at New York City; interment
6 January 1890 at Hicksville; cousin of Mrs.
John Braun of Hicksville
SEVIN, Catharine - 74 yrs 8 mos; d. 3 December
1886 at Hicksville; wife of John A. Sevin
SEVIN, John A. - 80 yrs 11 mos; d. 3 December
1886 at Hicksville
SEVIN, Margaret - funeral 24 February 1886 at
Hicksville
SEVIN, Philip - d. 13 September 1886 at
Hicksville; grocer
SEYMOUR, Horatio - d. 12 February 1886;
[Governor of New York State 1853-1855 and
1863-1865; Democratic candidate for U. S.
President 1868]
SHADBOLT, Amelia - 86 yrs 9 mos; d. 5 May 1879
at Huntington; widow of Alanson Shadbolt
SHADBOLT, Charles C. - 23 y 1 m 19 d;
d. 3 September 1887 at Huntington

SHADBOLT, Chauncey - 1 m 10 d; d. 17 January
1885 at Huntington; son of Florentine E. and
Fannie S. Shadbolt
SHADBOLT, Clifford E. - 2 y 1 m 6 d;
d. 25 July 1887 at Huntington; son of Edward
Shadbolt
SHADBOLT, Daisy O. - 13 yrs 2 mos; d. 7 June
1886 at Northport; daughter of Carll E. and
Adelia J. Shadbolt
SHADBOLT, Ethel D. - 5 months; d. 30 July 1890
at Huntington daughter of Alfred Shadbolt
SHADBOLT, Fannie R. - 32 y 6 m 11 d; d. 8 Aug-
ust 1888 at Huntington; wife of Florentine
E. Shadbolt
SHADBOLT, Henrietta E. - 37 years; d. 21 May
1885 at Huntington; wife of Theodore
Shadbolt
SHADBOLT, Laura - 25 years; d. 14 August 1885
at Huntington
SHADBOLT, Lorenzo S. - 62 y 3 m 10 d;
d. 17 September 1881 at Huntington
SHADBOLT, Nellie - 7 months; d. 29 March 1883
at Huntington; daughter of Henry C. and
Temperance Shadbolt
SHADBOLT, Theodore C. - 68 years; d. 1 Septem-
ber 1888 at Huntington
SHALER, Lizzie - 2 July 1880 paper; resident
of New York City; "Seawanhaka" fire on East
River
SHANLEY, John - 46 years; d. 11 March 1890 at
Brooklyn; Brooklyn City Clerk
SHAW, child - 5 years; d. 18 January 1880 at
Springfield; burned in fire; daughter of
John Shaw
SHAW, William - d. 14 May 1883 at Finderne,
New [Jersey]; former proprietor of Union
Trotting Course
SHAW, William - 56 years; d. 19 October 1884
at East Northport
SHEA, Edward - 8 years; d. 4 May 1884 at Long
Island City; hit by baseball bat
SHELDON, William E. - d. 30 June 1884 at
Boston, Massachusetts
SHELTON, Rev. Frederick W. - ca. 67 years;
d. at Carthage Landing, Dutchess County,
N. Y.; 29 July 1881 paper; son of Dr. Nathan
Shelton; native of Jamaica (b. 1814);

SHELTON, Rev. Frederick W. (continued)
graduate of College of New Jersey, Princeton, N.J.; ordained to Episcopal priesthood
1847; Episcopal minister who served in
Huntington about 1847 and later at Fishkill,
N. Y., Montpelier, Vt. and Carthage Landing,
N. Y.

SHEPARD, infant - d. at Staten Island; interment 3 June 1888 at Hicksville; child of
John Shepard; grandchild of Mr. Forgie

SHEPARD, Mrs. - "is dead" at Brooklyn; 10 May
1890 paper; mother of Charles S. Shepard;
Port Jefferson item

SHEPARD, George Elliott - 1 y 2 m 13 d;
d. 13 February 1884 at New York City;
interment at Huntington; son of George A.
and Josephine Shepard

SHEPARD, George H. - 63 y 10 m 27 d; d. 30 May
1879 at North Plainfield, N. J.; son of
Eliphalet Shepard and Mary Kellogg; former
editor of the Long Islander

SHEPARD, George Harvey - 8 y 9 m 15 d;
d. 1 August 1883 at Huntington; son of
Charles E. and Juliette L. Shepard

SHEPARD, Henry - 79 yrs 3 mos; d. 5 November
1883 at Comac

SHEPARD, Mary - 78 years; d. 4 December 1886
at Comac; found dead in bed; widow of Henry
Shepard

SHERIDAN, J. - 10 years; d. 15 July 1880 at
St. Johnsland

SHERIDAN, Philip H. - d. 6 August 1888 at
Nonquitt, Massachusetts; flags at half mast
in Northport "this week" in memory of General Sheridan 11 August 1888 paper; long
obit and articles 18 August 1888 paper

SHERMAN, Flora - 4 years; d. 2 November 1888
at Shelter Island

SHERRILL, Julia Anna - 1 y 2 m 13 d; d. 6 February 1883 at Litchfield, Minnesota; daughter of Rev. John and Julia E. Sherrill

SHERRY, Constantine - 2 July 1880 paper;
resident of New York City; "Seawanhaka" fire
on East River

SHILSKE, Pauline - d. at/near Jamaica; 30 November 1889 paper; "over indulgence in Polish
whiskey"

SHIPMAN, James I. - 74 yrs 4 mos; d. 29 February 1884 at Huntington; civil engineer who constructed railroads; native of Saybrook, Connecticut

SHORT, Julia A. - 45 years; d. 19 December 1890 at High River, Calgary, Northwest Territory, Canada; daughter of Charles Conklin; wife of Joseph W. Short; former resident of Huntington and Brooklyn; resident of Canada for past five years

SHRADY, Jeannie Lockhart - d. 15 January 1884 at New York City; daughter of Walter and Lucinda Sammis; wife of John Shrady

SHRIMPTON, John - 61 years; d. 30 May 1883 at Mount Sinai

SILLECK, Aaron - 35 years; d. 23 February 1880 at Oyster Bay

SILLIMAN, Benjamin - d. 14 January 1885 at New Haven, Connecticut; famous scientist

SILLS, George B. - 25 years; d. 31 December 1882 at Lumberville, N. Y.; interment at Huntington; son of Washington B. Sills of Centreport

SILLS, Isabella - 64 y 2 m 10 d; d. 9 October 1884 at Northport

SILLS, Joel Rogers - 77 y 7 m 4 d; d. 8 August 1886 at Northport

SILVIA, Joseph - 63 years; d. 31 July 1888 at Cold Spring

SILVIA, Ralph A. - 3 y 3 m 16 d; d. 2 October 1881 at Cold Spring; son of Joseph and Carrie Silvia

SIMBERG, Charlotte - 1 y 9 m 8 d; d. 23 August 1888 at Huntington; daughter of William and Annie E. Simberg

SIMMONS, Smith - 23 years; d. 15 August 1880 at Bayville

SIMONSON, Hannah - 54 yrs 11 days; d. 26 May 1888 at Brooklyn; interment at Hempstead; had 35 lb. tumor removed at Long Island College Hospital, but died after operation; resident of Plainview

SIMPSON, Clarence - 21 days; d. 25 August 1882 at Huntington; son of Robert T. and Ella Simpson

SIMPSON, Ella A. - 26 years; d. 13 August 1882
at Brooklyn; daughter of Richard E. Conklin;
wife of Robert T. Simpson

SIMPSON, Henry - 82 years; d. 6 December 1889
at Huntington Harbor; interment at Brooklyn;
father-in-law of Oscar Kissam

SIMS, Thomas - 80 years; d. 21 January 1882 at
Cold Spring

SINCLAIR, Rev. James - 59 y 9 m 23 d;
d. 6 February 1883 at Smithtown Branch;
interment at Yonkers, N. Y.; pastor of
Presbyterian Church at Smithtown Branch

SINGER, Bernard - found murdered 29 August
1886 at Ridgewood

SKIDMORE, Abram P. - 2 July 1880 paper; resident of New York City; "Seawanhaka" fire on
East River

SKIDMORE, Bryant - 80 y 10 m 18 d; d. 21 June
1881 at Northport

SKIDMORE, Esther A. - funeral 28 November 1889
at Riverhead; widow of Luther Skidmore

SKIDMORE, James H. - 2 July 1880 paper; resident of New York City; "Seawanhaka" fire on
East River

SKIDMORE, Joel - 45 y 9 m 19 d; d. 2 August
1884 at Northport

SKIDMORE, John H. - 39 y 3 m 16 d; d. 1 January 1887 at Northport

SKIDMORE, John H. - 36 y 5 m 8 d; d. 18 January 1890 at Northport; "serious injuries
resulting from the log falling on him"; son
of Capt. Henry Skidmore; oyster and clam
business

SKIDMORE, Mrs. Joshua - funeral 30 June 1890
at Riverhead; interment at Flushing; native
of Quogue and former resident of Great Neck

SKIDMORE, Mary Burr - 90 y 8 m 24 d;
d. 20 November 1888 at Huntington

SKIDMORE, Mary S. - 47 years; d. 18 March 1886
at Huntington; wife of William H. Skidmore

SKIDMORE, Mary S. - 86 y 10 m 22 d; d. 4 September 1890 at Northport; widow of Bryant
Skidmore

SKIDMORE, Mrs. Walter - 82 years; d. 25 February 1884 at North Sea, Southampton; mother
of William H. Skidmore

SKIDMORE, Woodhull - d. 3 June 1884 at North-
port
SKINNER, Charles - 28 years; d. 6 June 1888 at
Gravesend; hit by railroad train while
crossing tracks in a wagon; brother of
Herbert Skinner
SKINNER, Herbert - 24 years; d. 6 June 1888 at
Gravesend; hit by railroad train while
crossing tracks in a wagon; brother of
Charles Skinner
SKINNER, Susan - 75 y 7 m 8 d; d. 10 October
1879 at Centreport
SLACK, William - 58 years; d. 23 August 1881
at Huntington
SLECK, child - 5 years; d. 20 July 1889 at
Plainview; interment at Westbury; upset a
pot of scalding hot coffee on herself
SLEETH, infant - 27 days; d. 11 August 1884 at
Cold Spring; daughter of Isaac and Susan B.
Sleeth
SLEETH, Susan B. - 22 yrs 4 mos; d. 23 July
1884 at Cold Spring; wife of Isaac Sleeth
SLOCUM, John S. - 28 years; d. 12 July 1886 at
Cold Spring Harbor; resident of New York
City
SLOTE, Daniel - 53 years; d. 13 February 1882
at New York City
SMITH, infant - d. 28 July 1878 at Smithtown;
child of Alonzo Smith
SMITH, child - 9 years; d. 9 December 1879 at
Patchogue; burned in stove fire; daughter of
Brewster Smith
SMITH, child - 4 years; interment 16 November
1889 at Jericho; child of E. Smith
SMITH, child - d. "this week" at Comac; 7 Dec-
ember 1889 paper; interment at St. James;
son of Thomas Smith; child was blind and
paralyzed
SMITH, child - d. 12 December 1889 at New York
City; shot by father on 22 November 1889;
daughter of James Smith
SMITH, Mrs. - d. "last week" at Stelton, New
Jersey; 3 May 1890 paper; mother of Rev.
C. C. Smith, Baptist pastor at Hempstead
SMITH, Albert - 65 years; drowned 30 May 1881
in Great South Bay

SMITH, Alexander - 83 y 3 m 7 d; d. 9 November 1879 at Dix Hills

SMITH, Alice - 12 years; d. 3 August 1885 at Smithtown Branch; daughter of Norman L. and Carrie W. Smith

SMITH, Anna - 10 years; d. 4 August 1884 at Sag Harbor; hit by railroad train

SMITH, Benjamin R. - "nearly 90" years; d. at Freeport; funeral 24 March 1890 at Freeport; "prominent member of the Freeport M. E. Church"; grandfather of Rev. Nelson Edwards of Glen Cove M. E. Church; father of 10; grandfather of 36; great-grandfather of 22; married over 70 years

SMITH, Mrs. Caleb - funeral 4 February 1885 at Comac

SMITH, Caleb Tangier - 51 years; d. 2 May 1885 at Nissequogue; son of Ebenezer Smith; m. daughter of Edward Henry Smith; merchant with Smith, Archer & Company; lived in Hong Kong, China, for a time

SMITH, Caroline - 41 y 5 m 14 d; d. 2 June 1880 at Mount Sinai; wife of John H. Smith

SMITH, Charity - 81 yrs 13 days; d. 8 March 1883 at Long Swamp

SMITH, Charles (Indian) - 85 years; d. 20 February 1881 at Jamaica; interment at Shinnecock Reservation; "last full-blooded Shinnecock Indian"

SMITH, Charles - interment 9 January 1889 at Westbury; resident of Roslyn

SMITH, Charles P. - 55 years; d. 24 July 1881 at Roslyn; steamboat captain; "hero of the Seawanhaka"

SMITH, Churchill - d. 15 April 1885 at New York City; son of Samuel Arden Smith

SMITH, Clara Eva - 3 years; d. 14 September 1884 at Fresh Ponds; daughter of Orion M. and Alice M. Smith

SMITH, Daniel A. * - 1 yr 6 mos; d. 18 February 1883 at Oyster Bay

SMITH, Daniel Alfred - 73 years; d. 25 March 1885; Smithtown Branch

SMITH, Daniel L. - 78 years; d. 9 July 1889 at Jericho

SMITH, David - d. March 1884 at Flushing; 13 June 1884 paper

SMITH, David * - d. 19 July 1889 at Oyster
Bay; interment at Huntington
SMITH, David B. - 45 years; d. 6 December 1884
at Rocky Point
SMITH, David C. - 55 y 3 m 15 d; suicide
15 March 1881 at Long Swamp
SMITH, David Willis - 96 years; funeral
13 April 1886 at Smithtown
SMITH, E. Gertrude - 6 y 6 m 13 d; d. 12 April
1878 at Brooklyn; daughter of Edwin J. Smith
SMITH, Ebenezer - interment 15 March 1879 at
Hauppauge
SMITH, Ebenezer - 74 y 3 m 28 d; d. 24 April
1879 at Melville
SMITH, Ebenezer - 90 yrs 11 mos; d. 8 Septem-
ber 1881 at Norwalk, Connecticut; former
resident of Huntington
SMITH, Edith M. - 30 y 9 m 11 d; d. 1 February
1888 at Huntington; wife of Henry C. Smith
SMITH, Edna M. - 53 yrs 4 days; d. 22 January
1884 at Long Swamp; wife of Platt H. Smith
SMITH, Edward - d. 19 October 1890 at Patch-
ogue
SMITH, Mrs. Edward A. - d. 10 March 1890 at
Stony Brook; "member of Stony Brook Presby-
terian Church for over 60 years"
SMITH, Edward Henry - d. 7 August 1885 at Head
of Nissequogue River; son of Richard and
Eliza W. Smith; Supervisor Town of Smithtown
1854-1861; Member U. S. House of Representa-
tives from 1st District of New York as a
"War Democrat" during Civil War; [interment
at St. James]
SMITH, Edwin J. - 55 years; d. 22 September
1880 at Patchogue; interment at Huntington
SMITH, Egbert T. - 67 years; d. 8 July 1889 at
Mastic Neck; owner of St. George's Manor
SMITH, Mrs. Eleazer - d. 21 November 1882 at
Smithtown
SMITH, Eleazer H. - 71 years; d. 20 May 1882
at Smithtown Branch
SMITH, Elias * - 28 y 1 m 16 d; d. 16 April
1878 at Huntington
SMITH, Elias - 67 y 9 m 7 d; d. 1 September
1878 at Huntington; Democratic Party leader
at Long Swamp

SMITH, Eliphalet W. - 77 years; d. 13 January
1889 at Huntington; father of Phebe Smith,
Carrie Smith and Charles Smith
SMITH, Eliza - 68 y 4 m 7 d; d. 9 February
1882 at Northport; wife of Richard Smith
SMITH, Eliza - 73 y 5 m 22 d; d. 21 January
1887 at Northport; "suddenly of apoplexy";
wife of Henry Smith
SMITH, Eliza - 87 y 4 m 7 d; d. 27 August 1887
at Smithtown; widow of Theodorus Smith
SMITH, Eliza A. - 78 years; d. 15 November
1883 at New York City; widow of Ezra Smith;
former resident of West Hills
SMITH, Eliza J. - 32 y 7 m 3 d; d. 3 February
1885 at Melville
SMITH, Elizabeth - 77 y 5 m 18 d; d. 21 January 1879 at Centreport
SMITH, Elizabeth Jones - 78 y 10 m 10 d;
d. 10 January 1882 at Huntington; widow of
Carman Smith
SMITH, Elizabeth V. - 11 years; d. 12 August
1888 at Jericho; daughter of Alexander Smith
SMITH, Emma - d. at Sunk Meadow; 23 November
1889 paper; daughter of Richard Smith
SMITH, Emma E. - 30 y 11 m 22 d; d. 17 April
1884 at Huntington; daughter of Joseph
Sammis; wife of Edwin W. Smith; resident of
Northport
SMITH, Emmet - d. 2 May 1881 at Smithtown;
lockjaw; son of Moses R. Smith
SMITH, Epenetus - d. 8 September 1888 at
Smithtown
SMITH, Epenetus - 85 years; d. 18 August 1890
at Crab Meadow
SMITH, Ezekiel - 78 y 10 m 5 d; d. 19 October
1881 at Melville
SMITH, Fannie O. - 2 mos 13 days; d. 4 August
1881 at Comac; daughter of Sidney C. and
Marietta Smith
SMITH, Frank S. - funeral 21 July 1890 at
Huntington; "energetic business man";
partner of Joel S. Gardiner in Smith &
Gardiner; "the stores of the village were
closed during the funeral service"
SMITH, Freddie E. - 3 y 3 m 22 d; d. 12 Decem-
ber 1886 at Greenlawn; son of Henry J. and
Carrie R. Smith

SMITH, Frederick J. - 37 years; d. 6 September
1880 at St. Johnland
SMITH, George E. - 42 yrs 10 mos; d. 11 April
1887 at East Northport
SMITH, George M. - d. 13 November 1890 at
Brooklyn; "suddenly"
SMITH, George W. - 66 years; d. 3 December
1890 at Huntington; fell dead while walking
along New York Avenue; son of Oliver Smith;
father of S. Alonzo Smith of Hempstead,
Frank Smith of Huntington and Elizabeth
(Mrs. Addison) Brown of Riverhead; Elder of
Second Presbyterian Church; resident of Long
Swamp
SMITH, George William - 59 y 1 m 17 d;
d. 9 September 1890 at Greenlawn; funeral at
Huntington; gored by a bull; brother of Mrs.
Samuel C. Gaines; father of Mrs. Samuel
Smith, Mrs. T. William Smith and Ada Smith;
supported Democratic Party
SMITH, Georgianna - 7 mos 3 days; d. 17 April
1878 at Brooklyn; daughter of Edwin H. and
Georgianna Smith
SMITH, Georgie P. - 2 mos 18 days; d. 7 August
1881 at Comac; son of Sidney C. and Marietta
Smith
SMITH, Gertie M. - 6 mos 15 days; d. 5 Septem-
ber 1886 at Huntington; daughter of John W.
and Mary Smith
SMITH, Gilbert - 73 y 10 m 15 d; d. 22 May
1883 at Huntington
SMITH, Grace Ann - 67 y 4 m 11 d; d. 28 Sep-
tember 1886 at Huntington; wife of Daniel
Smith
SMITH, Gracie Annie * - 10 mos 10 days;
d. 6 March 1884 at Huntington; daughter of
Samuel Smith
SMITH, Gussie - 24 y 3 m 21 d; d. 17 August
1878 at Smithtown Branch
SMITH, H. Clifford - 9 mos; d. 5 October 1881
at Fresh Pond; son of Thomas and Ida Smith
SMITH, Mrs. H. T. - funeral 3 August 1888 at
Port Jefferson; interment at Lambertville,
New Jersey
SMITH, Hannah - 82 years; d. 13 January 1880
at New York City; interment at Brooklyn;
mother of Edgar M. Smith

SMITH, Hannah - d. "recently" at Jamaica;
   21 January 1888 paper
SMITH, Hannah K. - 79 years; d. 5 October 1878
   at Long Island City; interment at Huntington
SMITH, Harry - d. "last week"; 18 November
   1881 paper; interment at Smithtown Landing
SMITH, Harry E. - 30 y 5 m 27 d; d. 11 March
   1889 at Northport; interment at Comac
SMITH, Hayward Sidney - 11 mos 10 days;
   d. 10 May 1880 at Huntington; son of
   J. Abner and Lizzie Smith
SMITH, Henry - 60 years; d. 17 November 1884
   at Newtown Creek; accident at Havermeyer
   Sugar Works
SMITH, Henry - d. 26 November 1890 at Smith-
   town; typhoid fever
SMITH, Mrs. Henry - 58 yrs 4 mos; d. 25 July
   1880 at Smithtown
SMITH, Henry D. - d. 20 July 1879 at Sayville;
   bitten by mad dog
SMITH, Rev. I. Bryant - 55 y 8 m 25 d;
   d. 6 July 1878 at Greenlawn; New School
   Presbyterian minister; served at Vernon
   Valley, Long Swamp, Northport and Greenlawn
SMITH, Ida - 1 yr 6 mos; d. 6 April 1885 at
   Dix Hills; daughter of David H. and Sarah
   Smith
SMITH, Irving B. - infant; d. 26 February 1890
   at Smithtown; son of Herman T. Smith
SMITH, Irving C. - 8 yrs 11 mos; drowned
   10 May 1884 at Patchogue in a pond; son of
   George W. Smith
SMITH, Isaac - 18 years; d. 27 May 1890 in
   Oyster Bay; found dead in bed; son of
   Thomas Smith
SMITH, Mrs. Isaac - funeral 13 November 1889;
   interment at Smithtown Branch; mother of
   Emily Smith
SMITH, Israel - 68 y 3 m 2 d; d. 1 December
   1885 at Greenlawn
SMITH, Jacob - 71 years; d. 12 November 1882
   at Centre Island
SMITH, Mrs. Jacob - funeral 27 August 1885 at
   Oyster Bay; maiden name was Robbins; resi-
   dent of Centre Island
SMITH, Mrs. Jacob C. - d. 7 February 1883 at
   Amityville

SMITH, James E. - 8 mos 6 days; d. 16 August
1886 at Huntington; son of James E. and
Maria M. Smith

SMITH, James E. - 58 years; d. 20 November
1890 at Stony Brook; former resident of
Huntington

SMITH, James N. - 58 years; d. 5 August 1879
at Huntington

SMITH, James W. - 95 years; d. "a few days
ago" at Roslyn; 31 January 1879 paper; War
of 1812 veteran who served with Capt. Samuel
Williams' Company, North Hempstead Militia;
tailor

SMITH, Jamimaett - 68 y 2 m 2 d; d. 10 December 1886 at Huntington

SMITH, Jane - 93 y 9 m 11 d; d. St. Johnland
[date not copied]; wife of David Willis
Smith who survives at age 96; couple married
nearly 74 years having been married 11 April
1812

SMITH, Jeffrey - 74 years; d. 12 July 1885 at
Amityville

SMITH, Jennie J. - 28 years; d. 21 February
1881 at Bayville; wife of George Smith

SMITH, Jerusha - 75 yrs 3 mos; d. 6 January
1883 at Crab Meadow

SMITH, Jesse - death reported 25 January 1890
paper; "old time hotel-keeper" operated
hotel at Havemeyer's Point opposite Fire
Island; resident of Babylon

SMITH, John - 63 years; d. 3 September 1878
at Oyster Bay

SMITH, John * - d. 20 January 1881 at Smithtown

SMITH, John - 66 y 9 m 4 d; d. 19 May 1885 at
Elwood

SMITH, John - d. 20 October 1888 at Galveston,
Texas; son of Joshua B. Smith; Huntington
native; b. 10 November 1819; sea captain;
lived at Key West, Florida; before Civil War
ran steamboat between Charleston, Key West
and Galveston; during Civil War was a Confederate blockade runner; returned North
after Civil War and lived in Huntington and
Babylon, where he ran a hotel; moved to Galveston about 1876; see 3 November 1888 paper
for biography

SMITH, John C. - 81 yrs 17 days; d. 31 March
1885 at Brooklyn; former resident of Huntington

SMITH, John Egbert - d. 22 September 1888 at
Hauppauge; "accidental discharge of his
gun"; he was sitting on a fence while hunting; fence broke; gun fell and went off; son
of Henry Smith; resident of East New York

SMITH, John H. - 38 years; d. 5 May 1889 at
Bay Shore; interment at Huntington

SMITH, John H. - d. "suddenly" at Peconic;
28 May 1887 paper; former resident of Sag
Harbor

SMITH, John Lawrence - d. 17 March 1889 at New
York City; funeral at St. James; native of
Nissequogue b. 1816; lawyer; former member
New York State Assembly; former Suffolk
County District Attorney; former Suffolk
County Judge and Surrogate; active in
affairs of the Episcopal Church

SMITH, Josiah - 86 yrs 4 mos; d. 30 January
1882 at Long Swamp

SMITH, Julia Floyd - 52 years; d. 3 March 1881
at Smithtown; widow of Richard Smith

SMITH, Katie - 14 years; d. 21 February 1890
at Hicksville; niece of Joseph Steinert

SMITH, Laura E. - 1 y 11 m 13 d; d. 13 April
1884 at Northport; daughter of Theodore F.
and Annie A. Smith

SMITH, Lewis F. - 25 y 9 m 7 d; d. 12 February
1878 at Huntington

SMITH, Lizzie - 22 y 1 m 21 d; d. 1 February
1882 at Middleville; daughter of Thompson C.
and Isabella Smith

SMITH, Louis J. - d. 28 February 1890 at
Smithtown

SMITH, Louis N. * - 39 years; d. 8 January
1890 at Huntington

SMITH, Luther - 58 years; d. 27 May 1882 at
Huntington

SMITH, Luther I. - 31 years; d. 20 October
1882 at Huntington; typhoid

SMITH, Lyman Beecher - 77 yrs 7 mos; d. 21
August 1881 at Smithtown

SMITH, Mrs. M. A. - d. 22 August 1889;
Northport item

SMITH, Mahlon - d. 1 December 1885 at Lower
Melville

SMITH, Margaret H. - 59 yrs 8 mos; d. 15 November 1890 at Cold Spring Harbor; wife of
Sylvester Smith

SMITH, Margaret M. Hudson - 49 years; d. 27
April 1883 at Long Swamp; wife of George W.
Smith

SMITH, Mariam - 14 y 1 m 16 d; d. 27 May 1883
at Melville; daughter of William W. and Anna
J. Smith

SMITH, Mary - 67 years; d. 10 November 1878 at
Smithtown

SMITH, Mary A. - 58 y 2 m 8 d; d. 23 March
1883 at Nyack, N. Y.; interment at Huntington; widow of Platt Smith

SMITH, Mary A. - 64 years; d. 25 November 1889
at Brooklyn; wife of Carll Smith

SMITH, Mary B. - d. 2 February 1878 at Bay
Shore; widow of Joshua B. Smith

SMITH, Mary E. - 16 y 6 m 10 d; d. 30 January
1883 at Centreport; wife of William Smith

SMITH, Mary L. - 38 y 9 m 26 d; d. 27 June
1888; Jericho item; interment at Westbury;
wife of "Big Allec" Smith

SMITH, Matilda E. - 18 y 1 m 25 d; d. 6 April
1878 at Smithtown Branch; daughter of
Eleazer Smith

SMITH, Matthew - 56 years; d. 22 August 1888
at Hunter's Point; hotel keeper at Hunter's
Point

SMITH, Michael - drowned in sinking of
schooner off Eaton's Neck; 1 May 1885 paper;
resident of South Brooklyn

SMITH, Mordecai - 2 July 1880 paper; resident
of Brooklyn; "Seawanhaka" fire on East River

SMITH, Moses * - 53 years; d. 3 April 1879 in
[Wicomico River, St. Mary's Co.,] Maryland;
shipboard accident; interment at Huntington;
[accident noted in 10 April 1879 St. Mary's
Beacon published at Leonardtown, Md. This
located place of Smith's death, which the
Long Islander had called "Great Wicomico
River"]

SMITH, Nathaniel - 88 years; d. 5 February
1881 at Smithtown

SMITH, Nathaniel - 86 years; d. 4 March 1889
at Bethpage
SMITH, Nelson * - 84 y 11 m 14 d; d. 27 May
1888 at Huntington
SMITH, Newbury - 71 years; d. 18 May 1887 at
Old Fields
SMITH, Mrs. O. C. - 42 years; suicide 27 April
1878 at Bayport; hanged herself
SMITH, Olive L. - 63 years; d. 1 February 1883
at Brooklyn; wife of John Carman Smith
SMITH, Oliver - drowned in Long Island Sound
between Sand's Point and City Island;
30 November 1883 paper
SMITH, Oliver - d. 18 September 1885; fell
from truck; interment at Woodbury; resi-
dent of New York City
SMITH, Phebe - interment 11 February 1889 at
Westbury; resident of Jamaica
SMITH, Phoebe - 76 y 4 m 23 d; d. 27 September
1886 at Greenlawn
SMITH, Platt - 62 years; d. 25 December 1881
at Greenlawn
SMITH, Platt - d. 3 November 1882 at Nyack,
New York; former resident of Huntington
SMITH, Polly B. - 87 y 7 m 14 d; d. 13 March
1881 at Huntington
SMITH, Richard - d. 27 December 1878 at Nisse-
quogue; found dead in a wagon; funeral at
St. James; son of Ebenezer Smith; brother of
Timothy C. Smith; brother-in-law of ex-Mayor
Wickham; resident of St. James
SMITH, Richard - funeral 14 September 1886 at
Northport; resident of Brooklyn; formerly of
Northport
SMITH, Robert - d. 11 September 1883 at Long
Island City; railroad accident
SMITH, Robert M. - 19 years; d. 27 July 1879
at Huntington
SMITH, Ruth - 78 years; d. 24 May 1882 at Long
Swamp; widow of Woodhull Smith
SMITH, Ruth - 72 yrs 10 mos; d. 28 February
1883 at St. James; widow of Timothy C. Smith
SMITH, Samuel A. - 80 years; d. 19 October
1884 at St. James; interment at Smithtown;
Suffolk County Clerk 1841-1844; Superinten-

SMITH, Samuel A. (continued)
dent of Common Schools, Suffolk County 1844-1847; Suffolk County District Attorney 1866-1879; Smith family genealogist

SMITH, Samuel G. - 73 years; d. 6 August 1890 at Hempstead; father of Hempstead Town Clerk Thomas V. Smith

SMITH, Samuel O. - d. 28 January 1889 at Smithtown

SMITH, Sarah A. - 46 y 9 m 17 d; d. 7 February 1883 at Dix Hills; wife of Lewis Smith

SMITH, Sarah A. - d. 23 September 1885 at Babylon; daughter of Medab Smith

SMITH, Sarah C. - 83 years; d. 16 March 1879 at Hauppauge; wife of Ebenezer Smith

SMITH, Sarah Emma - 13 years; d. 30 September 1882 at Half Hollow Hills; daughter of David H. and Sarah E. Smith

SMITH, Sarah L. - d. 19 December 1890; Hempstead item; daughter of William Curtis; wife of Vandewater Smith

SMITH, Sarah M. - 76 y 8 m 14 d; d. 26 December 1887 at Huntington

SMITH, Sarah Nicoll - d. 20 April 1890 at New York City; interment at St. James; daughter of James Clinch; widow of J. Lawrence Smith; niece of Mrs. A. T. Stewart

SMITH, Sarah R. - 40 years; d. 16 March 1879 at Fresh Pond

SMITH, Selah C. - d. Babylon; 14 March 1884 paper; operated Watson House hotel in Babylon

SMITH, Sherman R. - 41 y 10 m 12 d; d. 23 March 1889 at Miller's Place

SMITH, Sidney - 29 years; d. 18 March 1886 at Amityville; son of John I. Smith

SMITH, Mrs. Sidney - "death by malpractice"; 21 September 1883 paper; Mrs. Margaret Carman of Hempstead convicted by Queens County Court

SMITH, Solomon - 82 yrs 22 days; d. 18 August 1888 at West Hills; son of Jacob Smith; trustee of West Hills M. E. Church

SMITH, Mrs. Solomon - d. 23 June 1888 at West Hills; mother of Rev. S. K. Smith, pastor of M. E. Church at Middlebury, Connecticut; active in M. E. Church affairs

SMITH, Stimas - d. 2 March 1886; resident of
Sweet Hollow
SMITH, Mrs. T. William - 30 y 3 m 14 d;
d. 8 October 1880 at Huntington
SMITH, Temperance - 83 years; d. 26 February
1888 at Smithtown Branch
SMITH, Mrs. Theodore - d. 16 November 1884 at
Brooklyn; interment at Northport; former
resident of Northport
SMITH, Mrs. Theodore - d. 18 February 1890 at
Brooklyn; sister-in-law of Mrs. Robert Dixon
of Northport
SMITH, Thomas - suicide 11 January 1880 at
Port Jefferson
SMITH, Thomas Bunce - 83 y 9 m 17 d; d. 17 May
1888 at Huntington; bookkeeper for Rogers &
Scudder in Huntington for 30 years
SMITH, Thomas E. - d. Philadelphia, Pennsyl-
vania; interment 8 July 1890 at Northport;
veteran of Union Navy in Civil War under
Admiral Porter; after war served as captain
of steamships of Reading Line between
Philadelphia and Boston; biography 12 July
1890 paper Northport column
SMITH, Timothy - 70 y 6 m 22 d; d. 10 April
1883 at Huntington
SMITH, Tredwell - ca. 45 years; fell overboard
and drowned 2 October 1883 in Long Island
Sound off Cooper's Bluff or off Cow Bay;
resident of Setauket
SMITH, Victor Edwards - 13 y 10 m 8 d;
d. 12 November 1888 at Brooklyn; funeral at
Centreport; interment at Dix Hills; victim
of gun accident previous August; son of Ward
B. and Sarah A. Smith
SMITH, William Paul - 82 yrs 9 mos; d. 14 Aug-
gust 1889 at Smithtown; funeral at Smithtown
Branch
SNEDEKER, Ann R. - d. "last week" at Brooklyn;
29 November 1890 paper; widow of Samuel
Snedeker; former resident of Hempstead
SNEDEKER, Eleanor - 98 yrs 22 days; d. 26 May
1883 at Hempstead; widow of Christian
Snedeker; oldest inhabitant of Hempstead

SNEDEKER, Lois Almy - d. "last week" at West
New Brighton, Staten Island; 22 November
1890 paper; interment at Hempstead; widow
of William Snedeker

SNEDEN, John - d. "recently" at Great Neck;
29 May 1885 paper

SNEDICOR, Charles - d. 20 January 1887 at Deer
Park

SNEDICOR, Mrs. Charles - d. "three weeks ago";
29 January 1887 paper

SNELLING, Mary Lewis - 79 years; d. 3 October
1890 at Elwood; widow of Stephen Snelling
(m. 13 March 1856); aunt of Thomas Lewis of
Elwood; former resident of Newtown; account
of contested will 22 November 1890 paper;
another account of contested will 18 July
1891 paper

SNOUDER, child - d. 28 September 1886 at
Oyster Bay; interment at Huntington; child
of A. Snouder

SOFFEL, infant - 5 days; d. 3 December 1890 at
Hicksville; interment at Westbury; daughter
of Joseph Soffel

SOPER, infant - 4 mos; d. 25 July 1880 at
St. Johnsland; child of George Soper

SOPER, Alexander - 1 yr 9 mos; d. 7 February
1885 at Northport; son of Joseph and Phebe
A. Soper

SOPER, Alexander - 85 years; d. at Brooklyn;
25 January 1890 paper; "fell and factured
his hip a short time ago"; interment at Dix
Hills; father of Mrs. Ward Smith; resident
of Northport

SOPER, Amelia - 79 yrs 5 mos; d. 24 April 1883
at Northport

SOPER, Amos - 75 years; d. 24 May 1890 at
Greenlawn; found dead in his chair;
interment at Huntington; father of Henry
Soper "who killed a young boy at Cold Spring
about three years ago"

SOPER, Brainerd C. - 39 yrs 7 mos; d. 21 April
1881 at Northport

SOPER, Mrs. Charles B. - 51 yrs 2 days;
d. 23 November 1889 at Northport

SOPER, Effie A. - 17 y 7 m 25 d; d. 31 March
1889 at Harlem, N. Y.; interment at Comac;

SOPER, Effie A. (continued)
daughter of Mrs. F. N. Rogers; granddaughter
of David B. Conklin
SOPER, Emmett R. - 34 y 6 m 2 d; d. 16 April
1879 at Dix Hills
SOPER, Franklin E. - 23 yrs 10 mos;
d. 12 January 1882 at Brooklyn
SOPER, George - 12 years; d. 14 August 1890 at
St. Johnland
SOPER, George S. - 50 y 6 m 26 d; d. 8 Decem-
ber 1888 at Elwood; funeral at Dix Hills;
son of Jacob and Hannah Soper
SOPER, Jacob - 86 y 1 m 18 d; d. 2 May 1885 at
Elwood; interment at Dix Hills
SOPER, Jane A. - 66 years; d. 27 December 1882
at Huntington
SOPER, Julia A. - 6 y 9 m 12 d; d. 26 August
1882 at Dix Hills; daughter of Emmett R. and
Frances Soper
SOPER, Julia E. - 6 years; d. 17 October 1884
at Northport; daughter of Brainard C. and
Emma Soper
SOPER, Lemuel - 85 yrs 4 days; d. 10 October
1878 at Melville; veteran of War of 1812
SOPER, Leonard E. - 27 years; d. 22 December
1881 at Flatbush; interment at Brooklyn
SOPER, Lewis - d. 28 May 1884 at Northport
SOPER, Mary A. - 71 y 4 m 13 d; d. 8 December
1885 at Greenlawn; interment at Comac; wife
of John R. Soper
SOPER, Nancy - 84 years; d. 4 December 1885 at
Babylon; interment at Lower Melville; widow
of Lemuel Soper
SOPER, Oliver - d. "a few months since" at
Euclaire County, Wisconsin; 29 December 1882
paper; son of Smith Soper
SOPER, Sarah Matilda- 49 years; d. 9 February
1890 at Norwich, Connecticut
SOPER, Smith - 62 years; d. 13 December 1882
at Potter's Mills, Wisconsin; former resi-
dent of Dix Hills
SOPER, V. Pembroke - 53 years; d. 3 March 1888
at Bozrahville, Connecticut; interment at
Huntington
SOPER, William Louis - infant; d. 3 August
1886 at Eau Claire, Wisconsin; son of Alfred

SOPER, William Louis (continued)
and Phebe J. Soper; grandson of A. A.
Bouton of Huntington

SOUTHWORTH, Hanna B. - d. 7 January 1890 in
New York City; interment at Louisville,
Kentucky; died in her jail cell; had
murdered Stephen Pettus, her "betrayer" in
November 1889

SPARKS, Hervey - d. San Francisco, California;
25 May 1889 paper (from 20 May 1889 New York
Herald); son of Rev. Peter Sparks; husband
of Stephanie Brandegee, who was sister to
Mrs. Henry Lloyd of Huntington; New Jersey
native who went to California during the
Gold Rush of 1849

SPECHT, Margaret - 50 y 6 m 18 d; d. 4 November 1879 at Northport

SPEEKS, Cassie * - 14 years; d. 22 July 1890
at Oyster Bay; daughter of Benjamin Speeks

SPENCER, Huldah - d. 31 December 1878 at
Smithtown Branch; "dropped dead"; wife of
Cornelius Spencer

SPIELER, Edmund - 45 yrs 25 days; d. 10 December 1889 at Cold Spring Harbor

SPRAGUE, Mrs. Jonathan - 85 years; d. 26 November 1880 at New York City; widow

SPRING, James - 72 years; d. 18 May 1889 at
Eaton's Neck; interment at Cold Spring

SPRING, Thomas - ca. 40 years; drowned
22 March 1882 in Long Island Sound; sloop
sunk off Rye Point

SPRINGER, William H. - d. 11 January 1888 at
Glen Cove

SPURGE, Mrs. William N. - d. 25 June 1885;
funeral at Comac

SQUIRES, Mrs. E. F. - d. 20 May 1888 at
Riverhead; sister of Rev. O. A. Down

SQUIRES, Joshua - d. 24 February 1885 at Sag
Harbor

SQUIRES, Stephen - drowned in Peconic Bay near
Sarbonac; 27 July 1883 paper; son of William
Squires

STACKER, Jane * - 54 years; d. 14 April 1890
at Northport; Northport laundress

STAHL, Matthew - 3 weeks; d. 16 October 1886
at West Hills

STANDER, John - suicide 28 February 1885 at
New Lots; shot himself; clothing manufacturer

STANLEY, Arthur A. - d. "recently" at Queens;
15 November 1890 paper; Mineola column;
widow received $3,000 from a beneficial
society

STANSBROUGH, James H. - d. 1 December 1887 at
Brooklyn; lawyer

STANSBURY, James Y. - d. at North Brattleboro,
Massachusetts; 19 May 1888 paper; Northport
item; brother of Rev. J. H. Stansbury of
Northport

STARKINGS, Caroline J. - 42 years; d. 10 December 1885 at New York City

STEAD, Rev. Benjamin F. - 64 years; d. 15 February 1879 at Astoria; Old School Presbyterian minister; member of Long Island Bible
Society and Home and Foreign Missions

STEARNS, Rev. Charles E. - 69 years;
d. 20 Dec December 1879 at Smithtown;
Methodist minister who served many Long
Island churches

STEELE, Albert J. - d. "few days ago" at New
York City; 10 January 1879 paper

STEHLIN, Joseph - d. in Germany; 11 October
1890 paper; remains shipped to New York City
for funeral; former resident of Lloyd's Neck

STEHLMAN, child - d. 16 January 1889 at Jerusalem; scarlet fever; daughter of Herman
Stehlman

STEIN, Joseph I. - 2 July 1880 paper; resident of New York City; "Seawanhaka" fire on
East River

STEINSIECK, Mrs. - d. 28 November 1887 at
Oyster Bay

STEINSIECK, Charles - d. 13 July 1880 at
Oyster Bay

STEINSIECK, Louis - d. 2 January 1889 at
Central Park

STEINSIECK, Myra - d. 12 November 1887 at
Oyster Bay

STEPHENS, Mr. - d. at Nyack, N. Y.; 15 May
1885 paper; brother of John Stephens of
Northport

STEVENS, child - 2 years; death reported
31 July 1885 paper; run over by railroad
train "two weeks ago"; child of Charles
Stevens of Little Neck, Queens County

STEVENS, James A. - 40 years; d. 17 January
1887 at Port Jefferson; son of John B.
Stevens

STEVENS, Sarah E. - 56 years; d. 18 April 1886
at Brooklyn; interment at Comac

STEWARD, Rev. Lanson - d. in Illinois;
18 April 1879 paper; Baptist minister;
formerly at Huntington

STEWART, Charles J. - d. 5 November 1887 at
Flushing; interment at Cold Spring Harbor;
insurance business with Atlantic Marine
Company

STEWART, Eugenia M. - d. 21 June 1890 at
Montclair, N. J.; funeral at Glen Cove;
daughter of E. M. Lincoln; wife of Thomas H.
Stewart; resident of Brooklyn

STEWART, George W. * - 1 y 3 m 19 d; d. 28 May
1881 at Huntington; son of John and Martha
Stewart

STEWART, Janet - 55 years; d. 2 October 1881
at Cold Spring; wife of Peter Stewart

STEWART, Mrs. Peter - 61 y 5 m 10 d;
d. 8 November 1888 at Miller's Place

STILLMAN, Henry - d. 27 December 1888 at South
Oyster Bay; student at Plain Edge School,
which closed due to diphtheria epidemic

STILLWELL, Sarah A. - 52 years; d. 9 September
1890 at Hempstead; resided with Charles
Sammis and family

STILWELL, Angeline H. - 56 yrs 7 mos;
d. 6 July 1887 at Woodbury; widow of Cornelius Stilwell; mother of Mrs. George H. Davis

STILWELL, Margaret E. - 81 y 1 m 28 d;
d. 3 January 1887 at Brooklyn; interment at
Huntington; widow of John Stilwell

STILWELL, Phebe E. - 21 y 5 m 21 d;
d. 10 September 1888 at Huntington; daughter
of George Stilwell

STILWELL, Ray Cleveland - 1 y 2 m 22 d;
d. 27 April 1885 at Huntington

STIMON, Cornelia - 67 yrs 4 mos; d. 11 August
1878 at East Northport

STOCKBEIN, Mrs. - d. 27 March 1890 at Queens; interment at Jamaica; "leaves three small children"

STOCKMAN, Theodore - 58 yrs 6 mos; d. 14 July 1879 at Melville

STONE, Charles B. - funeral 13 January 1889 at Riverhead

STONE, John - 2 y 2 m 20 d; d. 20 May 1880 at Melville; son of John H. and Esther Stone

STOOTHOFF, Mrs. - d. 30 January 1887 at Far Rockaway; drunk; died of exposure at railroad depot

STOOTS, Mary E. - 34 y 4 m 2 d; d. 7 July 1887 at Cold Spring Harbor

STOYLE, William H. - 3 years; d. 13 January 1888 at Huntington

STRAIGHT, Mary Bartley - d. 25 March 1888; Riverhead item

STRATTON, Mrs. - d. at Brooklyn; 13 September 1890 paper; former resident of Huntington

STRATTON, Anthony - 64 years; d. 19 March 1884 at Huntington

STRATTON, Edwin H. - d. 20 January 1887 at Amityville; suddenly of apoplexy

STRAWSON, Willetts A. - 11 mos 14 days; d. 14 January 1889 at Northport; son of William Strawson

STREET, M. Josephine - 7 weeks; d. 10 August 1884 at Huntington; daughter of Charles R. and Josephine E. Street

STREET, Naomi - 79 y 2 m 21 d; d. 12 July 1881 at Huntington; daughter of Gilbert Scudder

STRICKLAND, J. Thomas - 11 mos 22 days; d. 20 September 1881 at Brooklyn; interment at Huntington; son of John B. and Alma H. Strickland

STRICKLAND, Sarah A. - 1 mo 11 days; d. 17 September 1878 at Huntington; daughter of John B. and Alma H. Strickland

STRONG, infant - d. 22 July 1890 at Smithtown; son of F. A. Strong

STRONG, Cornelia Udall - d. 9 May 1882 at Setauket; widow of Judge Selah B. Strong

STRONG, Elizabeth * - 102 years; d. 10 April 1879 at Islip

STUDWELL, infant - interment 10 August 1887; Oyster Bay item ; son of Alexander Studwell

STUDWELL, child - d. 13 August 1888 at Oyster Bay; child of Alexander Studwell

STURGESS, Rev. Dr. Charles - 80 years; d. 1 May 1885 at Huntington; son of Nathaniel and Sarah Sturgess; husband of Margaret Kissam (m. 1833 d. 1853); husband of Sarah J. Kissam (m. 1856); b. Fairfield, Conn. 20 October 1804; studied medicine in New York City 1824-1826; settled in Huntington 1830; Presbyterian missionary to Omaha Indians 1857-1860 and 1862-1863; pastor of Yaphank and Middle Island Presbyterian Churches 1863-1872 and Hughsonville, Dutchess County, N. Y. 1873-1877; long obit 8 May 1885 paper

SUHR, John - d. "a few days ago" at Newtown; 27 May 1881 paper; fell off horse

SULLIVAN, child - 18 months; drowned 4 September 1890 at Old Westbury; fell into a cistern; interment at Westbury; child of Daniel Sullivan

SULLIVAN, Mrs. Daniel - d. 13 May 1890 at Westbury; "old resident of Westbury. She leaves two sons and three grown daughters"

SULLIVAN, Jane - 56 years; d. 1 August 1885 at Fresh Pond; funeral at Huntington; wife of Dennis Sullivan

SULLIVAN, Jeremiah - d. at Brooklyn; 17 September 1887 paper; son of Sylvester Sullivan

SUMMERS, Amy E. - 35 years; d. 16 July 1878 at Washington, D. C.

SURREY, Harriet - d. 30 August 1885 at Peconic; found dead in bed; widow of Benjamin Surrey

SUTTON, Albert - found 9 May 1889 floating in Oyster Bay; possible murder; coroner's jury ruled "accidental drowning"; 15 June 1889 paper

SUTTON, Charles - 28 years; d. 29 May 1890 at Hicksville; nephew of Mrs. Jane Heitz; native of Ireland; came to USA in 1882

SUTTON, Vera - 15 months; d. 8 August 1886 at Cold Spring Harbor; interment at Woodlawn Cemetery, New York City; daughter of William H. and Maria A. Sutton

SUTTON, William - d. 20 October 1890 at Patchogue

SUYDAM, Albert C. - 6 mos 10 days; d. 27 October 1881 at Centreport; son of John E. and Anna C. Suydam

SUYDAM, Frank - 8 years; d. 22 August 1881 at Babylon; son of Henry Suydam

SUYDAM, John R. - 74 years; d. 15 May 1882 at Sayville

SUYDAM, Nathaniel Kelso - 1 year; d. 28 October 1879 at Greenlawn

SUYDAM, Simonson - 71 years; d. 16 January 1890 at Oyster Bay

SWAN, Robert - d. 4 March 1890 at New York City; uncle of William Swan of Oyster Bay; resident of Geneva, N. Y.

SWEENEY, Ann Durkin - 45 years; d. 31 March 1889 at Fresh Pond

SWEENEY, John - d. 17 October 1890 at Toledo, Ohio; brother of Mrs. Samuel Powers of East Meadow

SWEENEY, Lizzie - 14 years; drowned 23 July 1878 at Great Neck; resident of Mineola

SWEENEY, Margaret A. - d. 26 September 1881 at Key West, Florida; wife of Douglas T. Sweeney

SWEEZEY, John - "old citizen"; d. 20 April 1890 at Riverhead; resident of Riverhead for 50 years

SWEEZY, Frank - d. at Brooklyn; interment 3 November 1890 at Patchogue; former resident of Bellport

SWEEZY, Halsey A. - d. "last week" at Riverhead; 13 June 1884 paper

SWEZEY, E. A. - funeral 2 June 1890 at Middle Island; father of Mrs. S. E. Randall

SWEZEY, Edward - 3 1/2 months; d. 4 October 1886 at Bedelltown; son of Edward Swezey

SYMINGTON, William S. - d. 21 April 1888 at Newtown Creek; explosion of boiler on tugboat

SYMONDS, Isabella - d. 16 July 1878 at Portland, Maine; teacher at Huntington Union School

TAFF, Mrs. Henry - funeral 22 August 1888 at Oyster Bay; widow; resident of Oyster Bay Cove

TALLCOT, Rhoda B. - 6 mos 23 days; d. 17 August 1889 at West Neck; daughter of Charles W. and Nellie W. Tallcot

TAPPAN, Charles I. - 45 y 3 m 15 d; d. 13 August 1886 at New York City; interment at Huntington; banker and broker; former resident of Huntington

TAPPAN, Charlotte - 71 years; d. 9 February 1882 at Jericho

TAPPEN, Andrew - 92 years; d. 24 May 1888 at East Norwich

TAPPEN, Andrew - 93 years; d. 12 January 1890 at Jericho

TAPPEN, Elbert - 74 years; d. 19 November 1889 at Mineola; interment at Oyster Bay

TAPPEN, Everett - infant; d. 17 September 1887 at Jericho; son of Andrew Tappen

TAPPEN, Maria - 83 years; d. 6 September 1889 at Huntington; wife of Hicks Tappen

TAPPEN, Philena - 87 years; d. 8 October 1880 at West Neck

TAPPEN, Sallie C. - d. 13 May 1886 at New York City; interment at Huntington; daughter of William H. Brown; wife of Charles I. Tappen; native of Taunton, Massachusetts; member of Holy Trinity Church, Harlem, N.Y.

TAULBEE, William Preston - d. 11 March 1890 at Washington, D. C.; Kentucky congressman; shot at the U. S. Capitol 28 February 1890 by Charles E. Kincaid, a Louisville newspaper man; b. Morgan County, Kentucky, 21 October 1851

TAYLOR, Eliza E. - 30 yrs 17 days; d. 5 October 1882 at Northport; niece of Elkanah Soper

TAYLOR, Eliza Estelle - 5 yrs 10 mos; d. 28 May 1882 at Northport; daughter of George L. and Eliza Taylor

TAYLOR, Frederick W. - 12 y 3 m 6 d; d. 9 December 1886 at Northport; son of Henry W. Taylor

TAYLOR, Isaac E. - d. 31 October 1889 at New York City; founder of Bellevue Hospital Medical College

TAYLOR, John - 71 years; d. 14 January 1881 at Cold Spring

TAYLOR, Laura E. - 6 y 8 m 18 d; d. 30 November 1886 at Northport; daughter of Henry Taylor

TAYLOR, Lucy H. - 64 y 8 m 3 d; d. 11 February 1885 at Cold Spring; widow of John Taylor

TAYLOR, Mary - 65 years; d. 31 March 1885 at Yaphank; resident of Huntington

TAYLOR, Mat - 8 years; d. 25 November 1888 at Shelter Island

TAYLOR, Sarah - 61 yrs 9 mos; d. 4 June 1886 at Farmingdale; wife of Francis J. Taylor

TAYLOR, Sidney B. - 41 years; d. 5 April 1887 at Northport

TAYLOR, Thomas - 85 years; d. 31 October 1889 at Westbury; interment at Hempstead; native of Ireland

TAYLOR, Thomas Henry - 8 mos 22 days; d. 24 July 1890 at Westbury; interment at Hempstead; son of Thomas Taylor

TAYLOR, William - drowned off Lloyd's Neck "2 weeks ago"; 25 November 1881 paper; resident of Port Chester, N. Y.

TAYLOR, William - d. 11 September 1882 at Glen Cove; shot while attacking a bartender in a saloon

TAYLOR, William - d. 25 December 1888 at Brooklyn; "distant relative" of Thomas Taylor of Westbury

TAYTOR, William R. - d. 13 December 1886 at New York City; interment at Riverhead; former resident of Sag Harbor

TEED, Willie - 14 years; drowned 13 February 1887 at Garden City; choir boy at Garden City Cathedral; resident of Brooklyn

TEMPLAR, John C. - d. 9 August 1879 at Bayville; also known as "John C. Cooney"

TEMPLE, Anna - 5 y 7 m 7 d; d. 14 March 1882 at New York City; daughter of James H. and Kate Temple

TENBROECK, Phebe - found dead in woods at Glen Cove; 20 January 1882 paper

TERRY, Mrs. - death reported 28 December 1883 paper; wife of Editor of Suffolk Times; resident of Greenport

TERRY, Caroline - 84 years; d. 31 August 1890 at Wading River; mother of William M. Terry,

TERRY, Caroline (continued)
Mrs. Samuel Trubee, Sidney Terry and Mrs.
Charles Woodhull
TERRY, Emma Cornell - 28 years; d. 7 July 1887
at Queens; wife of Everett E. Terry
TERRY, Frank C. - 18 months; d. 25 June 1885
at Queens; son of Everet E. and Emma A.
Terry; grandson of Rev. T. M. Terry
TERRY, Freddie A. - 6 1/2 years; d. 26 June
1881 at Aquebogue; struck by lightning; son
of George Terry
TERRY, Lewis H. - d. 1 March 1886; Riverhead
item; known as "Hampton Terry"
TERRY, Martha A. - d. at Brooklyn; interment
13 March 1888 at Riverhead; wife of Silas S.
Terry
TERRY, Mary E. - 68 years; d. 11 November 1882
at Cold Spring
TERRY, Mary J. - 53 y 8 m 5 d; d. 9 August
1884 at Northport; wife of John S. Terry
TERRY, William - lost at sea; washed overbroad
off schooner "Wyoming" on way to Nova
Scotia; 27 December 1878 paper
TEXIDO, Manuel - 78 years; d. 26 February 1890
at Plain Edge
THEALIS, Sarah - death reported 5 December
1884 paper; former resident of Cold Spring
THOMAS, Daniel - d. "about a week ago"; 6 Aug-
ust 1887 paper; Hempstead item; eccentric
who filled house with scrap and old tin
cans; wore multiple suits of clothing and
two hats at the same time
THOMAS, Virginia Clibborne - 35 years;
d. 4 July 1886 at Northport
THOMPSON, Dr. Abraham Gardiner - 71 years;
d. 26 September 1887 at Islip; son of
Jonathan Thompson; physician
THOMPSON, Daniel - 73 years; death reported
12 February 1886 paper; resident of New York
City; formerly of Northport
THOMPSON, Edward - d. 27 April 1890 at Hempstead
THOMPSON, Emeline - 4 years; d. 12 January
1889 at Greenvale; interment at Westbury
THOMPSON, Gracie - d. "last week" at Sag
Harbor; shot by friend while playing with a
gun; 25 December 1885 paper

THOMPSON, Hannah - 55 years; interment
18 March 1889 at Westbury; resident of
Jamaica

THOMPSON, James - 33 years; d. 23 December
1885 at New York City

THOMPSON, James - 2 months; d. 25 December
1885 at New York City; son of James and
Charlotte Thompson

THOMPSON, Joseph - d. 11 October 1885 at
Norwalk, Connecticut; former resident of
Oyster Bay

THOMPSON, Mary E. - 72 yrs 4 mos; d. 2 September 1879 at Huntington; widow of Floyd
Thompson

THOMPSON, Mary E. - 61 years; d. 14 January
1887 at Rochester, N. Y.; funeral at Cold
Spring; daughter of Joseph and Esther
Jarvis; widow of John N. Thompson; mother of
late Mrs. J. M. King

THOMPSON, William Adolph - 2 mos 15 days;
d. 26 July 1879 at Hauppauge; son of John
and Louisa Thompson

THORPS, Finetta - 75 years; d. 11 May 1886 at
Huntington, Connecticut; sister of Douglass
Jackson; native of Huntington [L. I.]

THUMB, Absolam - d. 28 July 1890 at Westbury;
father of Mrs. Rev. Gutweiler; former resident of St. Johnsville, N. Y.; involved in
lumber trade

THURBER, Ada - drowned "last week" in the
Connecticut River; 6 September 1890 paper;
Northport item

THURBER, Asa - drowned "last week" in the
Connecticut River; 6 September 1890 paper;
Northport item

THURSBY, Hannah A. G. - 84 years; d. 3 February 1881 at Brooklyn; widow of John Thursby

THURSBY, Jane A. - funeral 3 July 1884 at New
York City; interment at Brooklyn; widow of
John B. Thursby

THURSBY, Mrs. Joseph M. - d. "last week" at
Great Neck; 3 March 1888 paper; former
resident of Huntington and Northport

THURSTON, Elizabeth F. - 64 yrs 10 days;
d. 10 January 1879 at Huntington; wife of
L. M. Thurston

TICHENOR, William - drowned 15 July 1885 in
Great South Bay, off Patchogue; resident of
Patchogue

TILDEN, Gertie - 3 y 3 m 16 d; d. 9 December
1888 at Rockaway Beach; daughter of Thomas
H. Tilden

TILDEN, Israel - 89 yrs 1 mo; d. 6 November
1878 at Old Fields

TILDEN, Jarvis D. - 2 y 10 m 2 d; d. 12 December 1881 at Rockaway Beach; son of Thomas H.
and Annie Tilden

TILDEN, Keziah - 76 years; d. 29 August 1890
at Huntington; wife of Henry Tilden; member
of Second Presbyterian Church, Huntington

TILDEN, Nellie - 3 years; d. 24 November 1888
at Rockaway Beach

TILDEN, Samuel Jones - d. 4 August 1886 at
Yonkers, N. Y.; [Governor of New York State
1875-1877; Democratic candidate for President 1876; lost election by one electoral
vote to Rutherford B. Hayes]

TILDEN, Scynthia - 2 y 3 m 14 d; d. 23 October
1883 at Rockaway Beach; daughter of Thomas
H. Tilden

TILLESTON, infant - d. 3 May 1878 at Huntington; child of Jacob Tilleston

TILLOT, Almeda C. - 48 y 1 m 14 d; d. 10 August 1884 at Huntington; wife of William
Tillot

TILLOT, Susan - 69 y 1 m 19 d; d. 30 May 1884
at Huntington; wife of William Tillot

TILLOTSON, Mrs. - 99 years; death reported
23 November 1889 paper; Port Jefferson item;
grandmother of Selah Tillotson

TILLOTSON, Fannie E. - 9 y 4 m 17 d;
d. at Huntington; 19 June 1886 paper;
daughter of Selah and Catherine Tillotson

TILLOTSON, Isaac M. - 79 yrs 10 days;
d. 28 August 1887 at Comac; father of A. C.
Tillotson

TILLOTT, William - 80 years 14 days;
d. 16 April 1887 at Huntington

TIMBROOK, Pauline - 49 years; d. 28 April 1881
at Huntington

TITUS, infant - d. at Glen Cove; 9 June 1888
paper; perhaps strangled at birth; child of
Jacob W. and Mary Titus

TITUS, Alfred- 74 years; d. 10 September 1879
at Centreport

TITUS, Alice Ann - 41 years; d. 10 February
1885 at Huntington; wife of Joseph Titus

TITUS, Amelia - 31 y 1 m 13 d; d. 20 December
1880 at Northport; wife of Alfred Titus

TITUS, Buell - 65 years; d. 15 December 1889
at Cold Spring; native of Cold Spring;
"for many years prominently identified with
the public interests of the town"

TITUS, Edna - 6 weeks 1 day; d. 8 September
1884 at Syosset; daughter of James and Emma
P. Titus

TITUS, Eliza - 72 y 9 m 26 d; d. 9 April 1883
at Cold Spring; daughter of Edward Arrowsmith; widow of John P. Titus

TITUS, Elizabeth Kissam - 73 years;
d. 22 March 1880 at Brooklyn; daughter of
Samuel Sackett; wife of Thomas W. Titus

TITUS, Elma - d. 22 March 1880 at Smithtown;
former resident of Huntington

TITUS, Epenetus - 90 years; d. at Mineola;
14 January 1888 paper

TITUS, Hannah "half-breed Indian" - suicide
31 October 1888 at Patchogue; cut her
throat; wife of Stephen Titus *

TITUS, Hannah Maria - 85 y 1 m 20 d; d. 4 Nov-
ember 1888 at Cold Spring; fell while sit-
ting down and broke thigh bone; daughter of
Silas Conklin; widow of Isaac Titus
(m. 1827); mother of Mrs. Alfred Rogers,
Andrus Titus, Sidney Titus, Mrs. Warren
Rogers, Caroline Titus and Isaac Titus;
Huntington native b. 1803

TITUS, Harriet - d. 19 March 1889 at Brooklyn;
widow of William Titus; former resident of
Centreport

TITUS, Henry Buel - 29 y 7 m 10 d; d. 15 March
1885 at Cold Spring

TITUS, Isaac - 89 y 4 m 11 d; d. 19 June 1887
at Cold Spring Harbor; blood poisoning; son
of Jacob Titus, who served in the Revolution; brother of Zebulon Titus, Mrs. Nelson
Sands, Mrs. Stephen Hendrickson, Mrs. Elbert
Sammis and Jacob Titus

TITUS, Isadora - 31 yrs 2 days; d. 28 March
1885 at Cold Spring Harbor; daughter of
Platt and Helen R. Titus

TITUS, Jane - 77 years; d. 30 October 1889 at
Westbury; widow of Henry Titus; mother of
Henrietta Titus and Sarah P. Titus

TITUS, Jonas - 85 years; d. 19 April 1883 at
West Neck

TITUS, Keziah - 89 years; d. 26 March 1879 at
Syosset

TITUS, Lydia - 67 y 6 m 14 d; d. 9 September
1881 at West Neck; wife of Jonas Titus

TITUS, Mary J. - 80 yrs 6 mos; d. 20 August
1888 at Cold Spring Harbor

TITUS, Mary P. - 96 yrs 2 mos; d. 13 September
1884 at Westbury

TITUS, Platt - 50 y 2 m 9 d; d. 25 November
1878 at Cold Spring

TITUS, Sadie - 2 years; funeral 16 October
1888 at Jericho; interment at Wheatley;
daughter of Eugene Titus

TITUS, Samuel B. - 3 y 7 m 10 d; d. 4 August
1881 at Syosset; son of James and Emma Titus

TITUS, Sarah - 72 years; d. 28 February 1878
at Huntington

TITUS, Sidney - 55 y 9 m 21 d; d. 9 November
1887 at Cold Spring Harbor; son of Isaac and
Maria Titus; merchant in New York City for a
number of years

TITUS, Silas * - 80 years; d. 3 May 1889 at
Huntington

TITUS, Thomas W. - 83 y 5 m 5 d; d. 9 October
1887 at East Neck

TITUS, William L. - 78 y 1 m 19 d; d. 13 January 1884 at Centreport

TOBIAS, Charles * - 2 y 5 m 8 d; d. 24 August
1880 at Rocky Point; interment at Setauket

TODD, George - 65 years; d. 7 May 1887 at
Huntington; native of Ireland; Huntington
resident since 1850

TOEPFER, H. - 39 years; d. 31 January 1881 at
Fresh Pond

TOMLINS, Mr. -"old"; funeral 16 January 1887
at Oyster Bay

TOMPKINS, Lizzie Jenkins - 24 yrs 9 mos;
d. 2 November 1887 at Brooklyn

TOOKER, Charry - 78 years; d. 20 March 1888 at
  Mount Sinai; widow of Brewster Tooker
TOOKER, Selah D. - 3 months; d. 18 March 1889
  at Mount Sinai; son of John H. and Amelia
  Tooker
TOOKER, William - ca. 45 years; d. 8 July 1885
  aboard ship bound for Port Jefferson from
  New York City; "dropped dead"; resident of
  Port Jefferson
TOPP, John - d. 22 April 1878 at Syosset;
  found dead in bed; heart disease
TOPPING, Elias - 73 years; d. 12 February 1881
  at Centre Moriches
TOPPING, W. C. - d. "last week" 29 June 1889
  paper; Riverhead item; native of Port Jeff-
  erson
TOPPS, John - d. 25 August 1886 at Syosset
TORMEY, Mr. - interment 12 February 1889 at
  Westbury; resident of Glen Cove
TOTTEN, Alexander - 73 years; d. 2 April 1882
  at Half Hollow Hills
TOTTEN, Joseph C. - drowned 5 September 1878
  in Great South Bay, off Great River; former
  resident of New York City; lately of Patchogue; "taken with a fit, fell overboard and
  drowned"
TOWER, Sarah - d. at Holtsville; 15 January
  1887 paper; "distressing circumstances"
TOWNSEND, child - d. 3 January 1879 at Glen
  Cove; playing with matches; set clothing
  afire; daughter of James Townsend
TOWNSEND, child - 2 years; d. 14 December 1883
  at Little Neck; smothered by bed clothes;
  child of Benjamin Townsend
TOWNSEND, Amelia [Aurelia] - ca. 70 years;
  d. 16 April 1885 at Oyster Bay; died from
  injuries received 7 January 1884 when
  assaulted with a hammer by Charles H. Rugg,
  who left her and husband for dead; [called
  Aurelia in 11 January 1884 account of the
  assault on the elderly couple]; sister of
  General Winder "of Libby Prison infamy"
  "Being a southerner she was a strong secess-
  ionist"; [according to biography General
  John H. Winder C. S. A. by Arch F. Blakey
  (1990) she was born in Baltimore, Md. 14 May
  1820; her full name was Charlotte Aurelia.
233

TOWNSEND, Amelia [Aurelia] (continued)
Her father was William Henry Winder, a
commander of U. S. troops during the War of
1812. She was a member of an important
Maryland family.]
TOWNSEND, Charles * - 1 yr 2 mos; d. 3 April
1880 at Oyster Bay
TOWNSEND, Daniel J. - "is dead" at Niagara
Falls, N. Y.; 3 August 1889 paper; descen-
dant of Henry Townsend who settled Oyster
Bay in 1661
TOWNSEND, Edward * - 16 years; d. 11 February
1888 at Woodbury; fell dead; interment at
Glen Cove; son of Silas Townsend
TOWNSEND, Eliza * - 50 years; d. 22 January
1887 at Oyster Bay Cove
TOWNSEND, Elwood * - 18 years; d. 26 August
1890 at Glenwood Landing
TOWNSEND, George - 64 years; d. 5 September
1880 at Oyster Bay
TOWNSEND, James C. - d. 1 November 1882;
resident of Oyster Bay
TOWNSEND, James C. - 86 years; d. 27 January
1890 at Oyster Bay; "death hastened by the
beastly assault made upon him by murderer
Rugg several years ago"
TOWNSEND, John J. - 64 years; d. 5 December
1889 at New York City; "member of the well
known Townsend family of Oyster Bay"; law-
yer; President of Union League Club; thirty
years manager of the House of Refuge
TOWNSEND, Margaret - 86 years; d. 11 October
1888 at Oyster Bay; mother of Mrs. Daniel D.
Baylis, Mrs. Charles H. Baylis, William E.
Townsend, Stephen T. Townsend, George W.
Townsend, Henry A. Townsend, Mrs. Edgar S.
Baldwin, Mrs. Sylvester Holmes and Mrs.
Daniel Bennett
TOWNSEND, Mary * - 96 years; d. at Yaphank
Alms House; 10 August 1883 paper; resident
of Port Jefferson
TOWNSEND, Mary Embree - funeral 12 July 1890
at Locust Valley
TOWNSEND, Maude - 5 years; d. 27 March 1888 at
Brooklyn; granddaughter of Gideon Nichols

TOWNSEND, Robert C. - 41 yrs 15 days;
d. 20 May 1888 at East Neck; brother of Mary
Augusta McKeever, Annie Townsend, Elmira W.
Mills and Clara McGuire
TOWNSEND, Sarah - 92 years; d. 11 March 1888
at Glen Cove; found dead in her room
TOWNSEND, Solomon - 74 years; d. 2 April 1880
at Oyster Bay
TREADWELL, infant * - 14 days; d. 25 July 1879
at Smithtown; daughter of Emanuel Treadwell
TREADWELL, Mrs. Dr. - d. 13 March 1884 at East
Williston
TREADWELL, Annie G. - 18 yrs 10 mos;
d. 28 January 1884 at Brooklyn
TREADWELL, Jennette [*] - 94 years; d. 23 May
1884 at Flushing; former slave of Coles
Wortman of Oyster Bay
TRUBEE, W. E. - d. "last week" at Bridgeport,
Connecticut; 13 December 1890 paper; Port
Jefferson item
TRUE, Rev. C. K. - 69 years; d. 20 June 1878
at Brooklyn; Methodist minister; former
pastor of Cold Spring M. E. Church
TRUSLOW, Thomas - 65 y 5 m 12 d; d. 4 October
1884 at Northport; found dead in bed; inter-
ment at Brooklyn
TUCKER, Elizabeth - 93 years; funeral 9 Novem-
ber 1886 at Hicksville
TUCKERMAN, Mrs. Walter C. - d. "last week" at
Washington, D. C.; interment at Newport,
Rhode Island; summer resident of Cove Neck,
Oyster Bay; 19 March 1887 paper
TULLOCK, Robert J. - drowned 16 October 1878
on schooner sunk in gale off New Haven,
Connecticut; body found at Mattituck Creek
5 November 1878
TURKINGTON, Oliver - 69 years; d. 21 November
1887 at Woodbury; funeral at Bethel, Connec-
ticut; father-in-law of Rev. B. A. Gilman of
Woodbury M. E. Church; native of Redding
Centre, Connecticut
TURNER, Hannah - 75 y 7 m 1 d; d. 25 December
1881 at Mount Sinai; widow of David Turner
TURNER, Jeannette - 9 mos; d. 18 August 1882
at Woodbury; daughter of J. Clinton and
Katie Turner

TURNER, John - 40 years; suicide 1 August 1881
   at Hempstead
TURNER, Naomi - 84 yrs 5 mos; d. 20 January
   1881 at Manetto Hill
TUTHILL, Amelia - ca. 70 years; d. 4 March
   1886 at Mount Sinai; mother of George W.
   Rowland
TUTHILL, Daniel D. - 72 yrs 2 mos; d. 27 Sept-
   ember 1889 at Shelter Island; brother of
   David Tuthill
TUTHILL, Halsey C. - d. 14 January 1889 at
   Jamesport; deaf; hit by railroad train
TUTHILL, Ira Hull - d. 31 December 1890 at New
   York City; found dead in room at United
   States Hotel; former resident of Southold
TUTHILL, James - suicide 4 February 1884 at
   Shelter Island
TUTHILL, Noah - "aged"; d. 17 February 1888 at
   Yaphank; interment at Aquebogue
TUTHILL, Sylvester D. - 58 years; d. 3 March
   1885 at New Orleans, Louisiana; died while
   attending an exhibition in New Orleans;
   resident of Rocky Point
TUTHILL, Warren - 67 years; d. 11 February
   1890 at Port Jefferson; yachting captain;
   native of Manor
TUTTLE, Howard D. - 9 months; d. 20 August
   1884 at Centreport; son of Henry A. and
   Fidela V. Tuttle
TUTTLE, M. A. - d. 23 February 1882; interment
   at Huntington; daughter of Rev. Nehemiah
   Brown; wife of George F. Tuttle
TYLER, Mrs. Charles - funeral 22 April 1890
   at Smithtown Landing
TYLER, Mrs. John [Julia Gardiner] - ca. 70
   years; d. 10 July 1889 at Richmond, Va.;
   [daughter of David Gardiner; 2nd wife of
   President John Tyler; First Lady of U. S.
   1844-1845; b. Gardiner's Island 4 May 1820]
TYLER, Phebe - 82 years; d. 20 April 1890 at
   Smithtown; funeral at Smithtown Landing;
   widow of Joseph Tyler; "well known and
   respected"
UDALE, Mr. - d. 27 January 1884 at Patchogue;
   dropped dead in vestibule of Methodist
   church

UMBERFIELD, Harvey D. - 68 y 10 m 26 d;
    d. 9 January 1887 at Comac
UNDERHILL, infant - d. 15 July 1888 at
    Jericho; child of Samuel S. Underhill
UNDERHILL, child - interment at Oyster Bay;
    9 August 1890 paper; child of Sarah Under-
    hill
UNDERHILL, Almeda T. - 3 mos 15 days; d. 8 May
    1879 at Huntington; daughter of Charles and
    Mary Underhill
UNDERHILL, Annie E. - 1 yr 7 mos; d. 14 April
    1887 at Huntington; daughter of Charles and
    Minnie Underhill
UNDERHILL, Benjamin C. - d. 25 April 1888 at
    Mill Neck
UNDERHILL, Daniel - 69 years; d. 25 February
    1889 at Oyster Bay
UNDERHILL, Daniel C. - 55 y 8 m 26 d;
    d. 21 July 1884 at Yaphank; son of Jesse and
    Ruth Underhill; brother of Alfred Underhill;
    resident of Huntington
UNDERHILL, Frances Y. - 41 years; d. 9 July
    1890 at Locust Valley; daughter of John
    Wright of Oyster Bay
UNDERHILL, James - d. 26 August 1885 at sea;
    during storm on voyage from New York to
    Nassau; a huge wave knocked him into an open
    hatchway
UNDERHILL, Jessie - 7 years; d. 23 May 1889 at
    Jericho; daughter of Samuel S. Underhill
UNDERHILL, Mary A. - 32 y 8 m 7 d; d. 1 March
    1879 at Huntington; wife of Charles Under-
    hill
UNDERHILL, Mary W. - d. 28 November 1878;
    funeral at Oyster Bay; was to be married
    12 December 1878 to Solomon Townsend, Jr.
UNDERHILL, Phebe - 87 years; d. 12 March 1890
    at Mill Neck; widow of Smith Underhill
UNDERHILL, Phebe A. - d. at Hempstead; funeral
    26 October 1889 at Locust Valley; widow of
    Jacob Underhill; mother of Townsend D. Cox
UNDERHILL, Ruth - 82 years; d. 24 November
    1880 at Huntington; widow of Isaac Underhill
UNDERHILL, Sarah - d. "about three weeks ago";
    interment at Oyster Bay; 9 August 1890 paper
UNDERWOOD, Mrs. Edmund - 53 y 10 m 10 d;
    d. 10 April 1882 at Mount Sinai

UNDERWOOD, Edwin - 65 years; d. 11 November
1882 at Mount Sinai
UNDERWOOD, William G. - d. at Robbins Island;
27 July 1883 paper; lockjaw
URQUHART, Robert - death reported 7 May 1887
paper; Half Hollow Hills item
VAIL, child - 17 mos; d. 5 August 1882 at
Babylon; son of William Vail; great-grandson
of Almy C. Vail who d. same day
VAIL, Mr. - funeral 11 September 1886 at
Northport; resident of Yaphank; formerly
of Northport
VAIL, Mr. - interment 21 March 1890; Hicks-
ville item; father-in-law of I. R. Bricket
VAIL, Aaron S. - 84 years; d. 9 December 1881
at Smithtown; trout breeder
VAIL, Almy C. - 86 y 1 m 11 d; d. 5 August
1882 at Dix Hills; widow of Moses Vail
VAIL, Emma - 16 years; d. 1 November 1878 at
Hicksville; resident of Oyster Bay
VAIL, Israel R. - 70 y 7 m 8 d; d. 18 November
1880 at Vernon Valley
VAIL, Jane E. - 84 years; d. 13 September 1888
at St. Johnland; funeral at Smithtown
Branch; widow of Aaron S. Vail
VAIL, Lulu R. - 9 y 5 m 22 d; d. 13 August
1883 at Smithtown; interment at Riverhead;
daughter of Edward and Emma Vail of River-
head
VAIL, William Henry - 25 years; d. 13 January
1885 at Northport
VALENTINE, infant - funeral 1 August 1887 at
Westbury; infant grandson of Jackson Valentine
VALENTINE, infant - d. 27 February 1889 at
Westbury; son of William Valentine
VALENTINE, Brewster - ca. 70 years; d. 13 February 1878 at Sparkill, New York; Huntington
native (b. 1807); settled in Brooklyn 1836
and was a long-time grocer there with Carman
& Valentine and Valentine, Bergen & Company;
"one of Brooklyn's foremost and best citizens"
VALENTINE, Daniel - 81 y 7 m 6 d; d. 14 Decem-
ber 1890 at West Hills; "life-long member of
West Hills M. E. Church"

VALENTINE, Ella C. - 19 y 10 m 13 d;
d. 29 November 1880 at Babylon; wife of
Hosea Valentine of Long Swamp
VALENTINE, Ezra - d. "a few days since" at
Brooklyn; 14 May 1887 paper; son of Jesse
Valentine; brother of Mrs. Conklin Kellum;
lived in Long Swamp "many years ago"
VALENTINE, Hannah - 69 years; d. 28 January
1887 at Vernon Valley; fell dead in the road
VALENTINE, Henry - 70 y 10 m 3 d; d. 11 Janu-
ary 1889 at Huntington
VALENTINE, Hosea - 83 y 4 m 9 d; d. 13 Febru-
ary 1888 at Dix Hills
VALENTINE, Minnie E. - 2 y 4 m 29 d;
d. 19 January 1882 at Dix Hills; daughter of
Frank H. and Mary E. Valentine
VALENTINE, Richard - 84 years; funeral 24 Nov-
ember 1885 at Oyster Bay
VALENTINE, Ruth - 80 years; d. 19 October 1887
at Locust Valley; former resident of Wood-
bury
VALENTINE, Samuel - 58 years; d. 11 April 1889
at Woodbury; interment at Brookville
VALENTINE, William M. - d. 17 July 1884 at
Roslyn
VAN BRUNT, Mrs. James A. - d. 16 April 1890 at
Brooklyn; former resident of Huntington
VAN COTT, children - d. 2 January 1890 at
Farmingdale; two children of Alanson Van
Cott
VAN COTT, Elizabeth - 93 years; funeral 9 Aug-
ust 1887 at Farmingdale
VAN COTT, George R. - funeral 9 November 1890
at Farmingdale
VAN COTT, Tunis - funeral 27 January 1890 at
Farmingdale
VAN DE LINDE, Augustus - 19 years; suicide;
shot himself because news of his secret
marriage was published in Brooklyn Eagle;
5 October 1889 paper
VANDERBILT, Evelyn A. - 34 y 2 m 1 d;
d. 14 August 1878 at Northport
VAN DER HEYDON, S. - suicide 15 September 1883
at Winfield
VANDEWATER, Clarence - 4 years; 2 July 1880
paper; resident of Glen Cove; "Seawanhaka"
fire on East River

VAN NOSTRAND, child - 9 years; d. at Jamaica;
3 December 1887 paper; interment "last week"
at Northport; son of Benjamin Van Nostrand,
formerly of Northport
VAN NOSTRAND, child - 6 years; d. 17 November
1889 at Queens; interment at Elmont;
daughter of John Van Nostrand
VAN NOSTRAND, Benjamin S. - 66 y 9 m 12 d;
d. 19 July 1890 at Brentwood; interment at
Bay Shore; father of Mrs. Robert Purick,
Mrs. James Brush, Charles Van Nostrand and
William Van Nostrand; resident of Brentwood
since 1864; agent for Galenburg Medicine
Company; b. New York City 12 October 1823
VAN NOSTRAND, Cornelius - 79 y 11 m 21 d;
d. 12 September 1887; Jericho item
VAN NOSTRAND, George H. - 100 yrs 15 days;
d. 8 January 1886 at Farmingdale; funeral at
Bethpage
VAN NOSTRAND, Nancy Gardiner - d. 26 January
1890 at Lakewood, N. J.; widow of John J.
Van Nostrand
VAN NOSTRAND, Sarah - 91 yrs 3 mos;
d. 18 March 1884 at Northport
VAN SICLEN, Deborah - 45 yrs 1 mos;
d. 12 November 1881 at Northport
VAN SISE, infant - d. 17 August 1885 at
Syosset; child of Charles Van Sise
VAN SISE, Alfred - 39 y 3 m 26 d; d. 13 July
1880 at Syosset
VAN SISE, Charles - 10 years; d. 1 March 1886
at Plain View; interment at Woodbury
VAN SISE, Clarence J. - 1 y 1 m 22 d;
d. 6 March 1883 at Woodbury; son of Jeremiah
and Evelyn F. Van Sise
VAN SISE, Cornelius - funeral 9 June 1886 at
Woodbury; resident of Brooklyn
VAN SISE, Frederick - 22 years; murdered
1 April 1890 at Plainview; son of Nathaniel
Van Sise; political argument between bar-
keeper Charles Gunther Keil (age 74) and
Nathaniel and Frederick Van Sise and Charles
Duryea; led to Keil shooting Frederick and
attacking Nathaniel and breaking his leg by
hitting him with shotgun; long article on
murder 5 April 1890 paper

VAN SISE, Hannah M. - 57 yrs 12 days;
d. 21 August 1887 at Woodbury; wife of
Israel W. Van Sise

VAN SISE, Ida Lavinia - 4 y 7 m 19 d;
d. 19 June 1882 at Oyster Bay; daughter of
Ketcham and Sarah A. Van Sise

VAN SISE, Israel - 65 y 5 m 19 d; d. 27 April
1884 at Huntington; interment at Woodbury

VAN SISE, James - 83 y 9 m 8 d; d. 19 January
1888 at Woodbury

VAN SISE, James - d. at Brooklyn; interment
28 August 1889 at Plain Edge

VAN SISE, Martha - 80 years; d. 1 December
1890 at Plainview; widow of Robert Van Sise

VAN SISE, Othney - 82 yrs 4 mos; d. 17 July
1889 at Woodbury; widow of James Van Sise

VAN SISE, Robert - 74 yrs 5 mos; d. 25 July
1878 at Manetto Hill

VAN SISE, Ruth - 33 y 11 m 13 d; d. 13 October 1881 at Huntington; wife of Frederick
Van Sise

VAN SPLINDER, Aaron - 57 yrs 6 mos; d. 20 June
1879 at Lloyd's Neck; thrown from mowing
machine

VAN VELSOR, Elisha - 72 y 11 m 30 d;
d. 29 March 1882 at Oyster Bay

VAN WAGNER, Alexander - d. 10 February 1890 at
Brooklyn; brother-in-law of Sidney Walters
of Oyster Bay

VAN WICKLEN, child - d. at Westville; 19 February 1887 paper; blind daughter of Charles
Van Wicklen

VAN WICKLEN, Ann E. - 47 years; d. 8 April
1888 at Syosset

VAN WORT, Mrs. E. - 27 years; d. 29 September
1884 at Rocky Point

VAN WYCK, Ellen C. - d. 7 January 1881 at West
Neck; interment at New York City; widow of
Samuel A. Van Wyck

VAN WYCK, Frank - 24 years; d. 30 January 1890
at Denver, Colorado; interment at Oyster Bay
Cove; son of Whitehead H. Van Wyck; went to
Colorado for his health

VAN WYCK, Jennie - 15 years; d. 17 March 1878
at Jericho

VAN WYCK, Mary Kate - 43 y 3 m 13 d; d. 7 January 1884 at West Neck; wife of Whitehead H. Van Wyck

VAN WYCK, Theodorus - 82 years; d. 20 April 1882 at Woodbury

VAN WYCK, Whitehead H. - 50 y 2 m 17 d; d. 26 May 1888 at Huntington; son of Joshua Van Wyck; nephew of Samuel Van Wyck; lawyer at Jamaica; formerly of Oyster Bay Cove

VANCE, Samuel B. H. - d. 11 August 1890; former Mayor of New York City; had "summer residence on Long Island"

VARIAN, Joshua M. - d. 24 July 1882 at New York City; brother of Mrs. John Hopper of Huntington; ran wholesale meat packing business; officer in New York State militia; veteran of Civil War

VEGA, Alexis Leon - 6 m 18 d; d. 24 December 1890 at Hempstead; interment at Flatbush; son of R. J. Vega

VELSOR, Anna M. - 41 y 9 m 9 d; d. 9 February 1879 at Centreport

VELSOR, Charles M. - 7 years; d. 1 February 1882 at Long Island City; son of Lewis and Carrie Velsor

VELSOR, Cornelia - d. 6 September 1885 at Comac; daughter of Edgar Velsor

VELSOR, Edith - d. 18 April 1890 at Oyster Bay; interment at Woodbury; daughter of Alfred Velsor

VELSOR, Elijah - funeral 18 November 1889 at Woodbury

VELSOR, Ella J. - 2 mos 6 days; d. 12 June 1885 at Centreport; daughter of Ebenezer and Emma Velsor

VELSOR, Emma d. 25 December 1886 at Centreport; daughter of Ebenezer Velsor

VELSOR, Frances Ann - 50 years; d. 6 September 1882 at Cold Spring

VELSOR, Franklin - 19 yrs 3 mos; d. 19 September 1889 at Huntington

VELSOR, Jonas A. - 45 y 10 m 17 d; d. 19 December 1879 at Huntington

VELSOR, Joseph H. - 4 y 4 m 14 d; d. 30 January 1882 at Long Island City; son of Lewis and Carrie Velsor

VELSOR, Mortimer V. - 44 yrs 9 mos;
d. 15 March 1881 at Huntington

VELSOR, Olive L. - 41 yrs 8 mos; d. 11 August
1889 at Huntington; daughter of David V.
Lane; widow of J. A. Velsor

VELSOR, Phebe - 68 y 9 m 10 d; d. 29 October
1878 at Centreport

VELSOR, Sarah - 57 years; d. 2 September 1878
at Centreport

VELSOR, Susan L. - 62 y 7 m 12 d; d. 23 August
1879 at Woodbury

VELSOR, Susie Ketcham - 21 years; funeral
22 February 1888 at Farmingdale

VERITY, Gilbert - drowned at Greenport; 28
December 1883 paper

VERITY, Henry - 66 years; d. 12 June 1882 at
Yaphank; interment at Huntington; former
resident of Huntington

VERITY, Robert Seymour - 24 years; suicide
22 March 1886 at Roslyn; shot himself after
quarrel with parents; son of James Verity

VERITY, Mrs. William - death reported 12 March
1887 paper; Glen Cove item

VICK, James - d. 16 May 1882 at Rochester, New
York; florist

VINGERT, Gussie Floyd - 45 years; d. 27 August
1887 at Port Jefferson; wife of G. L. Vingert, a Cuban; resident of New York City

VOIGHT, James - d. 3 February 1885 at Hicksville; injuries from falling off a ladder

VON DER HEYDT, Edward - d. in Germany; 19 July
1890 paper; brother-in-law of Oscar E.
Schmidt of Lloyd Neck; former resident of
New York City

VON DER LUEHE, Dr. Carl - 60 years; d. 17 December 1878 at Williamsburgh; native of
Mecklenburg, Germany, who immigrated to the
U.S. in 1838; resident of Texas before
moving to Long Island; medical doctor with
large practice in Huntington and later in
Williamsburgh

VON STROMER, Charles - 9 years; d. 11 August
1890 at Glen Cove; broke neck when he was
thrown to ground when wagon upset; son of
Carl Von Stromer

243

VREELAND, child - 2 y 1 m 3 d; d. 10 March
1886 at Farmingdale; daughter of Robert H.
Vreeland
VREELAND, Mrs. - d. 17 September 1887 at
Hinsdale; diphtheria
VREELAND, children - d. 17 September 1887 at
Hinsdale; two children of Mrs. Vreeland;
diphtheria
WADDELL, Georgia A. - 13 y 7 m 25 d;
d. 24 April 1883 at Huntington
WADE, Esther - 53 y 1 m 10 d; d. 26 May 1880
at Cold Spring
WAGNER, Grover Cleveland - 4 years;
d. 19 November 1888 at Breslau; hit by
railroad train while crossing tracks with
a group of children
WAGNER, John - 57 years; d. 4 October 1885 at
Hicksville
WAGSTAFF, Dr. Alfred - 75 years; d. 26 April
1878 at West Islip; physician
WAINNER, George - ca. 63 years; suicide
20 February 1887 at Smithtown; cut his
throat
WAITE, Edward T. - d. 24 December 1889 at
Washington, D. C.; funeral at Toledo, Ohio;
son of U. S. Chief Justice [Morrison R.]
Waite
WALCOTT, Elenor (Nellie) M. - d. 23 November
1886 at New York City; former resident of
Huntington
WALCOTT, William T. - d. 15 August 1890 in
Texas; from "cancer of the mouth supposed to
have been caused by smoking"; 2nd wife was
Mrs. Phebe Ketcham, whom he m. "shortly
after the war"; father of William T. Walcott
and James Walcott; former resident of Huntington ca. 1848-1868; first wife died in
Huntington; was a wine and liquor importer
in New York City; moved to Texas after death
of 2nd wife to live with a nephew
WALDO, Henry - d. 10 November 1881 at Breslau;
found dead in barn to which he had gone
before breakfast; called to breakfast, but
he was already dead in the barn
WALDRON, Daniel - d. 17 November 1884 at
Woodbury; father of Mrs. George A. Velsor;
resident of East Norwich

WALDRON, Hannah - 94 years; d. at East Norwich; funeral 6 September 1890 at East Norwich; "oldest person in the neighborhood"

WALDRON, John - d. "a few weeks ago" 13 September 1890 paper; "suddenly while harvesting his crop of hay"; Oyster Bay item; son of Hannah Waldron

WALKER, Harvey - 82 yrs 6 mos; d. 17 March 1882 at Smithtown Landing

WALKER, John H. - 36 years; d. "last week" at Brooklyn; interment at Hempstead; 30 August 1890 paper; son of Mrs. C. W. Walker

WALKER, Maria A. - 68 y 6 m 20 d; d. 8 August 1879 at Mount Sinai; widow of William A. Walker

WALKER, W. James - murdered at Stamford, Ct.; 12 October 1889 paper; shot and killed by brother Edward Walker

WALKER, Wayland - 44 years; d. 12 December 1879 at Brooklyn; brother of Mrs. H. B. Horton

WALKER, William - 42 years; body found 11 February 1890 on beach at Lloyd's Neck

WALL, Alice L. - 18 y 5 m 29 d; d. 7 August 1883 at Huntington

WALL, Catherine - 55 years; d. 3 August 1878 at Laurelton

WALL, Ellen Murphy - 62 years; d. 21 July 1887 at Huntington

WALL, Mary E. - 31 y 6 m 26 d; d. 18 December 1885 at Huntington

WALLACE, Annie Allen - d. 25 August 1890 at Islip; thrown by her horse; hit a tree and fractured skull; wife of John Wallace

WALLACE, Irene - 2 years; d. 25 July 1889 at Brooklyn; daughter of John Wallace; granddaughter of Stephen Wallace of Hicksville

WALLACE, William - drowned 6 April 1888 in Nissequogue River at St. Johnland

WALLENHAUPT, Nancy - d. 17 September 1889 at Hicksville; wife of Henry Wallenhaupt

WALSH, James - drowned in Peconic Bay; 7 September 1889 paper; possible suicide; resident of Grace Harbour, Newfoundland

WALSH, Thomas H. - 71 years; d. 28 April 1881 at West Neck

WALTERS, child - d. at Brooklyn; 6 February
1885 paper; Cold Spring item; son of George
Walters
WALTERS, Elbert - 79 y 8 m 14 d; d. 20 Novem-
ber 1883 at Huntington; husband of Elizabeth
Oakley (m. 1825); son-in-law of John Oakley;
resident of Huntington since 1833; cabinet
maker; militia captain 1838; founder of
Huntington Mutual Fire Insurance Company;
Overseer of the Poor; Trustee Town of Hunt-
ington; school trustee; native of Plain Edge
WALTERS, Elizabeth - 76 yrs 7 mos; d. 28 Febr-
uary 1883 at Huntington; wife of Elbert
Walters
WALTERS, Jesse - drowned 13 July 1880 at Gilgo
Inlet; resident of Farmingdale
WALTERS, John - 66 y 3 m 28 d; suicide
26 March 1887 at Cold Spring Harbor; shot
himself
WALTERS, John S. - 86 years; d. 11 March 1883
at Farmingdale
WALTERS, Josiah - 84 years; d. 8 May 1888 at
Woodbury
WALTERS, Mary - 85 years; d. 1 September 1879
at Cold Spring
WALTERS, Mary Ann - 59 yrs 28 days; d. 23 Dec-
ember 1890 at Cold Spring Harbor; wife of
Albert Walters
WALTERS, Samuel B. - funeral 4 February 1890
at Farmingdale
WALTERS, Samuel D. - 85 yrs 4 mos; d. 16 July
1887 at New York City; interment at Hunting-
ton; native of Huntington
WALTERS, Samuel D. - 40 years; d. 29 December
1884 at New York City
WALTERS, Sarah - 86 years; d. 25 December 1882
at Cold Spring; interment at Woodbury; wife
of Abraham Walters
WALTERS, Treadwell S. - 63 years; d. 9 March
1889 at Syosset
WANSER, infant - found under a woodpile in
Little Neck; 20 July 1883 paper; son of
Julia Wanser
WANSOR, Benjamin - 86 years; d. 10 March 1890
at Brookville; "died in the poorhouse";
famous fox hunter

246

WANSOR, Thomas J. - 48 years; d. 11 August
    1890 at Glen Cove; wagon accident; shifting
    load caused wagon to upset; Wansor was
    thrown out and run over; cooper with
    L. Wansor & Sons
WARD, Abram Rapalyea - 63 y 2 m 5 d;
    d. 24 January 1884 at Dix Hills
WARD, General Elijah - d. 7 February 1882 at
    Roslyn; Judge Advocate General of New York
    State under Governor Seymour [1853-1855];
    [New York City lawyer]; former Member of
    U. S. Congress for four terms [1857-1859,
    1861-1865 and 1875-1877, serving as a repre-
    sentative from New York City]; President of
    Mercantile Library of New York; [b. Sing
    Sing, N. Y. 16 September 1816]
WARD, Ida - 22 years; d. 23 July 1884 at
    Setauket; interment at Elwood
WARD, James - drowned 12 March 1884 at
    Hunter's Point
WARD, Michael - 65 years; d. 21 August 1890 at
    Hicksville; "suddenly"; interment at West-
    bury
WARD, Stephen - 98 y 7 m 11 d; d. 28 October
    1880 at Dix Hills; funeral at West Farms,
    Westchester County, N. Y.
WARDLE, George S. - d. 20 March 1888; River-
    head item
WARMOUTH, John - d. "a month ago"; 29 January
    1886 paper; morphine adict; resident of
    Roslyn
WARREN, Horatio N. - 63 years; d. 11 August
    1882 at Marlborough, New York; former
    resident of Cold Spring
WARREN, James D. - death reported 1 January
    1887 paper; Editor of Buffalo Commercial
    Advertizer
WASHBURN, Edward Oakley - d. 26 November 1890
    at West Hills; son of Isaiah Washburn;
    son-in-law of Solomon Oakley
WASHBURNE, Elihu B. - death reported 5 Novem-
    ber 1887 paper; [Congressman from Illinois
    1853-1869; Republican leader of Congress-
    ional Reconstruction; U. S. minister to
    France 1869-1877; wrote memoir of service
    during Siege of Paris 1870-71 and Paris
    Commune 1871]

WASHKORKE, William - 3 mos 12 days;
d. 2 January 1885 at Lloyd's Neck
WATERBURY, Edward P. - d. 28 August 1889 at
Albany, N. Y.
WATERS, Edward L. - d. 10 November 1888 at
Jamesport
WATSON, Edward - 2 July 1880 paper; resident
of Whitestone; "Seawanhaka" fire on East
River
WATTS, child - 10 years; d. 13 December 1885
at Hell Gate Marsh, Jamaica Bay; froze to
death in an open boat; son of John E. Watts
WATTS, Jennie - d. "last week" at Bay Shore; 8
May 1886 paper; mother of Smith Watts who
was murdered on an oyster sloop in 1860
WEAVER, Jeremiah T. - 64 years; d. 17 March
1890; found dead in the road between Manetto
Hill and Central Park; resident of Beadle-
town [Bedelltown]
WEBB, Catharine L. - 78 y 2 m 5 d; d. 6 April
1878 at Huntington; resident of New York
City
WEBBER, Annie A. - d. 20 May 1888 at Mineola;
death caused by opium
WEBSTER, child - d. at Islip; 26 January 1889
paper; child of Rev. W. C. Webster
WEBSTER, Mrs. - d. 9 November 1889 at Wyan-
dance; "one of the oldest ladies of our
village"
WEEDEN, Nettie Hill - 46 years; d. 1 October
1889 at Jamaica; daughter of Rev. Francis C.
Hill; wife of David Weeden; active in M. E.
church work, evangelism and temperance;
former resident of Huntington
WEEKS, infant - d. at Watkins, N. Y.; 11 March
1881 paper; child of Rev. George E. Weeks,
formerly of Huntington
WEEKS, Mrs. - 93 years; funeral 7 February
1885 at Greenlawn
WEEKS, Daniel T. - 23 y 9 m 25 d; d. 31 March
1881 at Syosset
WEEKS, Delia R. - d. 27 February 1889 in
Montgomery County, Pa.; interment at South
Norwalk, Connecticut; wife of Rev. George E.
Weeks; former resident of Huntington
WEEKS, Francis - d. 27 February 1884 at
Yaphank; son of William J. Weeks

WEEKS, George - d. 9 September 1885; carriage
accident when horse was frightened by rail-
road train; son-in-law of Solomon Smith of
Babylon; resident of Comac; note: also
called George WICKS
WEEKS, Mrs. Rev. George E. - d. Watkins, New
York; 11 March 1881 paper; Rev. George E.
Weeks was formerly a Huntington resident
WEEKS, James - 68 years; d. "recently";
Hempstead item; 19 July 1890 and 30 August
1890 papers; brother of Hobart Weeks; "an
eccentric individual"
WEEKS, James H. - 81 years; d. 7 September
1879 at Yaphank; President of L.I.R.R.;
Yaphank resident since ca. 1840; member of
Episcopal Church at Yaphank; native of
Oyster Bay
WEEKS, Jane M. - d. "middle of January" 1885
at Glen Cove; wife of Samuel Weeks; separa-
ted from husband and disinherited him in
will
WEEKS, John J. - 82 years; d. 28 June 1880 at
Locust Valley
WEEKS, Mary Ethelinda - 5 mos 23 days;
d. 22 December 1890 at Huntington; daughter
of Henry Weeks
WEEKS, Miles - interment 8 January 1889 at
Babylon; father of Riley Weeks of Babylon;
resident of Dix Hills
WEEKS, Platt - 65 years; d. 2 September 1890
at Yaphank; fell from hay loft in Oliver
Carll's barn in Greenlawn
WEEKS, Samuel - d. 7 August 1887 at Centre
Island
WEEKS, William Penn - d. 2 February 1889 at
North Babylon; interment at Babylon
WEIDMER, infant - death reported 10 October
1884 paper; child of Robert Weidmer of
Hicksville
WEIHLING, John - d. 30 October 1887 at Hicks-
ville
WEINZ, child - 8 months; d. 15 July 1890 at
Port Jefferson; interment at New York City;
child of Louis Weinz
WEIR, John - 54 years; d. 29 November 1886 at
Dix Hills

WEISS, Frederick - d. 9 August 1887 at Brook-
lyn; killed when coal pocket collapsed
WELCH, infant - interment 19 December 1888 at
Westbury; child of John Welch of Red Ground
WELCH, Mary E. - 4 y 2 m 8 d; d. 21 September
1884 at West Neck
WELCH, Ralph - death reported 9 November 1883
paper; resident of Sag Harbor
WELD, Harvey S. - d. 20 March 1884 at Brook-
lyn; sexton of Plymouth Church, Brooklyn
WELLS, young man - 17 Years; d. 12 September
1880 at Riverhead; accidentally shot by
brother; son of John Henry Wells
WELLS, Amanda - d. "recently" at Northville;
15 January 1886 paper
WELLS, Eliza * - 45 years; d. 28 April 1879 at
Huntington; wife of James Wells
WELLS, I. Minor - d. 10 May 1888 at Northville
WELLS, Mrs. Jonathan H. - interment at River-
head; 20 July 1889 paper; resident of New
York City; formerly of Baiting Hollow
WELLS, Joshua - d. 15 March 1882 at Brooklyn;
interment at Riverhead
WELLS, Temperance - d. 20 April 1888 at River-
head; mother of O. O. Wells
WELLS, Waldo - suicide by drowning at Coney
Island; interment 24 June 1889 at Riverhead;
son of J. L. Wells
WEMHART, Henry - d. 10 December 1887 at Col-
lege Point; fell dead at railroad station
WENTWORTH, Gould - interment 5 December 1889
at Smithtown Branch; former resident of
Smithtown
WELING, Josephine - 19 years; d. 21 November
1888 at Hicksville; memorial notice from
Trinity Ev. Lutheran Church, Hicksville in
22 December 1888 paper; b. 21 December 1868
WESS, Eliza A. - d. 6 October 1889 at Port
Jefferson
WEST, Benjamin R. - 23 years; d. 3 March 1888
at East Setauket
WEST, Ellen - 39 y 1 m 5 d; d. 25 August 1884
at Huntington; wife of Samuel West
WEST, Stiles P. - 77 years; d. 13 September
1884 at West Hills
WESTCOTT, Edward - 2 July 1880 paper; resident
of Manhasset;"Seawanhaka" fire on East River

WESTERVELT, Eliza - d. 10 February 1880 at
Brooklyn; daughter of Jacob Westervelt;
sister of Mrs. A. T. Hurd

WESTERVELT, Rachael - 58 years; d. 20 May 1885
at Huntington; sister of Mrs. A. T. Hurd

WETTERAU, Kathrina - 59 y 10 m 18 d;
d. 15 November 1888 at Hicksville; wife of
George C. Wetterau

WHALEN, Margaret - 58 yrs 9 days; d. 3 May
1887 at Huntington; wife of Jerry Whalen

WHALEN, Mary - 65 years; d. 6 September 1885
at Melville

WHALEN, Sarah - 10 yrs 10 mos; d. 16 March
1881 at Huntington; daughter of Jerry Whalen

WHALEY, Nicholas - 23 years; d. 15 September
1889 at New York City; run over by train
which started moving while he was getting
off; interment at Westbury

WHEALEY, Stephen M. - d. 22 January 1887 at
Hempstead

WHEATLEY, William - d. 31 March 1885 at Oyster
Bay

WHEDON, Daniel D. - 37 years; suicide 19 August 1884 at Elizabeth, N. J.; son of Rev.
Dr. Whedon of Sag Harbor

WHEELER, Alfred E. - d. at Brooklyn; interment
23 May 1888 at Hauppauge; former resident of
Smithtown

WHEELER, Capt. Barnabas P. - 70 years;
d. 9 February 1887 at Smithtown

WHEELER, Charles E. - d. at Babylon; 3 September 1887 paper; builder

WHEELER, E. Frank - 20 yrs 7 mos; d. 30 October 1886 at Northport; son of George W.
Wheeler

WHEELER, E. Platt - 65 yrs 2 mos; d. 4 September 1882 at Babylon; interment at Northport

WHEELER, Mrs. Elnathan - d. Thanksgiving Day
1882 at Westport, Conn.; mother of Mrs.
George R. Rogers

WHEELER, Fannie E. - 20 y 4 m 25 d; d. 10 Dec-
ember 1887 at Brooklyn; daughter of William
H. and Naomi Warren; wife of Frank M.
Wheeler (m. 11 April 1887)

WHEELER, Lyman Beecher - d. 13 November 1888;
Smithtown item; funeral at Comac

WHEELER, Mrs. Treadwell - 33 years; d. 27
February 1880 at Smithtown
WHEELER, William A. - 67 years; d. "recently"
at Malone, N. Y.; 25 June 1887 paper; Vice
President of the U. S. [1877-1881] [served
in U. S. House as Representative from New
York State 1861-1863 and 1869-1877]
WHELAN, Martin - d. 9 February 1889 at
Babylon; former blacksmith in Huntington
WHELAN, Michael - d. 20 January 1889 at Islip;
"met his death in a sad manner on the rail-
road bridge over Stellenwerf's Creek";
brother of Martin Whelan of Babylon
WHIPPLE, Helen - 3 mos 16 days; d. 7 December
1879 at Dix Hills; daughter of Volney C. and
Vinnie Whipple
WHITE, Mrs. - "70 or 80"; d. 19 October 1887
at Jericho; fell dead from chair; mother-in-
law of William Titus
WHITE, Mrs. A. E. - 68 yrs 9 mos; d. 17 June
1883 at Smithtown; wife of S. E. White
WHITE, Charles - "advanced age"; d. 15 March
1888 at Newtown; founder of the Newtown
Register
WHITE, Charles - 82 years; d. 29 May 1890 at
Amityville; interment at Huntington; former
resident of Huntington
WHITE, Mrs. Charles E. - funeral 26 April
1885 at Babylon
WHITE, Coles W. - d. 11 May 1885 at Flushing;
funeral at Oyster Bay; native of Oyster Bay;
"costly monument erected over the burial
place" by Freelove A. White of Flushing,
widow; 29 October 1892 paper
WHITE, Elbert - 56 y 4 m 15 d; d. 11 December
1881 at West Hills
WHITE, George T. - 46 years; d. 25 November
1884; assistant editor of the Newtown
Register
WHITE, Gifford - funeral 25 March 1886 at
Oyster Bay
WHITE, Hannah Elizabeth - 49 yrs 3 mos;
d. 4 July 1881 at Huntington
WHITE, Herman - 2 mos 2 days; d. 1 February
1880 at West Neck; son of Henry and Matilda
White

WHITE, Henry - 6 years; d. 31 January 1881 at
New York City

WHITE, Nathaniel R. - 74 years; d. 12 February
1885 at Grahamsville, Florida; former shipbuilder in Northport

WHITE, Phebe - 28 days; d. 6 May 1884 at Cold
Spring; daughter of Edward and Eliza Jane
White

WHITE, Scudder - 79 years; d. 25 July 1882 at
Mineola; former resident of West Hills

WHITE, Thomas H. - d. 7 February 1884 at Cold
Spring; son of William H. and Abby A. White

WHITE, William E. - 3 months; d. 2 July 1884
at Huntington

WHITMAN, Deborah A. - 78 years; d. 18 February
1884 at Smithtown

WHITMAN, Martha - ca. 64 years; d. 16 April
1885 at Comac

WHITMAN, Sarah - 84 years; d. 21 February 1880
at Comac

WHITMAN, Zebulon D. - d. 23 December 1886 at
Comac

WHITMORE, Joseph - drowned 3 May 1878 off
Crane Neck Point; boat capsized; resident of
East Setauket

WHITNEY, I. Clausen - 25 years; d. 30 May 1883
in Vermont; former resident of Woodbury

WHITNEY, John J. - 51 yrs 9 mos; d. 7 December
1880 at Woodbury

WHITNEY, Mary Titus - 9 mos 9 days; d. 17 July
1885 at Brooklyn; daughter of Daniel D. and
Anna S. Whitney

WHITNEY, Nathaniel - 22 years; d. 26 October
1879 at Woodbury

WHITNEY, Phebe - 82 yrs 7 mos; d. 19 May 1878
at Woodbury

WHITNEY, Sarah Titus - 66 years; d. 26 Febr-
uary 1889 at Brooklyn; daughter of Henry
Titus; wife of Daniel D. Whitney; mother of
Mrs. Harvey A. Eames, Gerald Whitney and
Daniel D. Whitney; sister of James Titus of
Glen Cove, Mary Titus of Woodbury and Mrs.
Scudder V. Whitney of Woodbury; b. Glen Cove
11 June 1822

WHITNEY, Seymour D. - 24 years; d. 26 October
1879 at Jersey City, N. J.

WHITSON, infant - 6 mos; d. 31 October 1881 at
Syosset; son of Frank B. and Mary Whitson

WHITSON, Charles - 76 y 10 m 2 d; d. 13 December 1881 at Cold Spring

WHITSON, Charles H. - 25 years; d. 26 August
1885 at Melville

WHITSON, Isaac Youngs - 76 years; d. 8 February 1884 at Coney Island; son of Samuel
Whitson

WHITSON, Jennie A. - 2 years; d. 23 September
1886 at Syosset; interment at Melville;
daughter of Frank E. and Mary Whitson

WHITSON, John - funeral 1 June 1886; Farmingdale item

WHITSON, John H. - 2 y 4 m 6 d; d. 13 March
1886 at West Hills; son of Charles A. and
Ruth A. Whitson

WHITSON, Phineas J. - 36 y 2 m 13 d;
d. 26 June 1883 at Melville

WHITSON, Stanton - 24 years; d. 31 January
1886; member of Presbyterian Church at
Melville

WHITTAKER, Finetta Amelia - 42 y 6 m 12 d;
d. 3 December 1883 at Brooklyn; interment at
Huntington

WHITTAKER, Thomas - 69 years; d. 2 October
1882 at Northport; interment at Green-Wood,
Brooklyn

WHITTIE, Mrs. Edward - interment 29 December
1890 at Port Jefferson; body brought from
Bridgeport, Connecticut

WICKHAM, William - ca. 60 years; d. 24 February 1881 at Cutchogue

WICKLER, Eva B. - 46 years; d. 10 February
1888 at Hicksville

WICKES, Francis P. - 22 years; murder-suicide
20 April 1886 at New York City; shot Emma
Adams and then himself; interment at San
Francisco, California; parents reside in
Hempstead

WICKS, Capt. - drowned 23 December 1881 off
Lloyd's Neck; resident of New Brunswick,
New Jersey

WICKS, Adam C. - 78 years; d. 25 January 1879
at Old Fields

WICKS, Amanda - 78 yrs 6 mos; d. 3 November
1883 at Northport; widow of Adam Wicks

WICKS, Benjamin - 29 years; d. 10 December
   1886 at Northport
WICKS, Carrie Frances - 6 months; d. 21 July
   1888 at Greenlawn
WICKS, Clara E. - 17 y 9 m 4 d; d. 15 June
   1880 at Comac
WICKS, Conklin - ca. 90 years; d. 6 January
   1884 at Bay Shore; suffocated from smoke in
   house fire
WICKS, Emma A. - 2 y 10 m 4 d; d. 17 July 1889
   at Greenlawn; daughter of Theodore Wicks
WICKS, Ezra E. - 63 y 8 m 9 d; d. 11 September
   1881 at Comac
WICKS, Frank S. - 27 y 7 m 18 d; d. 2 December
   1878 at Comac
WICKS, George - 1 y 6 m 25 d; d. 6 March 1884
   at Huntington; son of William E. and
   Ethalinda Wicks
WICKS, George - see: George WEEKS
WICKS, Harriet E. - 26 y 5 m 27 d; d. 16 Aug-
   ust 1887 at South Dix Hills
WICKS, Isaac - 98 years; d. 23 February 1882
   at Brooklyn; resident of Fresh Pond; "always
   walked to and from Brooklyn"
WICKS, Mrs. Joel - d. 20 November 1890 at
   Southampton; interment at Patchogue; former
   resident of Patchogue
WICKS, John H. - 87 yrs 19 days; d. 4 November
   1885 at Half Hollow Hills
WICKS, Luther - 80 yrs 1 mo; d. 26 January
   1889 at Comac
WICKS, Mary A. - 14 days; d. 10 September 1889
   at Greenlawn
WICKS, Selah E. - 60 y 3 m 2 d; d. 18 July
   1881 at Comac
WIEHL, Solomon - ca. 38 years; suicide 8 July
   1884 at Jamaica; resident of Williamsburgh
WIGGINS, Mrs. Bradley - suicide 29 January
   1886 at Southold; hanged herself in a barn
WIGGINS, Joseph E. -"young man"; funeral
   7 November 1887 at Riverhead
WIGGINS, Tredwell - 79 y 5 m 6 d; d. 10 July
   1884 at Melville
WIGHTMAN, Mark - 73 years; d. 14 March 1889 at
   Babylon; died during prayer meeting at
   Baptist Church; interment at Springfield

WIGHTMAN, Mrs. Mark - d. 10 July 1885; Babylon
item; interment at Springfield
WIGHTMAN, William - 45 years; d. 3 August 1888
at Greenlawn
WILLETS, Amy - 80 years; d. 28 March 1880 at
Northport
WILLETS, Daniel - 60 years; d. 27 July 1884 at
Jericho; note: called Daniel WILLIS in
Hicksville column 1 August 1884 paper
WILLETS, Mrs. George - d. "last week"; Hemp-
stead item; 2 July 1887 paper
WILLETS, Gloriana N. - d. at Washington,
D. C.; 10 March 1888 paper; funeral at
Bayside; daughter of Samuel B. Nicoll of
Shelter Island; wife of Robert Willets;
resident of Bayside
WILLETS, Samuel - 86 years; d. 6 (or 7) Febr-
uary 1883 at New York City; banker with
Willets & Company, Pearl Street, New York;
native of Westbury
WILLETS, Samuel - 49 years; d. 22 June 1886 at
Roslyn; former Supervisor Town of North
Hempstead
WILLETS, Mrs. Theodore - funeral 3 April 1887
at Brookville (Reformed Church); "young
woman with four small children"
WILLETS, William - drowned 20 January 1889 off
Cape Hateras, N. C.; schooner "Alice K.
Chester," owned by Jesse Carll of Northport,
sank
WILLETS, Mrs. William - d. 8 February 1890 at
Jericho; funeral at Westbury; daughter of
Israel Hewlett
WILLIAMS, Augustine - 59 yrs 2 mos; d. 9 April
1888 at Huntington; wife of George Williams
WILLIAMS, Carrie A. - 5 years; d. 21 December
1886 at Northport; daughter of Christopher
and Mary Williams
WILLIAMS, Edith Grace - 5 years; d. 14 March
1886 at Chicago, Illinois; daughter of S. L.
and Mary Ballagh Williams
WILLIAMS, Esther - d. 23 March 1885 at George-
town, Connecticut; wife of Gilbert P.
Williams
WILLIAMS, Frankie - 6 y 2 m 12 d; murdered 24
June 1888 at Cold Spring by Henry Soper,
called "half-witted"; son of James Williams

WILLIAMS, Gilbert Potter - 83 y 4 m 6 d;
  d. 11 April 1888 at Huntington; son of
  Gilbert Williams; husband of Lucinda Finch
  (m. ca. 1828); father of Mary Elizabeth
  Williams, Robert B. Williams and Martha
  Lucinda (Mrs. Thomas) Young; brother of
  Henry Williams, Samuel Freebody Williams,
  Stephen K. Williams and Sarah Elizabeth
  Williams; b. Huntington 5 December 1804
WILLIAMS, James - 68 years; d. 8 April 1886 at
  Huntington
WILLIAMS, John - murdered 14 May 1884 aboard
  ship anchored off Whitestone; interment at
  Flushing; resident of Nova Scotia, Canada
WILLIAMS, Martha M. - 41 y 1 m 15 d;
  d. 31 January 1882 at Northport; wife of
  John D. Williams
WILLIAMS, Mary - 80 years; d. 2 September 1890
  at Hempstead; interment at Westbury; "old
  and respected lady"
WILLIAMS, Mary Ballagh - d. "lately" at Chica-
  go, Illinois; 5 March 1886 paper; wife of
  Wesley Williams
WILLIAMS, Obadiah - d. 1 May 1878 on board
  ship off Stratford, Conn.; interment at
  Northport
WILLIAMS, Phoebe - 77 years; d. 21 September
  1889 at Head of the River, Smithtown; inter-
  ment at Northport; wife of William Williams;
  native of Centreport
WILLIAMS, Richard - 74 years; d. 26 September
  1889 at Riverhead
WILLIAMS, Susan A. - 79 years; d. 4 February
  1885 at Huntington
WILLIAMS, Walter - 13 years; drowned 31 July
  1890 at Centerport on a picnic with West
  Deer Park Sunday School
WILLIAMSON, Anna V. - 31 years; d. 8 October
  1881 at Maspeth; daughter of Rev. C. B.
  Ellsworth; wife of George A. Williamson
WILLIAMSON, Deborah - 74 years; d. 13 August
  1888 at Comac; wife of John Williamson
WILLIAMSON, Edwin - 13 years; drowned 26 July
  1884 at Sag Harbor; son of Wallace
  Williamson

WILLIAMSON, John - 91 years; d. 25 February
1878 at Stony Brook; builder of Setauket
Presbyterian Church in which his funeral was
held

WILLIS, Benjamin A. - d. 21 October 1886 at
New York City; interment at Westbury;
[re-interment at Woodlawn Cemetery, New York
City]; elected to U. S. Congress in 1874
[served 1875-1879 from a New York City dist-
rict]; [lawyer in New York City]; [served
with 119th New York during the Civil War];
[elected to the New York State Assembly
1872]; native of Roslyn [b. 24 March 1840]

WILLIS, Daniel - see: Daniel WILLETS

WILLIS, George - d. at Newark, N. J.; funeral
2 September 1890 at Hewletts; interment at
Hempstead; son of George Willis

WILLIS, Mrs. Valentine - d. 19 February 1890
at Mineola

WILMOT, child - death reported from diphtheria; 15 January 1887 paper; son of Postmaster Wilmot of Whitestone

WILSON, infant - interment 25 September 1889
at Bethpage; daughter of Isaac Wilson

WILSON, Mrs. Alexander - d. 22 May 1886 at
Corona; struck by lightning

WILSON, Alfred D. - 10 mos; d. 1 June 1880 at
Miller's Place; son of Frederick M. and
Maria L. Wilson

WILSON, Annie - 54 years; d. 2 August 1880 at
St. James; interment at Green-Wood, Brooklyn

WILSON, George - d. "last week" at Riverhead;
9 April 1887 paper

WILSON, John - drowned in Peconic Bay; body
found off Shelter Island; 31 July 1886 paper

WILSON, John - d. at Hempstead; 6 August 1887
paper; resident of Williamsburgh

WILSON, Lizzie Combes - 33 years; d. 7 September 1887 at Ravenswood; daughter of John and
Catherine Combes; wife of George B. Wilson;
former resident of Deer Park

WILSON, Lulu - 13 years; drowned in Jamaica
Bay off Canarsie; [date not copied]; resident of Brooklyn

WILSON, Miles - 36 years; d. 5 January 1882 at
Huntington; interment at Green-Wood, Brooklyn

WILSON, William - 84 yrs 3 mos; d. 7 September
1881 at Dix Hills
WILSON, William F. - 72 y 2 m 7 d; d. 15 December 1889 at Brooklyn; interment at Hunt-
ington
WINCKLER, Eva B. - 40 y 4 m 26 d; d. 10 February 1888 at Hicksville
WINES, J. Edward - drunk; fell into water and
drowned; inquest held 15 October 1888 at
Riverhead
WINKLER, Peter - 42 years; d. 12 July 1887 at
Jamaica; lockjaw from being bitten during a
fight
WINKS, Maria - 89 y 1 m 3 d; d. 7 February
1885 at Greenlawn
WINSTED, Margaret - 108 years; d. 9 July 1882
at Far Rockaway
WITMER, Mrs. - d. 14 September 1890; Syosset
item; sister of Theodore F. Lewis
WOLFAUDER, Conrad - 70 y 5 m 14 d; d. 8 August
1890 at Hicksville; "wood carver by trade"
WOLFAUGER, Mary - 28 years; d. 13 December
1889 at New York City
WOOD, Mrs. - d. 30 May 1884 at Glen Cove; died
after hearing that her son cut his hand;
mother of William Wood
WOOD, Brewster - d. 4 November 1884 at Brook-
lyn "of apoplexy"; son of Brewster Wood;
brother of William J. Wood, Edwin Wood and
George Wood; wholesale jewelry and real
estate businesses; native of Huntington
WOOD, Catherine M. - 63 y 8 m 14 d; d. 8 May
1883 at Huntington; wife of George C. Wood
WOOD, Charity - 72 years; d. 15 July 1878 at
Oyster Bay
WOOD, Charles - 88 y 5 m 12 d; d. 14 November
1888 at Huntington
WOOD, Daniel I. - 51 years; d. 6 June 1887 at
Northport; consumption; member of the
G. A. R.
WOOD, David - 88 y 9 m 22 d; d. 19 December
1883 at Greenlawn
WOOD, Eliza - 84 years; d. 6 September 1885 at
Huntington; wife of Charles Wood
WOOD, Ella - 21 yrs 4 mos; d. 15 December 1882
at Huntington; wife of George Wood

WOOD, Frederick - d. 3 November 1884 at Garden
City; lockjaw

WOOD, George - 6 years; d. 17 May 1886;
Smithtown item; son of S. Wood

WOOD, Grace L. - 2 yrs 10 mos; d. 14 February
1879 at Brooklyn

WOOD, Henrietta S. - 32 y 2 m 9 d; d. 7 May
1881 at Brooklyn; daughter of T. Smith Roe;
wife of J. H. Wood

WOOD, James - d. 2 June 1884 at East Northport

WOOD, Mrs. James - d. 29 April 1889 at Brooklyn; widow; former resident of Northport

WOOD, Dr. James R. - 65 y 6 m 20 d; d. 4 May
1882 at New York City

WOOD, John - 67 years; d. 20 December 1886 at
Sayville; former Supervisor Town of Islip;
former Suffolk County Clerk

WOOD, John F. - 61 yrs 18 days; d. 8 November
1890 at Huntington; son of John Wood and
Deborah Fleet; husband of Sarah A. Slote;
father of John F. Wood and Daniel Slote
Wood; former Supervisor Town of Huntington;
b. 21 October 1829; see 15 November 1890
paper for biography

WOOD, Josephine - 28 years; d. 5 October 1884
at Southold; clothing caught fire; daughter
of John Wood

WOOD, Lester Meade - 1 y 4 m 9 d; d. 15 June
1886 at Brooklyn

WOOD, Mabel A. - 1 y 1 m 19 d; d. 2 August
1883 at Brooklyn; granddaughter of William
Meade

WOOD, Maggie Boyd - 8 yrs 6 mos; d. 20 March
1881 at Huntington; daughter of John F. and
Sarah Wood

WOOD, Margaret E. - 54 years; d. 29 January
1881 at East Northport

WOOD, Nancy G. - 80 yrs 3 mos; d. 1 February
1882 at Northport

WOOD, Phebe H. - 82 y 2 m 19 d; d. 25 September 1880 at Huntington

WOOD, Ruth - 71 y 8 m 9 d; d. 16 June 1885 at
Huntington; daughter of Zebulon Titus; widow
of Edwin Wood (m. 1 February 1830); mother
of Matilda (Mrs. Jacob) Crossman, Mrs. William D. Woodend, Mrs. Henry Sammis and Mrs.

WOOD, Ruth (continued)
George Hendrickson; Presbyterian; b. Cold
Spring 7 September 1813
WOOD, Mrs. Samuel - d. 4 February 1885 at
Mineola; widow
WOOD, Sarah - 84 y 3 m 12 d; d. 17 July 1887
at Huntington; mother of Mrs. Joseph Pettit
WOOD, Sarah - 53 years; d. 7 October 1887 at
East Northport
WOOD, William Jayne - 71 y 9 m 4 d; d. 4 May
1883 at Huntington; son of Brewster and
Matilda Wood
WOOD, William M. - 42 y 1 m 5 d; d. 7 May 1883
at Huntington; son of George C. Wood
WOOD, William W. - 59 y 6 m 28 d; d. 9 April
1878 at Huntington; son of John Wood
WOODBURY, Edwin - suicide 23 July 1883 at
Amityville
WOODBURY, Mary Shelton Nicoll - d. 4 February
1890 at Knoxville, Tennessee; daughter of
William Nicoll of Islip; wife of Coryton M.
Woodbury; funeral at Islip
WOODCOCK, Felix Mendelsohn - 8 mos 20 days;
d. 17 October 1884 at Huntington; son of
William H. and Rosalie E. Woodcock
WOODEND, Calvin C. - 51 years; d. 20 September
1881 at Cold Spring
WOODHULL, Abby C. - ca. 27 years; d. -- Nov-
ember 1880 at New Preston, Conn.; wife of
Joel B. Woodhull; former resident of Rocky
Point
WOODHULL, Ann Eliza - 63 y 4 m 4 d; d. 4 June
1886 at Huntington; widow of J. Amherst
Woodhull
WOODHULL, Annette - 65 years; d. 26 June 1884
at Miller's Place
WOODHULL, Gaylord - 14 years; d. 24 August
1880 at Brooklyn; interment at Huntington;
son of Caleb and Fanny D. Woodhull
WOODHULL, Gilbert C. - d. 21 January 1879 at
Brooklyn; cousin of J. Amherst Woodhull and
Caleb H. Woodhull
WOODHULL, Henrietta - d. 12 July 1885 at Port
Jefferson; died in chair at supper table
WOODHULL, Jeffrey Amherst - 59 years;
d. 14 February 1881 at Huntington

WOODHULL, John J. - d. 15 January 1889 at
Riverhead; hit by railroad train at Manor
on 14 January 1889; funeral at Wading River
WOODHULL, Sylvester - suicide; hanged himself;
11 December 1886 paper; resident of Wading
River
WOODRUFF, Rev. George W. - 60 years; d. "last
week" at Brooklyn; 24 March 1882 paper;
Methodist minister since 1845; served
Greenport, Riverhead and Flatbush M. E.
Churches as well as numerous churches in
Brooklyn, New York City and Connecticut;
native of New York City
WOODRUFF, Herman - "nearly 80" years;
d. 19 October 1887 at Greenport; constable
for 46 years
WOODRUFF, Jesse - d. 30 January 1886 at
Bridgehampton
WOODWARD, Elizabeth - 86 years; d. 2 August
1884 at Huntington
WOOLSEY, Ida W. - d. 17 February 1889 at
Cambridge, Illinois; daughter of William S.
and Sarah Woolsey
WOOLSEY, Lettie - 86 y 9 m 4 d; d. 26 November
1887 at Huntington
WORDIN, Clarissa - 72 years; d. 16 December
1883 at Cold Spring Harbor; wandered off and
died of exposure to cold weather; mother of
Mrs. George Mehan, Mrs. Thomas Barnes, Mrs.
Henry Gardiner and Juliette Wordin
WORDIN, George W. - 74 y 1 m 10 d; d. 28 Dec-
ember 1883 at Cold Spring
WORTH, J. L. - 66 years; d. 29 August 1879 at
Islip
WORTHINGTON, Mary C. - 48 years; d. 25 January
1885 at Shelter Island
WRIGHT, Albert - funeral at Oyster Bay (Bap-
tist Church); 6 February 1885 paper
WRIGHT, Bert - d. 28 January 1885 at Amity-
ville; resident of Oyster Bay
WRIGHT, Charity - 85 years; d. 25 January 1881
at Oyster Bay
WRIGHT, Mrs. Charles - funeral 30 March 1889
at Riverhead; daughter of Henry Griffing
WRIGHT, Edna May - 3 y 4 m 25 d; d. 20 October
1885 at Cold Spring; daughter of James and
Mary E. Wright

WRIGHT, F. A. - death reported; 1 October 1887
paper; Glen Cove item; father of J. W.
Wright
WRIGHT, George Walter - 15 y 9 m 1 d;
d. 2 September 1883 at Oyster Bay Cove; son
of John C. and Julia E. Wright
WRIGHT, James H. - d. 19 May 1883 at Hemp-
stead; artist
WRIGHT, John - 2 July 1880 paper; resident of
Glen Cove; "Seawanhaka" fire on East River
WRIGHT, Mary E. - 90 years; d. 12 January 1889
at Glen Cove; dress caught fire
WRIGHT, Sarah - 82 years; d. 1 March 1878 at
Oyster Bay
WRIGHT, Stephen - d. "last week" at Babylon;
11 December 1885 paper
WYCKHOFF, Mr. - suicide 6 August 1883 at
Gravesend
WYCKHOFF, Rev. Peter T. - d. 15 September 1890
at Hempstead; interment at Somerville, New
Jersey; brother of Mrs. Rev. J. A. Davis;
resident of Newark, New Jersey
WYLIE, Margaret - 93 year; d. 18 April 1890 at
Hicksville; sister-in-law of George Kay
WYMAN, Lizzie - 10 years; drowned 10 August
1886 at Breeze Point; daughter of Henry
Wyman of Far Rockaway
WYMAN, Nellie - 12 years; drowned 10 August
1886 at Breeze Point; daughter of Henry
Wyman of Far Rockaway
YATES, S. W. - found 28 November 1885 frozen
in a boat on beach at Baiting Hollow; stu-
dent at Yale College; on hunting trip; wind
blew boat across Long Island Sound and he
died of exposure; his father a banker at
Omaha, Nebraska; [student was Warren Samuel
Yates, son of Henry Whitfield Yates of
Omaha, who was b. St. Mary's County, Md.;
see St. Mary's Beacon 3 December and
10 December 1885 for more on the event]
YOUNG, child - d. 19 June 1887 at Hempstead;
interment at Riverhead; son of Willis H.
Young
YOUNG, Charlie B. - 5 years; d. 15 March 1883
at Brooklyn

YOUNG, Mrs. Daniel T. - d. 28 August 1879 at
Brooklyn; sister-in-law of William H.
Skidmore of Huntington; member of choir at
Plymouth Church, Brooklyn; native of Wading
River
YOUNG, Elizabeth - 73 y 4 m 10 d; d. 6 January
1881 at West Hills
YOUNG, Henry I. - 80 years; d. 19 February
1889 at Oyster Bay Cove; interment at Green-
Wood, Brooklyn
YOUNG, James H. - d. 30 January 1880 at
Aquebogue; lockjaw
YOUNG, John H. - 48 years; d. 2 November 1883
at Smithtown Branch
YOUNG, John Henry - 45 years; d. 15 May 1878
at Poughkeepsie, N. Y.; farmer at Mutton-
town; deranged; sent to Poughkeepsie Asylum
YOUNG, Lewis - 67 years; d. 1 June 1888 at
Baiting Hollow
YOUNG, Margaret B. - d. 14 January 1887 at
Brooklyn; wife of Anson S. Young
YOUNG, Thomas P. - 73 y 10 m 23 d;
d. 10 August 1880 at Franklinville
YOUNG, Warren - d. 23 March 1888 at Baiting
Hollow
YOUNGS, Bert - 19 years; d. 24 July 1890 at
Far Rockaway; struck by lightning
YOUNGS, Daniel T. - 68 years; d. 24 May 1878
at Oyster Bay; had sugar business in New
York City
YOUNGS, David Jones - 63 years; d. 4 May 1881
at Oyster Bay
YOUNGS, Graham - interment 30 January 1887 at
Oyster Bay Cove; son of Thomas F. Youngs
YOUNGS, Samuel - d. 28 or 29 December 1890 at
Oyster Bay; went to California in 1849 Gold
Rush; returned to Oyster Bay in 1884
YOUNGS, Thomas F. - d. 3 March 1883 at Oyster
Bay; shipping merchant with Youngs & Comp-
any, South Street, New York City; warden at
Christ Church, Oyster Bay
YOUNGS, Mrs. William J. - d. at Oyster Bay
Cove; 11 January 1884 paper; daughter of
David J. Youngs; granddaughter of Dr. James
C. Townsend

YOUNGS, Mrs. William J. - d. 22 March 1889 at
   Oyster Bay
ZEIGLER, Susan - d. 20 September 1886 at
   Hicksville; resident of New York City
ZERS, Charles - drowned 5 September 1886 at
   Flushing
ZIEGLER, John - 33 years; drowned 30 July 1887
   in Peter Neck Bay, Orient; squall upset his
   boat
ZORAMBISKI, --- - stabbed 10 April 1886 and
   "since died" at Winfield

LONG ISLAND GAZETTEER

SUFFOLK COUNTY

During the years 1878 to 1890, Suffolk
County was divided into ten towns. These are
the same ten towns into which the county is
divided in 1996. Generally speaking, the
boundaries of the ten towns are the same in
1996 as they were in the years 1878 to 1890.
There is one major boundary change which could
affect genealogical research in Suffolk County
and it must be noted by the genealogist. In
1886, Lloyd's Neck was annexed by the Town of
Huntington from the Town of Oyster Bay, then
in Queens County. The researcher must keep in
mind that records about residents of Lloyd's
Neck may be found in Town of Oyster Bay and
Queens County sources, especially for the
years prior to the annexation of the area by
the Town of Huntington.

Because some communities are located at
the edge of a town, it might be necessary for
the researcher to check the records of more
than one town or county. In cases where this
situation is especially important to notice,
a * has been placed next to that community's
name and a notation has been made in the notes
section immediately following. When a community has changed its name or spelling, a + has
been placed next to its name and the modern
name or spelling is given in the notes section. Special situations are marked by a # and
are explained in the notes section.

TOWN OF BABYLON

        Amityville *   Gilgo Inlet
        Babylon   Great South Bay *
        Breslau +   North Babylon
        Deer Park   West Babylon
        Fire Island *   Wyandance +
        Fire Island Inlet *

267

Notes: * Amityville borders on Oyster Bay
            Town, Queens County.
          * Fire Island extends eastward into
            Islip and Brookhaven Towns.
          * Fire Island Inlet is partly in Islip
            Town.
          * Great South Bay extends eastward
            into Islip and Brookhaven Towns.
          + Breslau is now Lindenhurst.
          + Wyandance is currently spelled
            Wyandanch.

TOWN OF BROOKHAVEN

Artist Lake	Moriches
Bellport	Mount Sinai
Centre/Center	New Village +
Moriches +	Old Field #
Crane Neck Beach	Patchogue
East Moriches	Port Jefferson
East Patchogue	Rocky Point
East Setauket	Ronkonkoma *
Fire Island *	Selden
Great South Bay *	Setauket
Holtsville	Setauket Bay
Lake Grove	Smith's Point
Lake Ronkonkoma *	South Haven
Manor +	South Setauket
Manorville	Stony Brook
Mastic	Waverly +
Mastic Neck	Woodville +
Middle Island	Yaphank #
Miller's Place +	

Notes: * Fire Island extends westward into
            Islip and Babylon Towns.
          * Great South Bay extends westward
            into Islip and Babylon Towns.
          * Lake Ronkonkoma and Ronkonkoma may
            refer to areas in Smithtown and/or
            Islip Towns.
          + Center Moriches is the modern
            spelling.
          + Manor is now Manorville.
          + Miller's Place is now Miller Place.
          + New Village is now Lake Grove

+ Waverly is now Holtsville.
+ Woodville is now Shoreham.
# Old Field should not be confused with Old Fields in Huntington Town.
# Many deaths listed in Yaphank were for inmates of the Suffolk County Alms House. Most of these people probably did not live in Yaphank during most of their lifetimes and it may be necessary to search elsewhere in Suffolk County for records of these people.

TOWN OF EAST HAMPTON

Amagansett	Montauk
East Hampton	Montauk Point
Freetown	Northwest
Gardiner's Island	Sag Harbor *

Notes: * Sag Harbor extends into Southampton Town.

TOWN OF HUNTINGTON

Centreport +	Huntington Harbor +
Centreport Cove +	Huntington Station
Clay Pitts +	Little Neck #
Cold Spring * +	Lloyd's Neck #
Cold Spring Harbor *	Long Swamp +
Comac * +	Lower Melville *
Crab Meadow	Melville
Dix Hills	Middleville *
East Neck	North Dix Hills
East Northport	Northport
Eaton's Neck	Old Fields +
Elwood	Pigeon Hill +
Fresh Pond * + #	Port Eaton +
Frog Pond +	Round Swamp *
Greenlawn	South Comac * +
Half Hollow Hills *	South Dix Hills
Half Hollows	Sweet Hollow +
Huntington	Vernon Valley
Huntington Bay	West Hills
Huntington Depot +	West Neck

Notes: * Cold Spring and Cold Spring Harbor
           border on Oyster Bay Town, Queens
           County and extend into that Town.
         * Comac and South Comac are located in
           both Smithtown and Huntington Towns.
         * Fresh Pond is located in both Smith-
           town and Huntington Towns.
         * Half Hollow Hills and Half Hollows
           border on Babylon Town.
         * Lower Melville borders on Babylon
           Town.
         * Middleville is located in both
           Smithtown and Huntington Towns.
         * Round Swamp borders on Oyster Bay
           Town, Queens County.
         + Centreport is now spelled Center-
           port.
         + Clay Pitts is located in the East
           Northport area.
         + Cold Spring is now Cold Spring Har-
           bor. This name should not be confus-
           ed with Cold Spring on the Hudson
           River in Putnam County, New York.
         + Comac is now spelled Commack.
         + Fresh Pond is Fort Salonga.
         + Frog Pond may be located in the
           South Huntington area.
         + Huntington Depot is now Huntington
           Station.
         + Huntington Harbor would include the
           area now called Halesite.
         + Long Swamp is located in the South
           Huntington area.
         + Old Fields is now Greenlawn and
           should not be confused with Old
           Field in Brookhaven Town.
         + Pigeon Hill is located in the South
           Huntington area.
         + Port Eaton is located on Eaton's
           Neck.
         + Sweet Hollow is now Melville.
         # Fresh Pond should not be confused
           with Fresh Pond in Newtown Town,
           Queens County.
         # Little Neck should not be confused
           with Little Neck in Flushing Town,
           Queens County.

Lloyd's Neck was annexed to Hunting-
ton Town in 1886 from Oyster Bay
Town, Queens County. All events 1886
and earlier would be found in Oyster
Bay and Queens County sources,
rather than Huntington Town and
Suffolk County sources.

TOWN OF ISLIP

Bay Shore   Great South Bay *
Bayport   Hauppauge *
Bohemiaville +   Islip
Brentwood   Lakeland
Central Islip   Ronkonkoma *
Fire Island *   Sayville
Fire Island Inlet * West Islip
Great River

Notes: * Fire Island extends westward into
          Babylon Town and eastward into
          Brookhaven town.
        * Fire Island Inlet is partly in
          Babylon Town.
        * Great South Bay extends westward
          into Babylon Town and eastward into
          Brookhaven Town.
        * Hauppauge is located in both Islip
          and Smithtown Towns.
        * Ronkonkoma may include areas in
          Brookhaven and/or Smithtown Towns.
        + Bohemiaville is now Bohemia.

TOWN OF RIVERHEAD

Aquebogue   Northville
Baiting Hollow   Peconic Bay *
Calverton   Riverhead *
Franklinville * +   Wading River *
Jamesport

Notes: * Franklinville is located in both
          Riverhead and Southold Towns.
        * Peconic Bay extends eastward into
          Southold and Southampton Towns.

271

* Riverhead is located on the border
  of Southampton Town and extends into
  that Town.
* Wading River is located on the
  border of Brookhaven Town and
  extends into that Town.
+ Franklinville is now Laurel.

TOWN OF SHELTER ISLAND

Shelter Island

TOWN OF SMITHTOWN

Bread & Cheese	St. Johnland +
Hollow *	St. Johnsland +
Comac * +	Smithtown
Fresh Pond * + #	Smithtown Branch +
Hauppauge *	Smithtown Landing
Head of the River	South Comac * +
Middleville *	Sunk Meadow +
Nissequogue	Sunk Meadow Creek +
Ronkonkoma *	Sunken Meadow
St. James	

Notes: * Bread & Cheese Hollow borders on
          Huntington Town.
        * Comac and South Comac are located in
          both Smithtown and Huntington Towns.
        * Fresh Pond is located in both Smith-
          town and Huntington Towns.
        * Hauppauge is located in both Smith-
          town and Islip Towns.
        * Middleville is located in both
          Smithtown and Huntington Towns.
        * Ronkonkoma may include areas in
          Islip and/or Brookhaven Towns.
        + Comac is now spelled Commack.
        + Fresh Pond is now Fort Salonga.
        + St. Johnland/St. Johnsland is in the
          Kings Park area.
        + Smithtown Branch is now the Village
          of the Branch
        + Sunk Meadow is now spelled Sunken
          Meadow

Fresh Pond is not to be confused with Fresh Pond in Newtown Town, Queens County.

TOWN OF SOUTHAMPTON

Atlanticville +
Bridgehampton
Flanders
Good Ground +
North Sea
Peconic Bay *
Poospatuck
Quogue
Sag Harbor *
Sarbonac +

Shinnecock
Shinnecock Bay
Shinnecock
   Reservation
Southampton
Speonk
Tianna
Water Mill
Westhampton

Notes: * Peconic Bay extends northward into Riverhead and Southold Towns.
    * Sag Harbor is located in both Southampton and East Hampton Towns.
    + Atlanticville is now East Quogue.
    + Good Ground is now Hampton Bays.
    + Sarbonac is now spelled Sebonac.

TOWN OF SOUTHOLD

Arshamamoque +
Cutchogue
East Marion
Fisher's Island
Franklinville * +
Greenport
Mattituck
Mattituck Creek

Oregon
Orient
Orient Point
Peconic
Peconic Bay *
Plum Island
Robins Island
Southold

Notes: * Franklinville is located in both Southold and Riverhead Towns.
    * Peconic Bay extends southward into Southampton Town and westward into Riverhead Town.
    + Arshamamoque is now spelled Arshamonaque.
    + Franklinville is now Laurel.

QUEENS COUNTY

During the years 1878 to 1890, Queens
County was divided into six towns and one
city. Major changes have occurred in Queens
County geography which the genealogist must
follow. In 1886, Lloyd's Neck, a part of the
Town of Oyster Bay, was annexed to the Town of
Huntington in Suffolk County. In 1898, the
western part of Queens County was annexed by
the City of New York and was organized as the
Borough of Queens. The City of Long Island
City and the Towns of Newtown, Flushing and
Jamaica plus the Rockaway Peninsula of Hempstead Town became the Borough of Queens and
kept the name Queens County. In 1899, the
remaining areas of old Queens County were
organized as Nassau County. The Towns of
Oyster Bay, without Lloyd's Neck, Hempstead,
without the Rockaway Peninsula, and North
Hempstead now form Nassau County. These
boundary changes and annexations are important
to understand.

The listing below shows the status in the
years 1878 to 1890, both before and after the
annexation of Lloyd's Neck to Suffolk County
in 1886 but before the creation of the Borough
of Queens and Nassau County. The modern cities
of Long Beach and Glen Cove were not established until much later than the period covered by this work and are included in the Towns
of Hempstead and Oyster Bay, respectively.

Please see the introduction to Suffolk
County for the use of the codes * + #.

TOWN OF FLUSHING

Bayside	Hinsdale * +
Black Stump +	Little Neck #
College Point	Whitestone
Douglaston	Whitestone Point
Flushing	

Notes: * Hinsdale is located in both Flushing
         and Hempstead Towns.
       + Black Stump is now Fresh Meadows.
       + Hinsdale is now Bellerose and Floral
         Park.
       # Little Neck is not to be confused
         with Little Neck in Huntington Town,
         Suffolk County.

TOWN OF HEMPSTEAD

Baldwins +	Meadow Brook
Bellmore	Merrick
Breeze Point +	Newbridge +
East Meadow	Northwest Point +
East Rockaway	Norwood
Elmont	Oceanville +
Far Rockaway	Pearsalls +
Floral Park	Ridgewood +
Foster's Meadow * +	Rockaway +
Freeport	Rockaway Beach
Garden City	Rockaway Inlet *
Hempstead	Rockville Centre
Hempstead Bay	Seaford
Hewletts	Smithville +
Hinsdale * +	Smithville South +
Island Trees	Uniondale
Jerusalem +	Valley Stream
Jerusalem South +	Washington Square +
Lawrence	Westville +
Long Beach	Woodsburgh

Notes: * Foster's Meadow is located on the
         border of Jamaica Town and extends
         into that Town.
       * Hinsdale is located in both Hemp-
         stead and Flushing Towns.
       * Rockaway Inlet is located between
         Hempstead Town, Queens County and
         Flatlands and New Lots Towns, Kings
         County
       + Baldwins is now spelled Baldwin.
       + Breeze Point is probably Breezy
         Point.
       + Foster's Meadow is now Elmont.
       + Hewletts is now spelled Hewlett.

275

+ Hinsdale is now Bellerose and Floral
  Park.
+ Jerusalem and Jerusalem South are
  located in southern Levittown and
  North Wantagh.
+ Newbridge is now Bellmore.
+ Northwest Point is located in the
  Inwood area.
+ Norwood is now Malverne.
+ Oceanville may be what is now Ocean-
  side
+ Ridgewood is now Wantagh and should
  not be confused with Ridgewood in
  Newtown Town.
+ Rockaway might be either the entire
  Rockaway Peninsula or the community
  of Lawrence.
+ Smithville and Smithville South are
  now North Bellmore.
+ Washington Square is now West Hemp-
  stead.
+ Westville is now Inwood.

TOWN OF JAMAICA

Clarenceville +	South Woodhaven +
Jamaica	Springfield +
Jamaica Bay *	Union Course +
Morris Grove +	Unionville +
Queens +	West Jamaica
Richmond Hill	Woodhaven
South Jamaica	

Notes: * Jamaica Bay extends westward into
          New Lots and Flatlands Towns, Kings
          County and southward to Hempstead
          Town, Queens County.
        + Clarenceville is located in the
          Hollis area.
        + Morris Grove is now Morris Park.
        + Queens is now Queens Village.
        + South Woodhaven is in the Ozone
          Park area.
        + Springfield is now Springfield
          Gardens.
        + Union Course and Unionville are in
          the Woodhaven area.

CITY OF LONG ISLAND CITY

Astoria	Long Island City
Dutch Kills	Newtown Creek *
Hunter's Point	Ravenswood

Notes: * Newtown Creek extends eastward along the border of Newtown Town, Queens County and the City of Brooklyn, Kings County.

TOWN OF NEWTOWN

Bowery Bay +	Laurel Hill +
Bowery Bay Beach +	Maspeth
Corona	Middle Village
Cypress Hills	Newtown
East Williamsburgh +	Newtown Creek *
Fresh Pond #	Ridgewood #
Glen Dale +	Winfield +
Hopedale * +	Woodside

Notes: * Hopedale borders on Jamaica Town.
* Newtown Creek forms the border between Newtown Town and the City of Long Island City, Queens County and the City of Brooklyn, Kings County.
+ Bowery Bay is now in the La Guardia Airport area.
+ East Williamsburgh is located in the Maspeth-Middle Village area.
+ Glen Dale is now spelled Glendale.
+ Hopedale is now Kew Gardens.
+ Laurel Hill is located in the Sunnyside area.
+ Newtown is now Elmhurst.
+ Winfield is located between Woodside, Maspeth and Newtown.
# Fresh Pond is not to be confused with Fresh Pond in Huntington and Smithtown Towns, Suffolk County.
# Ridgewood is not to be confused with Ridgewood in Hempstead Town.

TOWN OF NORTH HEMPSTEAD

Cow Bay +	Mineola *
East Williston	New Castle +
Flower Hill	New Cassel
Great Neck	Old Westbury
Greenvale *	Port Washington
Herricks	Red Ground +
Hyde Park * +	Roslyn
Lakeville +	Sands Point
Manhasset	Searingtown
Manhasset Valley	Westbury *

Notes: * Greenvale borders on Oyster Bay
          Town.
        * Hyde Park borders on Hempstead
          Town.
        * Mineola borders on Hempstead
          Town.
        * Westbury borders on Hempstead
          Town.
        + Cow Bay is now Manhasset Bay.
        + Hyde Park is now New Hyde Park and
          should not be confused with Hyde
          Park in Dutchess County, New York.
        + Lakeville is now Lake Success.
        + New Cassel is the modern spelling.
        + Red Ground is located in the East
          Hills - Old Westbury area.

TOWN OF OYSTER BAY

Bayville	Glen Cove
Bedelltown +	Glen Cove Landing +
Bethpage +	Glenwood +
Bethpage Junction +	Glenwood Landing
Brookville	Greenvale *
Cedar Swamp +	Hicksville
Central Park +	Jericho
Centre Island	Lattingtown
Cold Spring * +	Laurelton +
Cold Spring Harbor *	Lloyd's Neck #
Cooper's Bluff	Locust Valley
Dosoris	Manetto Hill +
East Norwich	Mannetto Hill +
Farmingdale	Matinnecock

Mill Hill +
Mill Neck
Muttontown
Oyster Bay
Oyster Bay Cove #
Pine Hollow +
Plain Edge +
Plain View +

Plainview
Sea Cliff
South Glen Cove
South Oyster Bay +
Syosset
Wheatley
Woodbury

Notes: * Cold Spring and Cold Spring Harbor
        are located in Huntington Town,
        Suffolk County and extend into
        Oyster Bay Town.
      * Greenvale is located on the border
        of North Hempstead Town.
      + Bedelltown is located in the north
        part of modern Bethpage.
      + Bethpage is now Old Bethpage.
      + Bethpage Junction is the area around
        the Bethpage railroad station.
      + Cedar Swamp is the Glen Head - Old
        Brookville area
      + Central Park is what is now Bethpage
        and should not be confused with the
        famous Central Park in Manhattan.
      + Cold Spring is now Cold Spring Har-
        bor and should not be confused with
        Cold Spring on the Hudson River in
        Putnam County, New York.
      + Glen Cove Landing is located within
        Glen Cove.
      + Glenwood is now Glenwood Landing.
      + Laurelton is now Laurel Hollow.
      + Manetto Hill is the modern spelling
        and the area is now Plainview.
      + Mill Hill is located northwest of
        Oyster Bay village.
      + Pine Hollow is located between
        Oyster Bay village and East Norwich.
      + Plainedge is the modern spelling.
      + Plainview is the modern spelling.
      + South Oyster Bay is now Massapequa.
      # Lloyd's Neck was annexed to Hunting-
        ton Town, Suffolk County in 1886.
      # Oyster Bay Cove is called "The Cove"
        in many newspaper citations.

KINGS COUNTY

During the years 1878 to 1886, Kings County was divided into the City of Brooklyn and five towns. In 1886, the Town of New Lots was annexed to the City of Brooklyn. During the 1890's the remaining four "county towns" of Kings County were annexed to the City of Brooklyn: New Utrecht, Gravesend and Flatbush Towns in 1894 and Flatlands Town in 1896. By 1896, the City of Brooklyn covered the same territory as Kings County. In 1898, the City of Brooklyn and all of Kings County were annexed to the City of New York and organized as the Borough of Brooklyn. It is important for the genealogist to follow these annexations.

CITY OF BROOKLYN

Brooklyn   Newtown Creek *
Brooklyn, E. D. +   South Brooklyn
East New York #   Williamsburgh
Greenpoint

Notes: * Newtown Creek is the border between the City of Brooklyn, Kings County and Newtown Town and Long Island City, Queens County.
        + The "Eastern District" were formerly separate Bushwick and Williamsburgh, annexed to Brooklyn by 1855.
        # East New York and New Lots Town were annexed to Brooklyn in 1886.

TOWN OF FLATBUSH

Flatbush

TOWN OF FLATLANDS

Flatlands   Jamaica Bay *

Notes: * Jamaica Bay extends into New Lots Town, Kings County and the Queens County Towns of Jamaica and Hempstead.

TOWN OF GRAVESEND

Brighton Beach	Manhattan Beach
Coney Island	Sheepshead Bay
Gravesend	

TOWN OF NEW LOTS

East New York	Jamaica Bay *

Notes: * Jamaica Bay extends into Flatlands
Town, Kings County and the Queens
County Towns of Jamaica and Hemp-
stead.

    # The Town of New Lots was annexed to
the City of Brooklyn in 1886.

TOWN OF NEW UTRECHT

Bath Beach

UNPLACED LONG ISLAND LOCATIONS

Cedar Springs
    Possibly a typo error for Cedar Swamp,
    Oyster Bay Town, Queens County
Gold Coin City
    Totally unknown reference. It is
    possible that Gold Coin City was in
    the Westbury area of present-day
    Nassau County, but this is uncertain.

NEW YORK STATE GAZETTEER

All New York State locations mentioned, except for those in the three Long Island counties of Suffolk, Queens and Kings, are in this listing by county only.

ALBANY COUNTY

    Albany

BROOME COUNTY

    Binghamton

CAYUGA COUNTY

    Auburn
    Weedsport

COLUMBIA COUNTY

    Hudson
    Lebanon Springs
    Livingston
    New Lebanon

DUTCHESS COUNTY

    Carthage Landing
    Fishkill Landing
    Pleasant Valley
    Poughkeepsie
    Rhinebeck

LIVINGSTON COUNTY

    Dansville

NEW YORK COUNTY

    Blackwell's Island +
    Governor's Island
    Harlem
    Morrisania +

ALLEGANY COUNTY

    Canaseraga

CATTARAUGUS COUNTY

    Sinclairsville

CHEMUNG COUNTY

    Chemung
    Dry Brook
    Elmira

DELAWARE COUNTY

    Delhi
    Lumberville

ERIE COUNTY

    Buffalo

GENESEE COUNTY

    Linden

MONTGOMERY COUNTY

    Fort Plain
    St. Johnsville

    New York City
    Randall's Island
    West Farms * +

Notes: In 1874, part of Westchester County west of the Bronx River was annexed to New York City and County. This area became part of Bronx Borough in 1898 and Bronx County in 1914

* West Farms bordered on Westchester County
+ Blackwell's Island is now Roosevelt Island
+ Morrisania is now in Bronx County.
+ West Farms is now in Bronx County.

NIAGARA COUNTY

Niagara Falls

ONONDAGA COUNTY

Skaneateles Lake

ORANGE COUNTY

Florida
Goshen
Highland Mills
Middletown
Newburgh
Salisbury Mills
West Point

RENSSELAER COUNTY

Bath-on-Hudson
Lansingburgh

ROCKLAND COUNTY

Haverstraw
Nyack
Sparkill

SCHUYLER COUNTY

Watkins

ONEIDA COUNTY

Rome
Utica

ONTARIO COUNTY

Geneva

OSWEGO COUNTY

Mexico

PUTNAM COUNTY

Patterson
Red Mills

RICHMOND COUNTY

New Dorp
Staten Island
West New Brighton

SARATOGA COUNTY

Mount Mc Gregor

SENECA COUNTY

Willard

ULSTER COUNTY
    Broadhead Bridge   Kingston
    Marlborough   Rondout/Roundout
    Stone Ridge

WESTCHESTER COUNTY

    City Island +   Scarsdale
    Mount Pleasant   Sing Sing +
    New Rochelle   Tarrytown Heights
    Peekskill   West Farms * +
    Port Chester   White Plains
    Rye   Yonkers
    Rye Point

Notes: In 1874, part of Westchester County
        west of the Bronx River was annexed to
        New York City and County. In 1895,
        part of Westchester County east of the
        Bronx River was annexed to New York
        City and County. These two annexations
        were organized in 1898 as Bronx
        Borough. In 1914, this area became
        Bronx County.
        *   West Farms was annexed to New York
            County in 1874 and bordered on
            Westchester County.
        +   City Island is now in Bronx County.
        +   Sing Sing is now Ossining
        +   West Farms is now in Bronx County.

UNITED STATES GAZETTEER

This listing includes all localities in the
United States, except for those in New York
State or on Long Island, which were mentioned
in the deaths found in the Long Islander from
1878 to 1890. This listing shows location by
present [1996] counties. Researchers should
check sources to learn if there have been
changes in county borders or the creation of
new counties which could effect their research
in these states. No attempt has been made to
do so in this listing.

CALIFORNIA
    SAN DIEGO COUNTY: San Diego
    SAN FRANCISCO COUNTY: San Francisco
    SANTA CLARA COUNTY: San Jose

COLORADO
    DENVER COUNTY: Denver
    PUEBLO COUNTY: Pueblo

CONNECTICUT
    FAIRFIELD COUNTY: Bethel, Bridgeport
      Danbury, East Norwalk, Five Mile River,
      Georgetown, Green's Farms, Huntington,
      Norwalk, Redding Centre, Rowayton,
      South Norwalk, Southport, Stamford,
      Stratford, Westport
    HARTFORD COUNTY: East Hartford, Windsor
    LITCHFIELD COUNTY: New Preston, North-
      field
    MIDDLESEX COUNTY: Haddam, Middletown,
      Saybrook
    NEW HAVEN COUNTY: Birmingham, Guilford,
      New Haven, Wallingford, Yatesville #
      # Probable typo for Yalesville
    NEW LONDON COUNTY: Bozrahville, Colches-
      ter, Griswold, New London, Norwich,
      Stonington, Waterford
    WINDHAM COUNTY: South Hampton

DISTRICT OF COLUMBIA
    Washington, D. C.

FLORIDA
    ALACHUA COUNTY: Gainesville
    BREVARD COUNTY: Cape Canaveral
    DUVALL COUNTY: Arlington, Jacksonville
    MONROE COUNTY: Key West
    PUTNAM COUNTY: Crescent City
    ST. JOHN'S COUNTY: St. Augustine
    unplaced: Grahamsville

GEORGIA
    FULTON COUNTY: Atlanta

ILLINOIS
    COOK COUNTY: Chicago
    DU PAGE COUNTY: Warrensville
    HENRY COUNTY: Cambridge, Galva
    LEE COUNTY: South Paw Paw

INDIANA
    MARION COUNTY: Indianapolis

KANSAS
    CHEROKEE COUNTY: Baxter Springs
    MIAMI COUNTY: Paolo +
    + now spelled Paola

KENTUCKY
    JEFFERSON COUNTY: Louisville
    KENTON COUNTY: Covington
    MORGAN COUNTY

LOUISIANA
    ORLEANS PARISH: New Orleans

MAINE
    CUMBERLAND COUNTY: Portland
    KENNEBEC COUNTY: Gardiner
    PENOBSCOT COUNTY: Corinna
    SAGADAHOC COUNTY: Bath
    YORK COUNTY: Lebanon

MARYLAND
    BALTIMORE CITY: Baltimore
    ST. MARY'S COUNTY: Wicomico River *
        * extends into Charles County
    Chesapeake Bay *
        * extends into Virginia

MASSACHUSETTS
    BARNSTABLE COUNTY: Chatham
    BRISTOL COUNTY: Fall River, Nonquitt,
        North Brattleboro #, Taunton
        # Probable typo for North Attleboro
    ESSEX COUNTY: Lynn
    HAMDEN COUNTY: Springfield
    HAMPSHIRE COUNTY: Amherst
    MIDDLESEX COUNTY: Cambridge
    NANTUCKET COUNTY: Nantucket
    NORFOLK COUNTY: Milton
    SUFFOLK COUNTY: Boston, Chelsea, East
        Boston
    WORCESTER COUNTY: Worcester

MICHIGAN
    BRANCH COUNTY: Coldwater

MINNESOTA
    MEEKER COUNTY: Litchfield

MISSOURI
    ST. LOUIS CITY: St. Louis

MONTANA
    ? Butter City
    Perhaps a typo for Butte City. Is this
    present Butte, Montana?

NEBRASKA
    DOUGLAS COUNTY: Omaha
    RICHARDSON COUNTY: Humboldt

NEW HAMPSHIRE
    CHESHIRE COUNTY: Walpole

NEW JERSEY
    ATLANTIC COUNTY: Atlantic City
    BERGEN COUNTY: Fairview, Fort Lee, New
        Bridge, Ridgewood, Tenafly
    CAMDEN COUNTY: Camden
    ESSEX COUNTY: Bloomfield, East Orange,
        Montclair, Newark, Orange, Orange
        Mountains
    HUDSON COUNTY: Arlington, Bayonne,
        Bayonne City, Harrison, Hoboken,
        Jersey City, Jersey City Heights

HUNTERDON COUNTY: Lambertville, Mount
    Pleasant, Stockton
MERCER COUNTY: Princeton, Trenton
MIDDLESEX COUNTY: Evona, New Brunswick,
    Perth Amboy, Stelton
MONMOUTH COUNTY: Long Branch, Neversink,
    Rumson
MORRIS COUNTY: Morris Plains
OCEAN COUNTY: Lakewood
SOMERSET COUNTY: Clover Hill, Finderne,
    North Plainfield, Somerville
UNION COUNTY: Elizabeth, New Providence,
    Plainfield, Union, Westfield

NEW MEXICO
    SANTA FE COUNTY: Santa Fe

NORTH CAROLINA
    BRUNSWICK COUNTY: Frying Pan Shoals +
    + Located off Cape Fear in Atlantic
        Ocean
    DARE COUNTY: Cape Hatteras
    HALIFAX COUNTY: Weldon
    NEW HANOVER COUNTY: Wilmington

OHIO
    LUCAS COUNTY: Toledo
    SANDUSKY COUNTY: Fremont
    WAYNE COUNTY: Fredericksburgh

PENNSYLVANIA
    BERKS COUNTY: Reading
    CAMBRIA COUNTY: Johnstown
    DAUPHIN COUNTY: Millersburg
    DELAWARE COUNTY: Chester
    FRANKLIN COUNTY: Chambersburg
    LACKAWANNA COUNTY: Scranton
    MC KEAN COUNTY: Bradford
    MONTGOMERY COUNTY
    PHILADELPHIA COUNTY: Frankford, Phila-
        delphia
    YORK COUNTY: York

RHODE ISLAND
    NEWPORT COUNTY: Newport
    WASHINGTON COUNTY: Block Island

SOUTH CAROLINA
    CHARLESTON COUNTY: Charleston
    GEORGETOWN COUNTY: Georgetown

SOUTH DAKOTA
    CODINGTON COUNTY: Watertown
    JERAULD COUNTY: Waterbury

TENNESSEE
    KNOX COUNTY: Knoxville
    SHELBY COUNTY: Memphis

TEXAS
    GALVESTON COUNTY: Galveston
    unplaced: Algiers

VIRGINIA
    ACCOMACK COUNTY: Modestown
    CAROLINE COUNTY: Sparta
    RICHMOND CITY: Richmond
    SHENANDOAH COUNTY: Woodstock
    Chesapeake Bay *
        * extends into Maryland

WISCONSIN
    EAU CLAIRE COUNTY: Eau Claire, Potter's
        Mill

WYOMING
    PARK COUNTY: Yellowstone National Park *
    TETON COUNTY: Yellowstone National Park *
        * Yellowstone National Park extends
        into Montana and Idaho

INDEX OF PERSONS MENTIONED

The following index includes the names of all persons mentioned in the death abstracts listed in "Deaths Reported by the Long Islander 1878-1890," except for the deceased subject. Since the listing of the deceased persons is done in alphabetical order, an index of these persons is not necessary.

To be found in this index are all listed parents, spouses, children, grandchildren, grandparents, siblings, nephews and nieces, cousins and other relatives. Most of the listings contain only a few of these relationships and in many cases none at all.

The only exception to the rule that a deceased person does not appear in this index involves married women. If the deceased married woman's maiden name is known, she is indexed under her maiden name, to provide an additional genealogical cross check. Likewise, if a deceased married woman had previous marriages listed, she would be indexed under these earlier married names, but listed in the body of the text only under the married name she used at the time of her death.

Many non-relatives are also listed in the index. Most frequently these would be employers or near neighbors, and in a few cases, former slave masters. If the person died at the hands of another, the person causing the death would found in this index.

This index should help the genealogist make the best use of the material contained in the abstracts.

INDEX OF PERSONS MENTIONED

ABRAMS, Jesse 181
ACKERLY, Elvena 1;
   Henry 2; James 2;
   Mary M. 2; N. S. 2;
   N. S. (Mrs.) 60;
   Orville B. 2;
   Philetus 2; William
   1, 2
ADAMS, Emma 254; Ben-
   jamin Franklin 2;
   James 2
AITKIN, Irving 3;
   Thomas 3 75
ALBERTSON, Benjamin
   157; Hicks 3 157
ALEXANDER, Celia Gar-
   diner 145; George
   W. 145
ALFRIEND, Edward M.
   3; Nellie 3
ALLEN, George 3,
   Tustram 3;
   William 105
ALMY, A. Curtis
   (Mrs.) 12
ALSOP, Margaret
   Rapelye 4
ANDERSON, Margaret
   C. 25; Maria 4
ANDREW, Redrick 4
APPLEBEY, Lucian O.
   4
ARCHER, Esther 5;
   Floyd D. 5; Thomas
   5; Thomas B. 5
ARMSTRONG, William 5
ARNET, Nelson 5
ARROWSMITH, Edward
   231; Eliza 231
ARTHUR, D. A. 5; Dan-
   iel A. 6; Isaac B.
   6; Nettie M. 6;
   Scudder 6
ATKINSON, John 84
AUER, George 6

AVERY, Charles 6;
   Mary J. 6
BAILEY, Annie 121;
   Theodorus 121
BAKER, Charles R. 7;
   E. Folsom (Rev.) 7;
   Edward 7; John 7;
   Mary 7; Sarah A. 7;
   Uriah 7; William 7
BALDWIN, Edgar S.
   (Mrs.) 234; Hannah
   8; John A. 8;
   Michael 8; Robert
   8; William 8
BALLAGH, Robert 8
BALLTON, Benjamin 9;
   Betty 9; Charles H.
   9; Samuel 9
BANKS, (Mrs. Dr.)
   148; George B. 9;
   Michael 9
BANVARD, John 9
BARKER, Israel A. 9
BARNES, Edward 9;
   Helen 9; Thomas
   (Mrs.) 262
BARNEY, David 10;
   Samuel 10
BARNHART, I. C.
   (Rev.) 10
BARRETT, Artemas 10;
   Arthur W. 10; De-
   witt C. 10; Dewitt
   C. (Mrs.) 82 83:
   Margaret 10
BARROWS, Isabella G.
   81; Napoleon (Rev.)
   10
BASSETT, John Mel-
   ville 54
BASSFORD, Byria W. 11
BAUKNEY, John N. 11
BAYARD, Thomas F. 12
BAYLES, Charles H.
   12; Desire Ann;

BAYLES (continued)
Hawkins 12; Elisha
12; G. Frank 12;
Hamilton T. 12;
Havens P. 12; Hen-
ry 155; James E.
12; James M. 12;
Joseph 12; S. Taber
12; Samuel H. 12
BAYLIS, Charles H.
(Mrs.) 234; Cornel-
ia 12; Daniel (Mrs.)
29; Daniel D. (Mrs.)
234; Daniel L. 12;
Elias Jr. 13; F. A.
12; Florence 13;
George 13; Jacob 12
13; John Smith 13;
Josephine 13; Oli-
ver 13; Phebe M.
12; Smith K. 12;
Thomas 12
BEARE, Henry 104
BEATTY, Alfred 14
BEDELL, Henry 14;
Jacob 169; Mary E.
141; Phebe Ann 169
BEEBE, Dora 15; Henry
14 15; Lyman 14;
Matilda 14
BEERS, Edward 15;
Hawley 15; John Z.
15; Lucinda 15;
N. T. 15; Nathan 15;
Nathan T. 15; W. S.
15
BELKNAP, Aaron B. 15;
R. L. 15
BELL, Peter A. 16
BELMONT, August Jr.
16
BENNETT, Aaron B. 17;
Abraham D. 16; Dan-
iel (Mrs.) 234;
G. H. R. 17; George
17; George I. 17;
John 17; Maria 17;

BENNETT (continued)
Nathaniel 17;
Nicholas 16
BENTLEY, A. 17
BERGEN, J. V. (Mrs.)
17
BERRY, Jane E. 109;
Richard D. 109
BETTS, George 18
BIALLA, John B. 19
BIERD, William 19
BIGGS, Alden 19
BIRDSALL, John 19
BISHOP, James 20;
Roscoe 20; Zebulon
20
BLACHLEY, Jarvis 20;
Mary Ann 20
BLAINE, James G. 20
BLAIR, William 20
BLANCHARD, F. Loring
20
BLAZINS, John 20
BLOXOM, Arabella 21;
Edward 21
BLOXSOM, Harver 21
BOCKUS, Isaac 21
BODIE, Henry 21
BOGGS, James 138;
Julia Augusta 138;
Sarah Lloyd Broome
138
BOLLER, Charles M. 22
BOOTH, William Chat-
field 22
BOSTWICK, Catharine
Elmore 70
BOUTON, A. A. 220;
Amos 22
BOYCE, William 22
BOYD, E. C. 23
BRAGAW, Daniel 23;
Richard 23
BRAND, (Mrs.) 67
BRANDEGEE, Jacob 23;
Stephanie 220

BRANDORSTEIN, Theresa 23
BRANNIGAN, Johanna 23
BRANT, Leonard 23
BRAUN, John (Mrs.) 201; Sebastian 24
BRAZIER, Charles 24; Georgianna 24
BREEN, Dennis 24; Maggie 24; Patrick 24
BREMNER, George 24
BREWSTER, James 24; Richard 24
BRICKET, I. R. 238
BRITT, J. W. 24
BROCK, William 24
BROOME, Sarah Lloyd 138
BROSS, Fannie Miller 24; William (Dr.) 24
BROWN, Addison (Mrs.) 210; Arden 58; Charles 25; Elizabeth 210; George 27; George W. 26; Henry 25; Isaac 152 153; James 26; Joel 26; John 25 125; John J. 25; Julia 27; Louisa Monroe 25; M. A. 236; Margaret C. Anderson 25; Mary 152; Mary R. 152; Nehemiah (Rev.) 236; Sallie C. 226; Stephen 25; Thomas F. 25; W. H. 25; William 26; William H. 226; William Jr. 26
BRUSH, Abel 185; Abner 27; Amanda Sammis 28; Charles 27; Charles E. 29; David 27 28;

BRUSH (continued) Elijah 27 28; Elizabeth 28; Elizabeth Carman 28; Ellie K. 29; Frederick 28 29; George 28; George W. 27; George W. (Dr.) 29; Gilbert 29; Harriet N. 29; Henry (Mrs.) 80; James (Mrs.) 240; James M. 28; James Madison 28; Jesse (Rev.) 27; John R. 27; John S. 28; Jonas Platt 27; Joseph 29; Lizzie 44; Lydia 185; Morris 27; Phebe 29; Samuel 27; Samuel J. 29; Skillman 28; Thomas F. 29; Thomas H. 44; Thomas Henry 28; Thomas P. 29; William 28; Zephaniah 28; Zophar 27
BRYAN, Ann 29; Frederick 29
BRYANT, Augustin 80; David (Mrs.) 28; Henrietta C. A. 20; John 29; Mary B. 80; Scudder 20; Thomas 29
BUCKINGHAM, Charles 30
BUELL, Matthew (Dr.) 30
BUFFETT, Chatfield E. 30; David 31; Eliphaz 31; G. Henry 31; Ketcham 31; Mary 31; Nancy 31; Nathaniel 31; Phebe 127; Sarah J. 31; Sarah Sammis 31;

BUFFET (continued)
William F. 31;
William P. 31
BUMSTEAD, Jacob 31
BUNCE, Albert 32; Albert S. 31; E. A.
32; E. H. 32; Edward 32; Elbert 32;
Fleet 32; Frank S.
32; Hannah M. 32;
Harriet N. 28;
Helen 28; John 32;
Louisa 32; Matthew
32; Samuel E. 32;
Selah 28
BUNN, Hannah E. 33
BURCH, Alfred 33
BURDEN, James A.
(Mrs.) 112
BURGER, Bertha 191
BURGESS, F. W. 33;
F. W. (Mrs.) 132
133
BURK, Emmett 33;
John T. 33
BURNS, John 34
BURR, Carll 34; Carll
S. 39; Elbert 108;
George W. (Mrs.)
177; Jarvis 34;
Lester H. 34; Mary
34 108; Ruth A. 40;
William 34
BURROWES, John N. O.
34
BURTIS, H. A. 8;
Rachel Smith 34
BUTTS, McCoskey (Mrs.)
70
BYRNE, Michael 35
CAIRE, Emilie A. 35;
Lewis H. 35
CALDER, Donald 35
CALLAHAN, William 35
CAMPBELL, George H.
36

CANAVELLO, Charles
36; John P. 36
CANVAN, J. J. 36;
John 36
CARLL, Ann E. 37;
Anne E. 36 37;
Charles 36; David
87; Edward 183; Elbert 138; Frances
A. 42; Gilbert 42;
Jesse 36 37 112
256; John 37; Julia
M. 37; Lemuel 37;
Oliver 249; Oliver
L. 37; Selah 37;
Silas 37
CARMAN, Caroline 37
38; Clarence 37 38;
Elizabeth 27 28;
Eva 136; Isaac N.
37; Joseph 37; Margaret 216; Samuel
38
CARPENTER, Alice 135;
Charles 38; James
38
CARR, William H. 38
CARTER, Emma 66; Robert T. 38; S. T.
(Rev.) 38 43; Samuel (Rev.) 38
CARTWRIGHT, B. C. 38
CASEY, Annie 39; John
39
CASH, Joseph 39
CASHAW, Emma 39; Thomas 39; Thomas A.
39
CASS, Mary E. 39;
Thomas 39
CERVOSKY, Joseph 6
CHALMERS, David B.
40; Ruth 40; Ruth
A. Burr 40
CHAPIN, E. H. (Rev.)
40

CHAPPELL, Barney 40;
Phebe 40
CHASTANT, Andre Dan-
iel 23; Jeannette
Caroline 23
CHESEBROUGH, Charles
A. 40; Elizabeth 40
CHESHIRE, Jeremiah
41; Lucinda 40;
Luther 40; Wilber
B. 41; William 41
CHICHESTER, Abigail
99; Asa 99 198;
Elizabeth 198
CHILDS, Hattie 176;
S. Russell (Dr.)
176
CHIPP, C. J. 156
CHURCH, Franklin
41; Susie 41
CHURCHILL, J. A.
(Rev.) 41
CLAFFLIN, Sanford 41
CLARK, Edward 159;
H. D. 42; J. Frank
42; James 42; Mary
Isabella 42; Nath-
an 42
CLEVELAND, Grover 99
CLINCH, James 43 216;
Sarah Nicoll 216
CLUNE, John 43; Mary
43
COBB, William (Mrs.)
22
COCK, Benjamin 43;
George 43
CODLING, W. B. 44
CODY, James 44
COGER, George 44;
George W. 44; John
44; Martha 44; Mary
Ann 44; William 44
COGGSWELL, Helena M.
44; William L. 44
COGSWELL, John 44

COLES, Butler 44;
Nathaniel 44
COLLIGAN, William 45
COLLINS, John 45
COLLYER, Annie B. 45;
Henry 45; Richard
37; Sarah L. 37;
Thomas 45; William
A. 45
COLYER, Charles 46;
Charles W. 46; John
L. 46; Mary Van
Wyck 46; Mary Whit-
son 46; Richard C.
141
COMBES, Catherine 46
258; Edward 46;
John 46 258; Lizzie
258; Phebe 46
CONANT, William A. 46
CONKLIN, Abel 46;
Abel Ketcham 50;
Addie 50; Addie E.
48; Alexander 50;
Amos P. 47; Annie
S. 49; Brewster 47;
Charles 47 49 204;
David B. 48 49 219;
Edward 75; Edward
H. 48; Edward T.
48; Elbert 49; Ella
A. 205; Emma L. 47;
Ezra 48; Frances O.
49; Frank A. 48;
George 49; George
A. 49; George H.
50; George Woodhull
50; Grace 49; Ham-
ilton 48; Hannah
Maria 231; Henry
47; Henry F. 49;
Imogene Earle 46;
James 50; James B.
48; Jesse (Mrs.)
174; John 49; John
(Mrs.) 39; John R.
47; Jonas P. 48;

296

CONKLIN (continued)
Joseph 46 49; Julia
A. 204; Louise 48;
Mary E. 48; Mary H.
Hahden 48; Millie
48; Moreland (Mrs.)
152; Phebe 47;
Philetus 46; Platt
49; R. M. 47; Rich-
ard E. 205; Rosa
47; Sabrina Valen-
tine 48; Sarah 49;
Sarah J. 49; Silas
231; Stephen 46;
Stephen A. 49;
Strong 49; Thomas
W. 47; Titus 50;
Warren 46; William
48; William F.
(Mrs.) 100
CONNERS, Luke 51
COOK, Edward 73;
Rockwell 51
COOKE, F. P. 51;
John 197
COOLEY, J. S. (Mrs.
Dr.) 42
COONEY, John C. 227
CORCORAN, Patrick 52
CORNELIUS, F. C. 52
CORNELL, C. E. 52;
E. T. 52; George 53;
James 52; Thomas
(Mrs.) 48
CORWIN, A. 53; Carrie
53; Hubbard 53;
James Barrett 53;
Nathan 53; Willie
M. 53
COSGROVE, Frank 191
COSTELLO, Emma 99;
Samuel 99
COTREL, Abraham 176;
Emma 176; Sarah 176
COULTER, Oliver 53
COURTNEY, John 53

COWHEY, Catherine 45;
Dennis 45
COWPERWAITE, Florence
Crozier 54; Howard
54
COX, Anne E. 154;
Elizabeth 155;
Stephen P. 54;
Townsend D. 237;
Walter 54 154
COYLE, Hannah J. 54;
James H. 54
CRAWFORD, Elbert 55
Henry 192; Isabella
E. 192; James M.
(Mrs.) 23; John W.
192
CROFT, Joseph 55
CROSS, George 55
CROSSMAN, Alfred B.
56; Elwood 56; Gil-
bert 55; Jacob
(Mrs.) 260; Jacob
R. 56; Mary McKay
56; Matilda 260;
William 55
CROZIER, H. P. 56;
Hiram J. 56
CRUM, Elizabeth 83
CUFFEE, Ira F. 56;
John 57; Sarah 56
57
CURTIS, Sarah L. 216;
William 216
CUSICK, James 57
DAISY, John 34; Sarah
34
DARLING, Jeremiah 58;
Oscar 58
DAUCH, Andrew (Mrs.)
58 59; John 33;
John (Mrs.) 151
DAVIDS, G. H. 59
DAVIDSON, H. H. 59;
Joseph C. 59
DAVIS, Buel 59; C.
Elsie 60; C. H.;

DAVIS (continued)
(Mrs.) 96; C. P.
59; Charles A. 59;
Charles G. 59; Ed-
gar 59; Elisha 59;
Elisha E. 60; Fanny
Havens 49, George
H. (Mrs.) 222; Ida
59; J. A. (Mrs.
Rev.) 263; J. Ben-
jamin 60; John 60;
Mary 49; Matthias
49; N. W. 59; Nath-
aniel T. 60;
William 59
DE FOREST, Lockwood
61
DE MOTT, George 62
DE PEW, John 62
DE PUY, Frances 62;
Talbot 62
DE SILVIA, Louis 62;
Mary A. 62
DELMONICO, Antenette
36; Peter 36; Rosa
36
DEMAREST, James (Rev.)
60
DENTON, Andrew J. 62;
Israel 62
DEWICK, George 63;
George N. 63
DEXHEIMER, Christian
63; Jacob E. 63
DICKERSON, Benjamin
63; Gilbert 63
DILL, James B. (Mrs.)
92
DILLER, Alonzo P.
(Rev.) 64
DILLON, William J.
64
DIXON, Robert (Mrs,)
217
DOANE, Etta 64
DOLAN, James 64,
Mary E. 64

DONALDSON, Fannie 64;
Wallace 64
DONLY, Charles 64
DOTY, Benjamin 101;
Hannah E. 101
DOUGHERTY, Andrew 65
DOW, Oliver 65
DOWDEN, James 65
DOWN, Azel (Rev.)
183; O. A. (Rev.)
220
DOWNING, Ananias 66:
C. M. 66; G. W.
66; Mary A. 28;
William L. 66
DOWNS, John P. 66;
William 66; William
T. 66
DOYLE, John W. 67
DRAKE, Fannie A. 158;
J. M. 158; John M.
67
DRIGGS, Abijah 67
Hannah Smith 67
DUDGEON, Frank 44 67
DUFFY, Hugh 67
DUMONT, Lucy 122
Van Gasbeck 122
DURYEA, Charles 68
240; Cornelius 68;
Egbert 68; John R.
68
DUSENBERRY, David 69;
Edward 69
DUVALL, Floyd 69
Melissa 69
DWYER, William 69
EAMES, Harvey A.
(Mrs.) 253
EARLE, Imogene 46
EATO, Andrew 69
ECKERSON, Fannie 69;
M. B. 69 70 166;
M. Bogart 69
EDDY, J. H. 70
EDEN, William 70

298

EDWARDS, Nelson
  (Rev.) 207; Silas
  C. 70
EGAN, Daniel 70;
  Emily B. 70; Thomas
  57
EINHART, Matilda 70
ELDRIDGE, Henry 70;
  William 70
ELLIOT, Joseph 71
ELLIOTT, Fanny E.
  71; James 71
ELLIS, Sarah 71;
  Thomas M. 71
ELLSWORTH, Anna V.
  257; C. B. (Rev.)
  257
EMMONS, Samuel (Mrs.)
  155
ETZEL, Jacob 72
EVERETT, John 128;
  Mary 128
EVERSELY, Mr. 193
FANCHER, Lysander 72
FANNING, John 72
FARRINGTON, George 72
FAWCETT, Leslie 72
FEEKS, John D. 73;
  Julius J. 73
FELTHOUT, John 73
FERRIS, D. O. (Rev.)
  73; Daniel O.
  (Rev.) 73
FIELD, George 174
FIELS, James 73
FIKE, H. 73
FINCH, Lucinda 257
FITTING, John 74
FLEET, Arnold 74;
  David 75; Deborah
  260; Hannah C. 191;
  John 74; John P.
  75; Laura A. 75;
  Luke 75; Naomi 191;
  Phebe 74; Samuel
  75; Thomas 191;
  Zebulon 75

FLEISCHBEIN, August
  (Mrs.) 144
FLOWER, William 171
FLOYD, John Woodhull
  76
FOLKS, James 76
FORDHAM, Albert 76;
  Sylvanus H. 76
FORGIE, (Mr.) 203;
  George 76
FORKIN, Bridget 76;
  Michael 76
FOSTER, (Mrs.) 155;
  Grace 83; John 83;
  Nat W. 76
FOWLER, P. P. 77
FOX, Elizabeth 77;
  George 77; John J.
  77, William 77
FRANCIS, Eben (Rev.)
  77
FRANK, Robert 77
FRANKLIN, John 77
FRAZIER, Aaron 77
FREZZA, Nicolo 190
FROECHLER, Mary 81
FUENFGELD, Joseph 78
FULTON, William 78
FUNNELL, Henry 92;
  Jessie E. 92
FURLONG, Eleanor 79;
  Francis J. 79
GABLE, Elizabeth 186
GAINES, Laura 79;
  Royal A. 79; Samuel
  C. (Mrs.) 210;
  Stephen W. 79
GALEBAIN, George 195
GALLOWAY, William 79
GALOW, Fritz 79; Lena
  79
GARDINER, Alexander
  (Mrs.) 116; Ann 80;
  Benjamin Franklin
  80; David 236; Ge-
  orge 80; George C.
  80; Harriet 196;

GARDINER (continued)
Henry (Mrs.) 262;
James 79 80; Joel
B. 79; Joel S. 80
209; John 79 80;
John H. 80; Julia
236; Warren 79;
William 80
GARFIELD, James A. 88
GASSETT, Harry 80
GASSNER, George S. 81
GATES, Edward A. 81
GAY, D. Nelson 64
GEARTH, John 81
GEORGE, Mary Froe-
chler 81; Walter
81
GERLACH, J. B. 81
GIBSON, John 81
GILDERSLEEVE, Ansel
B. 82 83; Charles
L. 82; David 82;
Elizabeth 82; Eliz-
abeth Crum 83;
Frances B. Griffith
83; Jonathan G. 83;
Mary Libbie 168;
Moses 162; Moses R.
82; Sarah 82; Sarah
J. 82; Smith 82;
Thomas 168
GILLIES, P. M. 83
GILMAN, B. A. (Rev.)
235; Robert 83
GILROY, James 83
GLASSEY, Margaret 84;
Samuel 84
GLOVER, H. C. (Rev.)
84
GOLDEN, Daniel 84;
E. P. (Mrs.) 140
GOLDSMITH, (Rev. Dr.)
84
GORRY, Christopher
84
GOULD, Conklin 85;

GOULD (continued)
David 85; Ebenear
85
GRADY, John 85
GRANDILENARD, (Mrs.)
98
GRAY, George G.
(Mrs.) 112; Joseph
86
GREEN, George 57 86;
Patrick 86
GRIFFIN, Patrick 86
GRIFFING, Cyrus 87;
Henry 262; Madison
W. 87; W. H. 87
GRIFFITH, Frances B.
83
GRIMES, James 87
GRINSTED, A. F. 88
GROHMAN, (Mrs.) 55
GURNEY, John 88; Jo-
sephine 88; Jose-
phine F. 88; Robert
88; Robert F. 88
GUTWEILER, (Rev.) 88;
(Mrs. Rev.) 229;
E. (Rev.) 88 89
HACKNEY, Robert W.
89
HAFF, Silas 89
HAHDEN, Mary Hannah
48
HAHN, John H. 89
HALL, (Colonel) 89;
Charles 90; Emma
90; George 89 90;
Henry 90; S. B. 90;
Scudder 129; Seely
90; T. K. 75; Will-
iam 90; William
King 90
HALLOCK, Edgar (Mrs.)
151; George W. 91;
James 90 91; M. W.
90; Peter 90; Phil-
ip 90; Richard 90

HALSEY, Oliver 91
HAMILTON, Eva 92;
   Viola 92
HANKINS, Samuel M.
   92
HARDING, George R.
   (Rev.) 93
HARNED, Edward 93;
   Francina 93; J. B.
   93; Jacob 93
HARRIS, Jennie Youngs
   93; Robert 93;
   William 93
HARRISON, Thomas 94
HART, John 94
HARTT, Abigail Smith
   95; Ada W. 94;
   Armenia 95; Charles
   S. 95; David G. 95;
   Erastus 94; Henry W.
   94; J. Fordyce 95;
   Joel 94; Joseph B.
   94; Phebe 94
HATTEL, Carl 96
HAUSER, August 96;
   Louisa 96, Thaddeus
   96
HAVENS, Fanny 49
HAWKINS, Desire Ann
   12; Francis Asbury
   96; Franklin 96;
   Gilbert 96; J. C.
   96; Sylvester 97
HAWLEY, Oscar F. 97;
   Oscar F., Jr. 97;
   Sarah C. 97
HAWXHURST, John 97
HAYDOCK, Charles
   (Mrs.) 61
HAYES, Rutherford B.
   97 230
HAYNES, Nathaniel 97
HAZELDINE, Ella
   Frances 98
HAZZARD, Charles 98
HEASLEY, James 98
HEDGES, (Judge) 98

HEGEMAN, Daniel 98;
   Edward 98; James
   98; William 98
HEIDINGSFELDER,
   Margarette 98
HEITZ, Jane 224
HELMS, Charles A. 99;
   Elizabeth 99
HENDERSON, Charles
   99; Joseph 99
HENDRICKSON, A. A.
   100; A. W. 100;
   Coles 100; Daniel
   99; David 99; Edwa-
   rd 99; Elbert 100;
   George (Mrs.) 261;
   George W. 99; James
   99; John C. 99;
   Stephen 100; Ste-
   phen (Mrs.) 231
HENGLE, W. F. 100
HENNESY, Charles 100
HENSLEY, James 101
HERBAGE, (Miss) 27;
   Elijah 101; Henry
   101
HERFORT, Andrew 101
HERMON, Henry 101
HERZOG, Fred 101;
   Henry 101
HEWLETT, Anne 94;
   C. 102; Divine 94;
   George 102; Hannah
   94; Israel 256;
   John V. 102; Lucre-
   tia 123; Oliver 102
HICKS, Benjamin 156;
   Benjamin D. 102;
   Emiline 119; Jacob
   102; James 102;
   Nelson 119; Rachel
   103; Theodore 103;
   Theodore S. 119
HIGBEE, Roger 103
HIGBIE, Altimont S.
   103; Benjamin S.
   103; Jonas 103;

HIGBIE (continued)
Nettie A. 103;
Richard 103; Richard S. 103
HIGGINS, A. S. 103
A. S. (Mrs.) 48
HILDRETH, Nathan 103
HILL, Francis C.
(Rev.) 248; Nettie
248; Phineas 103;
Sarah 103
HINES, Michael 104
HOBAN, Richard 104
HOFFMAN, Annie 201;
Ernest 201
HOGAN, Caleb 75;
Edith 104;
George W. 104;
William 104; William H. (Mrs.) 186
HOLBROOK, Arthur C.
104; Belle 104
HOLDEN, Randall 105
HOLMES, Edward 105;
Sylvester (Mrs.)
234; William 105
HOMAN, L. B. 105;
William 105
HOPKINS, Samuel 106
HOPPER, Alonzo 106;
John (Mrs.) 242
HORTON, Albert 106;
Calvin 106; Emily
A. 115; H. B. (Mrs.)
245; H. D. (Dr.)
106; James 115; Mary
115; Schuyler B. 107
HOWARD, Amelia M. 107;
Caroline A. 107; Eugene 107; Eugene H.
107; Farnam L. 107;
Gertie 107; Harold
107; James 107; Virgil 107; Warren N.
107
HOWARTH, George (Mrs.)
5

HOWATT, William 108
HOWELL, Frank G.
(Rev.) 108; Hannah
T. 108; J. H. 108;
John Frank 108;
T. B. (Capt.) 70
119
HOYLAHAN, Michael 108
HUBBARD, John O. 109
HUBBS, Alfred 109;
Amos 109; Samuel
109; William 109
HUDSON, Margaret M.
214; Mary 110;
Mary A. 109 110;
William S. 109 110
HULL, Isaac P. 110
HULSE, Daniel 110;
Selah 110
HULTS, Abram 110
HUNT, George 110;
Hattie 110
HUNTTING. J. G. (Dr.)
111; J. G. (Mrs.)
169; Jonathan W.
111
HURD, A. T. (Mrs.)
251; Arthur T. 111
INGERSOLL, William
112
IRELAND, Derrick 112;
Isaac (Mrs.) 128;
John H. 112; Tredwell L. (Dr.) 112
IRVIN, Richard 112;
William (Rev.) 112
IRWIN, Frank 113;
James 113; Joseph
42 113; Martha 113
IVENS, Zenias 113
JACKSON, Aaron 113;
Anselm 114; Douglas
114; Douglass 229;
Edward 113; Henry
113; Henry D. 113;
Jacob 114; James
113; Jeffrey 114;

JACKSON (continued)
Keziah 113; Sidney
W. 114; Solomon
176; Tamar 114;
William Henry
(Mrs.) 39; William
L. 22
JAMES, Alma 114;
David J. 114
JANSSEN, Amelia 115;
Herman 115
JARVIS, (Mrs.) 140;
Aaron 115; Abigail
118; Edward 116;
Esther 229; Henri-
etta 199; Ira 116;
Jackson 116; John
B. 117; Jonathan
115 116 143; Jose-
ph 229; Joseph R.
115; Mary E. 229;
Moses 115; P. C.
115; Rhoda 198;
S. Lee 115; Timo-
thy 117; William
116
JAYNE, Charles 138
JEFFREY, George 116
JENKINS, Abigail A.
117; Mary B. 117;
Samuel 117; William
117
JESSUP, Zebulon 117
JEWELL, James 117
JOHNSON, Abigail Jar-
vis 118; Alexander
118 119; Caroline
120; Charles 118;
Edmund 118; Ephraim
Henry 119; George
119; George R. 119;
Ida 118; James 119;
Jarvis 118; Joseph
118; Mary Hartt 118;
Mary S. 118; Matilda
118; Merritt 119;
Oscar 118 120;

JOHNSON (continued)
Reuben 118; Ruth
119; Samuel 118;
Samuel C. 118;
Stephen 120; Will-
iam (Mrs.) 118
JOHNSTON, Alexander
121
JONES, Charity 121;
Daniel (Mrs.) 60;
David 121; Edmund
122; F. A. 121;
Frank B. 112; Han-
nah Hewlett 121;
Hazel 122; Israel
C. 122; James 122;
James P. 121; John
121; John D. 123;
John H. 122 123;
John H. (Mrs.) 198;
Katharine H. 122;
Lucretia Hewlett
123; Lucy D. 122;
Nora J. 198; Samuel
A. 123; Samuel Van
Wyck 121; Townsend
122 123; W. R. T.
122; Walter 121;
Walter R. T. 121
123; William 122;
William H. 122;
William J. 122
KAGAAN, James 123
KALLY, William 123
KANE, Luella 123;
William 123
KAY, George 263
KAYLOR, James A. 124;
Laura 124
KEENE, G. Shepard
124; Sarah Louise
124
KEIFER, Antoine 124
KEIL, Charles Gunther
240
KEISLING, Augusta
Marie 196;
303

KEISLING (continued)
Charles 124 196
KELLOGG, Frederick
124; Mary 203
KELLUM, Conklin
(Mrs.) 239; Made-
line P. 193
KELLY, James 125;
Mary 125
KELSEY, Elizabeth
125; Hannah 185;
Hannah Amelia 186;
Joel (Rev.) 125;
Katie 125; Platt
125; William H. 125
KELSO, Mabel Suydam
126; Nathaniel K.
126
KEMPSTER, Kessiah
126; William 126
KERBS, August 126
KERPS, August 126
KERR, H. D. 126
KETCHAM, A. Mulford
127; Abial 129;
Andrew 127; Anne
Lefferts 128; Brew-
ster 127; Carll 127;
Daniel 129; Ells-
worth B. 128; Ells-
worth E. 129; Emily
167; Emma J. 129;
Eva C. 128 129;
Hannah 127; Henry
E. 129; Ira 127 128;
Isaac 129; Isaac H.
128; Jacob 127; Jer-
emiah 129; Jesse
128; Joel 128; Knee-
land (Rev.) 127;
Minnie 129; Nathan-
iel 128; Phebe 127
224; Stephen 127
128; William H. 129;
Woodhull 26 127 128;
Zophar 127 189; Zo-
phar (Mrs.) 172

KIERNAN, Patrick 147
KINCAID, Charles E.
226
KING, Albert N. 130;
Edward 152; Isabel
N. 130; J. M.
(Mrs.) 229; John A.
130; John A. (Mrs.)
181; Manuel 130;
Richard 130; Rufus
130
KINGSLEY, Daniel 70
KINSELLA, Charles
130; Daniel (Mrs.)
130; Mary 130
KIRBY, Hattie 130;
James 130
KISSAM, Daniel White-
head (Dr.) 130;
Elizabeth W. Rose
130; Margaret 224;
Oscar 205; Phebe
Ryerson 130; S. S.
130 ; Sarah J. 130
224
KITCHEL, Julia Ann
148
KLEIN, Joseph 131
KNOWLES, William 131
KNOX, W. W. (Rev.)
131
KORN, John 132
KRACK, Joseph 132
KREISCHER, John 81
KRULISCH, Frank 56
KUNTS, Louis 132
LANE, Adrienne E.
132; David V. 243;
Davis E. 132 133;
Davis V. 133; Henry
133; Olive L. 243;
Ollie 133
LANTON, Anna 121;
Cyrus 121; Sarah M.
121
LARRABEE, E. W. 133;
George 133;

LARRABEE (continued)
Robert 133
LAUCK, Albert 133
LAVELL, Annie 133;
David 133; Joseph
J. 133
LAWRENCE, Effingham
134; Jarvis 134;
Leonard W. 134
LEE, S. O. 134
LEEK, Fanny 135; Ida
51; Stephen T. 135;
Walter 51
LEFFERTS, Anne 128;
J. B. (Mrs.) 186;
Laura 185
LEGGETT, Abraham 135
LEONARD, John 135
LEUTH, Alice Carpen-
ter 135; Peter 135
136
LEWIS, Alvin 136;
Anna A. 136; Azel
32; David 32; Eg-
bert 136; Egbert
G. 136; Egbert S.
137; Ella 136;
Frank 136; Frank-
lin 136; Frederick
136; George 136;
Gloriannah Adeline
32; Joseph 137;
Joseph C. 136 137;
Joseph S. 137; Mar-
garet E. 137; Mary
218; Sarah Scudder
136; Solomon C. 136;
Theodore F. 259;
Thomas 218; Walter
L. 137; Wilbur R.
137; William B. 136
L'HOMMEDIEU, Charles
137; George 137;
John 137
LIMBERG, Frederick
138
LINCOLN, Abraham 138;

LINCOLN (continued)
E. M. 222; Eugenia
M. 222; Robert T.
138
LINSTEAD, Albertina
138; Theodore 138
LIVINGSTON, Lewis 138
LLOYD, Caroline B.
138; Henry 138;
Henry (Mrs.) 220;
James 138
LOCKE, Richard 139
LOCKWOOD, (Rev.) 139;
Edward 139; James
H. 139; Joseph 139
LONG, Hewlett J.
(Mrs.) 29
LOPER, Carrie A. 139;
William H. 139
LORD, Thomas 140
LOWNDES, Allison 140;
Ellison 140; Ruth
140; Sylvia 140;
William 140
LOWRY, J. J. 140
LUCE, Hallock F. 140
LUDLAM, Alfred 140
LUDLOW, Frances
Nicoll 140; Frank
140; Nicoll 140;
William 140
LUDLUM, George 140;
Henry 140; James H.
140
LUPTON, Emma A. 141;
John D. 141
LUSH, Carman R. 141
LUYSTER, Andrew J.
155; Charles 141;
Daniel 141
LYNCH, Peter 141
MAC GEUHY, Robert 142
MACK, Daniel T. 142
MAHAN, George 142;
John 142
MAHONEY, Daniel 142

MAITLAND, Jennet
  Lenox 15; Robert 15
Malloy, Adelia 142;
  William H. 142
MANLEY, John A. 143
MANN, Florence 12;
  Jacob 143; John 12
MANNY, Cornelius J.
  143; Mary J. 143
MARCHAY, Harriet 166
MARSH, E. T. T. (Dr.)
  144; Emma E. 144;
  John 144
MARSHALL, Thomas F.
  144
MARTIN, Louis 144;
  Susan 144
MATTDEUX, William 145
MATTHEWS, Harmon 145;
  Smith 145
MATTHIAS, Sarah 29
MAXIM, John 145
MAXWELL, Henry W.
  145; James 145
MAY, Francis 145
MAYBEE, Garrett 145
  146
MAYHEW, James 146
MC ALLISTER, Esther
  105; William (Rev.)
  105
MC BRIEN, Bridget
  146; William 146
MC CARTY, James 146
MC CAULEY, Thomas
  (Rev.) 146
MC CORD, Thomas 147
MC COUN, Charles 147
MC CULLOCH, Catherine
  147; David 147
MC CUSKER, J. J.
  (Rev.) 147
MC DOUGALL, Hugh 148;
  Julia Ann Kitchel
  148
MC EVOY, Dennis 148

MC FARREN, Robert 145
MC GONIGLE, (Miss)
  58
MC GREGOR, Henry 148
MC GUINNESS, John 141
MC GUIRE, Clara 235
MC KAY, Duncan 148;
  Margaret 148; Mary
  56
MC KEE, Thomas 3
MC KEEVER, Mary
  Augusta 235
MC KENNA (Judge) 6
MC LEAN, P. B. 149
MC MENOMY, (Mrs.) 180
MC MILLAN, Andrew C.
  149; Helen 149
MC NAMARA, Cornelius
  149
MC QUEEN, James 149;
  Julie 149
MEADE, Richard W.
  149; William 260
MEAGLE, Henry 150
MEHAN, George (Mrs.)
  262
MEIS, John 150
MEISCHEIN, Catherine
  150
MELTON, H. Ben 150
MERRITT, Daniel 151;
  Fowler 151
MERRY, Elijah 151
MESEROLK, Abby 166
MEYER, Henry 151
MILES, Rowland 151
MILLER, Edwin N. 152;
  George 152; John
  152 153; Jonathan
  152; Jonathan
  (Mrs.) 129; Lizzie
  166: Mary 46
MILLS, Elmira W. 235;
  Fannie 136; George
  A. 153; J. B. 153;
  J. Thomas 153;

MILLS (continued)
Jonas D. 153; Thomas 153; Wickham 153; William H. 153
MILTENBERGER, Antonia 153
MINOR, Ezra 154
MITCHELL, Edward (Rev.) 154
MONFORT, Elizabeth Cox 155; Emma 155; Frances A. 154; Franklin P. 154; George 155; Henry A. 154 155; Madison 155; Obadiah V. 154; Samuel V. 155; William 155
MOON, Joseph 155
MOORE, C. B. (Mrs.) 123; Charles L. 155; Clara 155; Thomas 156; W. H. (Rev.) 156
MORRIS, Stephen 156
MORSE, J. E. (Mrs.) 29
MOTT, Cornell 3 157; Ellsworth 157; Everett 157; George A. 157; Henry G. 157; J. S. 75; James S. 157; Jesse 157; Joanna 157; Mary C. 157; William 143; William J. 157
MOUNT, W. S. 122
MOWBRAY, Eliphalet 157; Mary 31
MULCAHEY, Patrick 157
MULFORD, Carrie E. 158; Henry 158; Henry D. 158
MULLINGS, Charles A. 158

MUNCY, Jesse 158
MUNSON, Levi 158
MUSANTE, Andrew 159
MYERS, Elbert 159; Louis H. 159
NATTIGAR, L. L. 128
NELSON, Alfred 159; Emma 159
NEVIUS, John 160
NEWINS, Joseph 160
NEWTON, Edwin S. 160; Emmett B. 160; William R. R. 160
NIBBE, Peter 197
NICHOLS, Ann 161; Gideon 160 161 234; Oscar M. 161; Rhoda A. 160; Susan 160 161
NICKERSON, Herman 161
NICOLL, Frances 140; Gloriana 256; Mary Shelton 261; S. B. (Dr.) 161; Samuel B. 256; William 140 161 261
NIGHTINGALE, James C. (Rev.) 161; Julia St. John 161
NINE, John 161
NOBLE, (Rev. Dr.) 161
NORTON, James 162
NOSTRAND, Jacob 162; Sarah 162
NOTT, William 162
NUN, A. 162
OAKES, Nathan 163; Platt 163
OAKLEY, Eliphalet W. 163; Elizabeth 246; George 164; Hannah 164; John 246; Marian 164; Samuel J. 164; Solomon 163 164 247; Whitson 163; Z. B. 163;

OAKLEY (continued)
  Zebulon E. 164;
  Zophar 75
OAT, George 164
O'BRIEN, Patrick 164
O'DONNELL, John 165
O'HARA, Michael 165
OLDS, George 165
OLMSTEAD, Eliza E.
  31; John 165
ONDERDONK, Benjamin
  T. (Rev.) 165
O'NEIL, Catharine
  165; John 165
ORR, Lizzie Miller
  166
OVERTON, Fanny 166
PAHDE, J. 167
PAINE, Henry Martin
  167
PALMER, Albert W.
  (Mrs.) 92; Augusta
  Temple 176; Walter
  167
PARISH, Richard L.
  167
PARKER, Emily Ketcham
  167; Frank 167
PARRISH, Richard L.
  167
PARSONS, S. (Mrs.)
  167; William 167
PASFIELD, Mary L.
  168; William G. 168
PATTERSON, Margaret
  168; Mary 168
PAULDING, Hiram 168;
  Virginia 168
PAYNE, B. K. 168;
  John (Mrs.) 82
PEARSALL, Daniel 169;
  James B. 168;
PEASER, Peter 169
PECK, Lily 169; W.
  Edward 169

PEDRICK, Emmet 169;
  Eugenie 169; I. B.
  169; I. B. (Mrs.)
  32
PENDERGAST, Mary 170;
  Michael 170
PENDELTON, George H.
  170
PERROTT, John W. 170
PERRY, Stephen 170
PETERS, August 170;
  Christina 170;
  John 170; John H.
  170
PETERSON, William
  171
PETTIT, Joseph (Mrs.)
  261
PETTUS, Stephen 220
PHAROAH, Aurelia 171;
  Eleazer 171; Steph-
  en 171
PHELPS, Frederick O.
  171
PIERSON, Casper H.
  172; Lottie E. 172
PIKE, Jonathan 172
PINE,P. Wesley 172
PITT, George E. 172
PLACE, Edward 172
PLATT, Edward 173;
  Eugene 173; Frank
  172; Gilbert 66;
  H. Maria 66; Hen-
  ry C. 173; Jennie
  D. 173
POLLARD, Dolly 116
POMEROY, Cyril B. 173
POOLE, Charles 173
POST, Birdsall 173;
  H. A. V. 72; Rich-
  ard B. 173; Samuel
  173
POTTER, Edward 174
POWELL, Andrew 175;
George 175; Isaac
174; Richard 174;

POWELL (continued)
Robert T. 174;
Susan D. 175
POWERS, James 175;
Samuel (Mrs.) 225
PRATT, Sidney 175
PRAY, Elias 175
PRIME, Augusta Temple
Palmer 176; Benja-
min Youngs (Dr.)
176; Benjamin Y.
176; Charles S.
176; Cornelia 176;
Cornelia Scudder
176; Ebenezer
(Rev.) 176; Edward
Y. 176; Fred E.
176; Henry R. 176;
N. S. 176; Nathan-
iel 176; Nathaniel
Scudder (Rev.) 176;
Temple 176
PRINCE, George 176;
George S. 176; L.
Bradford 176;
William 176
PROVOST, James C.
(Rev.) 177
PUGH, (Editor) 177
PURICK, Robert 81;
Robert (Mrs.) 240
PUTNAM, B. Van Vliet
(Rev.) 177;
Ella 177
QUIGLEY, James 177
QUINN, Margaret 177;
Thomas 177
RALSTON, Christopher
A. 177; Mary M. 177
RAND, George C. 178
RANDALL, Charles P.
(Mrs.) 121; S. E.
(Mrs.) 225
RAPELYE, Margaret 4
RAPELYEA, Simon 178
RAPPOLD, George 178
RAY, Joseph (Dr.) 178

REDMON, George R. 179
REEVE, Egbert 179;
Smith 179
REGENSBURY, Samuel
180
REGENT, Henry 180
REHBERG, Martin 180
REIKHERT, Charles G.
180
REINHARDT, Louis 180
REINHOLD, John 180;
Rosa 180
REMSEN, Abraham 180;
John 180; Wright
(Mrs.) 183
RENCE, Henry (Mrs.)
150
REUBERG, Matilda 190
RHODES, Henry E. 181
RICE, Augustus (Mrs.)
187; David 181
RICH, George 181;
Linnie 181
RICKS, Anthony 182
RIGGS, Timothy 182
RITCH, F. J. 182
RITCHIE, Charles 182
RITTER, Casper (Mrs.)
44; Casper H. 182;
Ferdinand 182;
Louise 182
ROAT, George W. 183
ROBBINS, (Miss) 211;
Benjamin T. 183;
Edward 183; Helen
A. 183; Sarah E.
183: William I. 183
ROBINS, Seth R. 17;
William 183
ROE, Charles F. 64;
Henrietta S. 260;
John C. 64; T. Sm-
ith 260; Thomas
Smith 184
ROGERS, Alfred 184;
Alfred (Mrs.) 231;
Alma 185 186;

ROGERS (continued)
C. S. (Rev.) 184;
Conklin 185 186;
Elizabeth 184;
F. N. (Mrs.) 219;
Flora 188; Frank W.
184; George 185
186; George R.
(Mrs.) 251; Henry
185; Isaac 184 185
186; Jacob 184; Jar-
vis 31; Joshua 184;
Lily 169; Louis E.
185; Lydia 186;
Maria L. 186; Mary
B. 184; Mary Mow-
bray 31; Mary Sea-
cord 185; Moses R.
184; Nancy 31;
Stephen C. 185;
Theodore 184 185;
Thomas P. 169 185;
Warren (Mrs.) 184
231; William 184;
William E. 185;
Zebulon 185
ROHRBACH, Elizabeth
Gable 186; Hartman
186; Henry 186; Mar-
tha K. Wagner 186
ROLLAND, Charles H.
186; Emma J. 186
ROOT, D. C. 187
ROSE, Catherine 187;
Elizabeth W. 130;
William 187
ROSELLE, James 187
ROSS, Eugene 187
ROWELL, (Mrs.) 4
ROWLAND, Carrie D.
188; Charles 188;
Charles H. 188; Ed-
ward 188; Emma J.
188; Frances 188;
George W. 236; Jere-
miah 188; Lewis M.
188; Mary E. 188;

ROWLAND (continued)
Smith 188; Warren
188; Warren (Mrs.)
40
RUEGER, Andrew 188;
Cornelius 188
RUGG, Charles H. 188
233 234
RULAND, Charles 189;
Darius 189; Flora
188; Samuel 189;
Wallace 188
RUNCIE, Amelia 189;
John T. 189
RUSCO, George P. 189
RUSHMORE, Benjamin F.
(Mrs.) 52; Edward
189; Elbert 189;
Howard 189; Stephen
177 189; William
(Mrs.) 120
RUSSELL, A. G. (Rev.)
36 156; Henry 190
RYAN, Mary 180
RYERSON, Jacob 131;
Phebe 130
SACKETT, Elizabeth
Kissam 231; Samuel
231
SAILSBURY, Edward 190
SALATA, Samuel 190
SALMON, A. M. 190
SAMMIS, Alexander
191; Alice E. 190;
Amanda 28; Betsy
192; Charles 222;
Charles F. 190;
Daniel B. 194; Da-
vid 85; Edgar 191;
Elbert 193; Elbert
(Mrs.) 231; Ellen
B. 35; Emma E. 209;
George 191; George
A. 191; Hannah 13;
Henry 13 191; Henry
(Mrs.) 260; Henry
S. 192; Jacob 193;

310

SAMMIS (continued)
Jeannie Lockhart
204; Jesse 190;
John M. 21; Jonas
193; Joseph 177 191
192 193 209; Joseph
E. 193; Joseph H.
192 193; Julia 193;
Julia S. 190; Juli-
et 191; Lewis 191;
Lillian 191; Lizzie
193; Louisa S. 192;
Lucinda 194 204;
Mary E. 177; Morti-
mer 193; Nathaniel
193; Phebe M. 192
193; Philander P.
193; Richard 193;
Rinaldo 193; Royal
193; Royal A. 190;
Ruth 85; Sarah 31;
Sarah Elizabeth 31;
Seaman 191; Stephen
190 191; W. Wood-
hull 192; Walter
194 204; William H.
191; William Wood-
hull 192
SAMSON, Annie 194;
John 194
SANDS, Nelson (Mrs.)
231
SANFORD, David H. 194
SANXEY, R. S. 194
SATTERLY, Thomas 194
SAUTER, Louis 194
SAXTON, Caleb 195
SCHACKWERTY, Joseph
195
SCHAEFER, Beyer 195
SCHAEFFER, August 78
SCHEIDWEILER, Philip
195
SCHENCK, Isabella 195;
William 195
SCHLIEMAN, August 195
SCHLING, Nicholas 196

SCHMIDT, Oscar E. 243
SCHNEPF, Christina
196; Martin 196;
Pauline 196
SCHOFIELD, Rachel 196
SCHRIEFER, Dora 196;
Henrietta 196;
Henry 196
SCHUCHMAN, Christina
Schnepf 196
SCHULER, Anton 197
SCHULTZ, Carl 197
SCHUYLER, Philip 34
SCHWARTING, Charles
197; Mary 197
SCHWARTZ, Joseph
197; Mary 197
SCOTT, John 24;
Libbie 24; Thomas
197
SCUDDER, Abigail 199;
Anne Cornelia 198;
Alonzo 199; Augus-
tus H. 198; Corne-
lia 176; Elizabeth
Hewlett 198; George
A. 198; George A.
(Mrs.) 100; Gilbert
198 199 223; Henry
198; Henry G. 122
198 199; Henry J.
199; Hewlett 198;
Isaiah 198; Israel
198; Jesse 199;
John R. (Mrs.) 118;
Louisa H. 199; Ma-
tilda 118: Naomi
223; Nora 122; Nora
J. 198; Rhoda Jar-
vis 198; Sarah 136;
Solomon C. 198;
Walter 35
SEABURY, Robert
(Mrs.) 101
SEACORD, Amelia A.
11; Daniel 199;
Mary 185

SEAMAN, Edward 200;
Esther 200; Henry
200; Jacob 200;
James 200; James
(Rev.) 200; Jesse
N. 200; John T.
200; Mary E. 200;
Oliver 200; Susie
Valentine M. 200
SEARLES, Joshua 201
SECOR, John W. 201
SEGELKEN, John 201
SELLECK, Sara 136
SELLS, Jerry 201;
Martha 201
SELTER, A. N. (Mrs.)
56
SEVAN, Edward 135
SEVIN, (Mrs.) 52;
Andrew 101; Cath-
erine 101; John A.
201; Philip 201
SEWICKS, (Rev.) 141
SEYMOUR, Hazel 122
SHADBOLT, Adelia J.
202; Alanson 201;
Alfred 202; Carll
E. 202; Edward 202;
Fannie S. 202; Flo-
rentine E. 202;
Henry C. 202; Temp-
erance 202; Theo-
dore 202
SHANESSY, Thomas 141
SHAW, John 202
SHELTON, Nathan (Dr.)
202
SHEPARD, Charles E.
203; Charles S.
203; Eliphalet 203;
George A. 203; Hen-
ry 203; John 203;
Josephine 203;
Juliette L. 203;
Mary Kellogg 203
SHERRILL, John (Rev.)
203; Julia E. 203

SHORT, Joseph W. 204
SHRADY, John 204
SHULOFF, (Mrs.) 52
SILKWORTH, (Mr.) 177;
Mary E. 177
SILLS, Washington B.
204
SILVIA, Carrie 204;
Joseph 204
SIMBERG, Annie E.
204; William 204
SIMMS, Isabella 153
SIMPSON, Ella 204;
Robert T. 204 205
SKIDMORE, Bryant 205;
Henry 205; Joshua
205; Laura 98; Lu-
ther 205; Walter
205; William H. 205
264
SKINNER, Charles 206;
Herbert 206
SLEETH, Isaac 206;
Susan B. 206
SLOTE, Sarah A. 260
SMITH, "Big Allec"
214; Abigail 95;
Ada 210; Alexander
209; Alice M. 207;
Alonzo 206; Andrew
I. (Mrs.) 109;
Anna J. 214; Annie
A. 213; Brewster
206; C. C. (Rev.)
206; Caleb 207;
Carll 214; Carman
193 209; Carrie
209; Carrie R. 209;
Carrie W. 207;
Charles 209; Dan-
iel 136 210; David
H. 211 216; David
Willis 212; E. 206;
Ebenezer 207 215
216; Edgar M. 210;
Edward A. 208; Ed-
ward Henry 207;

SMITH (continued)
Edwin H. 210; Edwin J. 208; Edwin W. 209; Eleazer 208 214; Eliza W. 208; Elizabeth 210; Emily 211; Ezra 209; Frances 136; Frank 210; George 212; George W. 211 214; Georgianna 210; Hannah 67; Henry 209 211 213; Henry C. 208; Henry J. 209; Herman T. 211; Ida 210; Isaac 211; Isabella 213; J. Abner 211; J. Lawrence 216; J. Lawrence (Mrs.) 76; Jacob 211 216; Jacob C. 211; James 95 206; James E. 212; John 183; John Carman 215; John H. 207; John I. 216; John W. 75 210; Joseph 120; Joshua B. 212 214; Josiah 80; Lewis 216; Lizzie 211; Maria 107; Maria M. 212; Marietta 209 210; Mary 210; Mary Elizabeth 193; Mary V. 80; Medab 216; Melancthon 67; Moses R. 209; Norman L. 207; Oliver 210; Orion M. 207; Phebe 209; Platt 214; Platt H. 208; Rachel 34; Richard 208 209 213; S. Alonzo 210; S. K. (Rev.) 216; Sadie E. 183; Samuel 210; Samuel (Mrs.) 210;

SMITH (continued)
Samuel Arden 207; Sarah 211; Sarah A. 217; Sarah E. 216; Sidney 216; Sidney C. 209 210; Solomon 216 249; Sylvester 214; T. William 217; T. William (Mrs.) 210; Theodore 217; Theodore F. 213; Theodorus 209; Thomas 206 210 211; Thomas V. 216; Thompson C. 213; Timothy C. 215; Vandewater 216; Ward (Mrs.) 218; Ward B. 217; Warren 67; Washington 147; William 2141 William W. 214; Woodhull 215
SNEDEKER, Christian 217; Samuel 217; William 218
SNEDICOR, Charles 218
SNELLING, Stephen 218
SNOUDER, A. 218
SOFFEL, Joseph 218
SOPER, Alfred 219; Brainard C. 219; Charles B. 218; Elkanah 143 226; Emma 219; Emmett R. 219; Frances 219; Frances O. 49; George 218; Hannah 219; Henry 218 256; Jacob 219; John R. 219; Joseph 218; Julia 85; Lemuel 219; Phebe A. 218; Phebe J. 220; Samuel 85;

SOPER (continued)
Smith 219
SOUTHWORTH, Hannah
R. 171
SPARKS, Rev. Peter
220; Stephanie
Brandegee 220
SPEEKS, Benjamin 220
SPENCER, Cornelius
220; Sophia 20
SPOONER, A. J. (Mrs.)
101
SPRAGUE, Jonathan 220
SPURGE, William N.
220
SQUIRES, William 220
STANSBURY, J. H.
(Rev.) 221
STANTON, P. V. B. 122
STEHLMAN, Herman 221
STEINERT, Joseph 213
STEPHENS, John 221
STEVENS, Charles 222;
John B. 222
STEWART, A. T. 154;
A. T. (Mrs.) 216;
Charles P. (Mrs.)
123; John 222;
Martha 222; Peter
222; Samuel S.
(Mrs.) 64; Thomas
H. 222
STILLWELL, John 139;
William 139
STILWELL, Cornel-
ius 222; George
222; John 222
STONE, Edward 195;
Esther 223; James
152; John H. 223
STOWE, Harriet
Beecher 15
STRAWSON, William
223
STREET, Charles R.
223; Josephine E.
223

STRICKLAND, Alma H.
223; John B. 223
STRONG, F. A. 223;
Selah B. (Judge)
223
STUDWELL, Alexander
223 224
STURGES, Charles
(Mrs. Rev.) 130
STURGESS, Margaret
Kissam 224; Nath-
aniel 224; Sarah
224; Sarah J. Kis-
sam 224
SULLIVAN, Daniel 224;
Dennis 224; Sylves-
ter 224
SURREY, Benjamin 224
SUTTON, Maria A. 224;
William H. 224
SUYDAM, Anna C. 225;
Henry 225; John E.
225
SWAN, William 225
SWEENEY, Douglas T.
225
SWEZEY, Edward 225
TAFF, Henry 225
TALLCOT, Charles W.
226; Nellie W. 226
TAPPEN, Andrew 226;
C. C. (Mrs.) 172;
Charles I. 226;
Hicks 226; Jackson
13; M. P. (Mrs.)
154
TAYLOR, Alec (Mrs.)
92; Eliza 226;
Francis J. 227;
George L. 226; Hen-
ry 227; Henry W.
226; John 227; John
(Mrs.) 19; Theus
87; Thomas 227
TEMPLE, James H. 227;
Kate 227
TERRELL, James O. 69

TERRILL, William N.
183
TERRY, "Hampton"
228; Emma A. 228;
Everet E. 228;
Everett E. 228;
George 228; John
S. 228; Sidney
228; Silas S.
228; T. M. (Rev.)
89 228; William M.
227
THOMPSON, Charlotte
229; Floyd 229;
Hester A. 130;
James 229; John
130 229; John N.
229; Jonathan 228;
Louisa 229; Mary
130; S. A. (Mrs.)
168
THORNE, I. C. 114
THURSBY, John 229;
John B. 229; Jo-
seph M. 229
THURSTON, L. M. 229
TILDEN, Annie 230;
Henry 230; Thomas
H. 230
TILLESTON, Jacob 230
TILLOT, William 230
TILLOTSON, A. C. 230;
Catherine 230;
Selah 230
TITUS, Alfred 231;
Andrus 231; Andrus
(Mrs.) 17; Caroline
231; Emma 232; Emma
P. 231; Eugene 232;
Helen R. 232; Hen-
rietta 232; Henry
232 253; Isaac 231
232; Jacob 231; Ja-
cob W. 230; James
231 232 253; John R.
231; Jonas 232; Jos-
eph 231; Joshua 102;

TITUS (continued)
Maria 232; Mary 102
230 253; Platt 232;
Ruth 260; Sarah
253; Sarah P. 232;
Sidney 231; Stephen
231; Thomas W. 231;
William 231 252;
Zebulon 231 260
TOMPKINS, Edward 100;
Hannah 100; Irene
Thompson 100
TOOKER, Amelia 233;
Brewster 233; John
H. 233
TOTTEN, J. C. 18
TOWNSEND, (Brothers)
84; Miss 23; Annie
235; Benjamin 233;
George W. 234; Hen-
ry 234; Henry A.
234; James 233;
James C. (Dr.) 264;
Silas 234; Solomon
237; Stephen T.
234; William E. 234
TREADWELL, (Dr.) 235;
Emmanuel 235
TRUBEE, Samuel (Mrs.)
228
TUCKERMAN, Walter C.
235
TURNER, David 235; J.
Clinton 235; Katie
235
TUTHILL, David 38 236
TUTTLE, Fidela V.
236; George F. 236;
Henry A. 236
TYLER, Charles 236;
John 236; Joseph
236
UNDERHILL, Alfred
237: Benjamin
(Mrs.) 30; Charles
237; Isaac 237;
Jacob 237;

315

UNDERHILL (continued)
Jesse 237; Mary 237;
Minnie 237; Ruth
237; Samuel S. 237;
Sarah 237; Smith
237; Townsend 95
UNDERWOOD, Edmund 237
VAIL, Aaron S. 238;
Almy C. 238; Edward
238; Emma 238; Hal-
sey 184; Ida 184;
Moses 238; William
238
VALENTINE, Frank H.
239; Hosea 239; Is-
rael 38; Jackson
238; Jesse 239;
Mary E. 239; Mary H.
38; Sabrina 48;
William 238
VAN BRUNT, James A.
239
VAN COTT, Alanson 239
VAN NOSTRAND, Benjamin
240; Charles 240;
John 240; John J.
240; William 240
VAN SISE, Charles 240;
Evelyn F. 240; Fred-
erick 241; Israel W.
241; James 241; Jer-
emiah 240; Ketcham
241; Nathaniel 240;
Robert 241; Sarah
A. 241
VAN WICKLEN, Charles
241
VAN WYCK, Joshua 242;
Mary 46; Richard
46; Samuel 242; Sam-
uel A. 241; White-
head H. 241 242
VEGA, R. J. 242
VELSOR, Alfred 242;
Carrie 242; Cornelia
99; Ebenezer 242;
Edgar 242; Emma 242;

VELSOR (continued)
George A. (Mrs.)
244; J. A. 243;
Lewis 242; Ollie
133; William 82
VERITY, James 243;
William 243
VINGERT, G. L. 243
VOGELSON, Lena 201
VON STROMER, Carl
243
VREELAND, (Mrs.) 244;
Robert H. 244
WAGNER, Martha K. 186
WAITE, Morrison R.
244
WALCOTT, James 244;
Phebe 244; William
T. 244
WALDRON, Hannah 245
WALKER, C. W. (Mrs.)
245; Edward 245;
William A. 245
WALLACE, John 245;
Stephen 245
WALLENHAUPT, Henry
245
WALTERS, Abraham 246;
Albert 246; Elbert
246; Elizabeth Oak-
ley 246; George
246; Josiah 170;
Sarah Ann 170;
Sidney 241; Susie
29
WANSER, Julia 246
WARING, C. B. 78
WARREN, Fannie E.
251; Naomi 251;
William H. 251
WASHBURN, Isaiah 247
WATERBURY, Amelia A.
168
WATTS, John E. 248;
Smith 248
WEATHERILL, Jane 167;
John 167;

WEATHERILL (continued)
Mary E. 167
WEBSTER, W. C. (Rev.)
248
WEEDEN, David 248
WEEKS, George E.
(Rev.) 248 249; Hen-
nry 249; Hobart 249;
Riley 249; Samuel
249; William J. 248
WEICKMAN, Conrad
(Mrs.) 196
WEIDMER, Robert 249
WEINZ, Louis 249
WELCH, John 250
WELLS, J. L. 250;
James 250; John D.
(Mrs.) 60; John
Henry 250; Jonathan
H. 250; O. O. 250
WEST, Samuel 250
WESTERVELT, Gertrude
111; Jacob 111 251
WETTERAU, George C.
251
WHALEN, Jerry 251
WHEDON, (Rev. Dr.)
251
WHEELER, Elnathan 251;
Frank M. 251; George
W. 251; Treadwell
252
WHELAN, Martin 252
WHIPPLE, Vinnie 252;
Volney C. 252
WHITE, Abby A. 253;
Charles E. 252; Ed-
ward 253; Eliza Jane
253; Freelove A.
252; Henry 252; Ma-
tilda 252; S. E.
252; William H. 253
WHITMAN, M. E. 117;
Zebulon 117
WHITNEY, Anna S. 253;
Daniel D. 253;
Gerald 253;

WHITNEY (continued)
Scudder V. (Mrs.)
253
WHITSON, Charles A.
254; Frank (Mrs.)
13; Frank B. 254;
Frank E. 254; I.
Youngs 164; Isaac
100 164; Mary 46
254; Phebe Ann 100;
Ruth A. 254; Samuel
254; Sarah G. 164
WHITTIE, Edward 254;
edward (Mrs.) 178
WICKHAM, (Mayor) 215
WICKS, Adam 254; Eth-
alinda 255; Francis
155; George 249;
Joel 255; Mary 155;
Theodore 255; Will-
iam E. 255
WIGGINS, Bradley 255
WIGHTMAN, Mark 256
WILLETS, George 256;
Robert 256; Theo-
dore 256; William
256
WILLIAMS, Christo-
pher 256; George
256; Gilbert 257;
Gilbert P. 256;
Henry 257; James
256; John D. 257;
Lucinda Finch 257;
Martha Lucinda 257;
Mary 256; Mary
Ballagh 256; Mary
Elizabeth 257; Rob-
ert B. 257; S. L.
256; Samuel 212;
Samuel Freebody
257; Sarah Eliza-
beth 257; Stephen
K. 257; Wesley 257:
William 257
WILLIAMSON, George A.
257; John

317

WILLIAMSON (continued)
Wallace 257
WILLIS, Daniel 256;
George 258; Valen-
tine 258
WILMOT, (Postmaster)
258
WILSON, Alexander
258; Frederick M.
258; George B. 258;
Isaac 258; Maria L.
258
WINDER, (General) 233;
Charlotte Aurelia
233; John H. 233;
William Henry 234
WINTERS, Isaac 155
WOOD, Brewster 259
261; Charles 259;
Daniel Slote 260;
David (Mrs.) 188;
Deborah Fleet 260;
Edwin 259 260; Geo-
rge 259; George C.
259 261; J. H. 260;
James 260; John 89
260 261; John F. 110
260; Mary F. 77;
Matilda 260 261; S.
260; Samuel 261;
Sarah 260; Sarah A.
Slote 260; William
259; William J. 259
WOODBURY, Coryton M.
261
WOODCOCK, Rosalie E.
261; William H. 261
WOODEND, William D.
(Mrs.) 260
WOODHULL, Caleb 261;
Caleb H. 261; Char-
les (Mrs.) 228;
Fanny D. 261; J. Am-
herst 261; Joel B.
261; O. J. (Mrs.)
122

WOODRUFF, Lawrence
V. B. 38; Mary S.
38
WOOLSEY, Sarah 262;
William S. 262
WORDIN, Juliette 262
WORTMAN, Coles 235
WRIGHT, Charles 262;
Frances Y. 237;
J. W. 263; James
262; John 237; John
C. 263; Julia E.
263; Mary E. 262
WYMAN, Henry 263
YATES, Henry Whit-
field 263; Warren
Samuel 263
YOUNG, Ann Eliza 54;
Anson S. 264; Dan-
iel T. 264; David
B. 54; Lewis 140;
Martha Lucinda 257;
Thomas (Mrs.) 83
257; Willis H. 263
YOUNGS, David J. 264;
Ira (Mrs.) 125;
Thomas F. 264;
William J. 264 265